GRANVILLE HICKS

in

The New Masses

GRANVILLE HICKS

KENNIKAT PRESS
Port Washington, N.Y. • London

in
The NEW MASSES

Edited by Jack Alan Robbins

Library of Congress Catalog Card No. 73-83265
ISBN: 0-8046-9042-1

Manufactured in the United States of America

Published by
Kennikat Press, Inc.
Port Washington, N.Y./London

CONTENTS

VII

Some Monuments

Editor's Introduction

The originator of radical journalism in America as we know it is the journal *The Masses* which was published between 1913 and 1917 under the editorial direction of Max Eastman. The material that appeared in *The Masses* was a strange admixture of muckraking reportage, bohemian poetry, socialist exhortation, realistic political cartoons, and some of the finest fiction of the times by writers such as Floyd Dell and Sherwood Anderson. The currents of bohemianism, anti-clericalism, revolutionary socialism and progressivism all blended in *The Masses* to create what is still regarded as the liveliest journal of the century. It is necessary to remember that nearly all issues of the *The Masses* appeared before the October revolution during a time when the Left was tolerant of its own divisions and intolerant and impatient of the ills within our society. Brutal class war was the fact of life then, as the Paterson strike and the Trinidad, Colorado massacre bear witness. Hypocrisy and corruption were established institutions in government and business.

The Masses, however, fell victim to the First World War. As revolutionary socialists the editors wanted either an immediate end of hostilities or the transformation of the war into a class war for the achievement of socialism. With the entry of the United States into the war the post office, through mail censorship, made circulation of *The Masses* all but impossible. Two attempts to try the editors for espionage and sedition ended in hung juries.

A successor to *The Masses, The Liberator,* appeared in early 1918 again under the guiding hand of Max Eastman. For nearly four years it continued to carry on in the spirit of its predecessor until internal conflicts over concepts of art and revolution, personalities and editorial responsibilities became too great. What had really happened was that the Bolshevik seizure of power in Russia had led to serious divisions within the American Left. Two Communists parties were founded (one heavily composed of Russian and East European immigrants). Later they merged, and in their zeal to import or imitate Bolshevik methods and manners to the American Left the Communists alienated many of the traditional leftists in the Socialist Party and De Leon's Socialist Labor party. The divisions became irreparable and in sharpening them the Communists made a virtue of what had been expediency. Rather than let *The Liberator* die, Eastman turned it over to the Communist party, which at that time (1922) had his sympathies. After two declining years the magazine died.

In May of 1926 an editorial board under the control of the Communist party raised the $25,500 needed to launch a new journal. The American Fund for Public Service, administering the Garland Fund, made a grant of $17,000 to the editorial board. The Garland Fund was created by a young Harvard graduate who, upon attaining his majority, turned his inheritance over to the service of the radical movement. The guiding spirit of the editorial board was Michael Gold, formerly of *The Masses*, and it was his intention that as much as was possible the new journal should reflect the style that had been so successful for a time for *The Masses*. And so the new journal was entitled the *New Masses*.

From 1926 through 1933 the *New Masses* was published as a monthly magazine. The editorial line was clearly Communist, policy reflected shifting decisions of the Third International in Moscow. (Lenin had died and Stalin was emerging as dictator after first eliminating from power the Left Bolsheviks of Trotsky, Zinoviev and Kamenev and later the Right Bolsheviks under Bukharin, Rykov and Tomsky.) The literary policy taken by Gold was to encourage the creation of a distinctly working class literature in America. The effort did not succeed, not in the early years. The prosperity of the Roaring Twenties was not reflected in the Communist movement. Sectarianism was the order of the day and it resulted in isolation. After the stock market crash of 1929 the tide began to change and the Communists found a growing audience for their ideas. But before the movement could really grow the Party had to change policy away from sectarianism. The rise of Hitler and the Nazis had been the direct result of the sectarian stupidity of the German Communist party, acting under Stalin's directives. The growth of fascism in France and Austria as well as Hitler's consolidation of power led Moscow to shift course, to adopt the popular front strategy. Already being tested in various places late in 1933 it was not formally adopted by the Third International until August of 1935. For the Party in America the change came at the end of 1933, tentatively, and from that point the Party grew rapidly in membership and influence.

Part of the shift to the popular front strategy entailed the reorganization of the *New Masses*. It was expanded from a monthly to a weekly and a new editor took over the literary section with the stated intention of developing a working class literature with a broader appeal to the American public. This new literary editor was Granville Hicks.

The writings of Granville Hicks for the *New Masses* in the 1933–1939 period mark the first sustained effort at developing a Marxist interpretation of literature in America. Previous schools of literary criticism examined literature from spiritual, narrowly cultural, or moral perspectives. Marxist analysis sought to ground works of literature in the socio-economic realities of their time. Social, political and economic changes in society helped to shape the consciousness of writers, more so than had been acknowledged previously.

Writers from the post-depression schools of literary criticism have pointed out a number of weaknesses in the Marxist method of the 1930s. Several of the Marxist critics carried their analyses to untenable extremes. Indeed, they claimed to see relations that could not be demonstrated to anyone's satisfaction. Non-economic factors were sometimes entirely discounted. Art gave way to propaganda for all too many Marxist critics. They saw economic factors that were really indirect and mediated as direct. Perhaps the worst sin was that a number of Marxist critics wrote in an irritating and arrogant manner. Fortunately, Hicks seldom struck this pose.

A major weakness actually lies with the very tool of analysis: the Marxist method. The Marxism of the 1930s in America, as elsewhere in the world, was mechanistic and dogmatic, deriving more from Engels, Plekhanov and Lenin. Two important early works by Marx had not yet appeared in translation: *The Economic and Philosophic Manuscripts of 1844* and *The Grundrisse*. It was not until the late 1930s that the Hegel renaissance got started with Alexander Kojève's lectures in Paris, which led to a reevaluation of the Hegelian influence on Marx's dialectic. The early works of Georg Lukács had been suppressed by the Third International and only rare copies were available. Moreover, the Marxism of the 1930s was more polemical than philosophical due to the aggravated character of the struggles in depression and thereby suffered.

Today Marxism is more complex, vibrant and philosophically more sophisticated. There is once again a wide audience for works of Marxism and many are interested in the development of the many schools of Marxist thought. In this light the early effort of Granville Hicks to fashion a Marxist critique of literature takes on added significance and commands itself to our attention.

The decade of the 1930s has been much distorted in the history written in retrospect of that decade. The McCarthy hearings, the witch hunts and books such as Eugene Lyons's *The Red Decade* have exaggerated the influence of the Communist party on the political and cultural life of America in that decade. The Communists have added to this distortion with their own brand of selective historicism. It has become Communist practice to treat people, who had been active in the movement but had left, as "non-persons," that is, as if they had never lived. In 1970 International Publishers brought out an anthology of selected writings of the *New Masses* edited from the current perspective on the 1930s. In this anthology will be found not one essay or book review written by Granville Hicks. True, Hicks is mentioned in passing in the introduction, but one would be led to believe from this omission that Hicks was not very important to the *New Masses*. The fact is that Granville Hicks was the most influential writer on the staff of the magazine during the 1933–1939 period. When the journal was converted from a monthly to a weekly and expanded in format Hicks became the literary editor. In this role he assigned books to certain reviewers, invited articles on specific topics, decided which books to review or not to review, and helped to promote various books with the reading audience. Granville Hicks, Edmund Wilson and Malcolm Cowley were the most widely read literary critics in the 1930s. They were the trend setters.

Over the past decade or so Wilson and Cowley have collected their literary writings of this period and have thereby taken their place in the annals of American literature. Granville Hicks has not, until now, been willing to have his literary writings of the 1930s collected. He has given two reasons: first, since he wrote them as a Communist, they are no longer fully representative of his views on literature; and, second, he considers many of these writings as journalism not having enduring literary merit. The reevaluation and reinterpretation today of the political and cultural movements of the 1930s has led Hicks to reconsider and at last consent to the collection of his *New Masses* writings. Thus it is now possible for Hicks to take his proper place in the literary life of the 1930s. This is the purpose of this collection.

                                                                            J.A.R.

Statement by Granville Hicks in 1973

When Jack Alan Robbins suggested that we might publish a collection of the articles and reviews that I wrote for the *New Masses* in the thirties, I was appalled. All that, I had felt, was well behind me, and buried under more than thirty years of social and personal history. In 1939, for reasons that seemed and seem to me sufficient, I resigned as a member of the Communist party of the United States. A little later on I wrote that I no longer considered myself a Marxist, although I acknowledged that I owed a great deal to Marx. That debt, I must add, has grown smaller and smaller as the decades have passed.

As I should have known, however, the past refuses to stay buried, especially today when young scholars are on the hunt for thesis subjects. You can count on it that, like the friendly dog in T.S. Eliot's *The Wasteland*, they'll "find your bones and dig them up again." For that reason, as Robbins argued, I might as well make sure that the digging was done under my auspices.

In the early thirties, as I have tried to explain in *Part of the Truth* and elsewhere, I began to feel that nothing less than a revolution could pull this country out of the Depression, and the only people who were talking about revolution were the Communists. The Communists offered a program of action and also a philosophy, Marxism, which undertook to explain nothing less than everything. Perhaps because I was brought up in a family of mildly skeptical Unitarians, I have never experienced a religious conversion, and my embracing of Marxism was not really of that order—as was that of Whittaker Chambers, for example, among many others. But in the end the result was pretty much the same, for, after I had studied the basic Marxist texts for a while, I acquired an exhilarating sense of certainty. I had not merely the world but the whole universe by the tail.

In the exploratory years I finished and published *The Great Tradition* (1933), a book about American literature since the Civil War. In this, as I pointed out in a new foreword and afterword for a paperback reprint (1969), I tried my newly-found Marxist wings. Some hostile critics felt that I never got off the ground, and some ostensibly friendly ones, other would-be Marxists, pronounced me guilty of horrible heresies, but the book, if it did nothing else, provided a target for people to shoot at.

The first essay in the present collection, which was originally prepared as a talk to be delivered to the John Reed club of New York City, was an attempt to formulate a theory of Marxist literary criticism. It was published in one of the final issues of the monthly *New Masses.* Originally representing several varieties of liberal and radical opinion, the magazine had come under Communist control and was staggering down hill. In the fall of 1933 I was invited to attend a meeting at which plans were announced for converting the senile monthly into a vigorous weekly. A nice trick if it could be done, and somehow it was.

It was at this preliminary meeting that I was asked to become literary editor of the new weekly, and I am a little embarrassed to remember how flattered I was. The amount of editing I did—assigning books, reading manuscripts, and the like—varied a good deal. I wasn't living in New York City, and most of the editing had to be done in the office. But I wrote something or other almost every week, and the present volume attests to my diligence if to nothing else.

Until Jack Robbins sent me proofs of this book, I had not looked at my *New Masses* articles and reviews in more than thirty years, and, as I have intimated, I had no intention of ever pulling them out of my files. The reading of them, however, proved less harrowing than I had expected. I am not saying that, like God, I looked on my work and found it good. On the contrary, I found much of it bad, but not quite so bad nor bad in quite the ways I had feared, and there were a few pieces and many parts of pieces that I could reread without too much dismay, perhaps even with satisfaction.

More than half the book is made up of book reviews, a literary form that is by nature ephemeral. It has pleased me, however, as I have read through them, to note that they constitute a kind of summary of the decade. We can see the kinds of situation that excited writers in the thirties, aroused controversies, and occasionally made best sellers. Perhaps the reviews also have some interest as examples, both good and bad, of the way my particular brand of Marxist criticism worked out in practice. A few of them I like rather well— for instance, what I wrote about Van Wyck Brooks's *The Flowering of New England;* at the end I put in a pointless plug for the Marxist interpretation of history, but otherwise there is little that I would change. About some writers—notably Henry James and T.S. Eliot— my judgments have moved steadily upward, and it is a relief to find that what I wrote about them in the thirties, though wrong in many ways, wasn't nonsense.

I suppose it is unlikely that anyone will ever want to analyze the old feuds and ancient wars, and I myself find them tedious enough. I can't help observing, however, that I was not guilty of all the sins of which I have been accused. It has sometimes been said, for instance, that I praised Sinclair Lewis's *It Can't Happen Here* because the Party line had changed; what you will see, however, if you glance at a paragraph or two, is that I praised it as an antifascist tract but called it a lousy novel. My great fault, as I have acknowledged more than once, was in the enthusiasm I felt for certain novels of a leftward tendency—e.g., Arnold Armstrong's *Parched Earth* and Clara Weatherwax's *Marching! Marching!* I have never reread these novels, and if I did, maybe I'd think they were great. But I doubt it; I believe that what I admired was their intention rather than their achievement—a mistake not to be easily forgiven.

It was a decade of strong antipathies and high-flying indignation. I have come to dislike the whole "off with their heads" school of criticism, but often in the thirties I took pleasure in playing the Lord High Executioner. Several of the longer pieces in this book are polemical, and perhaps there is not much else to say about them except that today some seem good examples of the genre and others bad. My article about the anti-Soviet and anticommunist bias of the *New York Times Book Review* seems to me to make its point whether that point was worth making or not. My contribution to the discussion of Malraux's *Man's Fate,* on the other hand, simply roiled water that was muddy enough to begin with.

From my present point of view, the most interesting controversy is that following my review of *New Voices in America,* which was edited by Horace Gregory. Gregory, himself a prominent poet as well as a fellow-traveler of long standing, had set out to publish work of young American poets and writers of prose who were less known than he thought they ought to be—more or less as John Lehmann had done for British writers in the three volumes of *New Writing.* Gregory felt that the new writers were likely to be Leftist in their policies, and of course I agreed with him there. What disturbed me was that these Leftists, even those who professed a faith in an inevitable revolution —"a better world's in birth"—sounded as lugubrious as the disciples of the early T.S. Eliot. If they had replied that that was a hell of a way to judge poetry, I would have disagreed with them then but would agree with them now. What they did insist, most of them, was that these youngsters were optimistic all the time and I didn't have brains enough to know it. So the quarrel of the pots and the kettle went on.

Less than a year after the publication of the review, that is, at the time of the Nazi-Soviet pact, this problem and many others came to seem quite unreal. Time, as has often been noted, disposes of many problems by throwing them out on the dump heap. On the other hand, history worries about keeping the record straight. If this collection helps even a little in that process, I shan't be sorry that I agreed to its publication.

Grafton, N.Y., 1973

GRANVILLE HICKS
in
The New Masses

I

THE CRISIS IN AMERICAN CRITICISM

By the time Granville Hicks joined the staff of the *New Masses* as literary editor in January 1934 he had already achieved some recognition as an earnest young critic and reviewer. In 1928 his first book appeared, *Eight Ways of Looking at Christianity*, a fictional conversation in which different theological perspectives were represented. Since January 1929 Hicks had well over a hundred essays and book reviews published in such diverse journals as *The Nation*, the *New Republic*, the *Forum, Hound and Horn, The Bookman*, the *Sewanee Review* and the *South Atlantic Quarterly.* The execution of Sacco and Vanzetti and the stock market crash led Hicks to make a more serious analysis of American society as it was then and not long after he embraced Marxism, though not yet joining the Communist party.

In fact Hicks did not join the Party until the spring of 1935, by which time it was clear that Moscow was abandoning the "third period" policy of attacking social democrats as an enemy worse than the fascists. In its place the Comintern favored "popular fronts" to unite all progressive elements against war and fascism. Hicks did not agree with third period tactics and it is clear that one of the main reasons for his joining the Party was to combat fascism more effectively on the cultural front.

By early 1933 Hicks, a Marxist, was beginning to develop a critique of American literature from his new perspective. "The Crisis in American Criticism" (February 1933) is an analysis of the impasse he felt literary criticism had come to with the onset of the Depression. It is also a call for young critics to articulate a Marxist approach to literature. And it is this task that he hopes the *New Masses* will fulfill and that as literary editor he will encourage, as he states in his "Open Letter" to *New Masses* readers in January of 1934.

The Crisis in American Criticism

Criticism, like American literature in general, has entered upon the second of two stages that are essential to its development as a vital force. The low estate of criticism in the latter half of the nineteenth century and the first years of the twentieth can be traced to its close association with the dominant section of the bourgeoisie. Most critics were confused and unoriginal and exceedingly timid. Almost the only standards they applied to literature were the moral standards of the period. The first task, then, was the emancipation of literature from Victorian morality, and this had been fairly well accomplished by 1925. In criticism the work was done by the impressionists, beginning with James Huneker, whose labors were carried on by H. L. Mencken. But the impressionists, though they were of considerable historical importance, avoided the fundamental questions of explanation and evaluation with which criticism must concern itself. Thus they lost their influence, and the younger critics took up the search for certainty.

Throughout the twenties confusion grew. The impressionists, who were trying to maintain their individualism by separating literature from life, continued to be active. The humanists, offering a ruling class philosophy for a period of capitalist stabilization, won a considerable following. And many of the younger critics sought to create a leisure class culture, suitable for persons who had no functional connection with the economic system. Purely technical criticism flourished, sometimes based on a theory of art for art's sake, sometimes associated with a reactionary philosophy, as in the work of T. S. Eliot. And, to mention still another factor, there was the school of Van Wyck Brooks, which recognized the close tie between the individual writer and the cultural situation, but failed to see the connection between culture and the economic and political situation.

The depression of 1929 brought clarity out of the existing confusion, and criticism, as I have said, entered the second stage. Before much time elapsed, it was clear that Marxism was the central issue in all critical controversies. There had been Marxist critics before 1929, but the leftward movement of a large group of intellectuals focussed attention upon all the literary implications of Communism. And it became apparent to most of these leftward moving writers that Marxism offered the only possible method for the solution of the

5

literary problems that the critics of the postwar period had so miserably bungled. At the same time, the rise of Marxism alarmed many critics of various schools, and they devoted themselves to attacking it.

It will be profitable to examine some of these attacks. There is little to be said about some of them. The sneers and denunciations in the daily press, for example—the work of Harry Hansen, Isabel Paterson, and William Soskin—are a mixture of misunderstanding and misrepresentation. They indicate very clearly that criticism and politics are not separate. More important is the liberal attack, led by Henry Hazlitt, Joseph Wood Krutch, and Elmer Davis—all of whom voted for Norman Thomas in the last election. As Obed Brooks demonstrated in his article in the *Modern Monthly* for February, 1933, these critics invariably fall back on the man-of-straw technique. Henry Hazlitt is peculiarly guilty of this fault, but he is not much worse than Krutch and Davis, and H. L. Mencken, Henry Seidel Canby, and M. R. Werner resort to the same device. The liberal critics have simply refused to meet the Marxists on their own grounds.

Even if the liberals' criticisms were more pointed than they are, the fact would remain that attacks are all they seem capable of. Attacks are, indeed, what most of them have lived on all their lives, and they have never shown much capacity for discovering new ideas or clarifying old ones. This gives us an idea of the sterility of bourgeois criticism. But the forthright reactionaries are no better off. When the editors of the *Hound & Horn* were accused of trying to create a leisure class culture, they began scurrying around to defend themselves. So far their defense has consisted of cheap attacks on the Marxists in the Hazlitt manner. But Archibald MacLeish, an associate of the *Hound & Horners,* has attempted in the *New Republic* for December 21, 1932, to create an up-to-date rationale of the leisure class. MacLeish is not only a well known poet; he is or was on the staff of *Fortune,* and a year ago he wrote for the *Saturday Review of Literature* an article called "To the Young Men of Wall Street." America, he said in this article, "requires of its governors a conception of capitalism in which a man can believe—which a man can oppose in his own mind to other and no longer visionary conceptions." And he cited Owen Young and Henry Ford as examples of the new capitalists. But MacLeish has advanced from this position, which after all belonged to the Golden Age of Big Business, and in the *New Republic* article he attempts to dispose of the Marxists for good and all. Borrowing a little from technocracy, he first says that power production has invalidated Marx, and then puts forth the bright idea that great social changes are coming without anyone bothering to direct them. And in this new society, which will effortlessly come into being, there will be a great number of people who will have nothing to do except to read what he calls "poetry itself" and "poetry as such." And so we have the new theory of the leisure class: the leisure class is all right now because some day everybody will have leisure and the present loafers will have set a good example.

Nonsense of this kind might lead us to suppose that the Marxists have a clear field. And, indeed, I can say that I have seen only one reasonably intelligent criticism of the Marxist position—James Burnham's "Marxism and Esthetics" in the *Symposium* for January, 1933. But there are real weaknesses in our work at the present time, weaknesses that are due not to Marxism but to Marxists. These weaknesses sometimes lend a kind of justification to the distortions of the liberals, and they expose us to very sharp attacks from critics of intelligence. They must be squarely faced.

The tasks of criticism are, as almost everyone will agree, explanation and evaluation. Unfortunately the first attempt on a large scale to apply Marxist methods to the explanation of American literature clearly reveals a great danger. Whatever one may think of V. F. Calverton's morals or his style or his brains, it is my contention that in *The Liberation of American Literature* he was applying the Marxist method to the best of his ability, and that, so far as an understanding of the broad class bases of our literature is concerned, his book is a useful one. But the great concern of Marxist historians of American literature in the future must be the avoidance of Calverton's failings, and especially of his sin of over-simplification. Obviously it does not help us much to know that James, Howells, and Mark Twain were all members of the bourgeoisie; we knew that all along, and knowing that, we want to find out why, though they were members of the same class, they wrote so differently.

Over-simplified Marxism of the Calverton variety reduces æsthetic categories, as Burnham points out, to economic categories. But it is possible to avoid this, and at the same time to show the fundamental dependence of literature on the economic organization of society. One way of doing this is to concentrate attention on the individual writer and his work. First of all, the writer's attitude towards life must

8 <small>GRANVILLE HICKS IN THE NEW MASSES</small>

be defined in terms of his work. This attitude can then be explained as one of the possible variations of the fundamental attitudes of his class. Certain limits, in other words, were imposed on the attitudes of Howells, James, and Mark Twain by the state of bourgeois thought in the middle of the nineteenth century; but within these limits variations were possible. The limits of possible variation can be still further narrowed by a consideration of the status of the particular section of the class to which the author belonged: this introduces, for example, the factor of the frontier in the case of Mark Twain and the factor of leisure and travel in the case of James. And within these narrower limits variations are still possible, variations which the present state of psychology may or may not permit the critic to explain.

Content and Form

Once the author's attitude towards life is explained as adequately as the resources of biography, history, and psychology will allow, the critic is prepared to examine the expression of that attitude in literature. It is at once apparent that an author's range of subjects is determined by the general condition of society, and is still further limited by his personal experience, and with these two factors the critic can deal objectively and more or less definitively. Since the author's choice within this range will be principally dictated by his attitude towards life, which the critic has already defined and explained, the remaining task is simply to examine the aesthetic forms in which the given attitude can express itself when concerned with the given material. There will still remain a variable factor, which is the just concern of purely technical criticism, but the basic questions of content and form will have been competently dealt with.

This is merely a rough suggestion of one practical way of bridging the gap between the analysis of the author's class status and the analysis of his finished literary product. It is possible that, once enough studies of individual writers have been made, a more generalized method can be evolved. But in any case the important point is that a refined and complicated method of procedure is necessary for the adequate understanding of literary phenomena. Many Marxist critics are working on the problem, but the temptation of over-simplification is always there, and we must beware of it.

The problem of evaluation is even more difficult, and there seems to be less evidence that a satisfactory solution is being arrived at, though here again the trouble is with Marxists and not with Marxism. Any discussion of the value of literature must begin with the assumption that literature is to be judged in terms of its effects on its readers. It is, after all, an integral part of life; the realm of art cannot be separated from the rest of human experience. But this leads us to consider, first, the kind of effect literature can have, and, secondly, the kind of effect it ought to have.

Marxists are often accused of dealing with the problem of evaluation rather summarily, and some of them do. These simplifiers, who are fortunately in a minority, argue somewhat in this fashion: if the class struggle is the central fact in life, and if the proletariat not only ought to win but is, historically speaking, certain to win, that literature is best which so affects its readers that they struggle better on behalf of the proletariat. There are at least two obvious objections to this analysis. In the first place, it means that the Marxist critic has no way of evaluating the greater part of literature past and present: he can only say that it is bad, inasmuch as it does not directly contribute to the advance of the proletariat. In the second place, it means that the critic's standard of value is shifting, almost from day to day. What served to inspire the proletarian yesterday will not necessarily inspire him today, when his tasks are different. This would force us to assume that what was a good novel in Russia could not be a good novel in the United States, and that no novel, however good today, could have any value after the establishment of a classless society.

A Theory of Effect

The underlying error here is, it seems to me, the conception of literary effect that is implicit in this standard of value. It implies that the effect of reading a book is such that the reader goes out and does some specific thing. But experience actually convinces us that books seldom have such an effect, and that the books that have influenced us most have had a different sort of effect, subtler, deeper, and more permanent. The simplified conception of effect is indeed, identical with that proposed by Kenneth Burke in his *Counterstatement*. Burke says that two completely separate judgments have to be made with regard to a work of art: its effect has to be judged in the light of the critic's social views, and the way it gains its effect has to be judged according to aesthetic standards. If literature had a narrow, direct, immediate effect, this would be true, but no one can define the effect of great literature in such terms. Burke's theory is really one more attempt to separate literature from life. He admits, of course, that the critic has a right to express agreement or disagreement with the author's purpose, but that is a more or less arbitrary matter, and the critic's real concern must be technique. The critic's insight, according to Burke, is in no way influenced by his philosophical and social views; the two things are in separate compartments.

Perhaps we can best understand the effect of literature if we define the aim of the creative writer. Stated in its simplest form, the aim of an author is to present, in terms of his chosen medium, life as he sees and understands it. Therefore literature affects the reader's attitude towards life. His attitude may be affected by the actual extensions of his experience; he may be brought into contact with kinds of persons or events he has not known. It may be affected by a change in the mode of experience; that is, his reading may lead him to look at events and persons in a different way. It may be affected by the re-interpretation of experience; he may understand more clearly his own thoughts, emotions, and observations. A great work of art will change the reader's attitude towards life in all these ways and perhaps in many others.

At this point our theory has to be concerned with a subjective element, though this is just as true of the cruder conception of effect. That is, what will affect one reader in the way described may not affect another reader. Perhaps the advance of psychology will some day permit us to eliminate subjective judgments altogether, but for the time being we have to proceed empirically. This does not mean, however, that we must surrender to the impressionists. Experience does demonstrate that not all the factors determining the response to a work of art are purely personal. We must, therefore, constantly strive to proceed from the personal to the general. In doing so we find that, as a rule, certain groups of people respond in certain ways. And the most important factor in determining the variations among groups is the class factor, because that is, when considered with all its ramifications, the most important factor in the creation of the individual mind.

In trying to generalize, then, about the effect of literature, the critic is aware that, though in some ways readers of all classes will make substantially the same response, in other respects the effect on one group will differ from the effect on another. If he is trying to arrive at some definite conclusion, he will therefore be forced to take sides. The Marxist critic's decision to ally himself with the proletariat is not merely emotional, nor is it based merely on political grounds. The emphasis placed by dialectical materialism on the role of the proletariat in history is of peculiar importance to the critic. Though there is objective truth, which human knowledge tends to approximate, there is no such thing as personal objectivity, in the sense of freedom from class influences. Therefore that class is most likely to approximate objective truth which has most to gain by such an approximation and least to gain by distortion. In our present society that class is the proletariat.

The critic is, therefore, justified in considering the effect of literature on the proletariat rather than on any other class. But since statistical information is not available, he must proceed by considering the historic role of the proletariat. He can largely eliminate the subjective element in his judgment by studying the possible effect of a piece of literature on the attitudes of persons performing the proletarian role. There is no doubt that this is difficult, but it is the process that any attempt to create objective aesthetic standards must follow in its development from the personal to the general, and the Marxist has a carefully evolved philosophy to guide him.

We are now in a position to formulate our conclusions. If the Marxian theory of history is sound, as I believe and as I am assuming throughout this article, an adequate portrayal of life as it is would lead the proletarian reader to recognize his role in the class struggle. Therefore a book could be judged by its ability to have that kind of effect. But the critic will judge the book, not by its direct effect on himself, but by the qualities that contribute to its possible effect on the attitudes of a certain class of readers. He will insist, for example, on centrality of subject matter: the theme must deal with or be related to the central issues of life. Obviously the novel must, directly or indirectly, show the effects of the class struggle, since, according to Marxism, that is central in life, and no novel that disregarded it could give an adequate portrayal of life. The critic also will insist on intensity: the author must be able to make the reader feel that he is participating in the lives described whether they are the lives of bourgeois or of proletarians. The peculiar function of literature demands this, since it is on intensity that all the various ways of affecting attitudes depend. But it is not to be thought that intensity is merely, or even principally, a matter of technique. On the contrary, intensity is primarily a result of the author's capacity for the assimilation and understanding of experience, and this in turn is related to his attitude towards life. For this reason and for others, the critic will demand, in the third place, that the author's point of view be that of the vanguard of the proletariat. The Marxian theory of knowledge, as I have pointed out above, requires this. And, inasmuch as literature grows out of the author's entire personality, his identification with the proletariat should be as complete as possible. He should not merely believe in the cause of the proletariat; he should be, or should try to make himself, a member of the proletariat.

A Sense of Solidarity

We have, then, a working statement of the qualities a Marxian critic will look for in literature. Literature that had these qualities would serve the purpose described earlier: it would rouse a sense of solidarity with the class-conscious workers and a loyalty to their cause. But it would do so, not by exciting the reader to go and do some particular thing, but by creating in him an attitude, an attitude capable of extension and of adaptation to any situation. It would, for example, force the reader to recognize the complete unworthiness of the existing system and the hope and power of the working class. It would give him a view of reality that, if he was by economic status a member of the proletariat or if he was intellectually and emotionally capable of identifying himself with the proletariat, would reveal to him the potentialities and destiny of that class and would galvanize him into action on its behalf.

Proust and the Bourgeoisie

But note that this list of qualities, admittedly rough and incomplete, gives us not only a standard by which to recognize the perfect Marxian novel, but also a method for the evaluation of all literature. No novel as yet written perfectly conforms to our demands; the question is one of imperfections and of relative successes and failures. It is possible, then, that a novel written by a member of the bourgeoisie might be better than a novel written by a member of or a sympathizer with the proletariat. Proust's *Remembrance of Things Past,* for example, gives a finer, clearer, more convincing picture of the decay of bourgeois civilization than I have found in any novel yet written from the revolutionary point of view. We must admit that Proust omits much that we should like to find in a novel, and that his own interpretation of events is shallow and confused; but the fact remains that he does one thing well, and that is better than doing several things badly. He gives us an enormously vivid sense of the corruption and unworthiness of the system under which we live; we see that that system is decaying and deserves to collapse. The novel, since it does not do more than that, since it does not carry us forward with a surge of determination and hope, is, needless to say, not so good as the perfect proletarian novel; it has not so much historical importance as the imperfect proletarian novel, for that, despite its failure, looks to the future. But Proust is, nevertheless, a better writer than the avowed revolutionary who cannot give us an intense perception of either the character of the proletariat or the character of the bourgeoisie. In any case, the important point is that *The Remembrance of Things Past* has some value and that value must be taken into account.

The same method, in a more complicated form, may be applied to the literature of the past. Calverton's idea that past literature can be evaluated on the basis of its technique—or, as he revises himself, execution—is ridiculous. Experience is all against it; we can learn from the technical achievements of earlier writers, but that is not our principal reason for reading their work. Calverton himself clearly reveals in *The Liberation of American Literature* that he actually applies other standards, though he has not taken the trouble to clarify them. Books do live for successive generations, and part of our task is to define the values that keep them alive.

But such a problem is outside the scope of this article. My purpose here, indeed, is merely to indicate the nature of our problems by tentatively proposing methods of attacking them. The conclusions I have offered are nothing more than suggestions. But the problems are important. The weakness of bourgeois criticism demonstrates the extent of our opportunities. There is no hope of converting the majority of these bourgeois critics, and little perhaps to be gained by converting them; but it is only by meeting their arguments and exposing their inconsistencies and evasion that we can reach the younger writers who can and should be brought to our side. We must not depend only on arousing their sympathy to our cause; we must also show them the soundness of our position. For this reason we must deal with the weaknesses and the difficulties of Marxist criticism as promptly and as definitely as possible. And it is not only the fellow-travelers we should consider; the proletariat is actually producing a literature that requires the kind of guidance only Marxists can give. The time has come for Marxists to make a tremendous effort to clarify their position and improve their practice. In this effort I hope all elements—proletarians, bourgeois intellectuals who have been connected with the movement for some years, and the newer fellow-travelers—will work together. Their labors cannot fail to have an important effect on American intellectual life, an effect that in many different ways will contribute to the overthrow of capitalism and the fulfillment of our hopes.

February, 1933

An Open Letter To
New Masses Reviewers

Before me as I write there is a list of nearly a hundred of you— nearly a hundred men and women who have been, or in the course of time will be, invited to contribute reviews to the *New Masses.** There are novelists and poets on this list, well-known critics, experts on painting and music, historians, economists, philosophers, scientists, labor organizers, journalists and pamphleteers, leaders of the Communist Party. Though I shall be writing you personally, I take this opportunity of greeting you collectively and of saying to you as a group certain things that you may be interested to hear.

There are a few practical considerations that had best be touched on first. Although I have no intention of making a fetish of publication dates, and although I hope you will never sacrifice the quality of your reviews to the demands of the deadline, I think you will agree that timeliness is important in revolutionary journalism. Our comments on books will have greater impact if they appear when the books are being read and discussed. This means that reviews must be written promptly; and if anything suffers in the process, it should be our convenience and not our reviews. Promptness is also necessary in the answering of letters, especially so, because I am handicapped in the editing of this department by living outside New York City. I do not apologize for stressing such points; for efficiency, even on the most mechanical level, is an essential part of the discipline of a revolutionary movement.

But of course what I want principally to speak about is the unusual opportunity in which we have been given a share. In the weekly *New Masses* it will be possible to review all the important books— all the books, that is, that are important to workers, farmers, and intellectuals who read the magazine. We shall, of course, review those books that grow out of the revolutionary movement. We will review them, needless to say, candidly and critically. We shall also review the books that are opposed to the revolutionary movement. We will review them intelligently and discriminatingly as well as searchingly. And we shall review many, many books that, in the minds of their authors and most of their readers, have nothing to do with the revolutionary struggle. We will review them thoughtfully and not unsympathetically, but we will review them from a particular point of view.

The gratifying, the encouraging thing about the *New Masses* is that it has a point of view. We constitute a diverse group. And yet any one of us can speak with confidence of the group's point of view. Every one of us believes that the capitalist system must be destroyed by the power of the proletariat, in alliance with the exploited farmers, the ruined middle class and the aroused intellectual and professional class. Every one is determined to fight such manifestations of capitalism as war and fascism. Every one is resolved to support the workers and poor farmers of America wherever they are struggling against injustice, starvation, and oppression. And these convictions and this determination are fundamental, the very basis of the attitudes and judgments that our reviews will express.

This does not mean that there will be no variety in the *New Masses* reviews. No dictator is going to impose some narrow and arbitrary interpretation of Marxism upon reviewers. Each one of us will work out for himself the application of the revolutionary point of view. And since our interests, knowledge, and experience are so varied, there is little danger of standardization and monotony. We are engaged, after all, in a co-operative venture, to which each contributes what he can. But we are united in our knowledge of our goal and our determination to reach it.

Moreover, the majority of our readers share our point of view. Some readers of the *New Masses* will undoubtedly be hostile to its purposes; we shall have to be accurate, logical, and well informed, not because we can convert these enemies, but because otherwise they will use our mistakes to fight our cause. Other readers will glance at the *New Masses* because they are beginning to feel a little doubt about the system in which they live; the more fully and fairly we set forth our point of view, the more likely we are to win them to our side. But most of the readers will be sympathetic towards— many, of course, active in—the revolutionary movement. It is to them that we are primarily responsible. That is why we must not be bookish or pedantic or abstract. Our task is not simply to write about books; it is to interpret the intellectual currents and the emotional forces of our time as they are reflected in literature.

"We ought to dream!" said Lenin, calling for a periodical that "would become part of an enormous pair of smith's bellows that would blow every spark of class struggle and popular indignation into a general conflagration." The *New Masses* may not be the most important weapon of the revolutionary movement, just as the literary section may not be the most important department of the magazine; but here our opportunity lies, and here we shall succeed or fail.

January, 1934

* In January 1934 the *New Masses* was converted from a monthly journal into a weekly and Granville Hicks became literary editor.

II

REVOLUTION AND THE NOVEL

As "The Crisis in American Criticism" was the call for a Marxist approach to literature in 1933, "Revolution and the Novel" was a statement of first principles through the reinterpretation of literature in 1934. Serialized over seven issues of the *New Masses* in April and May this lengthy essay was one of the most influential of the entire period. Indeed, it staked out the territory of a whole new school of novelists and critics.

The Past and Future as Themes

Of all literary types the novel is the hardest to define; any rigid definition excludes a certain number of books that by common consent are known as novels. This situation has driven Mr. E. M. Forster to define a novel as any largely fictitious narrative too long to be called a short story. The flexibility of the novel helps to explain its vogue: it lends itself to many purposes and all points of view. The most recent of literary forms—an infant when compared with the epic, the lyric, the ballad, the drama—the novel has dominated the literature of the western world for more than a century and a half. Its rise has closely corresponded to the rise of the bourgeoisie, and in the course of its history the mind of the bourgeoisie has been fully expressed, but it cannot be limited to any one class. Not only has the novel been adopted by all the various groups within the bourgeoisie; it has been taken over by proletarian authors, and it is in the novel that the greater and better part of proletarian writing has been done.

Forster's definition explains why the novel can be so naturally and effectively adopted by proletarian writers. Certain traditions have grown up around the drama, traditions with which the proletarian has to break. Each of the various types of lyric has a history that weighs more or less heavily upon the proletarian poet. But the only tradition of the novel is the tradition of flexibility, of almost complete freedom. The only reason for warning proletarian writers against bourgeois literary forms is that certain of those forms cannot be transferred without a transference of the intellectual and emotional conditions that created them. But the novel is not a form at all in that sense; the term is merely a convenient way of describing a great variety of literary forms that have in common only the two qualities Forster notes.

We do not know what kind of literature a classless society will bring forth, but apparently the novel is to have a prominent part in the literature of the transition period. It is therefore important for proletarian writers and readers, and for Marxist critics, to understand the novel's potentialities. Our youthful proletarian fiction has thus far exhibited a striking lack of variety, which possibly indicates a lack of resourcefulness. Not only have important themes been neglected; the best methods have not always been found for the themes that have been used. In these articles I shall try to point out the manifold possibilities of the novel by commenting concretely on both methods and themes. I shall draw as far as seems advisable on the past history of the novel, but I shall treat the past only in so far as it illuminates the opportunities of contemporary proletarian authors.

An obvious, but none the less useful, classification of novels is based upon time. A novel may be located in the past, in the present, or in the future. (By the present, I mean, roughly, the lifetime of the particular author.) Most authors have written of the present—of their particular present, that is—and I shall devote myself chiefly to the possibilities of dealing with the present. But we should not forget that the novelist has both the past and the future to write about if he chooses.

The two essential qualities in a novel of the past are authenticity and relevance. Authenticity we may define for the moment as correspondence to both the known facts about the period in question and the best possible interpretation of those facts. Relevance is relevance to the fundamental interests of the author and his readers.

Novels of the past are most commonly what we call historical romances, and the name indicates that authenticity is not the principal aim of their authors. The greater number of writers who have located their novels in the past have done so because they were thus freed from certain of the responsibilities of dealing with the present. Even the least critical reader, the one who is most eager to yield to illusions, cannot prevent himself from making some sort of comparison between a novel of the present and the reality he knows. Of course he goes through the same sort of process with an historical novel, but so much cannot be compared that he finds it relatively easy to forego criticism even when there is a legitimate place for the comparison. The author is thereby privileged to create characters and events in accordance with his own desires or his conception of his readers' desires, and the only checks upon his performance are his readers' knowledge, usually meager, of history and their sense, often not very sharp, of what constitutes consistency and plausibility in human conduct. The author's deviation from authenticity may be the result of ignorance or it may be conscious. It permits both the romanticism of Dumas and Stevenson, a romanticism of adventure and action, and the sentimental, nostalgic romanticism of Willa Cather's *Shadows on the Rock* and Wilder's *The Woman of Andros.*

The absence of authenticity would be enough to condemn historical romances, but in many of them we note the absence of relevance as well. In a sense any book that is read must have some reason for its appeal, but this need not be relevance to the fundamental interests of the reader. The typical historical romance appeals to the reader's desire to escape from the world in which he lives and to experience vicariously a more ideal life, a life unhampered by the restraining conditions of that world. To provide such an opportunity for escape is, according to Stevenson, the primary purpose of fiction, and he, as well as countless others, put his theory in practice. One does not need to engage in any profound psychological demonstration of the harmfulness of such literature; the infantile character of the satisfactions it offers is apparent; indeed, Stevenson frankly said that the function of literature was the function of day-dreams.

But historical romances may have relevance even when they lack authenticity, and, as a matter of fact, the leading historical romancers have sacrificed authenticity for the sake of relevance. Even when the author is permitting his readers to escape from the confines of contemporary reality, he may be seeking as well to impress upon them his own conception of that reality. So Sir Walter Scott, in his novels of the Middle Ages, gave his readers plenty of adventure, but took care at the same time to communicate to them the world-view of a Tory. Willa Cather, in *Death Comes for the Archbishop* and *Shadows on the Rock,* has a message for the modern world. Hervey Allen has admitted that he chose the period he did for *Anthony Adverse* because he saw in it a parallel to his own age. Miss Cather, Mr. Allen, Mr. Wilder, and a good many others have written of the past precisely because the lower level of authenticity—the result of the impossibility of the reader's making a direct comparison with reality—has permitted them to give to their conceptions of life an apparent relevance that they really do not have. They believe, for example, that religious faith is necessary in the modern world, but they find it easier to demonstrate that necessity in terms of the past.

It is also possible for an historical novel to have a high degree of authenticity with a low degree of relevance. Perhaps complete authenticity would necessarily involve relevance, but in practice, as Leonard Ehrlich's *God's Angry Man* shows, a novelist with wide knowledge of and considerable insight into a period may nevertheless fail to bring out its relevance for our times. Somewhat the same criticism may, at this point, be leveled against Josephine Herbst's *Pity Is Not Enough,* though perhaps subsequent volumes in the series will indicate that this flaw results from some defect in the author's treatment rather than from a fundamental weakness in her conception of the past. In general, authenticity without relevance is the mark of a serious novelist who has not quite found himself.

Enough has been said to indicate the importance of both authenticity and relevance. Authenticity, for the proletarian novelist, means correspondence to the best documentary evidence about the period in question as interpreted according to the Marxian theory of history. Relevance is relevance to the contemporary situation, interests, and demands of the working class. The historical novel further requires, of course, various qualities that are also demanded by the novel of the present, in connection with which I shall discuss them. But, these qualities being present, authenticity and relevance must be added to them.

There is obviously no reason why the proletarian author should not, on these terms, attempt the historical novel. Theoretically the entire past is open to him; there is no period of the past that is not, if one sees deeply enough, relevant to the present interests of the working class. In practice, however, the proletarian author will probably select some event the relevance of which is fairly clear: the French Revolution, Shays' Rebellion, the Paris Commune, the Chartist revolt. for example. Such events offer a magnificent opportunity for increasing the understanding of the present by increasing the understanding of the past. It is true that the proletarian author will probably find it easier to deal with the present, and will be far more interested in the present, but the past is open to him, and, as proletarian literature becomes richer and more diverse, it is safe to predict that the past will not be neglected.

The problem of documenting the historical novel differs little from the problem, which I shall discuss later, of documenting the novel of the present. Authenticity is not secured by the introduction of masses of material gleaned from the history books, nor does it depend on the inclusion of real persons and events. Every character and every incident in a book might be fictitious, and yet the book could have absolute authenticity. Authenticity depends, obviously, on knowledge and understanding, and, if these are great enough, the essential character of the period can be re-created wholly in the realm of fiction. On the other hand, the introduction of historical figures is always permissible and usually advisable.

One reason for urging proletarian novelists to attempt the historical novel is the great advantage they have over their bourgeois contemporaries. It seems almost impossible for the representative middle-class novelist to write about the past without romanticizing it; his vague discontent with the present and his lack of hope for the future almost force him to assume an elegiac tone, even when he is making the greatest effort to be honest. A proletarian author, however, expresses his dissatisfaction with the past in constructive labors for the future, and he would therefore feel little temptation to become nostalgic. The achievement of relevance could scarcely be a serious problem for him, since he would be fully aware of the significant tendencies of his own day. Moreover, the clarifying force of Marxian analysis would lay a firm foundation for the understanding of the past. This is not to say that the writing of a sound and valuable historical novel is easy, even for a proletarian novelist with all his advantages. These advantages entail high standards, and the proletarian writer would be intensely conscious of shortcomings. The difficulties are real, but the opportunities are not to be overlooked. The construction of an artificial parallelism, such as one finds in Upton Sinclair's *Roman Holiday,* is not worth the efforts of a serious writer; such work is as misleading as propaganda as it is defective as literature. But the actual and authentic re-creation of some past period— particularly a period in which the class struggle is sharp and its implications for the proletariat significant—offers opportunities for the artist that will compensate for the difficulties it involves.

If novels of the past have much to offer, novels of the future are less promising. We find a few novels located in the future, just as we find many novels located in the past, merely for the convenience of the author. We also find a few novels that are concerned with the future merely for the fun of prediction. These usually make some pretense to scientific authority, and they combine romantic entertainment with more or less serious efforts at instruction. The romances of Jules Verne and some of the earlier novels of H. G. Wells are the best examples of the type. Ordinarily, however, any novel that seeks seriously to predict the future does so in order to influence the present. Thus we

come to the largest and most important group of novels of the future,
the Utopian novels. We may legitimately consider all Utopian novels
as novels of the future, even though some of them are located in some
imaginary land in the present.

From the earliest times Utopian novels have been written because their authors thought to popularize their views by sugar-coating
the bitter pill of exposition. The Utopian novel is always more or less
expository, and has to be. Therefore it cannot be judged by the
criteria we would apply to other types of fiction. The fundamental
criteria must be sociological; it is the soundness of the author's views
that counts. On the other hand, we may recognize the presence of
literary values, though they are of secondary importance. The Utopian
novelist does not merely expound his conception of the future; he
tries to show the future itself in human terms. Morris does not content himself with saying that the men of the future will be happy and
free and artistic; he tries to show their happiness and freedom and
their pursuit of beauty. Huxley does more than condemn the dangers
of a mechanized, standardized society; he exhibits the minds and
hearts of the people of which such a society is composed. The more
fully an author can reveal the human inhabitants of his Utopia, the
more convincing he will be. And yet his work must ultimately be
judged by the views on which it rests. At best all his art can do is to
permit him to apply his knowledge of what human beings are like
under the existing conditions to his conception of what future conditions will be, and if he misunderstands the tendencies in the present
that are shaping the future, his work fails at both points.

The Utopian novel has been used for a multitude of purposes.
Occasionally the author paints the kind of future he hopes will be
avoided, as Huxley did in *Brave New World*. Jack London, in *The
Iron Heel*, though assuming that the revolutionary movement would
eventually succeed, portrayed an initial defeat and its consequences.
More commonly the author permits his own interests and desires to
shape his conception of the world of the future. After the appearance
and success of Edward Bellamy's *Looking Backward*, several score
of American writers embodied in narratives of the future their conceptions of the kind of world they desired and the ways in which such
a world could be achieved. Some authors are principally concerned
with ends, as both Bellamy and Morris were, in their different ways,
in *Looking Backward* and *News from Nowhere*, and describe briefly

or not at all the steps by which the better society is to be obtained. Others seek, as Wells has done in his *Shape of Coming Things* to describe the whole process of transformation.

It would appear that the Communist author would be in a position to write with particular effectiveness of the future, and this is probably true. The question, however, is whether it is worth doing. The general conception of the future he would express would be, of course, the property of all Communists, and his work could not have the "originality" of the famous Utopian novelists. So far as the structure of the future society is concerned, the pioneering work has been done, and all the writer could do would be to embody the conceptions of Marx and his followers in as richly human terms as possible. This might have value, in so far as it could bring home the desirability of the classless society and the necessity of the proletarian dictatorship as a means to that end. But there would always be the danger of fanciful and unscientific Utopianism, of the sort that Marxism has always condemned. Communism is rightly opposed to the kind of speculation that interferes with the realistic perception of objective facts, and it may be that a Communist Utopia is a contradiction in terms. Some Communist writer may some day prove me wrong, but I believe, especially when I think of all the other opportunities there are, that the novel of the future is not worth the efforts of a proletarian author.

Complex and Collective Novels

Although, as we have seen, the proletarian novelist might write about either the past or the future, he is far more likely to write about the present. No great virtue attaches to the present as a subject; it is possible to be evasive and untruthful in writing about the present, just as it is possible to be honest and courageous in writing about past or future. The important thing is for the author to live in the present; if he is part of the life of his own times, knows and responds to the currents of his age, faces squarely and seeks to solve the problems of his generation, it does not matter what he writes about. Shakespeare was not less fully an Elizabethan Englishman because he laid his dramas in Egypt, Greece, and Rome; nor can anyone accuse Wells, whatever else his faults may be, of seeking to escape from the present when he writes of the year 2100. Yet the fact remains that a great majority of writers have sought, not unnaturally, to express their concern with the present by writing about the present, and this and succeeding articles will be devoted to a consideration of ways in which this may be done.

Looking at any group of famous novels, we observe that most of them are concerned with individuals as individuals, and that usually there is in each novel one character who receives the greater part of the author's attention. In some quarters it has been assumed, both because the individualist novel has so persistently interested bourgeois writers and because Communism is anti-individualistic, that it is a mistake for proletarian authors to attempt this type of fiction. The theorists who take this position have some logic on their side, but experience is against them. We do not know what kind of novels will be written in a classless society, but it is already clear that, during the long period of transition, many, though by no means all, revolutionary writers will be concerned in their work with individuals. It is not to be assumed that such writers are indifferent to the play of social forces or to the ties that bind individuals into groups; they merely find it easier to communicate their perception of such phenomena in terms of individual lives.

All this must be said if we are to approach the subject of the collective novel without attaching to it a kind of political and theoretical significance that is really irrelevant. That the collective novel is important I do not deny, and I shall try to give it due consideration, but I refuse to believe that it is the only form for proletarian authors. Moreover, I think that we need to discover what we really mean when we speak of the collective novel. For some critics the important thing seems to be for authors not to have individual heroes, but, as I shall try to show, the absence of an individual hero does not necessarily make a novel collective. As I pointed out in reviewing the first volume of Jules Romains' *Men of Good Will* in The Anvil, a distinction between collective and complex novels is advisable. This distinction is not proposed as a hard and fast dogma, but I think its utility will become clear as we proceed.

The Collective Novel

The collective novel not only has no individual hero; some group of persons occupies in it a position analogous to that of the hero in conventional fiction. Without lapsing into the mysticism of those pseudo-psychologists who talk about the group-mind, we can see that, under certain circumstances, a group may come into existence that is independent of and more important than any of the individuals who compose it. Such a group could be portrayed through the eyes of a single individual—in other words, in terms of the traditional novel. But it might be more effective to portray the group as a group, to show forth objectively and unmistakably its independent reality. To do this requires a new technique, the technique of the collective novel.

So little work of this sort has been written that it is not easy to discuss the way in which it can be done. Most of the examples in existence spend a good deal of time in depicting the genesis of the group. Thus in the preliminary chapters of *Barricades in Berlin* one feels the group only as a potential entity, and in any case it is only in certain scenes that the group as a group is the dominating force. Kataev in *Time, Forward!* does not even try to bring the group into the foreground except in the chapters that portray the actual cement mixing; nevertheless, he creates a sense of the power of the group early enough in the story so that one is always aware of it as a factor in the situation. Fadeyev in *The Nineteen* almost takes the reality of the group for granted, in order to concern himself with the psychological relation to the group of the various individuals that compose it.

These examples suggest two generalizations. First, the existence of such a group depends on certain objective factors, and, in order to convey a sense of the group, the author must portray the conditions that call it into being. Second, it seems to be essential to depict at least some of the individuals in the group apart from the group. The first point is fairly obvious, but the second requires some explanation. The group is born, so to speak, and inevitably it dies. Its lifetime does not correspond to the lifetimes of the individuals who compose it. We therefore have to be sufficiently aware of them as individuals to be able to believe in their capacity to exist apart from the group, that is, both before and after the period of its existence. The problem this involves, the problem of creating credible individuals without destroying the sense of group unity, is the great problem of the collective novel.

If this problem can be solved, the possibilities of the collective novel are innumerable. Although the number of situations that would give rise to such groups as we are discussing is probably limited, each group is unique. Moreover, there is more than one way of treating each group. The author may be concerned with the relations of individuals to the group or he may be chiefly occupied with portraying the relation of the group to individuals outside it or to other groups. He may, as we have seen, treat the genesis of the group or he may indicate its genesis as he depicts it in action. And, though the situations are limited, they probably are increasing and, as the example of Russia shows, would undoubtedly increase with great rapidity in the course of building socialism. This may or may not mean that the critics are right in predicting that the collective novel will be the novel of the future, but in any case it is even now a legitimate form. At present there are many important and representative situations that could not possibly be treated in the collective novel, but there are other situations that demand such treatment, and the problems they involve challenge the ingenuity of any author.

The Complex Novel

What distinguishes the collective novel is, as we have said, the sense of the group as a group. This sense is not only communicated to the readers as an objective fact; it is also shown as a psychological reality for the members of the group. Without this sense the novel is not a collective novel, even though it has no individual hero; it is what I should call a complex novel. The complex novel has no individual hero, no one central character; but at the same time the various characters do not compose a collective entity; they may or may not have a factual relationship, but they do not have the psychological relationship that would entitle them to be called a group. Obviously there is a certain area within which the collective novel and the complex novel are very much alike; e.g., whenever the author of the collective novel is treating his characters as separate individuals. Apart from their group relationship, he follows the technique of the complex novel. But in the collective novel, if it is successful, the group sooner or later emerges as a character, so to speak, in itself, whereas in the complex novel there is not, and is not intended to be, any such development.

The complex novel might be regarded as a combination of two or more biographical novels. The author, that is, tells the stories of two or more individuals without giving any one of them a place of priority. There must, however, be some relationship between the stories if the novel is to have unity, and usually this relationship is both factual and thematic. Many degrees of complexity are possible. Family chronicles, for example, belong to a rather elementary type of complex novel. The factual relationship is provided by the family itself; the thematic relationship may be based, as in *The Way of All Flesh,* on a certain biological theory, or as in *The Forsyte Saga,* on certain social conceptions, or, as in *The Old Wives' Tale,* on a particular world-view. As these examples suggest, this elementary type of the complex novel is merely a simple variation, a simple extension, horizontally as in *The Old Wives' Tale* or vertically as in *The Way of All Flesh,* of the biographical novel. Equally simple is the organization of *Ulysses:* there are two characters, with the reader's interest very evenly divided between them; and the unity, insofar as it is not merely factual, is secured with the aid of the Homeric parallel.

These simpler types are suggestive, but we shall learn more about the complex novel if we turn to its more ambitious practitioners. In the latter part of the 19th century William Dean Howells attempted a complex novel, *A Hazard of New Fortunes.* Here the factual relationship is a matter of the magazine with which all the characters are directly or indirectly concerned; but when we seek for the thematic relationship, we are somewhat at a loss. It appears, not only from the novel itself but also from Howells' letters of the period in which it was written, that he was chiefly impressed by the diversity of city life and wished to record some of the magnificent variety of New York. The result of this triumph of the sense of diversity over the sense of unity is a kind of chaos for which the factual unity in no way compensates. The same fault weakens the effect of John Dos Passos' *Manhattan Transfer,* though his sense of unity, which manifests itself in the rhythm of the various lives he portrays, is stronger than Howells', and the book, despite the fact that it includes a greater number of characters and has much less in the way of factual relationship to depend on, makes a more solid impact than *A Hazard of New Fortunes*.

A sense of diversity is not enough for the creation of a complex novel. However, the desire to write complex novels originates to a considerable extent in such awareness, in the feeling that one character cannot be adequately representative. That is probably why the complex novel has become rather common in our times: authors are intensely conscious of the instability and artificiality of formal social relationships, and they wish to do justice to more than one aspect of experience. Presumably such a feeling explains Dos Passos' choice of form not only in *Manhattan Transfer* but also in *The 42nd Parallel* and *1919*. Dos Passos apparently felt that to tell the story of Mac alone, or of J. Ward Morehouse alone, or of Sister alone, would be essentially false. He therefore devised a form that would permit him to set side by side their stories and the stories of various other representative Americans. But the superiority of *The 42nd Parallel* and *1919* to *Manhattan Transfer* lies in the fact that their thematic unity is so much stronger.

The question naturally arises whether this thematic unity is simply a matter of the arrangement of the material or is the explication of the author's perception of relationships that elude the less sensitive observer. By means of a quotation from Philip Quarles' notebook Aldous Huxley expounds the theory of *Point Counter Point:* "The musicalization of fiction . . . All you need is a sufficiency of characters and parallel, contrapuntal plots. While Jones is murdering a wife, Smith is wheeling the perambulator in the park. You alternate the themes. More interesting, the modulations and variations are also more difficult. A novelist . . . shows several people falling in love, or dying, or praying in different ways—dissimilars solving the same problem. Or vice versa, similar people confronted with dissimilar problems. In this way you can modulate through all the aspects of your theme." The conception of unity here expressed is, in the most abstract sense, thematic; it depends wholly on the arrangement of material. But actually the characters in *Point Counter Point* are related and the events are unified, not by the adroit juxtapositions and contrasts but by the author's sense of the futility of any sort of endeavor. Only Rampion—and the exception is quite inexplicable in terms of the book—escapes from the general indictment. The arrangement serves to emphasize the pervasive sense of futility, but it is the latter that gives the book such unity as it has.

Both *Point Counter Point* and its model, Gide's *The Counterfeiters,* illustrate how far an ingenious ordering of materials may succeed in conveying to the reader the author's awareness of unity in diversity. But it is the actual perception of relationship that is important. I have analyzed elsewhere the structure of *The 42nd Parallel* and *1919,* and I need not repeat the analysis here. It is only necessary to say that, despite the fact that Dos Passos' intentions have not been completely revealed, and despite occasional weaknesses in characterization and conduct of the narrative, the work clearly illustrates the value of the Marxian interpretation to the writer of the complex novel. The same method of interpretation sharpened the insight of Arnold B. Armstrong, whose *Parched Earth* dramatically reveals the fundamental relationships of a considerable number of inhabitants of a California town.

If one wishes to see how other methods of unification have been employed, examples are easy to find. In Thornton Wilder's *Bridge of San Luis Rey* the factual relationship is accidental and the thematic relationship theological. In Frank Norris' *The Octopus* the various characters are in fact closely related, but the author's reliance on a naive and mystical philosophy, rather than on the genuine perception of social forces, for his thematic unity, robs the conclusion of the book of its force. The unifying ideology of Romains' *Men of Good Will* has not yet been made clear, but the first two volumes give evidence of a subtle distortion intended to make events fit a reactionary conception of society, perhaps derived from Pareto. For an example of the complete vulgarization of the method one has only to turn to Tiffany Thayer's *Twelve Men:* starting with the factual relationship of jury service, Thayer tries to secure thematic unity by revealing still another level of factual relationships, for the most part accidental and trivial.

No arbitrary limit can be set to the number of stories that may be woven into the complex novel. Both Romains and Dos Passos, planning works of considerable length, have not hesitated to introduce ten or a dozen leading characters. This process may easily be extended, but at a certain point the complex novel comes to resemble very closely a book of sketches. Dos Passos nearly, or perhaps quite, reached this point in *Manhattan Transfer,* and William March has deliberately built *Company K* out of a great many autobiographical fragments. It would be idle to try to decide whether *Company K* is a collection of sketches or a complex novel. The important question is whether it achieves thematic unity, and the answer seems to be that within limits it does. By arranging his sketches in chronological order March makes his book a picture of the war and its after-effects, and his pessimism reveals itself with cumulative force. Edwin Seaver's *The Company* achieves its effect in somewhat the same way: his many portraits of dissatisfied employees suggest the disintegration of the petty bourgeois as a class and the frustration of its individual members.

The importance of thematic unity in the complex novel has been made sufficiently clear. The factual relationship is less important, but it seems necessary in order to set convenient limits both for the author and for his readers. So far as the author is concerned, the factual relationship determines the boundaries within which he can reveal the more fundamental unity that is his primary concern. If his sense of unifying forces is really sound, there are no restrictions on its application; all life is unified, we may assume, in the light of his conceptions, and all life might be his theme. But limitation is a practical as well as an artistic necessity, even in a work of many volumes, and it is this kind of framework that the factual relationship provides. For the reader, on the other hand, the factual relationship is a kind of guarantee that the characters and the events have not been selected simply to prove a theory. The realization that these characters and events have some familiar kind of relationship creates in the reader a willingness to regard them as normal and representative, and therefore to accept the underlying unity revealed by the author as significant. Of course the factual relationship may be rather slight, as it is thus far in both Dos Passos and Romains, but some framework—even if it is no more than the presence of all the characters in a single city—seems essential.

For the proletarian novelist, his perceptions sharpened by the amplification of the Marxist method, the complex novel has much to offer. The fellow-traveler, the novelist of bourgeois backgrounds but proletarian sympathies, is particularly likely to find this form a satisfying means for the expression of his experiences. The complex novel permits a writer to make use of his knowledge of bourgeois life without restricting him to that life, for he may set over against representative bourgeois characters representative proletarian characters, using his Marxian understanding of both classes to give his work unity.

There are, of course other problems—problems that the complex novel shares with the novel of a single individual—but Marxian understanding can do much to solve the particular problem of thematic unity.

Drama and Biography as Models

There is a point at which the novel of the past or of the future cannot be clearly distinguished from the novel of the present; there is a point at which the novel without a hero cannot be distinguished from the novel with a hero; there is a point at which the collective novel cannot be distinguished from the complex novel. The distinctions I have been proposing in these articles are suggestive rather than definitive. This becomes particularly true and particularly important as we turn to the novel centered in individuals. The distinction that I use as a point of departure in this article, proposed by Edwin Muir in his *Structure of the Novel*, cannot be made with any great precision, but it is nevertheless useful. It is the distinction between the dramatic and the biographical novel.

The Dramatic Novel

The dramatic novel is dominated by a situation or a plot. Like the complex novel, it distributes the reader's interest among several characters, but these characters are closely related in terms of the plot and not merely in terms of some sociological or philosophical generalization. Moreover, the distribution of interest is not incompatible with the emergence of one character in a position of dominant importance—the hero, in short. As in the complex novel, the characters compose a group, but this group has no psychological unity; on the contrary, the plot usually demands opposition between two or more of these characters, as in the typical hero-heroine-villain situation. In their emphasis on individuals as individuals, biographical and dramatic novels are very much alike, and often the distinction is hard to make, but between fully developed forms the differences in treatment are obvious. No one, for instance, could hesitate to call *The Scarlet Letter* dramatic and *Tom Jones* biographical.

Edwin Muir contends that the dramatic novel develops in time and the biographical novel in space, and he compares the former to music and the latter to sculpture. This is merely a figure of speech, but it does indicate that the structure of the dramatic novel is determined by the development of the situation with which it deals, a development in which time is an important factor. The time element is not important in *Tom Jones* or *Tono-Bungay;* in fact it would be difficult to say, offhand, how much time either covers. In *The Scarlet Letter,* however, or in *Wuthering Heights,* the sequence of events is precisely measured. It is, of course, the emphasis on direct causation, rather than the emphasis on time, that is important, and the reader's consciousness of the passage of time is merely his recognition of the necessary orderliness of events. In most plays—not all plays are dramatic in this sense of the word—the time intervals are specifically denoted so that the spectator can have a precise framework of reference in which to locate the events he watches.

All this implies, and correctly, that the structure of the dramatic novel is more rigid than the structure of the biographical novel. This, in turn, demands a more careful selection. Thackeray in *Henry Esmond* or Dickens in *David Copperfield* could introduce any person or event that illuminated the life of the times and could even comment directly and personally on the progress of the story. Hawthorne, on the other hand, could tell us only so much about Chillingworth, Dimmesdale, and Hester as was necessary for our understanding of the situation of sin and punishment that is *The Scarlet Letter's* theme. Observe the rigorousness with which Henry James selects the material of *The Awkward Age* or *The Wings of the Dove.* And note, incidentally, how easily a novel by either James or Hawthorne can be arranged in scenes.

Obviously the dramatic novel must be self-contained. Every piece of characterization or description has a necessary relation to the sequence of events, and these events build towards a climax that is in itself their justification. This kind of limitation is not only difficult; it is genuinely restricting. The novelist may well be loath to exclude types of experience and kinds of events that he recognizes as important. Perhaps that is why dramatic treatment is more common in the short story than in the novel: the purely physical limitations of the short story make structural limitations acceptable and even desirable. The traditional expansiveness of the novel, on the other hand, encourages the writer to break through any such barriers.

Barriers are, however, absolutely essential in the dramatic novel. The impact of such a novel—like the impact of a play—comes from the fact that it is self-contained, that all the premises on which it rests are clearly stated, and that the end can be recognized, once it is reached, as having been foreshadowed by the beginning. This is precisely where the great difficulty arises. The traditional masters of the dramatic form in the novel have known how to select their material and how to order it. But the situation must be at one and the same time self-contained and relevant to the lives of the readers. Skillfully written melodrama may observe all the rules of dramatic structure and yet be valueless because the characters and events involved bear little relationship to ordinary human existence. The situation, in other words, must be representative; the characters must be recognizable men and women and not mere puppets; and the order of events must correspond to a credible conception of cause and effect.

Obviously no serious novelist would permit himself to take advantage of the kind of irrelevance we find in melodrama, but relevance is a matter of degree, and certain recognized masters of the dramatic form have achieved less relevance than is demanded in art of the highest order. The absence of relevance may be manifested in the selection of a situation of narrow reference, in the arbitrary and implausible manipulation of events, or in the distortion or imperfect creation of character. Henry James, for example, narrowed and narrowed his field of reference until the characters in *The Wings of the Dove* and *The Golden Bowl*, to say nothing of *The Sacred Fount* and *The Outcry*, live in a world as remote from that of his readers as if he were writing of another planet. The weakness of Hawthorne's characters has already been noted. Thomas Hardy did not hesitate to make excessive use of coincidence, not as the melodramatist does, to make his plot come out right, but rather to suit his philosophy, which is supposed to be the basis for the relevance of the drama he unfolds.

The dramatic form permits the novelist to make a strong and immediate impact upon his readers, and it is, furthermore, a form obviously adapted to certain situations. So far it has been neglected by proletarian authors. Mary Heaton Vorse approximates, but only approximates, a dramatic form in *Strike*. In comparison with *Call Home the Heart* and *To Make My Bread*, which are biographical, *Strike*, though inferior in other respects, shows the superiority of the dramatic form in the depiction of a situation so charged with emotional and social significance as that in Gastonia. A strike also invites either the method of the complex novel, as in William Rollins' *The Shadow Before*, or the method of the collective novel. The choice of method depends on the author's point of view and his plan of emphasis. When he wishes to bring out the conflict of personalities in terms of a rapidly changing situation, the dramatic method naturally suggests itself.

A strike is not, however, the only occasion for dramatic treatment, and perhaps not the best. Any situation essentially representative of proletarian life and involving representative proletarian characters—though very possibly characters from other classes as well—is a possible subject for such treatment. The conversion of a worker or intellectual, for example, to Communism, a theme frequently found in the biographical novel, might be more effectively presented in dramatic terms. Many incidents of the daily struggle invite dramatic treatment in the short story, and some of them in the novel as well. The personal psychological conflict between a Communist and other individuals—members of his family, for instance—is admirable material for the dramatic novel. There is no limit to the number of situations susceptible to presentation in this form, and certainly no proletarian author could be unaware of the relevance of the kind of situation we have been speaking of. His difficulty would be, not in showing the relevance of his material to the lives of his readers, but in shaping that material in accordance with the austere orderliness that dramatic presentation demands. It is important for some proletarian author to attack these problems of selection and structure, for if he succeeded in solving them, he might measurably enrich the literature of the revolution, not only by his work but also by his example.

The Biographical Novel

All the forms of the novel we have thus far discussed are relatively late innovations. Defoe, Richardson, Fielding, and Smollett wrote of Robinson Crusoe, Moll Flanders, Pamela Andrews, Clarissa Harlowe, Joseph Andrews, Tom Jones, Roderick Random, and Humphrey Clinker as if they were biographers—though, of course, biographers endowed with the privileges of the creator. Even Sterne used the biographical form as the basis for his eccentric experiments in *Tristram Shandy*. Certain of the Gothic romancers found that the maintenance of suspense demanded departures from the formula of the life-history, but biography provided the model for most nineteenth century novelists, including Scott, Thackeray, Dickens, and Meredith. By this time, it is true, Jane Austen and the Brontë sisters had broken almost completely with the biographical method, and such novelists as George Eliot, and to some extent Thackeray and Meredith, had found out how to select and order the events of a biography so as to approximate the dramatic effect. However, the general biographical form continued to predominate, not only in English and American, but also in French literature.

As I remarked earlier, it is only between extreme forms of the biographical and the dramatic novel that a clear distinction can be made. The difficulty of differentiating becomes apparent if we observe the novels of Thomas Hardy. Hardy's method is clearly dramatic, and the dramatic structure of *The Return of the Native* is obvious. In *The Mayor of Casterbridge* and *Tess of the D'Urbervilles*, however, he employs what seems to be a simple biographical method. Nevertheless, the selection of events in both books follows so rigorous a pattern that the novels resemble *The Return of the Native* far more closely than they do *Tom Jones* or *Roderick Random*. To turn to American contemporaries, Dreiser and Lewis have never departed from the biographical form, and on the other hand Ernest Hemingway has definitely followed a dramatic pattern. The problem of classification arises, however, when we come to such a writer as Edith Wharton, who is clearly dramatic in some works, such as *Ethan*

Frome, and in others, such as *The Custom of the Country,* is apparently but perhaps not actually biographical.

My excuse for dwelling on this problem of classification is not any idea that classification is at all important, but rather my desire to give the broadest possible scope to my remarks. Certain things that I have said about the dramatic novel are equally applicable to the biographical, and the greater part of my discussion of the biographical novel is more or less pertinent to the novel in general. I have reserved for discussion in subsequent articles certain practical questions about point of view, selection of material, method of narration, and use of documentation. I shall discuss these subjects in relation to the biographical novel, but, as I have indicated, my comments ought to have a more general bearing. The biographical form was the first to develop, and in a sense all other forms are variations of it. It should be possible, in the light of my analysis of the differentiating factors and special problems of these other forms, to make whatever re-interpretations are necessary for a wider application.

Characters and Class

In the biographical novel in its purest form one character dominates the book from beginning to end. The great virtue of the form is that, if the author is skillful, we come to know that one character thoroughly, and by virtue of knowing him so well we come to know his world. The form in itself makes no rigorous demands; the author may begin and end his story where he pleases, and he may loiter as long as he cares to at any attractive spot along the way. There are no questions asked so long as he succeeds in creating a character with whom the readers may identify themselves.

Obviously the selection of the central character is the first important step for the author of a biographical novel. Yet absolutely anyone might be chosen for the leading role, and each author has to make his choice on the basis of his experience, his interests, his conception of what is representative and important. This is as true for proletarian authors as for any others: the whole world stretches before them, and no critic can tell them they must write of this kind of man or that.

Because the choices are so nearly infinite, it may seem a little arbitrary to discuss them according to economic classification. But no Marxist will deny that the most important thing about an individual is the social class to which he belongs. Other things are important, too, and cannot be left out of account, but, since convenience demands some sort of systematic arrangement, we shall not go far wrong if we base our scheme on fundamental economic considerations.

The Millionaire

At the top of the scale, as things stand, is the major industrialist or financier, the ruler of modern society. He would seem to be as natural a theme for the contemporary novelist as a king was for the Elizabethan dramatist. Yet actually relatively few novels are written about multi-millionaires, perhaps because their activities are somewhat more mysterious than those of kings, perhaps because biographical novelists often prefer to write about characters they can admire. However that may be, enough biographical novels have concerned the very rich to warrant a few generalizations.

In the first place, the novelist who chooses an industrialist or financier as his central character has to define his attitude towards this figure of his creation. Usually he either approves of him or condemns him. If he approves, he may show his approval by exhibiting the great man's good deeds and revealing his contributions to civilization. As a matter of fact, I cannot think of a serious novelist who has ever done this, though apologies of this type are common in the *Saturday Evening Post* and the *American Magazine*. The serious novelist is far more likely to make his approval tacit. He usually refrains from spending much time on the economic functions of his multi-millionaire and dwells on his kindness to his family or his support of culture. This may be a largely conscious method of offering a subtle apology, as in Tarkington's *The Plutocrat* and some of Hergesheimer's short stories, or it may be an unconscious betrayal of ignorance and prejudice. Henry James, with his leisure-class contempt for money-grabbing, hated millionaires in their economic functions, but his non-functioning millionaires are very sweet. In *Dodsworth* Sinclair Lewis pried his character loose from his automobile factory before he placed him on display—a device that may account for the singularly silly ending of the novel.

It may be put to the credit of literature that far more novelists have disapproved of multi-millionaires than have approved of them. (It is really a striking comment on the status of authors within the class to which most of them have belonged.) Disapproval has traditionally taken a moral form: note Howells' *Rise of Silas Lapham*, Boyesen's *Mammon of Unrighteousness*, Herrick's *Memoirs of an American Citizen*, Phillips' *Master Rogue*, White's *A Certain Rich Man*, and Upton Sinclair's *Oil*. Such novels point out the evil deeds of their millionaires and usually dwell on their moral degeneration. Norris in *The Pit* tried to reconcile such a moral judgment with a mystical determinism: though the deeds of the individual are wicked, the good of society is secured.

Proletarian novelists certainly cannot be expected to approve of industrialists and financiers, but, on the other hand, they are not likely to fall into the liberal fallacy of attributing to personal wickedness the evils of a system. Certain bourgeois novelists have tried to avoid this dilemma, and with some degree of success. Theodore Dreiser sought to preserve a rigid objectivity in *The Financier* and *The Titan* by clinging to a thorough-going philosophy of determinism. In *Tono-Bungay* Wells sought to indict a criminally wasteful system, not to attack the morals of poor Edward Ponderevo. Both Dreiser and Wells suggest the method a proletarian novelist would employ. The trouble with *The Financier* and *The Titan* is not that Dreiser refuses to judge Cowperwood; the weakness lies in the inadequacy of the inflexible and old-fashioned determinism according to which he tries to explain Cowperwood's conduct. Wells' indictment of a system is certainly sound; the trouble is that he opposes to the wastefulness of capitalism the efficiency and intelligence of science instead of recognizing the class struggle.

The proletarian novelist would emphasize those elements in the millionaire's career that most fully illustrated his function in the economic system. That is, the proletarian author would see the millionaire as the class-conscious proletariat sees him. He might or might not illustrate the ways in which the millionaire falls below his professed moral standards, but he would not in any case assume that such delinquencies were the key to the man's character and career. He would certainly bring out the broad social effects of the millionaire's activities, thus illustrating the general waste of the capitalist system, but I think he would stress more than anything else the relation of the man to his employees. He would, in other words, recognize that the most important aspect of the man is his role as exploiter, and, without attempting to make him a monster, he would show clearly and concretely the process of exploitation.

Very few novelists have attempted to apply the Marxian method to the understanding of the multi-millionaire. Upton Sinclair, of course, has drawn to some extent on Marxism, but his liberal preoccupation with moral issues has made most of his millionaires mere caricatures. Some of the virtues of *Tono-Bungay* may be traced to Wells' slight acquaintance with Marx. Samuel Ornitz's *Haunch, Paunch, and Jowl* falls far short of adequacy, but it does indicate possibilities. The great obstacle to proletarian novels of this sort is ignorance: the proletarian author simply does not, as a rule, know enough about either the concrete economic activities or the personal life of a millionaire to make such a novel credible. It is fatal to the substance and reality of a book to reduce the central character to his economic function; the millionaire in fiction must be as many-sided as the millionaire in life. How far research may overcome this obstacle the work of Theodore Dreiser, Sinclair Lewis, and Upton Sinclair indicates, and Marxism offers a valuable guide for the conduct of such research, but the problems both of gathering and absorbing material can only be fully solved by a major talent.

The Worker

It would take too long to review all the different ways in which, since the rise of humanitarianism, the poorer classes have been treated in fiction. The pathetic treatment, for example, intended to arouse the emotions of the upper classes, had its vogue in the nineteenth century. Its greatest practitioner, Dickens, had fortunately had some firsthand acquaintance with poverty, and his principal vice, sentimentality, was balanced by notable virtues. In time the mood of pity yielded to the harsher methods of naturalism. It may be doubted, however, whether impartiality in the face of injustice and suffering is ever more than a pose. Sometimes, as in Stephen Crane's *Maggie*, that pose masks disgust and fear. Sometimes, as in Catherine Brody's *Nobody Starves* and in various other novels of the depression, it conceals the old attitude of condescending pity. Sometimes it is the refuge of desperate helplessness.

In writing of workers proletarian novelists are strong for precisely the reason that they are weak in writing of millionaires, and a considerable section of American revolutionary fiction is made up of biographical novels with workers as their central characters. Michael Gold, Jack Conroy, Robert Cruden, Louis Colman, Grace Lumpkin, Myra Page, and Fielding Burke have written such novels, and there are other writers whose novels and short stories illuminate the problem of the worker in fiction.

The novelist may choose as his central character a worker who is already class-conscious. The novel would then be a novel of the class struggle, not exclusively devoted, of course, to revolutionary activities, but centering in the hero's participation in the revolutionary movement. It seems to me a pity that no such novel has been written in this country, for the struggle is so dramatic, so intense, and so varied that it ought to yield a rich and vigorous fiction. Colman's *Lumber* is to some extent a novel of the class conflict, and it derives much of its interest and effectiveness from the fact. As Colman shows, preoccupation with daily toil and with the organization of labor need not lead to the neglect of the more narrowly personal life of the characters. Instead, personal relationships, as well as individual experiences, desires, and dreams, take on deeper significance when they compose the background of open class warfare.

In the second place, the central character may be a worker who, in the course of the story, becomes class-conscious. Perhaps we can point to so many examples of this type—*Jews Without Money, The Disinherited, Conveyor, To Make My Bread, Gathering Storm,* and *Call Home the Heart*—because our authors have themselves experienced the development of class-consciousness. This type gives excellent opportunities for portraying the backgrounds of proletarian life. Gold, for example, has given an extraordinary picture of the East Side; Conroy has shown a worker in a dozen different jobs and with no job at all; Cruden has recorded with convincing accuracy the details of the body-breaking routine in an automobile factory. All of these books are, however, more successful in their depiction of characteristic events in a worker's life than they are in describing the kind of psychological development that results in class-consciousness. Both Myra Page and Fielding Burke have also failed, for very different reasons, to make the process of conversion wholly convincing. Grace Lumpkin has come the closest to a record of such psychological growth that satisfies in every detail. I imagine that we shall have many more novels that portray a worker's conversion to Communism, and there is no reason why we should not, but I hope that other possibilities will be explored as well.

Perhaps the most difficult theme is the third one, the worker who is not and does not become class-conscious. As both Dahlberg and Caldwell have demonstrated, a novel on such a theme can be rich and powerful. Moreover, so long as the masses of the proletariat are not class-conscious, it can always be argued that the non-class-conscious worker is representative and important. On the other hand, the class-conscious worker is, when seen in historical perspective, more significant. The real difficulty, however, is a practical one: it is almost impossible to deal with the kind of people that appear in Dahlberg's and Caldwell's novels without giving an impression of absolute hopelessness. The revolutionary writer does not feel hopeless, and he is loath to convey to his readers such an impression, and yet he knows that slogans and sermons will not serve his purpose, and he will not resort to falsification. Perhaps, sufficient insight and sufficient skill could reveal in the most helpless group of workers the potentialities of revolutionary activity. In practice, however, this would be extremely difficult, and probably at best only sympathetic readers could perceive the full implications of the author's treatment of his characters and events. The charge of defeatism is not, of course, to be taken too seriously; books such as Caldwell's and Dahlberg's and Farrell's have a value that is not to be dismissed with an epithet. They deal with sectors of American life that ought to be treated, and they constitute an unanswerable indictment of the capitalist system. Such work cannot, however, communicate the militant hopefulness of the revolutionary, and is therefore likely to prove a little disappointing to author as well as readers.

The idea that the life of a worker is the only possible theme for a proletarian novel has been pretty well exploded, but it is likely that most proletarian novelists will find their subjects in the working class. Such a concentration need not lead to any lack of variety. There are not only the different kinds of treatment that have been indicated in

these articles; within the scope of the biographical form there can be
many different kinds of emphasis, and of course, in addition to all
other possibilities, there are the numerous types of work, each of
which offers special opportunities. Attention to specific detail, finally,
is important, but it need not, and must not, prevent the treatment of
proletarian character in the broadest human terms.

The Middle Class

Many of the writers who are helping to create proletarian literature come from middle-class backgrounds, and the middle class is
inevitably indicated as a theme for their novels. The selection of a
character from the lower middle class gives as good a chance to interpret class psychology and to show the workings of economic forces as
the choice of a worker. The trouble is, of course, that such a theme
does not give the author an opportunity to display the forces that are
working against the defeatism and incipient Fascism of the petty
bourgeoisie. As in writing of un-class conscious workers, the author is
bound to feel that his subject does not permit him to communicate
his total conception of life. He cannot be satisfied with the superficial
satire of *Babbitt,* much as he may admire the skill with which Lewis
has created a credible and significant character, nor will he imitate
the confused psycho-analytical approach of *Many Marriages,* though
he may recognize Anderson's flashes of insight. His treatment is likely
to be rather sombre and austere, for he realizes that he is dealing with
a class that is doomed. Sometimes he can suggest, as John Herrmann
does in *The Big Short Trip,* the existence of opposing forces, but this
remains merely a suggestion, and even so its introduction may seem
forced. Probably the only thing the author can do is to portray as
honestly as he can his representatives of the doomed class, and trust
to the sympathetic reader to reconstruct for himself the other half of
the story.

One particular section of the petty bourgeoisie that has played a
large part in recent fiction is the intelligentsia. During the years when
authors were struggling for emancipation from Victorian taboos, they
were naturally much concerned—and found an audience that was
also much concerned—with the trials of an artist among Philistines.
The semi-autobiographical novel of esthetic sorrows has pretty well

gone out of fashion since the depression, and a proletarian writer would be the last to try to revive it. There is, however, an opportunity for a clearer and more fundamental analysis of the status of the artist under capitalism. It is rather queer that the leftward movement of the intellectuals has not found a place in fiction, for it would seem that at least one good novel might be written on that theme. But whether the character in question found his way to Communism or not, there is much to be said about the American intellectual that the novels of the "renaissance" did not mention.

Another section of the petty bourgeoisie that deserves special mention is to be found on the farms. Of course a distinction has to be made between the poor farmers and the more prosperous ones, but even the latter class ought to be treated from the Marxian point of view. Rural life is so persistently presented in the romantic terms of a Gladys Hasty Carroll or a Phil Stong that a clear and realistic novel about farmers would be cause for cheering. And if the poorer farmers were introduced, there could be, as Whittaker Chambers' short story, *Can You Hear Their Voices?* shows a stirring presentation of the militant spirit of revolt. Ben Field's sketches and stories indicate the richness of the material, but the novel remains unwritten.

Thinking over the novels that revolutionary sympathizers have written about middle-class characters, I incline to the opinion that the complex novel offers a better way of presenting such characters than the biographical novel. It is obvious that bourgeois life is in no sense taboo; moreover, it would be a pity for knowledge of and insight into that life, such as many of our writers have, to be wasted. On the other hand, the very closeness of the fellow-traveler to the middle class makes it particularly difficult for him to free himself from attitudes that belong to that class when he writes about it. The problem of the artist, moreover, is always to express himself as fully as possible, and both the proletarian by birth and the fellow-traveler are likely to feel themselves unpleasantly cramped when they concentrate their attention on a typical middle-class character. Again I want to say—for I should rather appear indecisive than seem to bar any paths—that there is much that can be done with the biographical or dramatic novel of middle-class life, but the dangers and possible disappointments ought not to be ignored.

Selection and Emphasis

In the preceding article I made the not unreasonable assumption that the proletarian novelist would pay considerable attention to the economic functions of his characters. It is true that other novelists have not always done so. Occasionally, as in some of Henry James's novels, the characters have no visible means of support, and very often we catch only glimpses of the ways in which they earn their livings. The bourgeois novelist may defend himself by arguing that economic details are only of superficial importance, but the proletarian writer entertains no such illusions. He knows that not only the individual's role in society but also his character are to a large extent determined by his economic function. He insists on portraying those relationships that grow out of economic function and in showing their influence. It would be inconceivable to write a novel about an automobile worker without showing him inside the factory; to the proletarian novelist it is just as preposterous to try to present a millionaire without showing where his millions come from.

At the same time an intelligent recognition of the importance of a character's economic function need not lead to exclusive preoccupation therewith. Because, for example, novelists in the past have given a disproportionate amount of attention to sexual relationships, there is no reason for the proletarian writer to ignore them. It is clear that he will not adopt the romantic attitudes of popular fiction, nor will he share the mysticism of D. H. Lawrence or the obsessions of the pseudo-psychologists. He will trust, of course, to firsthand observation, and he will estimate as justly as he can the part that sexual relationships actually play in the lives of the kind of people he happens to be writing about. But, whether he sees that part to be large or small, he will refuse to limit himself to it. In an English novel of the depression, *Love on the Dole*, sexual interests and desires are made very important, but the author, Walter Greenwood, makes it perfectly clear, as the title implies, that love is not independent of economics. It is, indeed, his perception of the close relationship between the two dominant forces at work in his characters' lives that gives Greenwood's novel its power as well as its unity. Robert Cruden has tried to maintain the same sort of balance in *Conveyor*, and on the whole has succeeded remarkably well. In Conroy's *The Disinherited*, on the other hand, the episodes dealing with Larry's girls are not sufficiently integrated with the central theme.

Another major preoccupation of novelists is philosophical development, the groping of the central character towards a satisfying *Weltanschauung*. This theme has become more and more important in the literature of the twentieth century. One thinks, for example, of such diverse novels as *The Way of All Flesh, The Portrait of the Artist as a Young Man, The Remembrance of Things Past, Of Human Bondage, Victory, Sons and Lovers, The Magic Mountain,* and *Arrowsmith*. It is not my purpose here to criticize the particular philosophies set forth by these novels, but merely to call attention to the fact that, whatever other interests the authors may have had, the essential purpose of each of these books is to set forth the origins, growth, and usually the application of a certain conception of the nature and destiny of man. It may fairly be assumed that in all the novels I have mentioned the philosophy set forth by the hero is the philosophy of the author. It is possible, however, for a novelist to predict the origin, growth, and application of a philosophy of which he disapproves, and, in the course of his work, to justify his disapproval. In *Victory* Heyst begins with an outlook on life that Conrad condemns, but in the end he abandons it. Wells, however, lets Bulpington gather the sour fruit of his folly, and Lewis's *Babbitt* returns to his vomit.

For the proletarian novelist there is an obvious variation of the theme of intellectual development: the progress of a character, whether he be proletarian or intellectual, towards Communism. This has, indeed, been the theme of several novels and a number of short stories. (And there is no reason why the proletarian writer should not also utilize the reverse method and show the growth of some counter-revolutionary attitude—Fascism, for example.) The portrayal of intellectual growth is not, however, an easy matter, as we see if we examine some of the novels that have attempted it. The depiction of the creation of a Communist is easier, certainly, when the character is a proletarian, and when, as in *To Make My Bread* and *Conveyor*, class-consciousness develops in the course of daily struggle. Myra Page's novel *Moscow Yankee*, which is to be published soon, gives a fine example of the depiction of a slow and natural growth towards Communism. When, however, the character is an intellectual or a proletarian with intellectual aspirations, the task is more difficult. In both *Jews Without Money* and *The Disinherited,* the hero's enlisting in the revolutionary cause comes without sufficient preparation. The author not only has to understand the psychological processes by which an attitude towards life comes into being; he must be sure that each step is clear to the reader. The proletarian author is not likely to make the mistake, so common in bourgeois writers, of assuming that a philosophy develops in a vacuum, but he must be careful not to neglect the subtleties of temperament that help to determine what the results of experience will be.

These two examples—the treatment of sexual relationships and the treatment of intellectual development—will serve to emphasize the point that nothing is alien to the proletarian novelist. His field is not narrower, but broader, than that of the bourgeois writer. The whole of life is his province. He has his own conception of what is important and representative, and in his selection and emphasis he must follow that conception. But elimination is no solution of his problems; they can be solved only by his understanding of true relationships and just proportions.

Point of View

It will do no harm if we turn now to a consideration of some of the technical difficulties that arise in the course of writing any novel and that the proletarian novelist must meet in his own way. Henry James insisted that, once the novelist had his story in mind, he must strenuously seek for the method "that most presents it, and presents most of it." One particular aspect of this problem of presentation— and an aspect that specially interested Henry James—concerns the method of narration. James's disciple, Percy Lubbock, attributes far too much significance to this question in his *The Craft of Fiction,* but he does help to define the various points of view that the author may adopt in telling his story. By point of view I mean, in this connection, the position the author takes for the unfolding of his story, not his general attitude.

In the first place, the story may be told from the point of view of the central character, who is made the narrator. This method is in general adapted to simple, direct, objective narrative of adventure, such as *Roderick Random.* It sharply limits the scope of the novel, and it is therefore a useful guide in the selection and ordering of materials, but its limitations may prevent the author from making a comprehensive revelation of his own perceptions. For that reason it would seem to be unsuited for the subtler type of psychological analysis, and yet it has been used with considerable success in the most ambitious psychological novel of our times, *The Remembrance of Things Past*. Here, however, the narrator, who is closely identified with the author, is a person of unusual perceptivity. Mike Gold also uses the autobiographical method for the handling of autobiographical material in *Jews Without Money*, and again the success of the method may be attributed to the unusual sensitiveness of the narrator-author. When, on the other hand, the author is not identified with his central character, it is difficult, as Herrick's *Memoirs of an American Citizen* and Ornitz's *Haunch, Paunch, and Jowl* show, to avoid the suggestion of a split personality. Ernest Hemingway, though he is partly to be identified with the heroes and narrators of both *The Sun Also Rises* and *Farewell to Arms,* secures his effect because he eschews all analysis and permits his characters' states of mind to be inferred by the readers. This kind of indirect revelation, though immensely difficult to sustain, offers great rewards, for it adds to other satisfactions the joy of discovery.

Henry James came to believe that narrative in the first person greatly handicapped an author, and yet he appreciated the values of a clearly defined point of view. He therefore preferred to write as if he were looking over the shoulder of his character. That is, he limited himself rigorously to presenting only what the central character could see, but he substituted direct analysis of the character's states of mind for self-analysis. This method, which James followed so rigorously in *The Ambassadors*, for example, has been employed, in a much looser form, by a multitude of writers. Maugham in *Of Human Bondage* writes in the third person, but, except in three or four passages, in which the arbitrary change of method distresses the reader, he writes from Philip's point of view. Other novelists have been even less rigorous than Maugham, and at times the method collapses altogether. Cruden, Dahlberg, Colman, Fielding Burke, and Grace Lumpkin have all approximated this method. In *The Big Short Trip* John Herrmann exhibits the advantage of a rigorous observance of the method for purposes of indirect revelation.

When the author writes part of the time from the point of view of his central character, standing behind him and looking over his shoulder, as James would say, and part of the time writes from a point of view entirely outside the scope of the story, he is assuming the natural privilege of the novelist, omniscience. Very frequently, however, the author does not consider what such an assumption involves. He merely writes from the point of view of his character until he finds it necessary to tell the reader something the character could not know, and then he shifts his point of view. It must be admitted that the results of this mixture of methods often justify it, but more often there is confusion and even irritation for the reader. The advantage of writing from the point of view of one of the characters, whether in his words or not, is that it provides a principle of selection, and when the author abandons that principle, he has to make up his mind what principle he is substituting for it. Certain masters of the novel have taken full advantage of their omniscience, exploring the minds of one character after another, describing matters of which all characters are ignorant, even, some of them, appearing in their own persons and commenting directly on their own creations. Tolstoy, Fielding, Dickens, Thackeray, Hardy, and Dreiser are examples. Of these perhaps only Tolstoy and Hardy convince the reader that they have a clearly conceived principle of selection. The others introduce masses of apparently unassimilated material, and one feels that their success is a triumph of vitality over lack of method. That they do succeed ought to convince us that method is not of transcendent importance, but we must also remember the failures of countless other writers.

Authors choose a limited point of view as much because of the dangers of omniscience as because of the advantage of limitation. The author can, of course, limit himself to a point of view that is not that of the central character. There is, for example, the method of narration in the first person, with the narrator merely an observer. Examples indicate possible advantages. Butler chose this method for *The Way of All Flesh* because it permitted him to appear in two roles: as Ernest he relives the events of the story, and as Overton he comments, from the vantage point of age, on his own life. Willa Cather let Burden tell the story of *My Antonia* because he could legitimately adopt the faintly nostalgic tone that seemed to her suited to the story. Conrad, employing the method with some variations in *Lord Jim* and *Chance*, was apparently attracted by the possibilities of indirect revelation. As in the other type of first person narrative, there is always the problem of telling the reader what he needs to know, and in solving this problem novelists have sometimes defied the laws of probability. The narrator's style also presents a difficulty. At the same time, the method does localize the point of view and thus provide a principle of selection.

Another possibility is to tell the story in the third person, but to present events from the point of view of all or several of the characters. In its looser manifestations this method obviously approximates the method of omniscience, but it can be very closely and precisely followed, as James demonstrated in *The Awkward Age* and *The Golden Bowl*. It lends itself particularly well to the dramatic novel, but it can also be employed in the complex novel. It is essentially the method of *The 42nd Parallel* and *1919,* and Arnold Armstrong, who has unmistakably been influenced by Dos Passos, has used it, except in the first chapter, in *Parched Earth*. It is not always an easy method for the reader to follow, and that is why both Dos Passos and Armstrong label each section with the name of the character from whose point of view it is told. It does provide a principle of selection for each section, though the arrangement of sections has to be governed by other considerations.

In general the straight biographical novel suggests the use of a narrator, who may be either the principal character or merely an observer, or the adoption of the point of view of one or the other, usually the former. The author may, however, if he sees clearly enough what he wants to do, take his stand outside the events of the story and avail himself of the privilege of omniscience. In the dramatic novel, if the narrator is one of the central characters, there must be, as in Ford Madox Ford's *The Good Soldier,* a *tour de force*. It is also unlikely that any uninvolved observer could readily present all the necessary events in their dramatic order. Omniscience or the shifting point of view is indicated. These are obviously the only possible methods for the complex novel, which by its very nature cannot be limited to one person, and they are probably the best methods for the collective novel, since it would be extremely difficult, it not impossible, to present the reality of a group through the mind of a single individual. The collective novel, indeed, insofar as its group is a psychological unit, seems to require a new technique: narrative in the third person from a limited point of view, which is the point of view not of an individual but of a group.

The adoption of a limited point of view has two advantages. On the one hand, it materially assists the writer to solve the problem of selection, and, on the other hand, it encourages the reader's imaginative participation in the story.

Writers who employ this method have always maintained its superiority on the ground that it corresponds to human experience, for man's knowledge is always partial. But the assumption of omniscience is, if the author makes it really possible, a source of pleasure to the reader. Moreover, we must remind ourselves that no author actually believes he is omniscient, and the assumption is a matter of convenience. The author may well have a conception of events that cannot be rendered except from a point of view of one who, so to speak, surveys those events from above. This need not mean that the author is or thinks he is "above the battle"; it is perfectly compatible with an attitude of forthright partisanship.

What I have said makes clear that I have no desire to urge upon authors one method as opposed to others. It is ridiculous to maintain, as Lubbock does, the inherent superiority of a particular method under all circumstances and for all purposes. All I want is to indicate the variety of methods in order that novelists may be more acutely conscious of the possibilities offered to them. Given a particular author with a particular story to tell and a particular conception of its significance, there is, I believe, a particular method that is uniquely right. But what it is may not appear at first glance, and he must make sure he has discovered it.

The Problem of Documentation

In previous articles I have discussed the hero as millionaire, the hero as intellectual, or the hero as worker. To many persons this must seem a surprising procedure. The novelist is not concerned, such critics will say, with millionaires or workers as such but with men. Of course. But after all, certain men are millionaires and others are workers. They are not merely millionaires and workers; they may also be lovers, thinkers, voters, church attendants, creatures of mystery. But the novelist, though he tries to do justice to the many-sided character and varied activities of his hero, must follow a process of selection. If he does not discriminate, if he makes one act as important as another, one emotion as important as another, the result is chaos.

This is the barest commonplace, but it is a commonplace that has to be repeated again and again because so many persons refuse to accept its obvious implications. Let us take a very simple case. When Sinclair Lewis wrote *Babbitt*, he set out to write a novel about a business man, just as when he wrote *Arrowsmith* he set out to write a novel about a doctor, and when he wrote *Work of Art* he set out to write a novel about a hotel-keeper. But, certain critics say, that is not the proper way to write novels, and they point to Edith Wharton and Willa Cather, or perhaps to D. H. Lawrence and James Joyce. The assumption is, of course, that these authors are writing about men and women as men and women, not men and women in some special capacity. In fact, *O, Pioneers!* is as restricted as *Babbitt*, and *Sons and Lovers* is as restricted as *Arrowsmith*. What the critics should argue is that it is more important to write about the sex life of a man than it is to write of his business life, or that it is more important to describe the quasi-mystical responses of a frontier woman to the soil than it is to describe the artistic ambitions of the manager of a hotel. But they refuse to admit that there is simply a choice between one kind of selection and another. They try to maintain that there is completeness on their side and partiality on the other, instead of recognizing that there is partiality on both sides, and that the question of which side comes closest to comprehensiveness reduces itself to the problem of what aspects of human life are most important.

John Dos Passos says, "The business of a novelist is, in my opinion, to create characters first and foremost, and then to set them in the snarl of the human currents of his time, so that there results an accurate permanent record of a phase of history." The suggestion that the characters are created first and then set into their environment is unfortunate, for it postulates a separation between character and environment that does not exist in life and would be fatal in literature. But, assuming that this is merely a matter of unhappy phraseology, I should not quarrel with Dos Passos' definition. The typical bourgeois critic, however, would object to the statement because it implies that the novelist must deal with social forces. This objection rests on an assumption, tacit or not, that the fundamental qualities of mankind are independent of these forces. If Dos Passos had said that the business of the novelist is to create characters and then to place them in situations that reveal the true nature of mankind, the bourgeois critic would lean back and applaud. For Dos Passos, of course, the two statements are really equivalent, for he believes that any situation, if it is fully to reveal the nature of mankind, must portray the forces that shape that nature.

It is not only revolutionary novelists who try to show their characters in a living social environment and who seek to give an "accurate permanent record of a phase of history." After all, we must not forget Fielding, Jane Austen, Dickens, Thackeray, Tolstoy, Balzac, Zola, Howells. But we can agree that the revolutionary writer is particularly conscious of the intrinsic importance of social movements and of the decisive effect of economic alignments on characters. He is not likely to be guilty, on the one hand, of indifference and ignorance or, on the other, of cowardice. He must show his characters as part of "the snarl of the human currents of his time," or at least of the time he has chosen to write about, for he knows that they cannot be fully understood apart from their social environment.

This means that the revolutionary novelist must consider the problem of documentation. Let us not make the mistake, however, of assuming that this problem exists only for the writer who wishes to portray economic and political movements. The task of such a novelist is essentially no different from that of any other: any novel demands the selection of materials that embody the author's conception of life and permit the expression of his attitude towards it. The chief distinction is that the revolutionary novelist cannot indulge in any arbitrary manipulation of the materials of experience. The documentation of a novel by D. H. Lawrence, for example, consists of a series of descriptions and analyses of the responses of his characters to various situations, usually involving sexual desires. It is possible, of course, to compare these descriptions and analyses with one's own emotions and one's observations of the emotions of others, and on the basis of such comparison critics have praised or attacked Lawrence's work. The comparison is, however, personal and highly

debatable. When, however, the documentation of a novel consists
in a record of the events of a strike, let us say, the comparison between the strike in the novel and strikes in real life, though there is
still room for differences of interpretation and evaluation, offers
much more opportunity for impersonal exactness. Authenticity is
always essential, but in the novel that portrays social forces one can
tell much more easily when authenticity is lacking.

If we examine some of our revolutionary novels, we discover
that this problem of documentation has presented itself in many forms.
As is not unnatural, several of the best of these novels are essentially
autobiographical. The aim of their authors, however, has not been
so much to write about themselves and their lives as to describe the
particular environments they have known. Take, for example, Michael
Gold's *Jews Without Money* and Jack Conroy's *The Disinherited*.
Perhaps it may be objected that neither book is, strictly speaking,
a novel; but that does not matter, since both deserve to be called
literature. In both, that is, experience is seized upon, understood,
interpreted, re-shaped, and communicated to the reader. The important point, however, is that, having chosen the form of the novel,
both writers should have remembered what Dos Passos calls the
business of the novelist. If these books were frankly collections of
episodes, one would accept them as such. But both Gold and Conroy
felt—quite rightly, it seems to me—that their materials had a kind
of unity that demanded more than merely episodic treatment. They
were concerned not only with communicating certain experiences
but also with indicating the impact of those experiences. The proof
of this lies in the fact that each book ends with the awakening of the
central character to class-consciousness. But in both books this awakening comes as a surprise. Something is missing, for otherwise the
reader would feel that the climax of the book followed inevitably
from everything that had gone before. The trouble is not, I think,
in either the character or the amount of the documentation; it is in
the failure to portray in terms of the novel a relationship that must
have existed in life.

Essentially the same problem exists when the documentation is
not derived from firsthand experience. Certain critics assume that the
themes of a novelist are limited to the kind of life he has personally led.
Unfortunately for these critics—Mr. John Chamberlain, for example
—several of the greatest bourgeois writers have deliberately "worked

up" the documentation of their novels. At the present moment we can point to two novelists whom Mr. Chamberlain frequently praises— Sinclair Lewis and Theodore Dreiser. How did Lewis get his material for *Arrowsmith, Elmer Gantry,* and *Work of Art?* How did Dreiser get his material for *The Financier, The Titan,* and *An American Tragedy?* Both writers show that, at least under some conditions, an author can investigate a way of life that is largely foreign to him and can convert the results of his investigation into effective fiction. The difficulty with Lewis is not that his investigation is inaccurate or inadequate; his trouble is superficiality. Dreiser, on the other hand, for all his clumsiness, searches after fundamentals. Lewis does a brilliant job with surfaces, but he is satisfied to stop there. Dreiser at least tries to dig down into the roots, and his work shows that an honest effort at understanding compensates for many defects. Both writers refute Mr. Chamberlain.

The way in which the results of research can be converted into the material of fiction is little different from the process that personal experience must undergo. For purposes of analysis we can distinguish two elements in this process, though in fact they are not separated. One of these elements is essentially intellectual: the author must understand the relations of the different experiences with which he is dealing. The second is more purely emotional: the author must respond, positively and completely, to each of these experiences. The perception of actual relationships organizes his responses, and the result can be described as a unified pattern. This pattern constitutes an adjustment to reality. Communicated to the reader, it modifies the pattern that exists in his consciousness, which is presumably less inclusive and less satisfactorily organized. Thus it changes his response to subsequent experience.

Perhaps I can make this rather schematic statement clearer, at least in its implications for writers, if I cite two specific examples. In *The Jungle,* which is certainly the best of Sinclair's novels, most of the material was gathered during a comparatively brief stay in the stockyards. Nevertheless, in chapter after chapter, the lives of the people have for us the impact of firsthand experience. This means, I believe, that Sinclair has accurately understood the conditions of the stockyards, that is, not only what they are but also why they are. It means, moreover, that he has felt within himself essentially the emotions that would be felt by such persons as Ona and Jurgis. He sees, finally, both the conditions and the response to the conditions as parts of a larger whole, and his response to both the conditions and the emotions aroused in Ona and Jurgis is integrated with this perception. But there are also long passages of straight exposition, in which we are conscious of the author as observer and muckracker. Such passages indicate a lapse in the kind of process I have tried to describe. One-half of the process has stopped, and direct observation is suddenly substituted for imaginative re-creation; the book is no longer a book about Ona and Jurgis, but simply a book about Upton Sinclair and the stockyards. Since the integration I have spoken of is necessarily dynamic and progressive, every such interruption is destructive. That may explain why *The Jungle,* though aimed at the heart of a nation, only reached, in Sinclair's phrase, its stomach.

I do not know whether William Rollins, Jr., observed at first-hand the Gastonia and New Bedford strikes that provide the material for his novel, *The Shadow Before.* In any case I assume that he was only an observer and not a participant, and his situation is therefore comparable to Sinclair's. His perception of the strike made him want to show its impact on several kinds of persons, and he therefore introduces Harry Baumann and the Thayers as well as Mickey, Martin, and the renegade Ramon. (The success of the novel, incidentally, justifies what I said in an earlier article about the suitability of the complex form for the fellow-traveler.) What would ordinarily be called the documentation of the novel—the description of mill conditions, the conduct of the strike, and the trial—is subordinated to the portrayal of the characters. That is, we come to understand conditions through their effect on people as much as through direct description. The success of this method depends, in the first place, on Rollins' own understanding of conditions, which is in general adequate. It also depends on his understanding of the persons on whom those conditions are acting. Here, perhaps, there are momentary lapses, but they are only minor blemishes. In general, Rollins has shown a relationship that can reasonably be described as organic between character and conditions, between character and character, and between one set of conditions and another.

When so many elements are necessary for the success of a novel, it is impossible to say that one is more important than the other. There are certain qualities that are essential for any novelist, revolutionary or otherwise. What interests us now, however, is the way in which

these qualities operate in the imaginative processes of the revolutionary writer. I do not want to seem to over-emphasize the intellectual
element in the creative process, for I fully realize that by itself it can
accomplish nothing. But we ought not to ignore the fact that many
novelists, talented in other ways, have failed precisely for want of this
quality. There can be no excuse for such failure on the part of the
revolutionist. I grow tired, and I imagine others do, at the frequency
with which our critics point out that this author or that would have
written a better book if he had had a Marxist understanding of the
events with which he dealt. Yet it is the sort of thing that one is compelled to say again and again because it is so often both true and
important. No theory of social conduct can be a substitute for perception, but a sound theory is a most valuable guide. A knowledge
of the economic role of millionaires is not enough to provide an
understanding of any given millionaire, but it is a prerequisite for
such understanding.

    And the revolutionary movement offers the writer far more
than intellectual guidance. The notion of absolute objectivity, of complete withdrawal from the events presented in a work of fiction, is
one of the major fallacies of bourgeois literary theory. It is a fallacy,
because such objectivity is neither possible nor desirable. I am not discussing, of course, the theory of objective truth; I am merely maintaining that personal objectivity is unattainable. The class struggle is
so inclusive that, though one's allegiance may be divided, one cannot
remain aloof. And the attempt to remain aloof weakens and sometimes paralyzes the creative faculties. Understanding comes through
participation. All experience is a kind of struggle. Partisanship ought
to enrich one's understanding of enemies and friends alike. Sometimes,
we must admit, it has the opposite effect, and narrows and distorts the
vision. But I doubt if partisanship, even at its worst, is ever so
destructive as the attempt to reduce art to lifeless passivity.

    The problem of documentation reduces itself, as we have seen,
to the problem of the nature of the artist's experiences and the use to
which he puts it. The quantity of documentation is relatively important. It is a question to be settled in accordance with the novelist's
aim. If he is concerned, as Gold was, with evoking the life of a
particular place and a particular kind of people, there must be fullness
of documentation. So, too, if he makes a whole profession his theme,
as Lewis has done in several books. If he is portraying a particular

event, such as a strike, he must give details enough to make the strike a reality, but there is still much room for variation. Grace Lumpkin, for example, has given us, in *To Make My Bread,* a picture of the transformation of backward mountaineers into militant proletarians, and she has therefore, fully documented the lives of her characters before as well as after they go to work in the mills. Rollins, on the other hand, pays no attention to this particular aspect of his characters' lives, and his documentation is therefore entirely different.

It is very seldom, I believe, that the quantity of documentation offers any serious difficulty—though sometimes, as in the local color writers of the last century, there is far too much. The quality of the documentation is always the problem. That there is no easy solution is fairly clear. It is probably more difficult for a writer to assimilate material that is gathered by deliberate research than it is for him to draw directly on personal experience. This is not, however, invariably true, for the adaptation of autobiographical material demands a kind of self-understanding that many writers have not achieved. In either case there can be no substitute for the process to which experience is subjected when it passes through the sensitive mind of an artist.

The Future of Proletarian Literature

Several years ago I read the whole of Proust's *Remembrance of Things Past* in the course of a single summer. It was an "experience," if ever the reading of a novel deserved to be called by that name. Every day for two months the world of Marcel Proust constantly impinged upon my own world. I found myself stopping in the midst of my daily routine to wonder about the character and destiny of Swann, Charlus, Mme. Verdurin, Gilberte, Saint-Loup, Albertine, and of course Marcel. I became suddenly aware of the evocative power of certain experiences, and engaged in my own search for things past. Elstir's theories of painting and Bergotte's theories of literature, instead of having the academic remoteness of books on esthetics, took on the pertinence of personal discussions. I compared friends of my own with Marcel's friends, and because of the comparison—at least so it seemed to me—understood them better. At times, I recall, I was bored, especially when reading the fifth volume, *The Captive*. At times I revolted against Proust's preoccupation with his own emotions and against his theories about sex, which seemed to me then, as now, largely false—and false for rather obvious reasons. There were moments when I turned in disgust from the many trivial and irritating people and the solemn snobbery, and at the end I was offended by the obscurantism of Proust's philosophy. But occasional repulsions did not break the spell of the book, which played for a time a larger and larger part, not only in my thoughts and my conversation but also in my attitude toward my own world and in the equality of my emotional life.

Remembering all this, I have been asking myself two questions. First, would I have the same experience if I could read *The Remembrance of Things Past* for the first time now? Second, is it conceivable that any revolutionary novel, any novel that conformed to the demands I have tentatively proposed in these articles, could afford a comparable experience? In the articles of this series we have been proceeding from an examination of particular problems to a consideration of basic principles. The questions I have been asking myself about Proust set before us fundamental issues of Marxian criticism: the value of bourgeois literature for the proletariat and the potentialities of proletarian art. Though my treatment of these issues will necessarily be inadequate, they must be touched upon before I can leave the discussion of revolution and the novel .

The English critic, I. A. Richards, has tried to describe the effect of literary experience on the reader. "We pass," he says, "as a rule from a chaotic to a better organized state by ways which we know nothing about. Typically through the influences of other minds. Literature and the arts are the chief means by which these influences are diffused." "That organization," he further explains, "which is least wasteful of human possibilities is . . . best." He speaks of "those fortunate people who have achieved an ordered life," and goes on: "Their free, untrammeled activity gains for them a maximum of varied satisfactions and involves a minimum of suppression and sacrifice. Particularly is this so with regard to those satisfactions which require humane, sympathetic, and friendly relations between individuals. . . . Unfair or aggressive behavior, and preoccupation with self-regarding interests to the exclusion of due sensitiveness to the reciprocal claims of human intercourse, lead to a form of organization which deprives the person so organized of whole ranges of important values."

We may accept Richards' account of the psychological effect of art—which does seem to me, by and large, the soundest yet proposed—but we cannot accept his principles of evaluation. He has simply restated the utilitarian doctrine: when one acts in such a way that the best ends of society are served, he derives the highest personal satisfaction. But actually, the systemization or integration of which Richards speaks proceeds within the limits of class morality. If, for example, a man had a good income derived from what are called ethical investments, and if he was reasonably philanthropic, he would certainly enjoy "those satisfactions which require humane, sympathetic, and friendly relations between individuals"—despite the fact that he was living on the fruit of exploitation. He would be protected by his whole way of life—the character of his associates, the selection of his reading, the nature of his business relations—from any vivid realization of the human implications of his privileges and thus from the pyschological disharmony that might result from such a realization. Richards' theory not only assumes a reconciliation of all human interests, a manifest impossibility in a system based on exploitation; it also ignores the fact that the individual's norms of conduct, and therefore satisfaction, are determined by class factors.

Returning now to Proust, it becomes clear why I value *The Remembrance of Things Past* so much less highly today than I did five years ago. Though I still find plenty to praise, I find less than I did, and what I do find seems less important. I was particularly impressed, for example, with the way in which Proust shows how persons change and how one's ideas about persons change. That revelation still seems to me extraordinarily far-reaching and illuminating, but inasmuch as the persons he portrays have come to seem less representative than they once did, my admiration is tempered. There is truth here, but less truth than I once thought. The same thing may be said of Proust's portrayal of the whole society with which he deals. He has the appearance, if ever an author had, of creating a complete and self-sufficient world. Five years ago I accepted that world. Today I realize that it is not complete, and I realize that every character in it partakes of its incompleteness. How much more there is to be said about these people than Proust said in all his seven volumes! And what is unsaid now seems to me more important for an understanding of them—or, at least, of many of them—than what he does say.

There is another element that enters into my revised judgment of *The Remembrance of Things Past*. If one asks, in Richards' terms, what sort of organization Proust tries to create, the answer can be found in the last volume of the work, *The Past Recaptured,* with its climactic statement of the unifying philosophy of the entire novel. The climax of the novel comes with the decision of the autobiographical hero to write such a work. Life is given meaning only as the past is recaptured; significance lies not in experience but in the rediscovery of experience. The artist, then, is the master of us all. This is the most elaborate and probably the most ingenious statement ever made of the doctrine of art for art's sake. That doctrine I repudiated almost as emphatically five years ago as I do today; but the passivity that I rejected in theory I actually practiced, and, at the same time that I condemned Proust's mystical estheticism, I yielded myself with satisfaction to emotions with which it was indissolubly related. Today, emotional surrender would be as impossible as intellectual acquiescence. For me the reading of *The Remembrance of Things Past* would not be an "experience" in the sense that it was five years ago; it would, rather, involve a series of separate experiences, some of great value, it is true, but only in isolation, not as parts of an overwhelming whole.

What I have said of my response to Proust hints at my present attitude toward other bourgeois novelists. There is no bourgeois novel that, taken as a whole, satisfies me. I am not merely conscious of omissions and irrelevancies; I feel within myself a definite resistance, a counter-emotion, so to speak, that makes a unified esthetic experience impossible. On the other hand, portions of particular novels seem exciting and enriching—certain characters, incidents, descriptions. Here, I feel, is truth, a partial truth, of course, but for me a discovery, a realization, the beginning of greater awareness on my own part. It is even possible, when there are enough of these "truths," to perceive a relationship among them that the author himself did not understand. Edmund Wilson has said that it was Proust, rather than the Marxian propagandists, that made a revolutionary of him. I know what he means, though I am sure he is largely wrong. Proust does give the reader an overwhelming sense of the decadence of bourgeois society; he makes one feel that decadence far more strongly than any propagandist could. But recognition of social rottenness did not make Proust a revolutionary; nor would it have so affected Wilson if the preparatory work had not been done by the very propagandists he scorns. It is perhaps true of every work of art that there is more in it than the artist intended to put there. We salvage what we can and are grateful. But, for me and for many others, the complete surrender to bourgeois art is impossible.

With revolutionary novels the situation is reversed: the whole is usually more satisfactory than the parts. This is not quite true, of course, but the revolutionary reader is likely to feel the essential rightness of a revolutionary novel, even when he finds much in it to criticize. This is not purely an intellectual matter; the organization of emotion, as Richards calls it, is satisfying because it extends the pattern that is already formed in the reader's mind. Look, for example, at Grace Lumpkin's *To Make My Bread*. At times the reader is thwarted by the slowness of the movement and the absence of emotional intensity, and yet the climax sweeps him to a height of determination and strength. Or take Arnold Armstrong's *Parched Earth*, a faulty book, certainly, but one that seizes the emotions of the sympathetic reader and disciplines them to a vision and a purpose.

I am not talking about the rightness of the ideas of the revolutionary authors, for that is a relatively unimportant matter. What interests me is that these authors are discovering a new way of looking at and feeling about life. I call it new, though in many respects it is old, because it is new in literature. The reason why revolutionary authors so often seem clumsy is that they are trying to communicate the operations of what deserves to be called a new type of sensibility. And the reason why we respond so positively to their work, in spite of its manifest faults, is that we are moving in the same direction. Each of us finds his own experience clarified by what he reads and is better prepared to assimilate the experiences that the future brings.

Of the historical importance of this tendency we have no doubt. No critic, in evaluating a work of art, can afford to disregard the possible significance for the future of what the author has tried to do unless he thinks his duty is merely to give out grades. If he is conscious of his responsibility in shaping literary growth, he must reckon with personal intentions and historical tendencies. From that point of view a revolutionary novel that falls far short of its author's intentions is more important than a bourgeois novel that almost perfectly reaches its goal. This does not mean that the critic should relax his standards;

on the contrary, the most searching analysis is necessary. But that analysis is useful only if the critic can understand the author's aim and measure its importance.

In a classless society the integration of individual and social satisfactions, of which Richards speaks, can become a reality. Until that time the integration toward which the revolutionary writer aims is limited by the outlook and needs of the proletariat. This means, obviously, an emphasis on class-consciousness and militancy, but the author most effectively creates such attitudes, not by ignoring large sectors of life but by integrating them with the class struggle. "Proletarian art," Ernst Toller has said, "must ultimately rest on universal interest, must, at its deepest, like life and death, embrace all human themes." The class struggle is not something that concerns men and women for a few minutes during the day; it touches every thought and feeling and action of their lives. The scope of the proletarian novelist is not narrower but broader than that of the bourgeois. Thomas Craven, in a recent article in *Scribner's,* attacks the Communist painters and art critics, and argues that propaganda invariably narrows art. The attack rests on the assumption that Communism is merely the expression of special interests and is not a comprehensive philosophy of life. Communism does express the interests of a class, it is true, but so does the nationalistic liberalism to which Craven subscribes. The philosophy of Communism, Marxism, is broader than any philosophy the bourgeoisie has evolved. The sympathies of the Communist are more inclusive than the sympathies of even the liberal bourgeois. And the idea of Communism can broaden and grow, whereas the ideas and attitudes of liberalism are bound to shrivel in the violent heat of capitalism's last struggle.

As yet no revolutionary novelist has done for his readers what Proust did for the liberals and esthetes of the twenties. I have no doubt that, when the work of which *The 42nd Parallel* and *1919* are parts is finished, the reading of it will be an engrossing experience for any revolutionary. But Dos Passos is not Proust. He has not seen so many sides of his characters, does not provoke so much curiosity about them, does not make the reader so aware of the changes taking place in them. I would be the first to insist, of course, that what Dos Passos is trying to do is more difficult than what Proust tried to do. That may be sufficient explanation, but it does not alter the facts. Much as I admire Dos Passos, I cannot live in his world so completely as I once did in Proust's.

Proletarian literature, however, does not end with John Dos Passos, and his work is no more than a promise of what may be done. The achievement will require, obviously, even greater sensitivity than Dos Passos', as well as clearer vision and sharper understanding. But if we can imagine an author with Michael Gold's power of evoking scenes, with William Rollins' structural skill, with Jack Conroy's wide acquaintance with the proletariat, with Louis Colman's firsthand knowledge of the labor movement, with all the passion of these and a dozen other revolutionary novelists, with something of Dreiser's massive patience, we can see what shape a proletarian masterpiece might take. It would do justice to all the many-sided richness of its characters, exploring with Proustian persistence the deepest recesses of individuality and at the same time exhibiting that individuality as essentially a social phenomenon. And it would carry its readers toward life, not, as *The Remembrance of Things Past* does, toward death. The rare combination of circumstances necessary for the creation of such a masterpiece may not occur in our country and our lifetime, but there is nothing inherent in the nature of proletarian literature to prevent it. Our goal is apparent, and we can only battle our way toward it.

There may be a few skeptics who question the value of proletarian literature to the revolutionary movement. I would remind them that, as Richards says, the most powerful influences are often exerted upon us in ways of which we are not conscious. It is not merely direct experience of exploitation that makes workers class-conscious and brings intellectuals into the ranks of the Communists. It is not merely the study of Marxism that eradicates the patterns of thought and feeling that years of exposure to bourgeois education and propaganda have created. The making of a thoroughgoing revolutionary requires a long process of readjustment, involving the whole personality. In this process proletarian literature can play a crucially important part.

On the one hand, the growth of a proletarian literature is the mark of the power of the revolutionary movement, for it shows how deeply the ideas and emotions of revolution have penetrated and how insistently they demand expression. On the other hand, proletarian literature is an indispensable instrument for intensifying and organizing the vague impulses toward rebellion that are the foundation of the revolutionary state of mind. Perhaps those of us who are directly concerned with literature are tempted to exaggerate its importance, but I think it is better to do so than underestimate its power. We fight with what weapons we have, confident that when we have forged better ones there will be an opportunity to use them.

April–May 1934

III

AMERICAN WRITERS

The role that Granville Hicks has created for himself as a literary critic has been that of introducing young and promising writers to a reading audience and encouraging their careers. He was doing this in 1934 and is still doing it in 1973. Perhaps this has been Hicks's greatest contribution to literature. Some of the more recent writers he has helped in this manner include Wright Morris, Bernard Malamud, Flannery O'Connor, James Baldwin and Herbert Gold.

It is significant that most (though not all) of the writers Hicks reviewed in the pages of the *New Masses* are of interest to us today. Some had already made a name: Sinclair Lewis, Ernest Hemingway, T.S. Eliot and perhaps John Dos Passos. Others were soon to be well known: William Faulkner, John Steinbeck, James T. Farrell, Richard Wright and Van Wyck Brooks. It is a measure of a critic's judgment how many writers he has selected for review have endured the passage of time. Of course, how well the review itself endures is another measure.

As a literary critic Hicks has focused most of his attention on contemporary American and British fiction. His first major critical work, *The Great Tradition*, appeared in 1933, before he joined the *New Masses*. It is an interpretation of post–Civil War American literature. A provocative and persuasive survey, it was well received and exerted a strong influence in literary circles. A second edition was brought out in 1935 and included material on the "proletarian writters" he had reviewed for the *New Masses*.

Der Schoene Archibald

Poems, 1924–1933, by Archibald MacLeish

My original idea was to write a letter to Mr. MacLeish, a friendly letter, asking him if he really liked the idea of being a dirty Nazi. But there have been too many letters written. And I doubt if he would have read my letter anyway, for he doesn't like critics. He wrote a piece about them in the *Hound and Horn*—it was supposed to be a review of Stephen Spender's poetry, but it wasn't—and he said Marxian critics were sows and he was a lady up a tree. And, even if he did read my letter, it wouldn't do any good, for Archibald is a Nazi, at least a kind of ur-Nazi, whether he wants to be or not.

So, instead of writing a letter, I'd better write a serious critique of the poetry of Archibald MacLeish. I won't go back to the days when he was a promising lad at Yale; I'll start, as he does in this volume, with *The Hamlet of A. MacLeish.* When this poem was published, somebody headed a review with that fine line of T. S. Eliot's, "I am not Prince Hamlet, nor was meant to be." Of course Mr. MacLeish knew all the time that he wasn't Hamlet. That, in a way, was the point. Eliot had started the fashion of denigrating oneself and one's age by comparing them to dead heroes and past ages, and the *Hamlet* was MacLeish's *Waste Land.* One gathered from it that he felt awfully sick about something or other—though he artfully contrived to keep one from guessing just what. It was somehow connected with writing poetry in the twentieth century:

> Why must I speak of it? Why must I always
> Stoop from this decent silence to this phrase
> That makes a posture of my hurt? Why must I
> Say I suffer? . . .
> 　　　　. . . ease myself at the soiled stool
> That's common to so swollen many!

It would be cheap to reply, "Why, indeed!" especially when the answer is apparent. Mr. MacLeish belonged to a generation that had many misfortunes, not least of which was being labeled by Gertrude Stein the lost generation. (It is a relief to discover that Miss Stein was not half so worried about their being lost as they were.) He had to write about his troubles because there didn't seem to be any other subjects. And he developed an astonishing skill in making his troubles

69

sound as if they were worth writing about. There was the comparison-with-the-past trick, already noted in the *Hamlet* and actually used in many earlier poems. There was the concern with death in such a poem as *Voyage* ("Trade we our cargoes with the dead for sleep"), which is dedicated to the well-known author of *A Natural History of the Dead,* Mr. Ernest Hemingway. There was the device of referring to the uncertainties of science and the mysteries of metaphysics, as in *Einstein.* All these devices Mr. MacLeish mastered, and when he really abandoned himself to his melancholy he could turn out a pretty sad poem. I confess that I wept the first time I read *You, Andrew Marvell:*

>   And Spain go under and the shore
>   Of Africa the gilded sand
>   And evening vanish and no more
>   The long pale light across the land
>
>   Nor now the long light on the sea
>
>   And here face downward in the sun
>   To feel how swift how secretly
>   The shadow of the night comes on

I wept, but that was a long time ago, and MacLeish and I have both changed. So far as his change is concerned, he hinted at it in a volume called *New Found Land.* Much of the old nostalgia was there, but there was one poem, called *American Letter,* that caused a good deal of rejoicing in heaven. It was all about how it is a strange thing to be an American and he would like to be in southern France, but—

>   This, this is our land, this is our people
>   This that is neither a land nor a race. We must reap
>   The wind here in the grass for our soul's harvest:
>   Here we must eat our salt or our bones starve.
>   Here we must live or live only as shadows.

The critics threw their hats into the air, for another expatriate had been saved. MacLeish was settling down on American soil. (He did buy a farm in New England, I think.) And soon he was surpassing the critics' fondest dreams: he threw himself into the main stream of American life. Indeed, he became a veritable man of affairs, a member of the staff of *Fortune,* an authority on housing and technocracy, a person who could speak sternly to the young men of Wall Street. The critics stood aghast! (I didn't actually see them, but that's what

I hear.) Could this stalwart young American, they cried, be the same man as the pathetic wanderer of the waste lands? Surely, they said, this new, healthy, American MacLeish must give us a fine poem that comes out of the very heart of the country!

Conquistador was Mr. MacLeish's answer to the critics' prayers, and some of them were convinced it was just what they had ordered. Others were not so sure. Those who liked the poem praised its technique (especially if they had not read Ezra Pound's *XXX Cantos)* and spoke of its vitality, its eloquence, its sustained power, and what not. Lincoln Kirstein said that what we needed were heroes (he had used the same idea in an article on James Cagney) and that Mr. MacLeish had given them to us. The people on the other side of the fence looked around for the heroes and couldn't find them. The story of Cortez' march might be heroic, they pointed out, or it might not, but in any case it was here presented through the eyes of an elderly and infirm version of Mr. MacLeish. There were many nice details, they admitted, but they thought the poem, taken as a whole and on its own grounds, was rather limp and nostalgic and very much in the old manner. And they wondered why, if he was so deeply interested in twentieth-century America, Mr. MacLeish didn't write a poem about it.

Archibald has never felt the same about the critics since. In several poems (reprinted, perhaps unwisely, in this collection) and in several letters to the *New Republic,* he has tried to clarify his position. To some extent he has succeeded: he is at least certain that all Marxian critics ought to be shot. Beyond that his ideas are a little hazy. He devotes half his time to demonstrating that poets shouldn't write about social questions and the other half to writing about them. A great deal has been written about *Frescoes for Mr. Rockefeller's City,* and by now anyone can spot the elements that came, in Michael Gold's phrase, out of the fascist unconscious. One notes especially the attack on the Old Men of Wall Street (why is he so sure the young men are different from their papas?) and the splendid piece of dialect writing that, according to Carl Sandburg, is a contribution to the growth of an American language. But this is old stuff now, and I think that, instead of quoting from the *Frescoes,* I shall close with a few lines from another new poem, called *1933:*

> You had best—if you ask me—
> Push on from this place to the seaward

Laying your course close in
Where Tiresias' sirens sing of the

Dialectical hope
And the kind of childish utopia

Found in a small boy's school
*   *   *   *
You have only to push on
To whatever it is that's beyond us

Showing the flat of your sword and they'll
Lick the sand from before you!

Well, what do you think about it, Archibald? Do you suppose
that somewhere the American Hitler is pasting those lines on his look-
ing-glass? Are you applying for the job of chief sand licker?

Margaret Wright Mather
January 16, 1934

The Artful Dodger

Work of Art, by Sinclair Lewis

Ever since I read *Free Air* in the *Saturday Evening Post* I have
been a Sinclair Lewis fan, and I have read each new book (even
Mantrap and *Elmer Gantry*) with a lively pleasure. Whatever else he
may be, Lewis is a grand reporter. Agreeing with William Dean
Howells that every inch of this America is interesting, and not having
seen so very many inches for myself, I get a good deal of enjoyment
from Lewis's explorations. It is no wonder he is popular in Europe:
he covers an enormous amount of the American scene, and he makes
you think he is accurate even when he isn't.

This will explain why and in which way I enjoyed *Work of Art*.
The novel tells of Myron Weagle, son of a hotel keeper in a little
Connecticut town. Inspired by a desire to know all there is to be

known about hotel management, Myron works as a bellboy in a roadhouse, as a cook in a small hotel, and then, successively, as cook, waiter, and clerk in the Connecticut Inn of New Haven. His subsequent career, as an employee of the great Mark Elphinstone, takes him to St. Louis, Florida, and finally to New York. He becomes a power in the Elphinstone chain, but intrigue ousts him after Mark's death, and he takes a position as general manager of the Pye-Charian hotels. All the time he has dreamed of the perfect hotel, and at last, with Pye-Charian backing, he creates the Black Thread Inn. Bad luck and his backer's insistence on profits ruin the experiment—and almost ruin Myron. But he starts again as owner and manager of the Commercial Hotel of Lemuel, Kansas, makes it the best hotel in the state, and establishes a position for himself in the community. When the novel ends, Myron, urged on by his son, is contemplating the building of that modern counterpart of the old English inn, an overnight camp for tourists.

Work of Art just about brings Lewis clear around the circle, and he is now approximately where he was when he wrote *Free Air. Free Air,* which was the immediate predecessor of *Main Street,* was, as I remember it, a lively account of a young garage hand who takes a trip across the continent in search of romance, and finds it. It was admirably adapted, both because of its enthusiasm for America and because of its romantic elements, to the *Saturday Evening Post's* purpose, and at the same time it contained a good deal of excellent reporting. *Work of Art,* though rather lacking in sex appeal, has all the other qualities that made *Free Air* good material for the Post. It is, in other words, quite free from the bitterness that appeared in *Main Street* and its immediate successors. It also is considerably less important. *Main Street, Babbitt,* and *Arrowsmith,* are important books, not merely because they give a credible picture of the surface of American life, but also—and primarily—because they at least hint at the real forces that lie beneath the surface. And if they dealt more clearly and more convincingly with those forces, they would be better books. George F. Babbitt is not important because he is a realtor but because he is the type of business man that has been shaping American civilization. But Myron Weagle is just a hotel keeper.

If Lewis had any purpose other than the desire to show that an interesting novel could be written about hotels, it was to demonstrate that keeping a hotel can be a work of art. To drive home his moral, he made Myron's brother, Ora, a writer. Ora, who is full of talk about art and is very contemptuous of the materialistic Myron, actually is a hack-writer of the worst sort. He has no scruples, sponges on his brother, and in general lives a worthless life. Myron, on the other hand, takes his profession seriously, works hard, studies hard, has a good deal of integrity, and is far more idealistic and less mercenary than Ora. This is a rather obvious variation on a familiar theme, and it confirms the impression that Lewis is a victim of that very common disease among American men of letters, a sense of inferiority to men of action. What the novel proves, and all that it proves, is that a good hotel keeper is better than a bad novelist. Perhaps Mr. Lewis can find someone to debate that proposition with him, but I doubt it.

Many reviewers, I think, will agree with me that *Work of Art* is a superficial book, but there will be a division of opinion as to how that superficiality might have been avoided. One school, I suspect, will say that Lewis should have given us more insight into the soul of Myron Weagle. With that view I have no sympathy; we know all we need to know about Myron's soul. The other school will say that he should have given us more understanding of the world in which Myron functioned. That, of course, is my opinion. The worst of it is, one is driven to feel that Lewis deliberately dodged his responsibilities. There are just enough references to Myron's relations with his employees to show that Lewis is aware of the exploitation of the average hotel worker, but the incidents are carefully selected to permit him to ignore that exploitation. In the same way, he says just enough about hotel finance to explain some of Weagle's difficulties, but not enough to throw any light on the system of which these financial transactions are part. And finally Lewis makes three or four allusions, as if in a gesture of defiance to the class struggle, but the struggle itself never appears on his pages.

The ending of the book is the real give-away. Myron, we are to suppose, has not only found happiness in the small town, but has completely escaped from the influence of greedy investors, cut-throat competitors, and rapacious monopolists. The *Saturday Evening Post* should have serialized *Work of Art!* The happy ending of this novel demonstrates, even more conclusively than Dodsworth's housing project or Ann Vickers' enthusiasm for home and hubby, that Sinclair Lewis is really a constructive critic, a red-blooded American, and a first-class Rotarian—and that he will not face the fundamental facts of American life. Where is the labor novel that, five years ago, we heard he was going to write? It has not been written, though he has found time for a novel on careers for women and a novel on art for hotel keepers. And I suspect it never will be written. For even Sinclair Lewis couldn't write a labor novel without revealing himself as a double-crossing apologist for the existing order.

January 30, 1934

Symbol of Revolution

Parched Earth, by Arnold B. Armstrong

Revolutionary literature continues to thrive despite the blasts of hostile critics. Not only do the John Reed Clubs grow in strength and their members in ability; revolutionary writers appear, now as in the past, who have no connection with the organized cultural movement. Two such writers, having come by their own paths to an understanding and acceptance of the revolutionary position, are publishing books this spring. One of them is William Rollins, Jr., whose strike novel, *The Shadow Before,* will soon appear. The other is Arnold B. Armstrong, author of *Parched Earth.*

Parched Earth is set in the fruit-growing area of California. In a dramatic prologue Armstrong tells the story of the conquest and re-conquest of Tontos Valley: the docile Indians; the arrogant Spaniards, led by Don Miguel Vasquez; the Yankee squatters; and the Yankee entrepreneurs. The story proper begins with the spring fiesta in one of the years of the depression. With the local radio station furnishing a chorus, the author brings before us the life of the town and the principal characters of the novel. Everett Caldwell, whose father finally secured through chicanery the land that Don Miguel had seized by force, is the master of Tontos Valley. Only Maud Rathbone, last of the pioneers, and Belle Vasquez, last of the old Spanish family, dare defy him. Maud, an invalid, lives with her daughter Hattie in their old house, an eyesore to the town and a temptation to real estate agents. Not far away lives the daughter of Don Miguel Vasquez, long the town's prostitute, mother of an idiot son whose father is Everett Caldwell.

The novel covers the period from one fiesta to another. In the course of the year Caldwell tightens his hold upon the town that bears his name. Machinery replaces hundreds of men in his canneries, and the vagrant workers that pour into Tontos Valley each summer find no work. All unsuspecting, the men have rented Caldwell's houses in Slob Row, and they demonstrate under the leadership of Dave Washburn, a Communist organizer. But Dave is injured by Wally, Belle's idiot son, and the demonstration fails. Belle, also unemployed because the cannery workers are unemployed, and ill into the bargain, faces the problem of supporting Wally, who has the body and appetite of a giant. Hattie Rathbone, denied work by Caldwell's orders, walks eight miles a day to cut apricots at six cents a forty pound box.

Tenser and tenser the situation grows. It is impossible to follow all the various threads woven into the novel, but each of the various narratives repeats the theme of exploitation. Armstrong shows concretely how Caldwell extends his power and wealth at the expense of thousands of workers. He shows, too, the sliminess of the bourgeoisie, the soul-rotting subservience of the smaller business men of the town to their master. And he shows, through the actions of Dave Washburn and the words of Hop Collins, a brakeman and a friend of the Rathbones, that the workers must and will unite to overthrow this cruel and corrupt regime. By the time the end is reached there can be no doubt, at least in the mind of the sympathetic reader, that the situation the novel portrays must end in revolution. But the revolution has not come in California, and yet the novel must have its conclusion.

Armstrong's solution of his problem deserves comment. Mike Gold, the other day, answering an unreasonable attack on *Call Home the Heart,* said: "Anybody can write the first two acts of a revolutionary play. It is the last act, the act that resolves the conflicts, that has baffled almost every revolutionary playwright and novelist in the country. For you can't truthfully say in your last act or last chapter that there has been a victorious Communist revolution in this country." The trouble is, as Gold might have gone on to say, that the intellect can be satisfied by the conviction that a successful revolution must come, but the emotions aroused by the vivid presentation of a revolutionary situation demand nothing less than the revolution itself. That might be a good thing if it made the reader go out and fight for the revolution, but ordinarily it leaves him, as well as the author, in a state of confusion and helplessness.

This is how Armstrong solves his problem. Through a logical series of events the dam above Tontos Valley breaks and floods the town. In an extraordinary last chapter the author shows us character after character as the water sweeps over them. Then at last he comes to Hattie Rathbone and Hop Collins, who have been planning to be married. They, with Dave Washburn, who has returned to lead the unemployed workers again, climb the old-fashioned water tower on the Rathbone place and are saved. " 'That's Ev Caldwell's goddam buildin' for you!' said Hop, wringing out his coat. 'Well, ever'body's gonna have work now when the water goes down.' 'It sure looks like a rich harvest for us,' said Hattie." It is merely a symbol of course, but there is no getting away from the fact that this ending, when coupled with the skillful revelation of the rottenness of the bourgeoisie and the strength of the workers, gives a kind of emotional satisfaction that few revolutionary novels have achieved. And, for this particular novel, that satisfaction is valid, though perhaps the method can never be used again.

In dwelling on the resourcefulness with which Armstrong has attacked a particular—and important—problem, I have had to neglect various other qualities of *Parched Earth*. It would be pleasant to dwell on the satirical treatment of the Civic Improvement League, for example, or on the fantastic exploit of Wally Vasquez at the fiesta. I ought to comment, also, on the disproportionate amount of attention paid to the sexual frustration of Hattie Rathbone and the rather inadequate treatment of Dave Washburn. I ought to point out the superficiality in the characterization of some of the business men. There is no doubt that the book has faults, but they are of minor importance in a first novel that treats so complicated a series of incidents with so much clarity and force, that creates so many memorable characters, and that shows so profound and so truly Marxian an insight into the action of social forces and their effect on individual lives.

February 27, 1934

Notes of a Novelist

In All Countries, by John Dos Passos

The sketches in this book were written over a period of eight or nine years and have appeared in half a dozen magazines. They deal with Russia in 1928, Mexico in 1926 and 1932, Spain in 1933, and the United States from 1925 to 1934.

It is scarcely necessary to write a review, for Dos Passos has said almost all that needs to be said. In Moscow he writes, "Well, you're a reporter, you tell yourself. You're gathering impressions. What the hell good are impressions?" Some good, of course. These sketches are always lively, usually perceptive, sometimes shrewd. "Worthwhile writing," he goes on, "is made of knowledge, feelings that have been trained into the muscles, sights, sounds, tastes, shudders that have been driven down into your bones by grim repetition, the modulations of the language you were raised to talk." The best of the sketches are those on America, especially the restrained, terse, powerful summary of the Sacco-Vanzetti case, the description of the 1932 political conventions, and the account of the meeting of the unemployed. Next best are the sketches of Spain, where Dos Passos has spent considerable time.

As for the general attitude that underlies the book, Dos Passos has said the last word, said it deliberately in a prefatory piece called "Passport Photo." He is leaving Russia, and the director and company of the Sanitary Propaganda Theatre come to say good-bye. "They want to know," says the director. "They like you very much, but they want to ask you one question. . . . They want to know where you stand politically. Are you with us?" The Amerikan Peesatyel stammers, "But let me see . . . But maybe I can explain . . . But in so short a time . . . there's no time." The train pulls out.

And there you are. Some writers, as Dos Passos once pointed out, are born to be camp-followers. He is on the side of revolution, of course. He will fight for Sacco and Vanzetti or go on a delegation to Kentucky. He understands that "the function of the Socialist Party has been to give disorganized capitalism a breathing-space." But he hates to commit himself. Time after time you feel him drawing back. "But let me see . . . But maybe I can explain."

In All Countries is an interesting book because it has, though in lesser degree, the qualities we find in Dos Passos' novels: the vivid, authentic reproduction of sights and sounds, the lively sense of the paradoxical and the symbolic, the honest sympathy with working men and women. It exhibits also, and in an exaggerated form, the weaknesses of his novels: the absence of solid, inclusive, irrefutable knowledge of political and economic movements, and the absence of the kind of insight that only direct, disciplined participation in struggle can give.

Dos Passos, I believe, is superior to his bourgeois contemporaries because he is, however incompletely, a revolutionary, and shares, however imperfectly, in the vigor of the revolutionary movement, its sense of purpose, its awareness of the meaning of events, and its defiance of bourgeois pessimism and decay. He is also, it seems to me, superior to any other revolutionary writer because of the sensitiveness and the related qualities that are to be found in this book and, much more abundantly, in his novels. Some day, however, we shall have a writer who surpasses Dos Passos, who has all that he has and more. He will not be a camp-follower.

April 24, 1934

Surfaces and Realities

The Last Pioneers, by Melvin Levy
The Land of Plenty, by Robert Cantwell

These novels have only two things in common: both are located in the Northwest, and both are written by men who strongly sympathize with the revolutionary movement.

The Last Pioneers covers forty years in the life of a city, called Puget in the novel, Queen City of the Pacific. The central character is Herman Merro, born Chaim Shemanski, a Polish Jew, in Paris a pimp and a thief, in Russia a soldier, in Siberia a prisoner and refugee, in Alaska a waiter and entertainer, in Puget proprietor of a hotel and bawdy house, operator in real estate, amateur of politics, leading citizen. Herman Merro, Paul Dexter, Harvard graduate and banker, and Mick Delea, Irish lawyer, dominate the city for many years. Delea, twice mayor of Puget, is finally broken by a jail sentence. The depression drives Dexter to suicide and ruins Merro.

More than half of *The Land of Plenty* tells what happens in a single night in a factory, and the rest of the book covers only a few weeks. On this particular night the electric power gives out. First we see Carl, foreman of the night shift; then some of the workers, especially Hagen, the electrician, Carl's particular enemy; then MacMahon, the superintendent, interrupted in his perennial bickering with his wife by an appeal to come to the factory. There are arguments, quarrels, skirmishes between men and girls, and the rescue of an injured hoist-man. The class struggle emerges in its most elementary form, in the unceasing conflict, often merely personal in its manifestations but economic in its cause, between laborers and their foreman. We are prepared for the strike, ending in violence, that occupies the second part of the book.

To me, Cantwell's book is immeasurably superior to Levy's. This is not because Levy's is discursive, whereas Cantwell's is compact. It is certainly not because Levy deals with millionaires and Cantwell with workers. It is because Cantwell has seen his subject so closely, recognizing its implications and selecting with almost unfailing accuracy the incidents and the aspects of character that present his subject most truly and most completely. Levy, devoting much space to the personal eccentricities of his characters and to the sexual habits of Puget, gives a lively enough picture of the last frontier. But he seems constantly to be working on the margin of his subject, and the real drama of exploitation, which alone could have made the subject worth writing about, is only hinted at.

The Land of Plenty is far less personal, far less oblique, far less obscure than *Laugh and Lie Down*, Cantwell's earlier book. It is fully as sensitive and subtle as its predecessor, but it has much more meaning because it has much more purpose. There are remnants of old mannerisms, it is true, touches of the baffling harshness that belonged to the days of "the new barbarism." But the book gives the reader the mental atmosphere of a factory as no other novel does that I have read, and it shows in its essentials the unconquerable militancy of the workers. In the second part of the book, especially at the very end, Cantwell relies too much on obliqueness, and the heroism of the embattled workers is a little obscured. As a result *The Land of Plenty* fails to sweep the reader along, as William Rollins' *The Shadow Before* does, to high resolve and a sense of ultimate triumph. There remains, however, a feeling that one has been in contact with people and with forces that cannot be ignored.

May 8, 1934

Case Study of Conversion

A House on a Street, by Dale Curran

I don't know who was to blame, but it was a pity that this book wasn't reviewed in the *New Masses* when it appeared last spring. It is not so important a book as Cantwell's *Land of Plenty* or Rollins' *Shadow Before,* but it is a darn good novel, and it raises some very important problems. It not only raises these problems: it solves some of them. In its own right as a story of real people and also as a significant experiment, it is a book that the revolutionary cultural movement must take into account.

Dale Curran has told the story of an ex-bond salesman in the later years of the depression. Peter Twining, after a year's unemployment, has just got a job managing a small apartment house in Greenwich Village for a real estate firm for which he worked before he went into Wall Street. Peter is a pretty typical college graduate, an adroit salesman but otherwise dumb, violently prejudiced against radicalism, completely convinced that prosperity is just around the corner. His year of unemployment and his poverty have made him very unhappy, but they haven't taught him much. His education begins when he takes the job in the apartment house.

He learns from Graham, his predecessor, who disappears. He learns from Isabel, a rich girl he had hoped to marry. He learns from Levinsky, his employer, a decent fellow who sympathizes with the unfortunate but always does the thing that will benefit himself. He learns from Bullitt, an artist living in the apartment house. He learns from Eleanor, an ex-actress, with whom he eventually sets up house-keeping. And he learns from Tachibana, a Japanese Communist. After Peter has rescued Tachibana from the police in Union Square, he is ready to say, "I'll have to think it through for myself. I'll try."

The whole secret of Curran's success is his understatement—not rible agonies in the process of being declassed, and therefore the real the most usual quality in revolutionary fiction. Peter suffers no hor-significance of that experience is all the more apparent. There is nothing melodramatic about his break with Isabel, and the inevitability of that break is unmistakable. Levinsky is no villain; indeed, he hates the system more than Peter does; but the objective results of his actions are none the less devastating. Tachibana has his faults, personal and political, but he is strong because the revolutionary movement is strong. Even the portrayal of the demonstration in Union Square is moderate, but its implications are perfectly clear. And Peter's conversion, hesitant and tentative though it is, is, the reader feels, absolutely to be depended on.

A secondary source of Curran's strength is his frank, though restrained, idealism. Because Communists know that idealism is not enough, is often hypocritical and always unreliable, they distrust it. But Communism does, nevertheless, offer, in Rebecca Pitts' phrase, something to believe in, and for the declassed bourgeois that is enormously important. It was not enough for Peter Twining to be poor, though if he had not been poor his eyes would never have been opened; it was not even enough for him to see the rottenness of capitalism; he had to catch something of Tachibana's vision of a decent social order before he was ready for Communism.

Curran's weaknesses are closely related to his virtues. The book is almost too sweetly reasonable; it lacks emotional drive. It is also too much above the ears; it lacks the grossness and vividness of life. But it is straight and honest in every line. Curran makes the most of what he has; he doesn't go floundering about over his depth. And when he has more, he will undoubtedly do better. Unless something happens, we are going to be proud of him.

Margaret Wright Mather*
July 31, 1934

*Written by Granville Hicks just before the printer's deadline.

Germs of Frustration

Grammar of Love, by Ivan Bunin
Corporal Tune, by L. A. G. Strong
Dusk at the Grove, by Samuel Rogers
Slim, by William Wister Haines

John Howard Lawson, in his contribution to the "Authors' Field Day" in the recent quarterly of *New Masses,* pointed out that most bourgeois novels are very much alike and that "the news that another writer of fiction has written *another* story of middle-class decay is not especially revealing or important." It is impossible, of course, to disagree with him, and yet a simple assertion of that sort scarcely solves the problems of the *New Masses'* book review section. On the one hand, since the section tries to survey the whole field of books, it cannot ignore the novels to which pages are being devoted in the bourgeois press. Our readers presumably want to know what these books are about, why they seem significant to bourgeois reviewers, and why they have little importance for us. On the other hand, it is impossible, if we are to have space enough for the books that we do find important, to give each of these bourgeois novels a long review, "to isolate the particular germ of frustration," as Lawson suggests, "to show the author's *special* relation to bourgeois currents of thought."

So far as I can see, the only practical solution of this difficulty is to give long reviews only to a very few of these novels, the most representative and the most revealing, and to review the others as briefly as possible. One way of handling them is to give them unsigned brief reviews. The other way is to take them in groups. We shall continue to employ the former method, but I think that we shall use the latter method more in the future than we have in the past. Not only does it take care of the problem of space; it may serve to bring to readers of the *New Masses* the cumulative impression of decay that the extensive reading of bourgeois fiction produces on the revolutionary critic.

Certainly *Grammar of Love* is a perfect case study in futility. It is a book of short stories by a Russian emigré, who had lived for years in undistinguished obscurity until, for rather obvious political

reasons, he was awarded the Nobel prize. Of the ten tales here collected, two, *A Simple Peasant* and *On the Great Road,* belong to pre-
revolutionary Russia, and they are the only two that have any merit.
That merit, such as it is, derives from the fact that, before the revolution, Bunin regarded the peasants from a comfortable position of
unquestioned superiority to them. He could unflinchingly portray their
brutality, for he felt himself completely removed from their lives. He
could even sympathize with them, as one can safely sympathize with
whip-broken beasts. Bunin's callous acceptance of squalor and brutality is repellent, but one feels in the stories a limited kind of accuracy.
When he wrote them, neither fear of the peasantry nor any sense of
responsibility for its fate disturbed Bunin, and he could and did record
the more superficial aspects of its life.

But the world has changed, and Bunin's security has gone. The
three constant ingredients of his post-revolutionary work are nostalgia
for the Czarist past, hatred for the Soviet regime, and an eagerness to
find refuge in romantic trivialities. His neurotic bitterness against the
Soviet regime appears in *Comrade Dozorny,* which is so violent as to
seem almost a burlesque of all anti-Soviet fiction. His nostalgia reveals
itself in little details of *Sunstroke* and *Ida,* and all the stories in the
book, except the two early ones, are devoted to sentimental trifles.
Even at his best, Bunin was far from first-rate, but the conditions
that made his best work possible have vanished, and only a very poor
second-best is left.

L. A. G. Strong, Anglo-Irish poet, novelist, critic, and antholo-
gist, has told in *Corporal Tune* the story of the last weeks of a man
with a fatal disease. Although both Proust and Mann have portrayed
the psychological implications of sickness, I can think of no author
who has shown the part that illness and the threat of illness play in
the average life. Certainly Mr. Strong has no interest in anything so
gross as the economic causes and effects of disease. His hero, Ignatius
Farrelly is a successful author, with no worries about the cost of
medical attention or the fate of his dependents. Furthermore, Ignatius
has recently lost his wife and consequently his will to live. Thanks
to these two assumptions, Mr. Strong is permitted to concentrate on
Ignatius' observations of his surroundings, his analyses of his own
sentiments, and his semi-mystical reflections on death. The result
is a "kind grave very sorry" book, like Mr. Garfield's reading voice
in *The 42nd Parallel,* of no possible importance except to literary

club women who seek their occasion for a good cry on a higher level than Bess Streeter Aldrich.

Samuel Rogers, whose *Dusk at the Grove* won him the Atlantic's $10,000 prize, is an American schoolteacher. Though this is his first novel, he has the polished literary manners of a professional vendor of pseudo-profundities. It is the story of the disintegration of a family, a process that Mr. Rogers, in common with a great many other novelists, seems to regard as fascinating and completely mysterious. The War and a bad marriage ruined Dicky, and Brad became another of these frustrated business men, and Linda got a divorce, and finally the Grove, which is the family place at Newport, had to be sold to help Brad out of the depression. And that is that, except that Linda, for no good reason, still has faith in life, and Mr. Rogers, for the very good reason that he has just won $10,000, ought to have.

To contrast these three books with William Wister Haines' *Slim* is to see the enormous difference between the frustration and despair of bourgeois fiction and the potential vitality of working-class literature. *Slim* is not a very good novel; it is certainly not a revolutionary novel; but it is a lively, first-hand record of a workingman's experience. One of the many advantages of proletarian writers, as this book, with all its defects, suggests, is the freshness of their material. They don't live in a world in which everything has been said before and the only chance of originality is in finding a new way of saying something. This story of linemen, by a man who has been a lineman for seven years, humanizes a large sector of life that for most of us is completely blank. And it shows that there are, even among non-class-conscious workers, many of the elements of a true culture, a warm solidarity, a body of traditions, a code of ethics. Mr. Haines has not idealized his workers, but you feel that there is something strong and healthy in their way of life.

I have said that *Slim* is not a very good novel. Mr. Haines unfolds the story with a simplicity that is almost mechanical, describing Slim's apprenticeship as a helper, then introducing an adventure, describing Slim's experiences in the Southwest with an adventure thrown in, describing the death of Slim's friend Red, describing Slim's love affair, describing Slim at work on the electrification of a railroad. The conversation is frequently lit up by magnificent phrases of linemen's jargon, but the narrative style is consistently banal. The details of the job, though extremely illuminating, are often difficult to comprehend; an adroit novelist could have smoothed the reader's path by more judicious selection.

I have also said that *Slim* is not a revolutionary novel, and that is not the least important reason for its relative ineffectiveness. The central theme of the novel is the workman's pride in his own independence and in the difficulties and dangers of his job. That is all to the good; we need to realize that the worker, exploited though he is, is not a cower slave. But it is impossible, even for the naïve and hopeful Mr. Haines, to describe independence and craftsman's pride as if they had no economic foundation. Towards the end of the book he comes to the depression, the dropping of electrification projects, and the consequent unemployment of Slim and thousands of his fellow linemen. What are these jobless linemen to do? Mr. Haines knows that their pride and independence will make gangsters of many of them, but he also knows that this is neither a personal nor a social solution. What is the alternative? Mr. Haines calmly dodges. Slim escapes marriage, and by study and hard work is able to get along. It is a solution that could only work for one lineman out of a thousand, and Mr. Haines knows it.

It is not merely the lame ending, however, that indicates what a revolutionary attitude might have given Mr. Haines. That is merely a symptom of a lack of understanding of forces that are as much a part of linemen's lives and as much a menace to those lives as the voltages that pass through their wires. Without that understanding, *Slim* tells only half the story, but it tells that half effectively, and it suggests that our revolutionary writers would do well to remember the freshness, the drama, and the human value of work as well as the causes and the necessity of revolt. It also suggests that even a fifty-fifty proletarian has an edge these days on the average bourgeois.

August 28, 1934

Salamanders and Politics

Now in November, by Josephine Johnson

Sensitivity of a very high order has been fatal to more than one novelist and poet, or perhaps I should say that such sensitivity is often found in combination with fatal qualities. There is Emily Dickinson, for example, who at her finest completely transforms everyday experience and sharpens the senses of even the dullest reader, but who rather more often is merely fanciful or absurd or trivial. Then there is Willa Cather, who, in her earlier novels, drew vitality from her extraordinary responsiveness to the smallest detail of Nebraskan farm life, but who has in later years become a kind of genteel antiquarian. Miss Dickinson, one gathers, was so remote from the normal course of human existence in her own age that she could not evaluate her experiences, could not distinguish the ephemeral and eccentric from the representative and profound. Miss Cather, on the other hand, has been precipitated into a world in which her earlier values are no longer pertinent, and she prefers to falsify life rather than adjust herself to it.

By virtue of her perceptiveness and her ability to communicate to her readers something of her own awareness, Josephine Johnson deserves to be compared, as she already has been, with Emily Dickinson and Willa Cather. The theme of her novel suggests, furthermore, comparison with an author who was perhaps greater than either of them, Emily Brontë. In *Now in November*, as in *Wuthering Heights*, the sense of doom colors the very first page. One knows that this is not simply an account of a Missouri farmer's struggle against drought and debt. One knows that there is more involved than the simple but intense revelation of a Dickinsonian appreciation of beauty in nature. From the first the novel builds towards the madness of Karen and her suicide, towards the catastrophic fire and the death of the mother, towards the frustration of both Merle's and Marget's love.

I would be the last to deny the power of this strange and almost unearthly tragedy that Miss Johnson unfolds. Yet I am most grateful for those elements in the book that are least reminiscent of the Brontes and Emily Dickinson, for the importance attached to the mortgage, for the casual talk about farmers' organizations, for the little glimpse of the milk strike, for the insistence on the general tragedy of which the Haldmarnes' tragedy is a small part. The novel ends, it is true, on the theme of resignation, but Miss Johnson takes refuge neither in mysticism nor in melodrama. There is, moreover, the hint, significant because of what has been said about organization: "It is not possible to go on alone."

I stress these things, not because they play a very important part in *Now in November,* but because their presence is an indication of the way Josephine Johnson's mind is working. She seems to be honest. She has said, "Salamanders and fungus seem more important than war or politics, but it is cowardly and impossible to ignore them and try to escape." It is well that, with her peculiar temperament and talents, she has learned that lesson so early. A concern with salamanders and fungus and all they symbolize is not wrong in itself, but it may all too easily mean a refusal to think about war and politics and all they symbolize. That is the way that Willa Cather and Elizabeth Madox Roberts, for example, have gone. Miss Johnson seems to see its dangers. The other way is our way. It, too, has its dangers, but the disintegration of the backbone is not one of them.

September 25, 1934

A Study in Comparative Literature

Isidor Schneider's collection of poems, *Comrade-Mister,* is divided into two sections, the first, I take it, containing poems that he wrote before he became a Communist, the second those written since. There are important differences between the two sections, and these differences are worth examining.

In a note on revolutionary poetry Schneider points out that the two most common themes of the poetry of the last three or four hundred years are love and nature. These are also the dominant themes of the first section of his book. His treatment of them, however, is by no means that of conventional romantic poetry. There are, for example, two parallel poems, one describing a tree on a city street, the other a well-cover in the country, and the two observations suggest "the two eternities," the power of nature and the power of man. The hanging of clothes in an orchard brings the reflection that nature "can set anything at home." An overheated room reminds the poet that city life breeds its own kind of strength. The five or six poems concerned with travel in Europe pose serious questions of the destinies of men and nations. A visit to the Louvre, for example, calls attention to the dual nature of man, his need for security and peace and his need for action and change. And a poem in praise of France ends:

> We shrank to see distend your armies,
> your ranks of beetles wasting green
> your youth. You have the maw imperial
> whereon men, steel-edged, hinge for teeth.
> It rends the strength of nations: you
> it nourishes never. Oh train out
> this canine towardness to the stools of death.

Obviously Schneider is a poet whose mind reaches out from simple experiences to far-reaching questionings and bold generalizations. The same trait appears in his poems of love. "A Night of No Love" is a rather simple and very poignant expression of longing for the beloved one, but usually he strives to transcend the immediate experience by finding in it ultimate significance. "You Are My Sun," for example, suggests the limitations of passion: after a stanza that is pure tribute, it concludes:

> When you are away
> I sit in cold silence, and my hands knot in the cold,
> and a night hollows my mind and the hollowness is sealed.
> And then, as in the absence of the sun, the stars can glitter,
> remote and struggling, tinily flare up and flicker
> the little constellations of ideas.

It is apparent that Schneider, in his pre-revolutionary phase, belonged to the school of poets we call, rather inaccurately, metaphysical. Not only his concern with ideas and his striving to discover the far-reaching implications of simple experiences but also the originality and difficulty of his figures of speech and the hard-packed terseness of his style place him among the followers of John Donne. The resemblance is particularly striking in the poems of life. The first part of "Marriage" has the same ecstatic quality as have Donne's love poems, and the conclusion raises a question that Donne might have raised. "Harlem from a Bus Top" rests on a "conceit" that would have delighted either Donne or Marvell, and line after line of the poem explodes with the startling effectiveness so characteristic of them.

But Schneider's metaphysical poetry does not escape, could not escape, from the dark shadow that has hovered over Eliot, MacLeish, Tate, Gregory, and the other poets who, despite their many differences, have alike turned to Donne and his school for inspiration. These poems have an air of perplexity that comes dangerously close to despair. It is not only that some of them, such as "Sleep" and "In the Syrup See Dead Flies," echo the concern with death that Eliot has celebrated in his "Whispers of Mortality"; they all strain, almost in agony, toward some sort of release from the meaninglessness of life. The attempt to twist by sheer brutality more meaning out of words than they have symbolizes the poet's effort to assault the universe and make it deliver an answer to his questionings.

Turning to the revolutionary poems, one finds, naturally, that Schneider has not wholly changed. He is still an intellectual poet. But at last his mind has found something that will nourish it. It seems to me that, in the earlier poems, he was not quite convinced himself that his themes were worth the effort he spent on them. They were the best he could find, but I feel in his treatment of them a certain self-distrust, as if one part of him knew that all his tense striving could win no fruitful victory. In the revolutionary poems there is self-confidence; the assurance of a man who has found allies and has come to terms with his world. He no longer needs to tear himself to pieces to find his theme; he has been released from sickly subjectivism and has learned to contemplate fearlessly the men and movements of his day.

One consequence of this release from self-preoccupation is the development of a notable talent for satire. The first two stanzas of "For the Tenth Anniversary of the Daily Worker" and the whole of "In a Hotel Lobby" and "Dollars" magnificently combine shrewdness and savage contempt. "Portrait of a False Revolutionist" not only defines a type; it inoculates against contamination.

Furthermore, without losing any of that extraordinary terseness that is perhaps his greatest gift, Schneider has sloughed off the kind of deliberate, literary obscurity that occasionally vitiated his earlier work and that is found in Eliot and his followers. His poetry demands an effort of comprehension, just as it always did, but there is no willful concealment of meaning behind forced figures of speech and private references. Note, for instance, the first stanza of the eloquent and richly burdened poem, "To the Museums":

> Come to the museums, workers; and under every landscape
> paste this label: "Workers! Is the earth as beautiful where you live?
> You on the poverty farms, boarded to hogs,
> your sore fields scratched to the stone by the chickens?
> You in the slums who can span between two fingers
> all you can have of the free horizon; who must lean,
> somehow, over a tenement's shoulder to see the sun?
> This is your homestead, farmer. Worker, this is your summer place.
> It has been kept beautiful by your labor. Enjoy its grace."

The same quality is to be found in most of the poems in the second section. "Comrade-Mister" explores with soundness and ingenuity the meanings of the two barricade-separated forms of address, and "The Reichstag Trial" catches some of Dimitroff's own eloquent fire. Best of all, it seems to me, are the four revolutionary orations which appeared in the *New Masses*. It is a fine theme that Schneider has chosen, the theme of the great deception. In the first of the orations the priest speaks to the people, to exploit them. In the second the king, to further his own greedy ends, allies himself to the priest. In the third the priest and king are made part of the profit-machine of the business man. And in the fourth the workers rise to overthrow this unholy trinity.

In the first three of these orations Schneider has written with insight, with sardonic wit, and with power, illuminating both the process and the psychology of exploitation. The fourth oration seems to me less successful. Written in a slangy prose, it sometimes achieves the sharp eloquence of working-class speech and it is always vigorous and hard. But there are passages in which the language is overdone, and as a whole it seems forced.

If I am right, I think the explanation is not hard to find, and it is the explanation of other weaknesses in these revolutionary poems. Like many other revolutionary writers, Schneider knows so well what he wants to be that he is not quite content to be what he is. We are all like that; we all want to force the process of adaptation to revolutionary ways of thought and proletarian ways of feeling. But the process takes time and much experience in the radical movement, and it is always a mistake for anyone, and perhaps especially for a poet, to substitute what he thinks he ought to feel for the feelings he actually has.

In "Prophecy to Myself" Schneider writes:

> So, vain and doomed is personal love.
> If it has destiny, it is like a potted tree,
> that as it grows must break the pot,
> and if it reach not more abundant earth, must die.
> My love has cracked its pot; but has struck
> the more abundant earth, the earth of comradeship;
> and I can, all my length grow out,
> in revolutionary act.

This seems to me less than completely sincere. It is commentary, of course, on the love poems of the first section, and I suspect that the reversal of attitude it describes is scarcely an accomplished fact. I have a similar complaint against "Seed on my Desk," in which the wind-blown seed suggests to the poet the teachings of revolution. Nature still, I am sure, has meaning for Schneider other than its power to provide illustrations of revolutionary processes. If his enjoyment of nature and his eagerness for revolution are not fully integrated, that is no great matter at the moment; better frankly recognize the division than create a false integration.

I could find other examples of essentially the same weakness, but to dwell upon them would give a false impression of their importance. I do not want to obscure from the reader my conviction that Schneider is the most fully developed revolutionary poet in America. There are younger American poets who in occasional poems have given promise of going beyond Schneider, but at the moment they are his inferiors. His methods are stronger than theirs, more disciplined, more appropriate. His sensitivity is surer, less erratic. His imagination has deeper roots in revolutionary thought and action. His work has much of the sturdiness and vigor of the proletarian movement of which he is an important part.

December 4, 1934

Sinclair Lewis—Anti-Fascist

It Can't Happen Here, by Sinclair Lewis

It Can't Happen Here is not a great novel. It is a political tract, a novel with a message, and it can no more be judged by ordinary standards than could *Looking Backward* or *The Iron Heel.* That the tract was written in the form of a novel will greatly increase its sale, but the story is to be judged only by its success in sugar-coating the pill. What really matters is the pill itself.

The novel begins in the spring of 1936, with the nomination of Buzz Windrip as the Democratic candidate for president. Competing with Windrip are Senator Trowbridge, a sober and intelligent Republican, and Franklin Roosevelt, running independently with the backing of the liberal Congressmen and Norman Thomas. Windrip is elected, and on his inauguration assumes the power of a dictator, crushing opposition with his private army of Minute Men. The usual fascist policies are adopted: the breaking of the labor unions, the suppression of criticism, the burning of books, the redistricting of the country to facilitate Windrip control and Windrip graft, the establishment of concentration camps, the persecution of minority races and the use of elaborate ballyhoo to conceal the lowering of standards of living. In 1938, Windrip is deposed by his secretary and brains, the homosexual Lee Sarason, who, in 1939, is assassinated by General Dewey Haik. A war is on with Mexico when the book ends.

All this is seen through the eyes of Doremus Jessup, a middle-aged liberal who edits a Vermont newspaper. Jessup criticizes Windrip, is arrested, paroled and forced to help the pro-Windrip editor who is put in his place. After his son-in-law is shot, he joins an underground anti-fascist organization. Finally discovered, he is sent to a concentration camp, with beatings, castor oil, bad food, vermin, filth and all the rest. His escape is maneuvered from the outside, and he goes to Canada, where he works at the headquarters of Walt Trowbridge's New Underground. After a time he is sent to the West to do active work, and we last see him making his escape from the fascists.

Although Jessup comes to life in certain episodes, it would be foolish to compare him with George Babbitt or Martin Arrowsmith or even such lesser heroes as Myron Weagle. The only thing that can or needs to be said is that he is convincing and interesting enough to hold the story together. His private life, which consists mostly of an affair with Lorinda Pike, is of no importance except as a concession to readers who want love-interest. The various characters just barely serve their functions in the tract and that is all.

The book must, then, be discussed as a piece of political writing, and it might as well be made clear here and now that Sinclair Lewis has written a courageous and tremendously useful book. If John Jones had written the novel, it would be considerably less important. But here is our illustrious Nobel Prize winner, whose poorest books cannot help selling. His tract is going to be read by tens and probably hundreds of thousands; editorials will be written about it; every women's club in the country will listen to a paper about it in the course of the winter. And whatever the novel's shortcomings, it does make two things perfectly clear: first, fascism is entirely possible in the United States; second, it would be damned unpleasant. Oh, I know plenty of readers will say, "But really, it *can't* happen here," but the book is going to make quite a dent just the same.

Because the novel is likely to raise the issue of fascism more sharply than it has ever been raised in America before, it is important to find out just how well Lewis understands the phenomenon and just how effectively he is arming people against it. First of all, he knows that fascism is related to capitalism and that is the beginning of wisdom. Secondly, he realizes that fascist demagogues rise to power on the strength of their radical promises. And finally he is fully aware that the liberal suffers as much from fascism as the Communist or Socialist.

On the other hand, it must be recorded that he seldom emphasizes the capitalist basis of fascism. Despite his occasional references to Wall Street's support of Windrip, he has not quite freed himself from the notion that fascism is directly caused by the gullibility of the masses and the knavishness and sadism of its leaders. This is particularly apparent in his account of the beginnings of Windrip's regime. He gives no reason for the emergence of fascism at just that moment. There is no explanation of why Roosevelt has failed, no indication of working-class militancy of the kind that Wall Street would want a fascist to crush, no discussion whatever of the economic condition of the country.

In the second place, the scope of the book seems needlessly limited. Lewis says nothing, for example, about the international reverberations of fascism in the United States, beyond his references to its extreme nationalism and its war with Mexico. More striking is his failure to give the reader more than a sketchy idea of what is happening throughout the country as a whole. His choosing a corner of Vermont as his locale was wise, for it enables him to show how fascism strikes at the most secluded spots, but he pays too much attention to Fort Beulah to do what he really wants to do.

Thirdly, Lewis' liberalism, though genuine enough and in a way admirable, does not conduce to intellectual clarity. This is a tract, remember, and a tract that is intended to get results. What, then, is one supposed to do to prevent fascism? Lewis does not know. The only time he copes with the problem is when Jessup reflects: "The tyranny of this dictatorship isn't primarily the fault of Big Business, nor of the demagogues who do their dirty work. It's the fault of Doremus Jessup! Of all the conscientious, respectable, lazy-minded Doremus Jessups who have let the demagogues wriggle in, without fierce enough protest." It sounds a little like a civil-service reformer: don't let the rascals get into power; keep good men in office. Practically speaking, indeed, the moral seems to be that one should vote for Franklin D. Roosevelt in 1936.

The same confusion appears when the question is raised of what, supposing Jessup's counter-revolution is successful, will take the place of fascism. It will be recalled that the leader of the counter-revolution is Walt Trowbridge, last Republican candidate for president. Jessup is "content to know that, whatever happened, Trowbridge and the other authentic leaders would never go back to satisfaction in government of the profits, by the profits, for the profits." Trowbridge talks about "a new feeling" and "a universal partnership," and Jessup—and Lewis—are content.

Lewis makes no pretense, of course, of being anything but a liberal, but it can scarcely be said that his case for liberalism is convincing. The whole book demonstrates the helplessness of the liberal in the face of capitalist terror. Jessup himself, though he disapproves of violence, is forced to resort to it. He refuses to accept the view that Communism is the only alternative to fascism, but he has nothing convincing to propose.

It is obvious throughout that Lewis is terribly afraid the Communists may be right, for he cracks at them on every possible occasion. They are "Puritanical, hortatory and futile"; they are dogmatists; Russia is their Holy Land; they refuse to make a united front with Franklin Roosevelt; they are theocratic, intense and narrow. The one Communist who plays much of a part in the book illustrates all this by regarding his fellow-prisoners as comrades "only if they were saved, baptized Communists." There is another Communist, who is a pretty decent fellow, but he is expelled from the party for saying that the revolution ought not to be run from Moscow.

It is difficult not to feel that, so far as Communism is concerned, Sinclair Lewis is both worried and ignorant. His ignorance is inexcusable; there are plenty of Communists not so very far from his Vermont home who are living demonstrations of the falsity of most of his ideas. His worry is more understandable, but, I think, a little excessive. He feels that the Communists are putting up a pretty good fight against fascism, but he refuses to ally himself with them. We can assure him that, despite all his fears about dogmatism, the Communists will welcome him—do, in fact, welcome him right now for the fight against fascism he has made in this book. We can also assure him that he need not be afraid of the results of the alliance. We only ask him to go as far as his strong and fine hatred of fascism carries him. If we are wrong in holding that Communism is the only alternative to fascism, he has nothing to lose, for history will go his way and not ours. If, on the other hand, we are right, and he has got to choose between what he regards as two evils, it ought not to be hard to determine what is, for him, on any ground, the lesser of the two.

This is a political review of a political book, and the upshot of it is that Lewis has done a magnificent job so far as warning his readers against fascism is concerned, but that he has not understood fascism well enough to be able to show how to fight against it. But there is one literary comment that ought to be made. If it is not a great novel, it is a very significant phenomenon in the career of a highly important novelist. After a good deal of inglorious wobbling, Lewis has discovered the great issue of his day and he has not been afraid to tackle it. The effect on his future writing should be tremendous. Lewis is looking at America with new eyes. Instead of third-rate stuff like *Ann Vickers* and *Work of Art,* he ought to give us the kind of book that *Babbitt* promised, a book alive with understanding, warm with sympathy, a full, rich, honest, courageous book. If *It Can't Happen Here* is an event in American politics, that would be an event in American literature.

October 29, 1935

Better Than *Call Home The Heart*

A Stone Came Rolling, by Fielding Burke

More than thirty years ago, Olive Tilford Dargan, who now writes under the name Fielding Burke, published her first book, a collection of plays in verse. Other books, both of plays and lyrics, appeared during the next two decades and she became known as a poet with a strong love of natural beauty. From such of her verse as I have read, I gather that she was always a humanitarian, but certainly the reader was less conscious of her social sympathies than of her intense and perhaps mystical preoccupation with nature.

Then, three years ago, *Call Home the Heart* was published. In its early chapters it showed a rare ability to portray the beauty of the Carolina mountains and what seemed to be a thorough understanding of their people. But the novel did not fall into the mistake that has vitiated so much regional literature: it did not try to set forth the dead past as if it were the living present. On the contrary, it bravely carried its characters from the mountains to the industrial towns of the South, and showed how new forces were creating new problems. It did more than that: it selected types of experience that indicated how these problems could be solved. The humanitarianism of the early work had grown into revolutionary passion.

Call Home the Heart was a sincere and moving novel, but its faults were obvious. The description of its industrial struggle seemed incidental, an episode between the heroine's departure from the mountains and her return. That she should return was natural enough, but the emphasis was unfortunate. Moreover, the impression that the strike was only of secondary importance was heightened by the fact that the author was unmistakably much more at home in describing the mountains than she was in describing industrial conditions and labor organizations. No one could doubt the genuineness of Fielding Burke's revolutionary sympathies, but they were not given integrated expression in the book.

Whatever its faults, *Call Home the Heart* was, in its own right, a remarkable novel, and it was even more remarkable in the light of its author's previous work. It is, then, as extraordinary as it is pleasant to report that *A Stone Came Rolling* is a much better book than *Call Home the Heart,* and is strong precisely where its predecessor was weak. Not only is the struggle of labor an integral part of the book; it is handled with knowledge and insight. Fielding Burke understands the economic problems of southern industry, the difficulties that face organized labor and the tactics that are being evolved to meet those difficulties. From this point of view, *A Stone Came Rolling* is a challenge to the revolutionary novelists who have allowed themselves to be beaten by ignorance: Fielding Burke has shown that writers can learn.

The novel is not, of course, a strike handbook, but simply the story of a group of southern people, especially Ishma Hensley, the heroine of *Call Home the Heart,* her husband Britt, and Bly Emberson and his family. The strike that takes place in Dunmow is a crucial event in their lives and, therefore, Fielding Burke makes it her business to describe the strike intelligently. But she is primarily interested in the characters, as she should be, and she handles them beautifully. Britt, who was a little shadowy in *Call Home the Heart,* emerges very clearly in this novel and shares the honors with Ishma. Bly Emberson, a manufacturer who wants to be good and is beaten by the system, is a character worthy of a place beside them. And the whole picture of life in Dunmow is firm and well-rounded. One of the incidental weaknesses of the first novel was the unconvincing portrayal of the upper class; here even the most reactionary employers are real persons.

The great quality that Fielding Burke has in both her novels is warmth, and it is a quality that is too often lacking in revolutionary fiction. One never feels for a moment that she is outside the struggle she portrays; she is in it, heart and soul. The reader cannot help but respond to her admiration for Ishma, her tenderness towards Britt, her respect for Bly Emberson. These are real persons to her, and she makes them real to us, and makes us feel about them as she feels. Her dislikes are as strong as her loyalties: she understands Verna Emberson but detests her; she shudders at the stinking hypocrisy of most of the clergymen; she is grieved and angry at the treason of some of the workers. And her revolutionary hope is real, too; one feels it as a living, irresistible force in her life.

It is perhaps only in the matter of language that Fielding Burke betrays the fact that her literary powers developed in an earlier day than ours. Her appreciation of natural beauty is certainly an asset and one is glad that she is not, like some of our writers, ashamed to express the emotion that a lovely scene arouses in her. But her imagery sometimes seems too purely romantic, and in describing emotional crises—the death of Britt, for example—she occasionally comes to the very edge of the gulf of sentimentality. This is a minor criticism, though justice requires that it be recorded. Its chief significance is that it reminds us of the Olive Tilford Dargan who had written for twenty-five years before Fielding Burke appeared. It reminds us that Fielding Burke has come by a more difficult path than most of our young writers have had to follow, and the fact that she belongs, as she indubitably does, with men and women who were not born when her first book was published is a tribute to the creative force of the revolutionary movement, to the power of the poetic imagination and to Fielding Burke.

December 3, 1935

The *New Masses* Prize Novel

Marching! Marching! by Clara Weatherwax

"She has discovered the true poetry of proletarian life and revolutionary struggle, and out of it has written a strong and beautiful book."

The judges of the *New Masses*—John Day proletarian prize

novel contest chose *Marching! Marching!* as the best of the more than a hundred novels submitted. By the terms of the contest, the winning novel had to deal with working-class experience, and we were pretty well in agreement that it ought to portray that experience from the workers' point of view. Otherwise there were no prerequisites. Some of us, however, felt that the prize novel ought not to be merely a good piece of work; it ought to contribute to the further growth of proletarian literature. And in *Marching! Marching!* we found what we were looking for.

Marching! Marching! tells a simple story of workers, mostly lumbermen, on the Pacific Coast. At the outset a lumberman, Tim, is killed as a result of a defective cable. Pete Bayliss, supposedly the illegitimate son of the town's big business man, sees the accident. The men believe he is a stool-pigeon, as indeed Mr. Bayliss wants him to be; and Mario, a Filipino, in his wrath over Tim's death, beats him. Pete, instead of resenting the beating, resents his own equivocal position. He informs Bayliss that he is not really his son, repudiates the privilege Bayliss has given him and takes his place with the workers.

Attention shifts to Joe Strong, Tim's brother. Joe and his girl, Mary, are, like Mario, hard workers in the Communist Party. The forces are gathering for a strike in the Bayliss mill, and Bayliss decides to eliminate Mario. Gangsters waylay the Filipino and nearly kill him. Through an accident, Joe and Mary discover him in time to save his life. Other persons are drawn into the struggle, many lumbermen, a couple of clam-diggers, some of the unemployed, and even members of the middle class. At last, at a stirring mass meeting, the strike is called. Bayliss and the town officials immediately resort to violence. Joe Strong is framed, taken to jail, beaten up. Homes of Communists are raided. The militia is brought in. But the fight goes on.

It is a simple story of workers' lives as they are actually lived. I can think of no proletarian novel that is more authentic or more intimate. Here are Joe and Mario and Mary and a host of others at their work, in their homes, in their militant organizations. Miss Weatherwax is particularly successful in her treatment of the Communist Party, for she sees it as something growing directly out of the lives of the workers, and she appreciates the ardent heroism of the leaders of the Party and the stubborn courage of the rank and file. But she never treats her characters as merely political beings; they have fears, hopes, passions, weaknesses, dreams.

It is because Miss Weatherwax so effectively portrays her characters that *Marching! Marching!* is a fine novel, and it is her method of portraying them that makes the book a significant contribution to proletarian literature. I do not know how to describe her method except by saying that the incidents of the strike are treated as events in the minds of the people of the book. Everything is given as it impresses itself on the consciousness of some character, sometimes Pete Bayliss, sometimes Joe, sometimes Mary, sometimes Mary's paralyzed mother, sometimes respectable old Granny Whittle. The novel turns from character to character, and yet always sweeps triumphantly toward its climax.

Such a method is difficult to sustain, but Miss Weatherwax has a rich, poetic style that grows out of a sensitive mind. Take, for example, her description of Nick's beer joint: "From outside, the voices seemed coming and going with the door's swinging—shouted orders and talking and laughing, sweeping out like brief gusts to be lost in the slapping wind. And the outside swung shortly in, carrying a taste of the town too familiar for noticing: the waterfront ship-salt-tar smell, oil on the river, decaying flotage, and the dank weed-mud bitterness of the tideflats under the mouldy pilings; wet lumber tangy as medicine; smoke, with a faint whiff of pulp far off."

Or look at the very end, in which the author suddenly talks about "we," seizing the reader and bringing him into the action of the story: "Everyone laughs and talks. We look forward and back at our strength and numbers. A feeling of live power ripples through us like electricity, feeding and renewing itself on the charged air round us, full as it is of the sounds we are making, of the sweaty smell of our own flesh in movement, and of the oil, fish, wood, pulp, gasoline, factory smells of our working clothes. Our hearts nearly burst thumping so loud. Feet find a common rhythm as we settle into our stride and the ranks flow smoothly forward with the force of a river. We get quieter. Not much talking now. Even the kids step strong like men." The marching strikers confront the militia. "For a few seconds we hear only the sound of our own feet, the steady pound of ourselves marching forward. Then suddenly Annie turns and waves a signal to our marshals. Each lifts a hand for a moment while a word is spoken from rank to rank. The signalling hands go down in unison and we're all singing:

"Hold the fort for we are coming;
Workingmen be strong . . . "

It is the power of Miss Weatherwax's imagination, as shown in such wholly representative passages, that holds the book together. Disregarding the conventional forms of narrative, she relies on the sensitive recording of impressions. And she does so with complete success. She has discovered the true poetry of proletarian life and revolutionary struggle, and out of it has written a strong and beautiful book.

January, 1936

Eliot In Our Time

The Achievement of T. S. Eliot, by F. O. Matthiessen

Mr. Eliot's achievement is considerable enough to deserve the careful, intelligent, and resourceful treatment that Professor Matthiessen has given it. If one were to judge Eliot only by his influence on his contemporaries, one would have to regard him as an important figure, certain of a place in literary history. But he has been not merely a stimulus to poets but also a satisfaction to readers, including some readers well over on the left. For more than one radical, indeed, Eliot is almost the only modern poet who will bear re-reading. Why this is true Mr. Matthiessen helps to explain, and in giving his explanation he has made so many significant comments on the nature of poetry that his book immediately takes a prominent place among the critical works of our time.

The book is important in spite of what I regard as Mr. Matthiessen's confusion on the interminably and inconclusively debated topic of form and content. At times he seems to take a firm position with the formalists. At the outset, for example, he laments "the increasing tendency to treat poetry as a social document and to forget that it is an art," and says that the one quality that gives a poet's work permanence is "his quality as an artist." Later on he observes that what makes Rivera great is "the complete mastery of the demands of his form."

Yet Mr. Matthiessen also points out, "That does not mean that either the poem or the poet can be separated from the society that produced them, or that a work of art does not inevitably both reflect and illuminate its age. Nor does it imply that a poet is necessarily lacking in ideas, or that the content of his work, the material he chooses to write about, and the interpretation he makes of it, is without cardinal significance in determining his relation to life and to the currents of thought in his time." And, as a matter of fact, Mr. Matthiessen devotes much of his attention to Eliot's ideas and their relation to the life of our times.

In short, Mr. Matthiessen very properly regards both form and content as important. What disturbs me is that he fails to investigate the relation of the two. He says shrewd things about both, but he talks about them separately.

It is this lapse, I believe, that makes Mr. Matthiessen unduly hostile to what he calls sociological criticism. Every critic, no matter how far to the left, acknowledges, even if he sometimes appears to forget, that there is no ideological equivalent for a poem. He also knows that there is a difference between good expression and bad expression. But what some of us hold is that a thing well expressed and a thing badly expressed are two different things. If two men paint the same landscape, and one painting is a masterpiece and the other a collection of daubs, the difference is not wholly in form. There is also a difference in content, not in the actual physical content of the landscape, of course, but in the mental content, so to speak—in what the two men perceived.

For us, therefore, the problem is not so simple as it is for Mr. Matthiessen. He can always dismiss a difficult question by talking about the poet's quality as an artist or his mastery of form. We, however, cannot separate artistic quality and formal mastery from the poet's perceptions and even, if he has any, his ideas. That it requires great talent and long apprenticeship for the expression of any perception, even a simple one, we do not deny, and we do not willingly overlook the intricacies of the process. But we cannot forget that the perception and the expression must always be examined together, for we are certain that they are integrated in the actual functioning of the poet.

It would be extravagant to try to define, in the space of a review, the interrelation of perception and expression, but the existence of that interrelation ought to be obvious. For this reason, I am unwilling to accept Mr. Matthiessen's phrases about artistry. I think Eliot is important because he says something. That "something," I will repeat, cannot be reduced to ideas. The way he says it, I will add, is important. But the way he says his "something" is part of what he says. The form of his verse, in other words, is in large measure determined by the subtlety of his perceptions, and his artistic mastery in no small degree lies in his understanding of their demands.

What Eliot has to say is obviously concerned with the present mood of the bourgeois intelligentsia. I need not apologize for regarding that mood as important. It grows, as Mr. Matthiessen admirably shows, out of conditions that affect us all. It is a mood that most revolutionary intellectuals have felt and perhaps, at some moments and to some extent, still feel. It is a mood that even those who have never felt it or have completely overcome it have to reckon with. Eliot registers that mood in a hundred phrases, as it enters into personal and political relationships, as it affects education, science, religion, history. "What gives authority to the interpretation of life emerging from both his poetry and prose," Matthiessen says, "is the fact that it is authentic, that it corresponds closely not to any preconceived standard of what he ought to think and believe, but to what he has actually felt and understood by listening to himself, by studying the deepest elements in his nature." What he has found in himself is not unique; it is different in degree but not in kind from what many of his contemporaries have found in themselves. His poetry is representative, not because it states some familiar idea, but because it expresses what a representative man thinks, feels, is. That is why it is illuminating, enriching, and in a sense emancipating.

But this is for the most part true only of the poetry Eliot had written by 1925. Mr. Matthiessen, defending *Ash Wednesday* and the later poems, quotes Allen Tate: "The reasoning that is being brought to bear upon Mr. Eliot's recent verse is as follows: Anglo-Catholicism would not at all satisfy me; therefore, his poetry declines under its influence." This, I must say, with all deference to Mr. Matthiessen, is nonsense. Some critics may have agreed that, since Anglo-Catholicism is intellectually untenable, an adoption of this faith argues a relaxation of integrity that is bound to be reflected, sooner or later, in the poet's work. But even such *a priori* judgments, though probably sound, are unnecessary. Mr. Matthiessen knows well enough that *Ash Wednesday* has not spoken to Eliot's contemporaries as *Gerontion* did, and that there is small likelihood that phrases of *The Journey of the Magi* will enter, as did phrases of *The Love Song of J. Alfred Prufrock,* into our daily speech. He himself, after tenaciously defending the later poems, admits that "they do not give expression to so fully packed a range of experience," though he tries to cover up his admission by rebuking the sociological critics for expecting an artist's career to be plotted on a steadily rising curve.

Mr. Matthiessen, indeed, seems to find himself placed in a rather uncomfortable position by his hero's Anglo-Catholicism. He admits that, when a poet has ideas, as Eliot does, they are important, and he does not quite like to put himself on record as saying that it makes no difference to the resulting poetry if the ideas are pure nonsense. But he will not make the effort to analyze Eliot's religious and political theories. He says of *Triumphal March,* quite rightly that it is not a Fascist poem, but he gives himself away when he adds, "I am not here concerned with the direct applicability of Eliot's ideas." If he were, he would realize that the ideas are not directly applicable; in the modern world they could not possibly be; but some one might try to apply them, and the attempt would give the strongest support, whether Eliot liked it or not, to fascism.

It is Mr. Matthiessen's overemphasis on form, or at least his failure to clarify the relation between perception and expression, that has resulted in his evaluating Eliot's later poems—against his own better judgment, I feel—so highly. He has approached Eliot's later work from only one side, and so he has failed to understand its significance. He appreciates the great technical ingenuity of these poems, but he does not see that this ingenuity is functionless, or, rather that its function is to conceal a lack of perception. Expression is communication, and Eliot is saying less and less to fewer and fewer persons.

Eliot once spoke to many men, saying to them and for them what needed to be said. To say that the mood he expressed was negative is not to dismiss it nor to minimize the poetry that grew out of it. But major poets have seldom been satisfied with negation, nor indeed with any single mood. Growth, as Mr. Matthiessen insists, does not follow a regular curve, but change does take place. Where, we asked after *The Hollow Men,* will Eliot go? He went towards an irrelevant philosophy and a dangerous politics. At the same time his poetry lost breadth, subtlety and strength as well as pertinence and influence. Are we justified in believing that he reached the inevitable crossroads and took the wrong turning? Mr. Matthiessen thinks not, but the evidence of much of his own book is against him.

February 11, 1936

In Defense of James Farrell

Isidor Schneider's recent review of James T. Farrell's *A Note On Literary Criticism* points out that Mr. Farrell seems to be at some pains to dissociate his critical theories from the body of ideas known as Marxism. This is true, and yet perhaps it ought not to be said without qualification. Unqualified, the statement contributes to a danger that is already real enough, the danger that Mr. Farrell's theories may be discredited just because he holds them.

This is a danger for which Farrell is himself in no small measure responsible. In the course of his book he misrepresents the opinions of half a dozen revolutionary critics. Not only does he, as Schneider points out, ignore the historical context of the articles and books he quotes; not only does he wrench his quotations from the surroundings that explain them; he performs obvious feats of distortion in the face and eyes of his readers.

It is, therefore, easy to conclude that Mr. Farrell's theories are as untenable as his polemics are unscrupulous. But we must not be too hasty. We must not be deceived, either by Mr. Farrell's methods of literary warfare or by the praise the book has had in anti-revolutionary quarters. The anti-Marxists are applauding Mr. Farrell, not for his ideas, which very possibly they do not understand, but for his attacks on specific Marxist critics. Even the editors of the Catholic Book Club, though they too have had the advantage of a parochial-school education, are taken in by Mr. Farrell's abuse of his comrades in the revolutionary movement. But revolutionaries must keep their thinking straight.

There are not many ideas in the book, and it will not take us long to run through them. Mr. Farrell begins by saying, "I think that literature must be viewed both as a branch of the fine arts and as an instrument of social influence." He goes on to explain that, "for purposes of intellectual convenience," we "may divide human experience into two generalized categories: the esthetic and the functional, the subjective and the objective." The former "deals with the pleasure, value, and elations which we derive from things, from qualities, and from intellectual, emotional, and physiological states as ends in themselves"; the latter "with objects and actions in terms of their use-value."

This means that literature is both pleasurable and useful. The statement cannot be questioned if the adjectives are satisfactorily defined. Does Mr. Farrell, one has to ask, conceive of usefulness in too narrow terms? The answer is no. He says, for example, that "living literature . . . cuts beneath stereotyped feelings and crystallized thoughts, furnishing the material from which extended feelings and added thought are developed. It is one of the agents serving to work out within the individual consciousness the twin processes of growth and decay in a way corresponding to the objective working-out of these processes in society." And so the passage goes on, quite an eloquent passage, not altogether precise, perhaps, but on the right track.

And what of pleasure? Mr. Farrell introduces this aspect of literary experience so portentously that at first one fears he is going to exaggerate its importance. But not at all. When he speaks of the Humanists, he says they were guilty of functional dualism, which means that they ignored the pleasure element in literature. He does not, however, rest there; he goes on, like any sensible person, to show that their philosophical and sociological ideas were reactionary and untenable. More than that, he quotes approvingly from Chernishevski: "Only subject matter worthy of the attention of thoughtful man can save art from the reproach that it is the empty amusement which it all too frequently is." If literature that gives pleasure but has no use is to be condemned in this way, then we need have no fear that Mr. Farrell is exaggerating the importance of the pleasurable element. Rather he is in danger of becoming a Puritan.

He does not even maintain that the amount of pleasure one gets from a book can be regarded as a standard of judgment. He tells us that he likes both *Alice in Wonderland* and *The Remembrance of Things Past,* and goes on: "I should not be able to present any measurement or standard of feeling and experience to prove that Proust affords me a more enjoyable experience than *Alice in Wonderland* does." All he asks is "at least passing acknowledgment" of the "refreshment-value" of literature. This is certainly not an exorbitant demand, and, though it may be questioned whether Mr. Farrell does justice to the pleasurable element in literature, he cannot be accused of overrating it.

His second contention is that some literature of the past has value in the present, both esthetic value—as he, for some strange reason, calls the pleasurable aspect of the literary experience—and use value. Here, if anywhere, one would expect an un-Marxian concept, the concept of absolute, universal human values. But Mr. Farrell is no believer in the absolute. He contents himself with saying what dozens of Marxists have said before him, namely, that "there is a relative objective validity to some works of formal art." Any two Marxists might disagree forever as to what is valid, and why, in some particular piece of literature, but they would never think of denying that its value can survive the period and the class for which it was written.

His third counterclaim is a quotation from Marx: "It is well known that certain periods of highest development in art stand in no direct connection with the general development of society, nor with its material basis and the material structure of its organization." This quotation has proven a stumbling-block to certain critics who have overlooked its too obvious implications: first, that in certain periods art *does* stand in direct connection with the general development of society; second, that it always stands in an indirect connection. Mr. Farrell does not clearly recognize the first of these implications, but he does not deny the possibility of a direct relationship, and he is well aware of the indirect connection. His understanding of these relationships might not always be dependable, but in theory he recognizes them.

We must hurry on. Mr. Farrell says that a book is not necessarily altogether bad because it was written by a bourgeois, and that a good revolutionary novel can be written about an individual. If there is anything un-Marxist about these two statements, he deviates in the best of company. He does not like the slogan, "All art is propaganda," but all he asks is to be allowed to substitute the phrase, "Literature is an instrument of social influence." Permission to do this will, I am sure, be granted by unanimous consent. He says that a novel of decay—such, I presume, as *Studs Lonigan*—may be revolutionary. His reasoning will, I think, convince anyone who was not previously convinced.

And that is all. Observe that I do not say Mr. Farrell's discussion of literary criticism is clear, comprehensive, or original. These adjectives do not apply. The discussion is so beclouded by Farrell's personal grudges and his elementary confusions that, as has been noted, it has been loudly welcomed by anti-Marxists. It fails, moreover, to deal incisively with a single one of the problems it raises. In its treatment of the connection between literature and social development it largely disregards the knowledge of social forces that has been given by the Marxian analysis of class alignments. Its examination of the qualities that give literature "relative objective validity" is superficial and unrevealing. Even the distinction between pleasure-value and use-value is no contribution to criticism because Mr. Farrell does not treat the close relationship between pleasure and use. It may be doubted, indeed, if there is any point at which *A Note on Literary Criticism* is genuinely valuable. But we must be careful not to assume that, because the book is an inadequate statement of Marxism, its central ideas are anti-Marxist. Mr. Farrell has built badly, but it is on a Marxist foundation. This we must recognize, for the sake not of the book, but of Marxism.

July 14, 1936

Wisdom And Insight

The Flowering of New England, by Van Wyck Brooks

Of this book I can only say, as Brooks says of Prescott's *Ferdinand and Isabella,* "One might well ask for different things, but one could scarcely ask for anything better." With *The Flowering of New England,* Brooks's talent appears in its fullest bloom, and I do not see how anyone can today deny that he is, and for twenty years has been, the most fruitful literary critic in America. This is not to say that I regard him as, in Eliot's phrase, "the perfect critic," but he is the least imperfect we have thus far seen. His imperfections are important; to most readers of the *New Masses* they must seem, as they do to me, to set a definite and regrettable limit to Brooks's participation in the future growth of American literature; but in our present situation they have only a relative significance. Not only does Brooks tower above his contemporaries, all of them guilty of the same imperfections; he reveals to younger writers—I am thinking particularly, of course, of the Marxists—that, though they may have found a way to remedy his particular defects, they are far from having realized the manifold obligations and possibilities of literary criticism.

The *Flowering of New England* describes the astonishing renaissance of the half-century before Appomattox. Beginning with the Boston of Gilbert Stuart, the codfish aristocracy, and colonial culture, Brooks sets forth the first signs of the change: the coming of the German influence, the rise of Webster, Channing, and Everett, the appearance of Bancroft and Prescott. It is almost impossible to describe his method, the combination of erudition and insight that enables him always to write from within the cultural situation he describes. He slips easily from Stuart to John Quincy Adams to Andrews Norton to Nathaniel Bowditch to Theodore Dwight to Noah Webster. By the time we come to George Ticknor and Edward Everett, first of the pilgrims to Germany, we are ready to understand the effect on the New England mind of German erudition and German idealistic philosophy.

The story of the early years, presented in terms of the experiences of a score or more of writers, paves the way for the renaissance itself. Brooks is generous to Longfellow, recognizing not only that he had more virtues than it is now fashionable to admit but also that his influence on the literary growth of New England was of great historical importance. But he reserves his highest praise and his finest powers of interpretation for Hawthorne, Emerson, and Thoreau. They are seen as part of a vital growth. Their world includes philosophers, historians, the reformers of Brook Farm. Alcott,

Margaret Fuller, Brownson, Ripley, Elizabeth Peabody, Christopher Cranch, Ellery Channing, Richard Henry Dana, Motley, Parkman, Lowell, Dr. Holmes—Brooks touches all these and dozens more with a respectful intimacy that makes us know their lives as well as their books. From the furthest corners of New England, as well as from Boston, Cambridge, and Concord, he draws evidence of growth and power. As he unfolds it, the story of this renaissance is exciting, even romantic. Greater writers have, no doubt, flourished in one place and period, but has there ever been a more sudden and startling burst of talent? Out of apparently barren soil came, in two generations, a literature that deserved and won the respect of the world.

What Brooks has given us, first of all, is a masterly piece of interpretation. In describing the novels, poems, essays, and histories, he is not merely just; he is consistently revealing and stimulating. Thus he performs the first task of the critic: he takes a body of literature, much of it grown unfamiliar, and makes it once more a part of the imaginative experience of the American people. And, more than this, he shows us the intellectual life out of which this literature grew. Nothing in the book is more amazing than its wealth of detail, the knowledge it shows of the thoughts, emotions, and interests of hundreds of authors. This knowledge comes, of course, from biographies, journals, and letters, read not merely with scholarship but also with imagination. It enables Brooks to show the renaissance as a complex whole. A writer is never presented as an atomic individual; always we see how his mind is being acted upon by and is acting upon others. With this grasp of relationships, Brooks can carry effortlessly the burden of his erudition, moving easily from writer to writer, unifying great masses of information, presenting his story in a style that has ease and flexibility and distinction.

It seems unfair to demand more than this, but I am afraid we must. I have said that Brooks is careful never to give the impression that a writer can be an isolated entity; every writer he shows to be part of a social process. But that process is, except on rare occasions, presented as wholly intellectual, imaginative, cultural. Minds, Brooks shows, influence minds, as most certainly they do. But is this, as he seems to suggest, a closed circle? Are minds independent of material circumstances? Brooks writes as if they were, or rather, as if

any relationships that might be found to exist were of no importance for his purposes.

Leaving theoretical objections to one side, I believe his interpretation would be more valuable, would make the literary history
of his period even more vivid and significant to us, if he showed
the relation of cultural to political and economic activity. In one
of the few passages that hint at such a relation, he says, "In all these
centres of the seaboard life, there had arisen a buffer generation
that lay between the hard old Puritan ways and the minds of the
younger people." He knows, vaguely, that this buffer generation was
made up of the merchant princes and those they carried to prosperity
with them, but he refuses to see that here lies a body of facts that
might be significantly related to the phenomena that are his special
concern. I am not suggesting that a direct connection can be shown
between the tonnage carried in Massachusetts bottoms and the appearance of Ralph Waldo Emerson, but I do think there are some
pertinent questions that might be asked. Why did the merchant
princes turn away from Puritanism, even formally rejecting it, as
many of them did when they embraced Unitarianism? How does it
happen that, in New England, theological radicalism became associated with social conservatism? How far was the theological radicalism of the codfish aristocracy, as it was passed on to the next
generation, colored by commercial interests? To what extent did the
generation of Emerson and Thoreau revolt against the ideas of the
merchants and to what extent did they take them over? Was this
process affected by the fact that mercantile capitalism was being
transformed into industrial capitalism? In their revolt against the
mercantile philosophy, were the New England writers affected by
the rise of the common man, the emergence of Jacksonian democracy? These are only a few of the questions that I think it would
be interesting to have answered. If such questions were answered,
we should, I believe, have an even stronger feeling for the literature
of the period than Brooks, with all his gifts, can impart to us. And
they are questions that Brooks's fine imagination could have answered
if he had thought them important.

If Brooks had asked these questions, perhaps he would have
had a better answer for a question that he is forced to ask: why did
the New England renaissance flourish so briefly? He tries to explain
its decline by reference to Spengler's thesis of the culture-cycle. I

am skeptical about both the thesis and its applicability to this situation. I see, moreover, a much more obvious explanation. During the fifty years from 1815 to 1865, the economic basis of New England life was changing from agriculture and commerce to industry. This change affected the habits of the ruling class, altered the way of life of a large section of the population, destroyed the religious and racial homogeneity of the region, and ended the possibility of maintaining the cultural semi-independence that New England had previously enjoyed. The change was so rapid that writers could not adjust themselves to it. They went on making the old assumptions, and the old assumptions were no longer valid. The post-Civil War writers in New England were not facing the world as their predecessors had faced it. More and more, to protect the assumptions they cherished, they built bulwarks against reality. The process was infinitely varied and complicated, and I cannot even suggest it; but Brooks could have shown it in something like its entirety, if he had thought it important to do so.

And it is important. The more we understand the forces that enter into the creation of literature, the more fully we can respond to it. Moreover, the point of understanding the world is to be able to change it. So far as literature is concerned, Brooks would admit this. It is he, after all, who invented the phrase, "the usable past." One of his great services has been the shaping of a tradition that could contribute to the growth of American literature. But if literature is closely related to social conditions, then the clarification of a tradition, the establishing of standards, and the preaching of artistic integrity—important though they all are—are not enough. Ultimately, some of us believe, the only thing that can save literature is drastic social reconstruction.

But I come back, after asking for different things, to the statement that the book, taken for what it is, could scarcely be better. I wish that Brooks had felt the importance of looking further afield, because I know how valuable his perceptions would be, but, after all, we can, in a rough way, supply the deficiency. And what we do get from the book is something that only a man with Brooks's patience, wisdom, and insight could give us. To put it quite simply, he has read these hundreds of books, and, as he speaks to us of them, those we have read take on new meaning and even those we have not, become, in some measure, part of our cultural being. This is a service for which we, who believe in Communism as the heir of the finest American traditions, cannot be too grateful.

September 1, 1936

Small Game Hunting

Green Hills of Africa, By Ernest Hemingway

It ought to be said that I approached *Green Hills of Africa* with a sincere desire to find something to praise in it. Hemingway's piece in the *New Masses, Who Murdered the Vets?* put me in a frame of mind to forgive everything, even *Death in the Afternoon*. I have always admired most of *The Sun Also Rises*, some of *A Farewell to Arms* and several of the short stories. I have always felt that Hemingway was by all odds the clearest and strongest non-revolutionary writer of his generation. The passion of *Who Murdered the Vets?* not only strengthened my conviction; it made me want to emphasize the good things that can be said about Hemingway, not the bad. This was not because I had any notion that Hemingway would become a revolutionary novelist if the *New Masses* patted him on the back; it was because *Who Murdered the Vets?* had a quality that has been disastrously absent from his previous work. A reviewer has a right to interpret an author's work in terms of his direction. *Who Murdered the Vets?* suggested that Hemingway was going somewhere, and I hoped to find further evidence in *Green Hills of Africa*.

This autobiographical preface is advisable, for what I have to say about *Green Hills of Africa* is that it is the dullest book I have read since *Anthony Adverse*. There are perhaps ten pages that are interesting, and of these I shall speak later on. The rest of the book is just plain dull. Hunting is probably exciting to do; it is not exciting to read about. Hemingway got up very early in the morning and went out and chased a lion or a rhinoceros or a kudu, and he either shot him or he didn't, and if he did, someone named Karl shot a bigger one. So that evening they all got a little tight. This went on for a month, and finally they found themselves beside the Sea of Galilee, drinking, and Karl made a good crack about not walking on the water because it had been done once, and Hemingway said he would write a book so that P.O.M. (Poor Old Mama, i.e., Mrs. Hemingway) could remember what Mr. J. P. (their guide) looked like. And so we have *Green Hills of Africa.*

After a good deal of thinking about why the book is dull, the only reason I can see is its subject-matter. On page 148–150, Hemingway has a very long sentence—which proves that he does not have to write short ones, and that, I suspect, is what it is intended to prove. The sentence begins by talking about the feeling that comes "when you write well and truly of something and know impersonally you have written in that way and those who are paid to read it and report on it do not like the subject so they say it is all a fake, yet you know its value absolutely." Now I do not like the subject of *Green Hills of Africa,* but it would never occur to me to say that it is in any respect a fake. It is a perfectly honest book, and that is why I think it is dull because the subject is dull. Another clause in the same sentence concerns the feeling that comes "when you do something which people do not consider a serious occupation and yet you know, truly, that it is as important and has always been as important as all the things that are in fashion." This applies, I suppose, to either bull-fighting or hunting, and the only possible comment is that though they may be important to Hemingway, they aren't to most people. The proof is in the response to *Death in the Afternoon* and *Green Hills of Africa.* Since they are, it seems to me, as good books as are likely to be written on bull-fighting and hunting, the trouble must be with the subjects.

A certain amount of nonsense is written about the subject-matter of literature. No critic in his right mind will try to prescribe an author's subjects; the author has to start with what he feels and knows. But that is not equivalent to saying that one subject is as good as another. "To write a great novel," Herman Melville said, "you must have a great theme." The whole history of literature proves that he was right. When an author, starting out to write on some trivial theme, has produced a great book, it is because the trival theme hitched on to a great one. (You might have a great novel about people who were hunting, but it wouldn't be about hunting.) A great theme concerns the issues of life and death as they present themselves in the age in which the author lives.

It comes down to an argument over values, in which Mr. Hemingway's judgment is set against the judgment of history. The ten interesting pages in the book are all given over to discussions of the nature of literature and the function of the author. It is a subject on which Mr. Hemingway feels deeply, and when he feels deeply he writes well. But he is always on the defensive, just as he was in the literary conversations in *Death in the Afternoon.* He is very bitter about the critics, and very bold in asserting his independence of them, so bitter and so bold that one detects signs of a bad conscience. No one will deny that sports are pleasant and even important, but to be wholly wrapped up in them is not a sign of intellectual maturity. And the truth is, as he constantly reveals, that Hemingway is not wholly wrapped up in them. He has ideas about war, revolution, religion, art and other adult interests; ideas that the readers of the *New Masses* wouldn't always like, but ideas. And still he goes on writing about bulls and kudus.

Would Hemingway write better books if he wrote on different themes? *Who Murdered the Vets?* suggests that he would, for in that piece all his talents were suddenly lifted onto a higher level. That is why a great theme is important: it calls out so much more of what is in an author. I should like to have Hemingway write a novel about a strike, to use an obvious example, not because a strike is the only thing worth writing about, but because it would do something to Hemingway. If he would just let himself look squarely at the contemporary American scene, he would be bound to grow. I am not talking about his becoming a Communist, though that would be good for the revolutionary movement and better for him. I am merely suggesting that his concern with the margins of life is a dangerous business. In six years Hemingway has not produced a book even remotely worthy of his talents. He knows that the time is short and that it is difficult in this age and country for a writer to survive. There is bigger game in the world than kudus, and he had better start going after it now if he ever wants to get it.

November 19, 1936

Hemingway's Pirate

To Have and Have Not, by Ernest Hemingway

Harry Morgan, the hero of *To Have and Have Not,* is a rum-runner and a murderer. He lives in Key Kest, owns a motorboat, gets his living when he can by taking out fishing parties, and picks it up when necessary in less legal fashions. The principal incidents of the story concern such illegal exploits. After Morgan has been cheated by a wealthy sportsman, he undertakes to smuggle Chinese from Cuba to Florida, and kills the man who has hired him. Later, when the depression has diminished the number of sporting visitors, he smuggles liquor, and loses an arm. Finally, in taking a group of quasi-revolutionary bank robbers to Cuba, he is fatally shot.

He is Hemingway's most completely realized character. He has his prototype, perhaps, in Manuel in *The Undefeated* and Jack in *Fifty Grand,* but these are, by comparison with *To Have and Have Not,* mere sketches. Jake Barnes and Frederic Henry, in the earlier novels, are fully enough developed, but they are too closely identified with the author's unconscious needs to be fully independent individuals. Morgan is both objectively conceived and admirably portrayed. His life, we feel, goes on outside the pages of the novel. (When Hemingway skips three or four years, we have no sense that Morgan was put away in mothballs during the interval.)

Hemingway displays—as he has been displaying almost from the beginning of his career—an extraordinary mastery of the art of indirect exposition of character. In life our ideas of other persons are inferences based on what they do and say. Hemingway chooses to let us learn about his characters in the same way, and therefore reports, for the most part, only what could be known to the eye and ear. To do this, with the economy he demands, requires a high order of craftsmanship. We know Morgan because of what he does, because of what he says, sometimes because of what he thinks. We know him, too, because we understand the relations of other persons, particularly his wife, with him. All this Hemingway gives us in a few scenes, each of them relatively brief. We see Marie Morgan, for example, only three or four times, and yet we know her well enough not only to understand her but also to see Harry through her eyes.

For this craftsmanship Hemingway deserves full praise, but it is not the only explanation of his success with Morgan: we can know him because he is placed in a recognizable world. The statement may seem unreasonable: Key West and Havana, sportsmen and rum-runners, bank robbery and murder, what do most of us know of them? But Hemingway has succeeded, as he never has succeeded before, in showing us that what he writes about is part, and a representative part, of the world we know.

Harry Morgan is an individualist. He says to Albert, who gets seven dollars a week on a W.P.A. job, "Let me tell you, my kids ain't going to have their bellies hurt and I ain't going to dig sewers for the government for less money than will feed them. I don't know who made the laws, but I know there ain't no law that you got to go hungry." That is his code. When the sportsman robs him, he does not complain, but makes up for what he has lost by taking a dangerous job. When the depression and bad luck have brought him close to pennilessness, he risks and loses his life.

Hemingway respects him, and rightly. At the very outset Morgan is compared with Johnson, the cheating sportsman. In the next episode he suffers from the spite of a pompous politician. Later we meet Key West's literary colony: Richard Gordon, currently a novelist—for fashion's and profit's sake—of the class struggle; his dissatisfied wife; Professor MacWalsey, drunkard by choice; the fatuous Laughtons; Crazy Harold Spellman; and the insatiable Mrs. Bradley. Finally, on the night that Morgan lies fatally wounded on his boat, we make a tour of the yachts in the harbor—meeting Wallace Johnson, pervert, and Henry Carpenter, sycophant; meeting a ruthless businessman and the other kind who doesn't have to be ruthless because he can sell for a dollar a pint something that costs three cents a quart; meeting a professional son-in-law of the rich and his mistress, a director's wife on her way to bitch-hood.

These are the "haves," of course, and Hemingway sets them on his pages with a kind of quiet fury that I have never felt in his work before. Then there are the "have nots": Albert, working for his seven dollars a week, licked when he tries to strike, killed when he attempts to follow Morgan's example; and the veterans from the Keys, many drunkards, some masochists. Morgan rejects both slavery and oblivion. He is a man; he has *cojones;* and he takes a man's way.

We can all admire Morgan, as Hemingway does, but we can see

that his way of individual lawless violence, however heroic in itself, could not work. The remarkable thing—remarkable in view of certain passages in *Death in the Afternoon* and *Green Hills of Africa*— is that Hemingway sees it, too. We feel this all through the book, and finally he makes it perfectly clear. Morgan, dying, says, "A man. One man alone ain't got. No man alone now. No matter how a man alone ain't got no bloody——chance." And Hemingway, for almost the only time in the novel, allows himself the luxury of comment: "It had taken him a long time to get it out and it had taken him all his life to learn it." Harry Morgan is different from all Hemingway's other characters because he is so firmly rooted in a real world. And the world is real because Hemingway sees an essential fact about it: that no "have not," however brave, can single-handed defeat the "haves."

To realize what this means to Hemingway, it is only necessary to compare the scenes of violence in this book with those in its predecessors. Like many of his contemporaries, he has always dealt largely with violence, which is not surprising in a world in which every day's headlines prove violence to be the rule. But the violence in Hemingway's earlier novels and stories has always seemed curiously wanton, almost mystical in its irrationality. There is nothing mystical about the murders and fights in *To Have and Have Not*. The raid on the Cubans in the first chapter, the death of Mr. Sing, Harry's loss of an arm, the veterans' fights, Richard Gordon's twice-slapped face, and the almost Elizabethan slaughter on the boat, all fall into a pattern. Violence, perversion, frustration, and debauchery are inevitable parts of the world Hemingway is writing about, and they have the quality of inevitability in his novel because he knows why they are there.

Hemingway, like so many others, has always been wiser as a creative writer than any direct expression of his ideas would indicate, but there has always been a danger that his imagination would be corrupted. After *Green Hills of Africa*, I frankly wondered if he would ever write as good a novel as *The Sun Also Rises* and *A Farewell to Arms*. He has written a better one, and the explanation is, quite simply, his increasing awareness of the character of the economic system and the social order it dominates. I am not saying, of course, that that awareness alone makes him a good novelist. I do say that, without it, his talents might easily have gone to waste. That fact stands, no matter what one may think about the present limitations

of Hemingway's knowledge. It is a fact of importance for American
literature.

October 26, 1937

Halper Humanizes the Mail-order Company

The Chute, by Albert Halper

As a country dweller I do some business with mail-order houses,
and especially with the concern that Albert Halper—for no very good
reason, it seems to me—refers to as Montaigne, Warren Co. Their
eastern headquarters are not far away, and I go there once in a while,
either to make retail purchases or, as more often happens, to complain
about the filling of mail orders. The company makes an extraordinary
number of mistakes, and, as I follow the buck that is passed from
clerk to clerk and manager to manager, I usually grow nastier and
nastier. So impersonal is the establishment that I am led to treat the
employees as I do not treat human beings when I am conscious of
them as such.

We have to accept the large-scale methods of production and
distribution that are so essential and important a part of modern life,
and the only way to eliminate the impersonality they encourage is
through an effort of the imagination. But most of us, unaided, are
incapable of this, and need the assistance that men and women of
greater sensibility can give us. Certain novelists are doing this. Many
writers have helped to humanize factories. Leane Zugsmith has humanized the department store. Now Albert Halper has humanized
the mail-order company.

You look in a catalog, you mail an order, and sooner or later
you receive, if you are lucky, the goods you want. What happens in
the meantime? Suppose you order men's clothing of the Golden Rule
Mail-Order House. That part of your order, copied by harried stenog-
raphers, is borne by a boy on roller skates to Department 2. The goods

are selected, checked, and wrapped. Thirty minutes after the order reaches the department, bells ring out their intolerant demands, and the goods must be sent hurtling down the chute, to be assembled and shipped with the rest of your order. The chute dominates the department, and boys and girls draw on all their youthful reserves of energy to meet its demands.

Who are these boys and girls whose mistakes you damn so heartily? Well, there's Paul Sussman, for example, son of a hard-pressed tobacconist, who goes to work in Department 2 because he can't afford to study architecture. He suffers from the frustration of his hopes and from the strain of a constantly intensified speed-up. He dreams of escape and so does his family. His sister Rae, working in a garment shop, postpones her marriage to Moe Weiner and tries to save money to send Paul to college. Paul does not know of this, nor does Rae know that he is working for, and finally gets, a chance to go into an architect's office. Their plans are fruitless: Mrs. Sussman has to have an operation, and Rae, who has been relying on Golden Rule contraceptives, has to get married after all. Paul resigns himself to working for the Golden Rule Co., not knowing, even as the story ends, that the business has been captured by one of its larger competitors.

It seems foolish to say that Halper has made the employees of the mail-order companies seem like human beings. Who ever thought they were anything else? Yes, but to realize it, to realize it fully and deeply, that is a different matter. He makes you feel all the noise and tension of Department 2, and he makes you feel the human stuff that is subjected to this pressure. Not everyone is a Paul, ambitious and sensitive, but everyone has his dreams. Halper, always fecund, gives us a variety of characters: man-hunting Helen and Eve, sweetly childish Rosanna, wisecracking Joey, Killer Howard, philosophical Mr. Cohen, tubercular Jimmy Kirby. And the bosses: neurotic Myerson, beaten Mangan, ambitious Sidell, the big shots who are not quite big enough to hold on to their business.

Halper's obviously accurate account of the working of a mail-order house is impressive, but it would not accomplish his purpose if he were not able to set human beings before you. His characters are victims of a cruel type of exploitation, but they are remarkably resilient, full of hope, capable of joy. No one can accuse the author of a false optimism: most hopes are undeniably doomed to disappointment;

the union that is organized conducts no victorious strike; the business itself has collapsed when the novel ends, and most of the characters, though they do not yet know it, are facing unemployment. Nevertheless, the reader feels in these young people the ability to rise, not forever of course, but again and again, above the strain of their exploitation. Their dreams and quarrels and romances prove they have not been crushed. They are good human stuff, the stuff out of which rebellion can and will be made.

The Chute is a feat of humanization, entitling Halper to respect and admiration, but that does not mean that the reader can take pleasure in every page. Disciple of Zola and Dreiser, Halper relies on the amassing of details, relevant and irrelevant. On the first page Paul Sussman's father looks out the frost-covered window.

> The dull morning, lightening perceptibly, showed through the scratchings a piece of Chicago he was sick and tired of looking at— a small view of hardened dirty city snow, two pairs of shiny car tracks (steely), a lamp post with an old election sign pasted against its face with the command, "Vote for me!," and a large white horse-radish, minus its plumage, which had been dropped unnoticed to the ground by Mrs. Sussman, or by God knows whom.

Any college freshman could point out how the same effect could be achieved with half as many words.

The same freshman could criticize Halper's repetitions and his tricks of characterizations: Freddie's stuttering, the Dutchman's "Dorpat iss the name," Fritz Steucken's amateur detective antics, Joey's chatter about Algeria. Such tags, as Dickens long ago found out, will do much to fasten a character in the reader's mind, but they are likely to become substitutes for understanding.

And the comments! Surely no one since Dreiser has interrupted his narrative so often to speak in his own person or has spoken to such bad effect. For example: "After all, he was not made of straw; he became aroused as she held him, every part of him. In the fierce hot combat of life he began to assert himself, with all his seventeen-year-old fire. After all, he was not made of straw, not at all!" And what could have possessed Halper to send Myerson down the chute to his death? The incident, so easily predictable, so cheaply symbolic, is as wrong as anything could be.

All this ought to be said, and yet one wonders how much it should be allowed to weigh against the total achievement. Halper has borrowed from Dickens, Zola, and Dreiser certain of their least valuable devices. But fortunately he has also acquired something that cannot be borrowed from anybody: the ability to observe facts truly and to present them so cogently that their significance becomes apparent. The same thing might be done in other ways, but it is the doing of it at all that is important.

The Chute confirms what I have recently said in the *New Masses* about the continuing vitality of realism. Let us by all means recognize its faults but at the same time let us see and say that the book is readable, fundamentally sound, and significant, that it extends our experience by opening up for us a truly important segment of the world, that it makes a valuable contribution to the task of humanizing modern life, and that it does this, as the novel immemorially has, by giving us real people in a real environment. This is the point, so far as I am concerned, at which discussion must begin.

November 23, 1937

Sinclair Lewis's Stink Bomb

The Prodigal Parents, by Sinclair Lewis

Among the many persons annoyed by Sinclair Lewis, none has a better right to be irritated than the Marxist critic. The Marxist holds that there is a fundamental relationship between content and form. He argues that you cannot say a novel is bad as politics and good as literature, because he believes that the political qualities and the literary qualities are inextricably intermingled. But he insists that the relationship is subtle and only to be stated with a hundred carefully formulated qualifications. And then Sinclair Lewis comes along and illustrates the thesis in its simplest and baldest form.

During the past twenty years Mr. Lewis's political views have varied considerably, sometimes swinging fairly far left and then again fairly far right. If you arrange his books in order of their political astuteness, counting from left to right, they fall in some such order as this: *Babbitt, Main Street, Arrowsmith, It Can't Happen Here, Dodsworth, Elmer Gantry, Ann Vickers,* and *Work of Art.* Now judge the books by other standards—the convincingness of the characters, the verisimilitude of the situations, the vigor and veracity of the dialogue, the distinction of the writing, the little touches of insight—arrange them in order of merit, and see how they fall into very nearly the same pattern.

This is a distressing situation. Here we are, demanding more subtlety in evaluation, insisting that political correctness must not be regarded as synonymous with literary virtue, and here is Mr. Lewis, engaged in exhibiting a very unsubtle parallel. And to add to our dismay, his latest novel, *The Prodigal Parents,* which is by all odds the most reactionary, turns out to be by every standard the worst.

The Prodigal Parents is the story of Frederick William Cornplow, who owns an automobile agency in Sachem Falls, N.Y. Fredk Wm, as Mr. Lewis humorously calls him, and Hazel have two children, and they are a trial! The older, Sara, a Vassar graduate, is snobbish, bossy, and grabbing. (She was christened Sarah, but, as Mr. Lewis—the same Mr. Lewis who was recently castigating authors for their careless misuse of words—puts it, she "decapitated" the name.) The younger, Howard, a student at Truxon, is brainless, spineless, and shiftless. Both Sara and Howard expect their father to support them in luxury and get them out of all their fixes. Howard falls in love with Annabel Staybridge, daughter of Sachem Falls's prime snob, and Mr. Cornplow, who likes Annabel and thinks she is too good for Howard, proceeds to support them after they are married. But he is beginning to feel a little resentful, and he and Hazel run away for a vacation in the Berkshires. They are traced down, however, by the children, and brought back alive. When Mr. Cornplow continues to indicate his resentment, Sara tricks him into an interview with a psychiatrist. Then Frederick and Hazel flee in earnest, to Europe. This is enough for Sara, who gets married and settles down, but Howard goes completely to pieces. Fred comes back, takes his son on a camping trip, and Makes a Man of him.

If the summary suggests that the novel is both trivial and unconvincing, it may prepare you for what is to come. For the truth is that *The Prodigal Parents* is superlatively and fantastically bad. It is cheaper than *Mantrap,* duller than *The Man Who Knew Coolidge,* more amateurish than *The Trail of the Hawk*. Its badness is grotesque, embarrassing, and not quite credible.

The characterization is thin to the point of invisibility. The reader learns that Howard looks like "a Norse god" and has one silly idea after another, that Sara has a sharp tongue, that Annabel is pretty sweet, and that Hazel, despite her "slavery to possessions," is a fine pal to Fredk Wm. Mr. Cornplow himself would be considerably more substantial than the other characters except that every time he exhibits what might be regarded as an individual trait, the reader gets him all mixed up with George F. Babbitt or Myron Weagle or Sam Dodsworth. There are indeed, whole scenes that stir up recollections of earlier books in the way that bad parodies evoke and at the same time destroy pleasant memories. And the dialogue might have been written by someone with a rather bad ear who had listened inattentively to a slovenly reading of *Arrowsmith* or *Babbitt*.

But the worst is yet to be told. The Cornplow children, at the outset of the novel, have fallen under the influence of a Communist named Eugene Silga. Now Sara and Howard are so completely unreal that one cannot say what they would or would not do. Perhaps the only thing one can state with any confidence they would not do is go through the process of reform that Mr. Lewis assigns to them. But next to that in degree of improbability is their displaying the slightest interest in Communism. Each little scrap of insight into their characters that we gather argues against such a development. The neurotic Sara might just possibly fall in love with Silga and hence accept his political views, but Howard—no, if Mr. Lewis is worrying about the radicalism of the Howards of this generation, he is wasting his time.

This is so obvious, and Mr. Lewis is so uninterested in concealing it, that we can only conclude that Eugene Silga was introduced quite simply to serve the author's purposes.

Silga, "a radical agitator," is "slim and taut." He steals and he lies. He calls his young converts "cursed sons of aristocrats," and he has a habit of humming the *Internationale* in emergencies. He talks about "a real honest-to-God dictatorship of the rednecks like me." And he has "a reckless smile."

Now perhaps a certain amount can be forgiven Lewis, the anti-

Communist agitator. Silga, he says, "wanted power and revenge; he was willing to risk death in the hope of smashing the entire democratic system and winding up with the factory workers dictatorially running the country and himself running the workers. . . . He was neat and quiet-voiced; he smiled affectionately; and he was, to the world of Fred Cornplow—to the world of Franklin and Emerson and Mark Twain, of Willa Cather and William Allen White—as dangerous as a rattlesnake." A crusader who has taken on, practically single-handed, the job of saving the world of Franklin, William Allen White, et al., ought to be permitted an epithet or two.

But it is impossible to forgive Lewis the novelist for the creation of Eugene Silga. After all, Mr. Lewis rode 7382 miles in smoking cars, consuming 346 cartons of cigarettes and unknown gallons of highballs, in order to learn how realtors talk. He called in a medical expert to help him with *Arrowsmith*. He appeared in pulpits while gathering material for *Elmer Gantry*. He prepared for *Work of Art* by making a minute study of the hotel business. He married Dorothy Thompson before writing *Ann Vickers*. He might have talked for half an hour with a Communist organizer before he put Eugene Silga on paper.

Mr. Lewis once had a reputation for accuracy. Silga is a Communist Party organizer. He goes to Sachem Falls, an industrial town, and his only activity is to form something called the International Workers' Cohesion, the membership of which is drawn mostly from college students. There is no mention whatsoever of there being a unit of the Communist Party in Sachem Falls or of his trying to build one. His chief function, aside from lying and stealing and insulting the Cornplows and Staybridges, is publishing a magazine called *Protest & Progress*. (One gathers that the major concern of the Communist Party is the founding of such magazines in all communities of upstate New York.) And in the magazine Silga, who, it is carefully specified, is acting under orders from Communist Party headquarters in New York City, publishes an article calling on the workers of the Pragg Glassworks "to buy rifles, to form classes in marksmanship, to study Georges Sorel," in order to organize the plant.

The stupidity of this piece of Red-baiting surpasses anything said or written by Hamilton Fish and has, indeed, been equalled in this country only by Colonel Frey and Harold Lord Varney. Moreover, since it is made clear that Silga had previously been involved in a strike and that he subsequently was active in the automobile strikes in Detroit, we perceive that Lewis, like Frey and Varney, is as anxious to malign the entire labor movement as he is to attack the Communist Party. (And rightly, for if the world of Sinclair Lewis is threatened by the Communists, it is threatened by the entire labor movement.) Nor does his service to reaction stop there. In the spring of 1936 Silga is trying to collect money for Spain, "where, everyone said, there would be a dangerous right revolution before long." This, I take it, is Mr. Lewis's pleasant way of lending support to Franco's thesis that the rebellion was started to defend the Spanish people from a horrible Red plot. And there are some juicy—but not very original—bits about W.P.A. loafers.

Neither the venom of Mr. Lewis's anti-communism nor the confusion of his political thinking can surprise anyone who has been reading his contributions to *Newsweek*. Mr. Lewis opened his series of book-notes with an attack on Communist writers. "A surprising number of new talents," he wrote, "plod up the same dreary Communist lane, and produce, all of them, the following novel: There is a perfectly nasty community—mining or pants-making or sharecropping—but in it one Sir Galahad who, after a snifter of Karl Marx, rushes out, gathers the local toilers into an organization of rather vague purposes, and after that everything will be lovely, nobody will ever have hay fever again nor the deacon ever wink at the widow." Mr. Lewis, whose familiarity with Communist novels is probably only slightly greater than his acquaintance with Communist organizers, has continued with a nasty crack in every second or third issue. In between somewhat belated assaults on Dale Carnegie and Gertrude Stein and somewhat ponderous advice on what the young should read, he has made his catty little jibes. And once, in what purported to be a review of *The Writer in a Changing World*, he printed a long list of Trotskyite books—furnished, no doubt, by one of Miss Thompson's research assistants. Indeed, Mr. Lewis cannot say that Americans are "friends, kind, shy, and loyal," or that "Willa Cather has greatly pictured the great life," without a reference to Moscow.

So we knew what to expect on the political level, but, as I have suggested, we could scarcely have anticipated that this peculiar frenzy of anti-Red hysteria—I am afraid Mr. Lewis's psychiatrist did not do a very good job—could have undermined so promptly a literary talent as considerable as I, at least, believe Lewis's to have been. Silga is, I suppose, the key character. Lewis had to have a Communist villain. But I take it that even he knew that he could not, with his preposterous ignorance of Communists and Communism, write a whole novel about Silga. Therefore he hastily threw together a little fable about middle-class Americans and their children, something that he thought would be comforting to his readers, and let it go at that. Or perhaps the Cornplows were in his mind first, and he really intended to do something with them, but became so distraught in thinking about the Red menace that he had to abandon the attempt. Or possibly *The Prodigal Parents* started out to be nothing but a pot-boiler, and Mr. Lewis's determination to be a really solid citizen like Dorothy Thompson got in the way.

Whatever the explanation, the novel is so bad that one can only hope it is never translated into Swedish to embarrass the gentlemen who award the Nobel prizes. In fact, I am all for forgetting it as quickly as possible. When *It Can't Happen Here* was published, I said that, displaying a new kind of awareness, it might mark the beginning of a new and more significant phase in Lewis's career. I would normally say about *The Prodigal Parents* that, exhibiting a singular asininity, it might mark the beginning of a descent to the level of the *American Mercury*. And, by gosh, I will say precisely that—hoping that Mr. Lewis will again prove me a bad prophet.

Of all his contributions to *Newsweek,* the saddest was his review of *To Have and Have Not.* The peroration began: "Please, Ernest! You could have been the greatest novelist in America, if you could have come to know just one man who wasn't restricted to boozing and womanizing." (This means, of course, that Hemingway has known only dirty foreigners, for Americans are kind, shy, and loyal.) "Perhaps you can still be," Mr. Lewis continued. "Please quit saving Spain and start saving Ernest Hemingway." Mr. Lewis hasn't wasted any of his time saving Spain, but the salvation of Sinclair Lewis seems pretty remote. If he discovered precisely why Spain—and all it represents—is worth saving, there might be hope for him yet.

January 25, 1938

Confederate Heroism

The Unvanquished, by William Faulkner

Ever since Faulkner wrote the opening chapters of *Sartoris* in 1929, it has been clear that he would some day write the book. Of all the families with which he has peopled his Jefferson, Miss.—the Snopeses, Sutpens, Compsons, Benbows, and so on—only the Sartorises command his admiration. In general he is as complete a skeptic as our age has produced, but he retains an enthusiasm for Confederate heroes almost as unadulterated as that of Margaret Mitchell or Stark Young. And the Sartorises are the embodiment of Confederate heroism.

The Unvanquished is for the most part made up of stories that appeared in the *Saturday Evening Post*, and that too seems appropriate, because this is almost the only theme on which Faulkner could write in a way that would be satisfactory to *Post* readers. Not that these tales are free from gruesomeness, for "Vendee" is as brutal a piece as he has ever written, but they are cloaked with a glamour that he can summon up only when he is writing of the Old South. The dashing splendor of the narrator's father, the romantic (and incredible) audacity of his grandmother, and the general atmosphere of chivalry have their appeal to persons whose lives are unsplendid, unaudacious, and certainly unchivalrous.

The best of the stories—they have unity enough to be called a novel if the publishers insist—is "An Odor of Verbena," which had not been published before. In this study of conflicts, baffling emotions, and strange decisions, there is some of the insight that made it worth our while to puzzle our way through *The Sound and The Fury* and *As I Lay Dying*. But for the most part the book is unpleasantly close to the general level of the Stars and Bars school.

In one respect, however, it is quite unlike any other Confederate novel. In *Soldier's Pay*, his first novel, Faulkner hinted at a deep hatred of war. The hint recurs in *The Unvanquished*, rather surprisingly since the book is intended to glorify the Confederate dead. It is in no sense the book's theme, and it does not save Faulkner from the charge of triviality, but it is there, reminding us that there is more in the man than he has allowed to appear in his recent novels.

With every book he writes Faulkner becomes a more complex problem. But unfortunately with every book the incentive to try to solve the problem diminishes. Certainly *The Unvanquished* does not do much to encourage us, but it does make us conscious that this is one more tragedy of frustration, and a very real one.

February 22, 1938

Richard Wright's Prize Novellas

Uncle Tom's Children, by Richard Wright

You cannot read these four stories without realizing that the literature of the left has been immeasurably strengthened. Although Richard Wright is certainly not a new name to readers of *New Masses,* and although the talents of this young Negro have not gone unrecognized, *Uncle Tom's Children* will not only make the name familiar to all literate Americans but also startle those whose expectations have been high. The truth is that the revolutionary movement has given birth to another first-rate writer.

It is Wright himself who gives the revolutionary movement credit. Born in Natchez, he wandered about the South with his parents until, at the age of fifteen, he went on his own. In Chicago, where he worked as a clerk, a waiter, and a street sweeper, he joined the John Reed Club. There, he says, he learned to understand the significance of his harsh boyhood. "I owe my literary development," he has said, "to the Communist Party and its influence, which has shaped my thoughts and creative growth. It gave me my first full-bodied vision of Negro life in America."

These are four tales of Negro life. The first tells how, of four good-natured, easy-going boys, two were shot, one became a murderer, and the fourth was burned, mutilated, hanged. The second concerns the special tragedy of a Negro in a time of general tragedy, a flood. In the third a white man seduces a Negro woman, whose husband is burned to death in his own house after he has killed the seducer. The fourth is a story of a minister who, after a beating, leads a successful demonstration for relief.

They are bitter stories, cruel stories. Each one tells of the white man's discrimination against the Negro, of his stark, irrational, savage prejudice. In the first story it is not the barbaric, sadistic fury of the lynch mob that impresses the reader, but the white man who shoots first and asks questions afterward. In the second one notes the colonel who, just after a Negro's wife has died, turns to his soldiers and says, "Give this nigger some boots and a raincoat and ship him to the levee." The white man in "Dark Black Song" not only combines seduction with salesmanship but also salesmanship with seduction. ("I'm leaving that clock and graphophone. You can have it for forty instead of fifty. I'll be by early in the morning to see if your husband's in.") And it is instructive to see how easily the mayor's patronizing friendship for Reverend Taylor ("It's not every nigger I'd come to and talk this way") yields to the Chief of Police's brutality ("A nigger's a nigger! I was against coming here talking to this nigger like he was a white man in the first place. He needs his teeth kicked down his throat.")

Each story tells also of resentment deep beyond any reckoning. The carefree boys in "Big Boy Leaves Home" interpret the No Trespassing sign: "Mean ain no dogs n niggers erllowed." The husband of the seduced Sarah says: "From sunup to sundown Ah works mah guts out t pay them white trash bastards whut Ah owes em, n then Ah comes n fins they been in mah house! Ah cant go into their houses, n yuh knows Goddam well Ah cant! They dont have no mercy on no black folks; wes just like dirt under their feet! For ten years Ah slaves like a dog t git mah farm free, gives ever penny Ah kin t em, n then Ah comes n finds they been in mah house." It is no wonder he and countless others feel that there is nothing better for them to do than die defiantly.

But there is something better, as Wright knows, and he is not content to leave his knowledge unexpressed. That is why, in the fourth story, he shows a Negro beginning to learn what he himself has learned so well. "Its the people!" the minister tells his son. "Theys the ones whut mus be real t us. Gawds wid the people! . . . Ah been wrong erbout a lotta things Ah tol yuh, son. Ah tol yuh t work hard n climb t the top. Ah tol yuh folks would lissen t yuh then. But they wont, son! All the will, all the strength, all the power, all the numbahs is in the people. Yuh cant live by yoself!"

So Wright says what he wants to say, or rather, lets his stories say it for him. He writes with an intensity that makes you clench your fist. Big Boy, in the cave, watching the mutilation of his comrade; Mann, brought to his death by the woman he has rescued; Silas, calmly waiting for the cruel end of a barren life, glad to pay any price for revenge; Taylor, thinking his way out of confusion as the lash falls on his back: these are things one feels rather than reads about.

Wright's technique is simple: straightforward narrative and beautifully direct dialogue. But there is no lack of artistry. He is always reaching beyond the simple event to catch all the complexity of emotion that surrounds it. The horseplay of the first part of "Big Boy Leaves Home" adroitly leads up to and contrasts with the frenzied tragedy of the shooting and the lynching. Sarah's downfall is not a rape but a complicated emotional experience that she cannot understand, and Silas's response is no conventional indignation at a sexual affront but hopeless resentment of the ultimate invasion of his personal life. Taylor becomes the focal point of innumerable forces in his community: white fear, white hatred, white tyranny; black desperation, black timidity, black courage.

If there is any weakness that Wright reveals, it is in construction. Two of the stories move with magnificent speed and clarity. In "Down by the Riverside," however, the author has difficulty in handling the rapid sequence of events after Mann reaches the hospital. And in "Fire and Cloud," when the mayor, the two "Reds," and the deacons are all in Taylor's house, the situation, instead of seeming dramatic, has for a page or two the confusion of a bad movie. Apparently Wright is so eager to move ahead with the main action that he will not pay sufficient attention to subordinate details even when they are essential.

This is a defect that can be remedied without too much difficulty, and I am confident that Wright will remedy it in the novel on which he is reported to be working. Certainly he has all the other gifts that go to make a novelist. *Story Magazine* made no mistake when it selected *Uncle Tom's Children* from the five hundred manuscripts submitted by authors on Federal Writers' Projects. It is not only a fine piece of writing; it is the beginning of a distinguished career.

March 29, 1938

The Moods and Tenses of John Dos Passos

U.S.A., by John Dos Passos
Journeys Between Wars, by John Dos Passos

John Dos Passos' publishers are wisely doing their part to make the country conscious of him as a major literary figure, and they have accordingly issued two omnibus volumes of his work. *U.S.A.* is, of course, his famous trilogy: *The 42nd Parallel, 1919,* and *The Big Money. Journeys Between Wars* is made up of his travel books: much of *Rosinante to the Road Again* (1922), almost the whole of *Orient Express* (1927), and most of those sections of *In All Countries* (1934) that deal with foreign lands. It also contains some sixty pages on Dos Passos' visit to Spain a year ago.

Comparison of the two books makes it quite clear that Dos Passos' deeper experiences go into his novels, leaving his more casual impressions to be recorded in the travel essays. *Journeys Between Wars* shows that he is at his best when he is describing the persons he meets or recording his own moods. The *padrone* in the Spanish restaurant, the Sayid on the Orient express, the Danish accountant on his way home from America—these are effectively drawn. And the journal of the camel ride from Bagdad to Damascus is as pleasant a personal record as can be found in modern literature. But there is not much—and I have now read most of these essays twice—that the mind holds onto. Other novelists—Gide, Lawrence, Huxley—have written travel books that belong with their major works, but not Dos Passos.

The explanation, which has some importance for the understanding of Dos Passos as a writer, seems to me fairly clear. He deals, consistently and no doubt deliberately, with impressions—the specific scene, the precise emotions, the exact conversation. The seeing eye—even "the camera eye"—is admittedly the first virtue of the travel writer. But it is equally certain that the memorable travel writers have not been afraid to draw conclusions from what they saw. Dos Passos is afraid: no milder word will do. What one feels in *Journeys Between Wars* is neither a casual holiday from the job of thinking nor a conscientious elimination of ideas for some literary purpose but a deep emotional unwillingness to face the intellectual implications of things seen and heard.

And the extraordinary thing is that this shrinking from conclusions is to be found even in the last section, the section dealing with Spain in 1937. Dos Passos tells of crossing the border from France, of a night on the road, of executions in Valencia, of a bombardment of Madrid, of a fiesta of the Fifteenth Brigade, of a trip through some villages, and of an interview with officials of the P.O.U.M. But there is not a word about the issues between the loyalists and the fascists, not a word about the differences between the loyalist government and the P.O.U.M. It seems incredible that any author, considering all that is involved in Spain today, could keep silence. Do not suppose that Dos Passos is merely maintaining an artistic objectivity, holding back his own opinions so that the reader can arrive unhampered at the truth. He simply has refused to think his way through to clear convictions. He has sympathies—with the loyalists as against the fascists and apparently with the P.O.U.M. as against the government. But even the Spanish crisis cannot shake him into thought.

The only approximation to a conclusion comes as Dos Passos is leaving Spain, and, characteristically, it is in the form of a question: "How can they win, I was thinking? How can the new world of confusion and crosspurposes and illusions and dazzled by the mirage of idealistic phrases win against the iron combination of men accustomed to run things who have only one idea binding them together, to hold on to what they've got?" This passage has been quoted by almost every conservative reviewer of the book, and quoted with undisguised satisfaction. "We told you so," one could hear them saying. "There's no sense in trying to help Spain. It's all foolishness to hope for social justice anywhere. Let's make the best of things as they are."

The truth is that it is impossible to avoid having opinions, and the only question is whether or not they are based on adequate information and clear thinking. If Dos Passos had faced the responsibility of the writer, and especially the radical writer, to use his intellect as well as his eyes, if he had been concerned, not with avoiding conclusions, but with arriving at sound ones, I think he would have come out of Spain with something more to say than these faltering words of despair. Afraid to think, he has yielded to a mood, and the reactionaries are delighted with his surrender. Both that surrender and his flirtation with the P.O.U.M. are results of an essential irresponsibility.

Dos Passos' irresponsibility takes two forms: unwillingness to think and unwillingness to act. Several years ago, I remember, at the time when he was perhaps closest to the Communist Party, he said something to the effect that he was merely a camp-follower. In *Journeys Between Wars* there is a revealing passage. (It is, of course, creditably characteristic of Dos Passos to reveal himself.) When he was leaving the Soviet Union in 1928, the director and the actors of the Sanitary Propaganda Theatre came to see him off. The director said, "They want to know. They like you very much, but they want to ask you one question. They want you to show your face. They want to know where you stand politically. Are you with us?" Dos Passos continues: "The iron twilight dims, the steam swirls round us, we are muddled by the delicate crinkly steam of our breath, the iron crown tightens on the head, throbbing with too many men, too many women, too many youngsters seen, talked to, asked questions of, too many hands shaken, too many foreign languages badly understood, 'But let me see. . . . But maybe I can explain. . . . But in so short a time . . . there's not time.' The train is moving. I have to run and jump for it."

The passage, so palpably sincere and so pleasant, reminds us that, even in a broader sense, Dos Passos has always been uncommonly detached. Indeed, detachment is almost the keynote of *Journeys Between Wars*. In the extracts from *Rosinante* Dos Passos is "the traveler"; in *Orient Express* he is "the eastbound American"; in the Russian section he is "the American Peesatyel." Perhaps it is no wonder that in writing about Spain in 1937 he is still merely an observer. It is no wonder that he has seldom tried to write about the revolutionary movement from inside, and, when he has tried, has failed. It is no wonder that he has never communicated the sense of the reality of comradeship, as Malraux, for example, communicates it in *Days of Wrath*.

Yet there was a time when Dos Passos seemed willing to try to think clearly and to feel deeply. His second play, *Airways, Inc.*, was bad dramatically, but in it Dos Passos at least made an attempt to be clear. There was a sharp difference between that play and *The*

Garbage Man, and an even greater difference between *The 42nd Parallel,* first novel of his trilogy, and *Manhattan Transfer.* In *The 42nd Parallel* Dos Passos seemed for the first time to have mastered the American scene. The technical devices used in this novel and *1919* perplexed some readers, but Dos Passos himself appeared to be relatively clear about what he was trying to do.

Airways, Inc. was published in 1928, *The 42nd Parallel* in 1930, and *1919* in 1932. Here, then, are three or four years of comparative clarity. And in those years Dos Passos was close to Communism. At this time he actually believed in something like the Marxian analysis of history, and it worked. He also felt a stronger confidence in the working class. Communism did not make him a novelist, but it made him a better novelist.

What I failed to realize at the time of the publication of *1919* was the extent to which Dos Passos' interest in the Communist Party was a matter of mood. He had not sufficiently overcome his fear of conclusions to make a serious study of Marxism, and he had only partly subdued his passion for aloofness. Little things could—and, as it happened, did—disturb him. He was on the right track, but not much was required to derail him.

In the four years since he left the track Dos Passos has gone a long and disastrous way. Last summer, as has been said, he came out of Spain with nothing but a question mark, and committed himself to a hysterical isolationism that might almost be called chauvinistic. Last December he and Theodore Dreiser held a conversation that was published in *Direction.* Dos Passos' confusion—equaled, I hasten to say, by Dreiser's—is unpleasant to contemplate for anyone who expects some semblance of intellectual dignity in a prominent novelist. He is still looking for an impartial observer of the Soviet Union, and thinks he has found one in Victor Serge. His new-found devotion to the United States continues to run high: "America is probably the country where the average guy has got a better break." "You can't get anywhere," he says, "in talking to fanatic Communists." He talks about revolution: "A sensible government would take over industries and compensate the present owners, and then deflate the money afterwards." And this is his contribution to economics: "Every time there is a rise in wages, prices go up at A. & P."

After one has noted the banality, the naïveté, and the sheer stupidity of most of Dos Passos' remarks in his talk with Dreiser, one knows that politically he is as unreliable as a man can be and is capable of any kind of preposterous vagary. But I am interested in Dos Passos' politics only insofar as they influence his writings, as of course they do. When *1919* appeared, I believed that Dos Passos had established his position as the most talented of American novelists—a position he still holds. As early as 1934, however, I was distressed by his failure to shake off habits of mind that I had thought—quite erroneously, as it turns out—were dissolving under the influence of contact with the revolutionary movement. At that time, reviewing *In All Countries,* I said: "Dos Passos, I believe, is superior to his bourgeois contemporaries because he is, however incompletely, a revolutionary, and shares, however imperfectly, in the vigor of the revolutionary movement, its sense of purpose, its awareness of the meaning of events, and its definance of bourgeois pessimism and decay. He is also, it seems to me, superior to any other revolutionary writer because of the sensitiveness and the related qualities that are to be found in this book and, much more abundantly, in his novels. Some day, however, we shall have a writer who surpasses Dos Passos, who has all that he has and more. He will not be a camp-follower."

Now that Dos Passos is not in any sense a revolutionary and does not share at all in the vigor of the revolutionary movement, what about the virtues that I attributed to his association with the Communist Party? I am afraid the answer is in *The Big Money,* most of which was written after 1934. One figure dominates *The Big Money* to an extent that no one figure dominated either *The 42nd Parallel* or *1919.* It is Charley Anderson, the symbol of the easy-money Twenties, the working stiff who gets to be a big shot. ("America is probably the country where the average guy has got a better break.") His desperate money-making and drinking and fornicating take place against a background of unhappy rich people and their unhappy parasites. Further in the background are some equally unhappy revolutionists, who are either futile or vicious. ("You can't get anywhere in talking to fanatic Communists.")

It seems to me foolish to pretend that an author doesn't choose his material. Dos Passos didn't have to lay his principal emphasis on the hopeless mess that the capitalist system makes of a good many lives. He didn't have to make his two Communists narrow sectarians.

He didn't have to make the strongest personal note in the book a futilitarian elegy for Sacco and Vanzetti. There must have been a good deal in the Twenties that he left out, for large masses of people did learn something from the collapse of the boom, and the Communist Party did get rid of factionalism, and the workers did save Angelo Herndon and the Scottsboro Boys, even though they failed to save Sacco and Vanzetti. *The Big Money,* in other words, grows out of the same prejudices and misconceptions, the same confusion and blindness, as the conversation with Dreiser.

The difference is, of course, that there is a lot in *The Big Money* besides these faulty notions. I have written elsewhere about Dos Passos' gifts, and I need only say here that I admire them as strongly as ever. I know of no contemporary American work of fiction to set beside *U.S.A.* But I also know that, because of the change in mood that came between *1919* and *The Big Money, U.S.A.* is not so true, not so comprehensive, not so strong as it might have been. And, though I have acquired caution enough not to predict Dos Passos' future direction, I know that, if he follows the path he is now on, his claims to greatness are already laid before us and later critics will only have to fill in the details of another story of genius half-fulfilled.

April 26, 1938

Steinbeck's Powerful New Novel

What John Steinbeck has previously done—whether he knew it or not, and I don't suppose he did—has been in preparation for this book (*The Grapes of Wrath*). *Tortilla Flat* was a rich, loving study of the color and romance and fundamental decency in people the world calls bums. The world read into it a condescension of which Steinbeck is incapable, laughed heartily, and went on talking about bums. *The Grapes of Wrath* has the same warm feeling for both the vices and the virtues of the common people, but the most insensitive reader will not find it quaint. *In Dubious Battle* was an exciting strike novel, so vigorous, so dramatic that you could forget the strikers were fighting for the right to live. You will not make that mistake with *The Grapes of Wrath*. *Of Mice and Men* rested on Steinbeck's understanding of the migratory worker and his dreams, but Steinbeck got to playing a game with himself. *The Grapes of Wrath* shows a far more impressive mastery of technique than *Of Mice and Men*, but you never think about the form, just because it is so perfectly right.

Hitherto, whenever anybody asked us what we meant by proletarian literature, we had to say, "Well, it ought to have this quality that you find in so-and-so's work, and that quality as exemplified by the other fellow, and such-and-such as found in somebody else." (You can fill in the blanks yourself, and then I won't have the bricks thrown at me.) We shan't have to offer that kind of composite illustration any more. We can now say, "Proletarian literature? Oh, that means a book like John Steinbeck's *The Grapes of Wrath*. Of course, that isn't the only kind of novel that deserves to be called proletarian literature, but it has all the qualities proletarian literature has to have. That is the real thing."

What are these qualities? First of all, there's power, beauty, imagination—whatever you want to call it. It's hard to define but easy to recognize, and I think you can see it in Steinbeck's paragraph:

To the red country and part of the gray country of Oklahoma, the last rains came gently, and they did not cut the scarred earth. The plows crossed and recrossed the rivulet marks. The last rains lifted the corn quickly and scattered weed colonies and grass along the sides of the roads so that the gray country and the dark red country began to disappear under a green cover. In the last part of May the sky grew pale and the clouds that had hung in high puffs for so long were dissipated. The sun flared down on the growing corn day after day until a line of brown spread along the edge of each green bayonet. The clouds appeared, and then went away, and in a while they did not try any more. The weeds grew darker to protect themselves, and they did not spread any more. The surface of the earth crusted, a thin hard crust, and as the sky became pale, so the earth became pale, pink in the red country and white in the gray country.

I have read hundreds of novels in manuscript, and I begin to believe that one can tell on the first page or two whether an author has this kind of imaginative power or not. (Some very considerable novelists, by the way, haven't it, and get along after a fashion without it.) Steinbeck shows it on page one, and it doesn't seem to me that there is any serious diminution of it on any of the following six hundred pages.

The second quality is knowledge. In certain literary circles one of the most heretical things you can say is that a novelist has to know what he is talking about. This is somehow taken as a reflection on the literary imagination. But no serious novelist believes he can show people unless he knows how they live. Steinbeck, who obviously can pick up a good deal of information effortlessly, has not spared effort in preparing for this novel. He knows about dust storms and tenant farmers and tractors and automobiles and Hoovervilles and cotton picking and fruit picking. When the car breaks down, he is with Al and Tom every step of the way as they repair it. He knows the big things, and he knows the little things.

Then of course there are people, and people make or break a novel. The introduction of Tom Joad is one of the most adroit pieces of craftsmanship I can think of. Steinbeck knows Tom, and he finds the best way to make us know him. Tom and Casy and poor Muley, and then the whole Joad tribe—Oklahoma tenant farmers, kicked off their land and starting for California. Steinbeck doesn't idealize them; he shows them as they are, and he likes them as they are. There are moments of crazy comedy as hilarious as anything in *Tobacco Road* or *God's Little Acre*. But the Joads are never brainless clowns, nor are they ever loathsome monsters. They are human beings, and pretty good representatives of the species, rising at moments to an inspiring heroism. Cheated, starved, and beaten in California, they merge with the mass of victims, but Steinbeck never loses his hold on them as individuals. The Joads live if ever people in a book did.

But are the Joads representative? That is always a relevant question today. There have been times when an author could present a character and know that his readers would see exactly where that character belonged in the existing organization of society. Today there is such confusion that little can be taken for granted. Characters and situations have to be defined and explained in relation to their times. Authors have found various ways of doing this, and some—notably John Dos Passos—have invented elaborate and ingenious techniques. Steinbeck employs a simple but immensely effective device. Every other chapter is the story of the half-million emigrants from the Dust Bowl. This antiphonal device—first the

Joads, then the half-million, then the Joads, then the half-million—enriches the novel. But it also—and this is the real test—helps the story. At the end of each of the short antiphonal chapters, the story of the Joads has advanced. They are representative, you see, and Steinbeck has found the right way of making this clear.

The development of so effective a form as this indicates careful consideration of formal problems and is proof of the value of Steinbeck's technical apprenticeship. But valid form must rest on genuine understanding. Last spring the Simon J. Lubin Society of California brought out in pamphlet form, under the title *Their Blood Is Strong*, some newspaper articles Steinbeck had written on the homeless migrants. To compare this pamphlet with *The Grapes of Wrath* is to gain considerable insight into the problems of the two types of writing. But the point I want to make here is that the pamphlet proves beyond any question that the novel is based on firsthand knowledge and on a carefully acquired knowledge of economic forces.

Any sensitive reader would, to be sure, learn this from the novel itself. There is, for example, a remarkable passage about the driving of the tenant farmers from their Oklahoma land:

> Some of the owner men were kind because they hated what they had to do, and some of them were angry because they hated to be cruel, and some of them were cold because they had long ago found out that one could not be an owner unless one were cold. And all of them were caught in something larger than themselves. Some of them hated the mathematics that drove them, and some were afraid, and some worshiped the mathematics because it provided a refuge from thought and from feeling. If a bank or a finance company owned the land, the owner man said, The Bank—or the Company—needs—wants—insists—must have—as though the Bank or the Company were a monster, with thought and feeling, which had ensnared them. . . . The bank—the monster has to have profits all the time. It can't wait. It'll die. No, taxes go on. When the monster stops growing, it dies. It can't stay one size.

Steinbeck's understanding of economic forces is best indicated, for purposes of a review, in a brief passage such as this. But actually he is never abstract. If one had space, one could show how his insight into capitalism illuminates every chapter of the book. There is, for instance, a magnificent passage about the selling of secondhand cars, and there is another fine passage that describes an incident at a filling station. Steinbeck knows both how things happen and why they happen, and he shows the why working itself out in the how.

No writer of our times has a more acute sense of economic forces, and of the way they operate against the interests of the masses of the people, and yet Steinbeck is never for a moment close to despair. The Joads at the end of the book face certain disaster, and, having got to know and love them, one bitterly resents it. But, though the book ends on the note of pathos, it is an optimistic book. Steinbeck can afford to show without mitigation the tragedy of the Joads because he knows so well the only basis for hope in our times. He writes:

The Western land, nervous under the beginning change. The Western states, nervous as horses before a thunderstorm. The great owners, nervous, sensing a change, knowing nothing of the nature of the change. The great owners, striking at the immediate thing, the widening government, the growing labor unity; striking at new taxes, at plans; not knowing these things are results, not causes. Results, not causes; results, not causes. The causes lie deep and simple—the causes are hunger in a stomach, multiplied a million times; hunger in a single soul, hunger for joy and some security, multiplied a million times; muscles and mind aching to grow, to work, to create, multiplied a million times. The last clear definite function of men— muscles aching to work, minds aching to create beyond the single need— this is man. To build a wall, to build a house, a dam, and in the wall and house and dam to put something of Manself, and to Manself to take back something of the wall, the house, the dam; to take hard muscles from the lifting, to take the clear lines and form from conceiving. For man, unlike any other thing organic or inorganic in the universe, grows beyond his work, walks up the stairs of his concepts, emerges ahead of his accomplishments. This you may say of man—when theories change and crash, when schools, philosophies, when narrow dark alleys of thought, national, religious, economic, grow and disintegrate, man reaches, stumbles forward, painfully, mistakenly sometimes. Having stepped forward, he may slip back, but only half a step, never the full step back. This you may say and know it and know it.

Many authors today would agree with that; some might have written it; few indeed could so perfectly make the idea a living reality in fiction. We all talk about the hope that lies in the masses, but it is a very different thing to make that hope palpable. Steinbeck does it because he knows where to look. Not in Casy's eloquence, moving as that is, not in Tom's heroic decision, not in the glimpse of the strike, but in Ma Joad's unshaken determination lies the hope of the future. "We're the people that live," she tells Tom. "They ain't gonna wipe us out. Why, we're the people—we go on."

So we come to the end of our list of qualities. There are others: there is humor, for example, much of it unprintable in a family journal such as *New Masses;* there is pathos ("Why, you can't get through nine months without sorrow"); there is sentiment of a perfectly legitimate kind. But the main thing is that there is a deep knowledge of people and the forces that move them, together with a remarkable, carefully acquired skill in communicating what is known.

It would be a crime to break up into parts a book of the stature of *The Grapes of Wrath* if it were not that its stature is being fully realized. We can afford to learn what we can from Steinbeck, to make this novel an occasion for clarifying our views of proletarian literature, because it is becoming widely known that this is a book that must be read. However, it may be worth saying, to avoid any chance of misunderstanding, that *The Grapes of Wrath* is an experience, as every novel ought to be and few are, a significant experience, a heart-rending experience, a tremendously encouraging experience. Other critics can argue whether it is a book for the ages. I am content to say that it is preeminently and beautifully a book for our times. Posterity can take care of its own literary judgments.

May 2, 1939

Three Novels

At the opening of a new publishing season three novels seem noteworthy. Vardis Fisher's *Children of God* is a lively chronicle of the Mormons, interesting rather because of its material than because of any creative force on the author's part. Kenneth Fearing's first novel, less distinguished than his poetry, deals with a subject in which almost everyone is interested—sickness—and has its exciting moments. *Christ in Concrete* gives us the measure of an unusual and hopeful talent. None of the three is first-rate, but all are worth reading.

Children of God, by Vardis Fisher

Vardis Fisher tells the story of the Mormons from Joseph Smith's first revelation in 1820 to the virtual collapse of the movement seventy years later. In the first part Smith is the central figure, in the second Brigham Young, and in the third a family by the name of McBride. So completely objective a study seems pleasant after Mr. Fisher's autobiographical tetralogy, and there is no denying the fascination of the narrative. From many points of view, the rise of Mormonism is one of the most fabulous episodes in American history. In the whole pageant of human follies and superstitions, no more fantastic gospel was ever preached than Joseph Smith's. Compared with him, such a contemporary as John Humphrey Noyes seems a model of enlightenment and practicality. Yet Smith's preaching inspired thousands of people, sustaining them not only through martyrdom but also in a heroic and wholly magnificent constructive enterprise.

As one reads Mr. Fisher's book, one is divided between amazement at Mormon folly and admiration of Mormon courage. Towards the enemies of Mormonism, on the other hand, one feels only indignation and contempt. That Mormon doctrine could legitimately be opposed on rational grounds goes without saying, but there can be no defense of the persecution of the Mormon people. One reads the record of massacre, pillage, rape, of the perversion of justice and the misuse of civil authority, with a chastening kind of horror. It is the sort of thing that couldn't happen here—but it did. And it was all done with a hypocrisy so nauseous that one cringes as one reads of it.

It is good for us to know the story, and on that ground *Children of God* is worth reading. A big book, it moves swiftly, and so far as I know it is dependable. The reader, however, is likely to wonder why the Mormons behaved as they did and were persecuted as they were. On this score he will find the novel disappointing. In his essay on Vardis Fisher, published last year, David Rein commented on his reliance on psychological methods to explain social phenomena, and in the same little volume Mr. Fisher defended himself and expounded what he regards as the true psychology. Yet here, where psychological insight is surely called for, Mr. Fisher has little to offer. His treatment of Joseph Smith's visions is inept and evasive, and the whole question of conversion, which is central to the novel, is gingerly handled. Yet, bankrupt as the psychological approach proves, he remains true to his theories and pays no attention to similar movements of the period. I do not suggest that a study of social conditions in the twenties, thirties, and forties would immediately yield a satisfactory explanation of Mormonism, but a student, examining the whole wave of religious hysteria, might find some significant clues.

It is fair to ask Fisher for some more adequate treatment of Mormonism, for the emphasis all the way through falls on history rather than fiction. But even on literary grounds there is reason to demand a sharper understanding. There is not a single fully developed and wholly credible character in the book. The historical novelist today has a difficult task, for readers insist on accuracy, and his imagination is allowed to function only within the limits set up by documentary evidence. This means, in effect, that he can make characters live only if he thoroughly understands their role in history. That is why *Children of God* is no more than a competent retelling of noteworthy facts.

The Hospital, by Kenneth Fearing

Mr. Fearing has been less ambitious, and done rather better. The idea has occurred to many authors of trying to show what was happening in a given place—a ship, say, or a hotel, or a city block— in a given period of time. The idea is tempting, for the arbitrary grouping of many people is characteristic of our age and symbolic of its complexity. And it is a perfectly good idea, no matter how many people have had it.

The Hospital describes what happens in less than an hour on a hot afternoon. A girl is being examined for tuberculosis, and another is being operated on for a tumor, which turns out to be malignant. The first girl's doctor has just learned that his father-in-law is penniless and perhaps insane. The second girl's doctor is staking his reputation as a surgeon. An ambulance doctor sees a victim of acid-throwing. A famous old surgeon is dying. Nurses, technicians, and washerwomen are going about their work. And an old timekeeper gets drunk, goes berserk, and cuts off the electric power in the whole hospital.

Mr. Fearing handles all this very well, skillfully solving the chief technical problem, which is that of time sequence, since many events happen simultaneously. He shows how people live apart even when they are together, and at the same time he shows how strangely their lives may be related. He remembers, furthermore, that the hospital is not a world by itself. Not only is each character influenced by what happens outside the walls; the institution itself—in its income, its management, its labor relations—is part of an economic system that is functioning rather badly.

The book's most impressive quality is knowledge. In a note Mr. Fearing thanks "the many doctors, nurses, technicians, maintenance workers, hospital and city executives" who have helped him. He can well say that the book could not have been written without their aid, for every page reflects what appears to be precise technical information. This information is not, of course, important in itself, though it is interesting. It is, however, essential to the success of the novel. The only way Mr. Fearing can get at these human beings is by showing exactly what they are experiencing. Lafcadio Hearn once said that a great novel could never be written about high finance, fascinating as the subject is, because no author knew enough. Today writers realize that they must acquire the information they need, and *The Hospital* shows that it can be done.

The novel does not compare in either originality or intensity with Mr. Fearing's poetry. One of the best of modern poets, he seems in this his first novel, merely one of the better novelists. The book, however, is easy and exciting to read, and sound as far as it goes. Mr. Fearing may not have aimed very high, but he did score a bull's eye.

Christ in Concrete, by Pietro di Donato

Both *Children of God* and *The Hospital* are uncommonly objective; *Christ in Concrete* is autobiographical and personal; yet it is concerned with the recreation of a world rather than the revelation of the author's soul. It is a story of Italian immigrants, bricklayers and their families. The first chapter, which received high and well deserved praise when it was published as a short story, describes the death of Geremio. His son, Paul, who is twelve, takes up the burden of supporting the family, and begins laying brick. The family struggles along, and he adjusts himself to his job. There are incidents in the lives of his associates—an injury, a marriage, a debauch, a death. And the book ends with Paul's disillusionment and the death of his mother.

Donato has a great talent for dramatic scenes, and in particular episodes the book is magnificent. As yet, however, he has not a comparable talent for the creation of character, and one remembers scenes, not people. The style is supposed to reflect the rhythms of spoken Italian, and perhaps it does. In any case Donato is on the way to creating a style of his own, but as yet he has not mastered it, too often relying on such devices as the omission of articles, the inversion of sentences, and the concocting of unusual word combinations. On the other hand, there are times when he picks the reader up and soars with him. He has, I think, a great gift, and some day he will know how to use it.

The fine thing is, of course, Donato's saturation in the life he describes. He brings to our literature the deepest, warmest, most intimate feeling for the essentials of proletarian life. He knows not only the job, with all its dangers, but also the home, with its joys as well as its worries. He is not afraid of sentiment, and he knows how to create color. If the novel is fragmentary and often overstrained, it is alive, and out of such vitality great fiction can come.

September 5, 1939

IV

BRITISH WRITERS

It seems that Granville Hicks's literary criticism of British writers is not very well known. He has been more strongly identified with American literature. Yet, in the view of the editor, a selection of Hicks's best criticism would include as much material on British fiction as on American fiction. His finest interpretative literary study, *Figures of Transition,* was published in November 1939. It is an examination of British literature at the end of the nineteenth century, with a focus on six writers: William Morris, Thomas Hardy, Samuel Butler, George Gissing, Oscar Wilde, and Rudyard Kipling. This focus enabled Hicks to devote more discussion to specific writers than he was able to do in *The Great Tradition,* which covered a longer span of time.

Throughout the period during which Hicks was writing for the *New Masses,* 1934 to 1939, he was conducting the research for *Figures of Transition.* This will perhaps explain why many of the British writers he reviewed here were of a period earlier than the 1930s: H. G. Wells, Ford Madox Ford, Kipling, Wilde, D. H. Lawrence, G. K. Chesterton, E. M. Forster.

Three of the contemporary writers Hicks found so promising have, alas, not weathered so well: Phyllis Bentley, Walter Greenwood and Ralph Bates. A lengthy novel, *The Olive Field,* Ralph Bates wrote about the Spanish Civil War does merit attention today and should not be ignored any longer. Bates served with the International Brigade in Spain and this novel presents an excellent account of the origins and early days of that conflict.

Liberalism And Tragedy

A Modern Tragedy, by Phyllis Bentley

The scene of Miss Bentley's new novel—Yorkshire, the textile district of England—is the scene of her earlier novels, *Carr* and *Inheritance;* but *A Modern Tragedy,* unlike its predecessors, is set in the present, in the era of the depression. All the characters are, directly or indirectly, involved in the textile business. The central character, Walter Haigh, happens to be chosen as the tool of Leonard Tasker, a shrewd and unscrupulous manufacturer. Tasker's exploits involve not only Walter and his family, but also other business men of the district, including the honest and aristocratic Henry Clay Crosland, the town's oldest and most respected manufacturer. On the other hand, depression creates a shortage of work, and thousands of craftsmen are thrown out of their jobs. So far as the book is concerned, the unemployed are represented by Harry and Milner Schofield, who are victims of their own stubbornness rather than of the depression. The former, after a long period of unemployment, takes a non-union job with Walter; the latter eventually joins an unemployed council. The climax of the book comes with the collapse of Tasker's schemes, resulting in suicide for Crosland and jail sentences for Tasker and Haigh.

Miss Bentley is one of the ablest of the younger English writers. *Inheritance,* based not only on a thorough knowledge of the growth of the textile industry, but also on a strong and affectionate sense of the industry's importance and the toil that created it, showed how rich and dramatic a story of business and business relationships could be. The reader was, however, distressed by the weakness of the conclusion: after balancing capital and labor against each other in a record of a century of struggle, Miss Bentley suddenly preached a sermon on love and brotherhood, and, though she was dealing with a period of obvious intensification of the class struggle, asked the reader to believe that all problems could be solved by the exercise of a little good will. Such a conclusion, distressing enough as anti-climax, was even more distressing in its indication of Miss Bentley's shortcomings. Her longing for class collaboration, which in practice meant a strenuous effort at impartiality in the record of earlier conflicts between employers and employed, could be effective within limits in dealing with the past, but it was easy to see the dangers Miss Bentley

151

would run in treating the present. Moreover, the publication in America of her earlier work, *Carr*, increased this alarm. A solid novel, carefully wrought in the Victorian manner, *Carr* enhanced one's respect for the author, but at the same time it showed how much better she understood employers than she did workers. Her liberalism led her to prefer a generous and honorable employer to a callous and unscrupulous one; it made her sorry for workers who were badly treated; but it was, after all, the liberalism of a textile manufacturer's daughter, and she could not go against her class. The most she could do was to assert that classes ought not to exist.

Miss Bentley has, of course, carried her liberalism into *A Modern Tragedy*, and the novel confirms all our fears. For her spokesman in the book, she has chosen Rosamund Haigh, Walter's sister, an intelligent, liberal-minded, and sensitive young woman. Rosamund, on the last day of the trial, sees the unemployed, led by Milner Schofield, starting on their hunger march to London. "There was some connection between the hunger-marchers and the trial, she felt. . . . Outside, hungry and desperate men paraded; within, the men who had most experience in organizing their industry were being tried for a crime of personal greed." Rosamund wonders if employers have ever stopped to consider the effect of their actions on their employees. "Henry Clay Crosland had thought of his work-people, Rosamund felt sure." (Crosland, like Carr, is the benevolent employer, probably modeled on some ancestor of Miss Bentley; it is his type she really admires.) But if Crosland had been thoughtful, certainly such men as Tasker and her brother had not been. She goes on: "Had the leader of the hunger marchers considered anyone but his own class? Rosamund thought not . . . And she began to think that it was this universal limitation of vision which had caused the frightful, the altogether terrible, the tragic waste represented by that column of marchers outside and the men on trial within." And lest anyone should fail to understand the moral, Miss Bentley has an epilogue spoken by Rosamund: "I can see that not till men have learned the mutual love which casts out fear can the economic problem be solved."

If we believe that Miss Bentley is sadly mistaken in her conception of the solution of the industrial problem, we can see how she comes to hold such an opinion, and we can grant that such sincere humanitarianism as hers has elements of nobility. The question we have to ask, however, is whether this position has enabled her to write a moving and satisfying novel. There are two reasons for saying it has not. In the first place, Miss Bentley, by stating her problem in ethical terms, has suggested that there were alternatives, that her characters might have acted differently. But this is simply not true; though Miss Bentley does not say and probably would not admit it, her book clearly shows that there were no fine, honorable, socially useful ways in which Tasker and Walter could have expended their talents. Henry Clay Croslands are the product of a period of expanding capitalism when the evils of the system are largely hidden from sight in far-away India; they cannot exist in an era of world-wide depression. Tasker and Haigh had to be what they were or starve. The tragedy is the tragedy of a system, not of the evil in men's hearts.

In the second place, the tragedy of Haigh and Tasker and Crosland is a minor tragedy when compared with the sufferings of the myriads of workers brought by unemployment to starvation or to mental and physical decay on the dole. Miss Bentley refers to these unemployed just often enough to make her concern with the unhappiness of the industrialists seem as irrelevant as it really is. But this tragedy, the real tragedy of the crisis, does not appear in her book. Why not? Does she really know, though afraid to confess it to herself, that, in the face of these millions of jobless, her talk of brotherly love is nonsense? Is that why the principal representative in her book of the working class is a half-educated blatherskite who is out of work because of his own pigheadedness? If, instead of portraying Milner Schofield, who lost his job in an extremely unusual way, she had taken one of the millions who have simply been thrown out of work and perhaps thrown off the dole as well, it might not have been so easy to advise employees to think about their masters.

It is a hard saying, but Miss Bentley might have written a better novel if she were a less generous and sympathetic person. That is, since she was apparently barred by class affiliations from dealing with the real tragedy of the crisis, since she was forced to concern herself with employers rather than workers, she could have attained greater clarity if she had frankly accepted the actions of the manufacturers, honest and dishonest, weak and strong alike, as results of the economic system. But of course, though she would have gained clarity, she would have lost the pervasive tenderness that is one of Miss Bentley's, if not of the book's, virtues. It is rather paradoxical that this tenderness, which makes one look on Miss Bentley as half an ally,

is the source of much of the book's weakness. The belief that men
are at fault and not the system is the only consolation left for tender
minds, and Miss Bentley, for obvious reasons, needs that consolation.
If she did not, she would be, I venture to say, on our side.

February 13, 1934

Philistine's Progress

Seven Famous Novels, by H. G. Wells

No doubt it was the Hollywood success of *The Invisible Man*
and *The Island of Dr. Moreau* that inspired the reprinting of these
seven scientific romances, written by Mr. Wells between 1895 and
1906. They are mildly interesting in themselves, and they are very
instructive because so much of the later Wells is in them. Not only
do these novels suggest the ideas around which his hundred and more
books have been built; they employ the methods that he has used in
his subsequent and superficially very different types of fiction. "In
all this type of story," he says in his preface to this volume, "the
living interest lies in their non-fantastic elements and not in the in-
vention itself. . . . The thing that makes such imaginations interesting
is their translation into commonplace terms and a rigid exclusion
of other marvels from the story." In other words, what gives these
fantasies such interest as they have is a vivid, superficial, journalistic
realism, very similar to what we find in *Tono-Bungay, Mr. Polly,*
and *Kipps.* As in Dickens, who has influenced Wells, and in Sinclair
Lewis, whom he has influenced, this realism is often heightened to
the point of caricature, and it affords the reader a pleasant combination of surprise and recognition.

But it is with Mr. Wells' ideas that we are primarily concerned.
It has not, I think, been observed that the type of literature represented in this volume belongs to a much wider genre, a genre very
common in England in the nineties. It was in the eighties and nine-

ties that English writers began to revolt against the solid bourgeois smugness that had been induced by so many years of prosperity. That this prosperity was based on exploitation at home and abroad seldom struck these writers; they were much more concerned with its psychological effect on the kind of persons they knew. So they began to *épater les bourgeois*—to use the phrase that was invented to describe a similar but much earlier movement in France. It was the period, remember, of the *Yellow Book,* Oscar Wilde, Aubrey Beardsley, Ernest Dowson, Lionel Johnson, and Baron Corvo. They were poseurs, of course, though some of them were much more than that, but the important thing is that English writers, who had previously either completely conformed to middle-class standards or tried seriously to modify them, now felt it was their supreme duty to defy those standards and shock the men and women who held them. Thus they expressed, without knowing it, both their unhappiness and their helplessness.

It seems a little difficult to make Wells fit into this picture. On the one hand, his seriousness of purpose and his realistic method seem to raise him above all the art-for-art's-sakers; on the other hand, he was always, as Lenin was to observe, a good deal of a Philistine. But nevertheless we find him saying: *"The Island of Dr. Moreau* is an exercise in youthful blasphemy . . . *The War of the Worlds* like *The Time Machine* was another assault on human self-satisfaction." And *The Invisible Man, The First Men in the Moon,* and *The Food of the Gods* are quite as obviously intended to reveal what Wells calls the "hideous grimace" of the universe and to raise disturbing doubts about the future of the race. It is probably true that these books were, from this point of view, failures, that they merely amused the complacent British bourgeois, but it seems to me that, so far as Wells had a serious purpose, it was deliberately to affront and distress his middle-class contemporaries, quite as deliberately as if he had walked down Pall Mall with a lily in his hand.

The only exception to the general rule among these seven stories is *The Tail of the Comet,* the latest of them all. By the time he wrote this Wells had entered a new phase, and this is one of the first of his Utopian and "constructive" works. It follows *Anticipations* by several years and, if I remember correctly, just precedes *Tono-Bungay.* The smugness of the British bourgeoisie had been pretty well dispelled by 1906: the Boer War, colonial revolts, the approaching war with

Germany, and the rise of the Labor Party had seen to that. It no longer seemed so necessary to sting and harry the bourgeois; moreover, the diminution of their strength had made it possible to hope for a more fundamental attack on them. Wells, in common with many other writers, now turned to the making of designs for a new society. This has, of course, been his principal concern down to the present time.

It is significant that in *The Tail of the Comet* the transformation of society comes through the dissemination of a mysterious gas which works the moral regeneration of mankind. That is most typical of Wells, who has always been seeking for some miraculous means of achieving the Utopia he desires. Never, so far as I know, has he granted that a revolution could come—much less, must come—through the overthrow of the existing state by the working-class. In his most recent book, *The Shape of Things to Come,* it is the aviators who, in the latter part of the twentieth century, save civilization. That is, indeed, the most common method: some group of scientists or technicians perform the miracle. Occasionally, as in *The World of William Clissold,* faith is pinned in the capitalists themselves. Wells has imagined all sorts of dictators, committees, intrigues, religions; new Machiavellis, researches magnificent; anything but a working-class revolution.

Wells came from far enough down in the bourgeois scale to see the rottenness of the capitalist system, and the perception was strengthened by a scientific education. At the same time he was incapable of trusting in or allying himself with the working-class. As a result he has never been able to find a theory of society that could long satisfy him. He has leaped so rapidly, indeed, from theory to theory that his avoidance of a genuine revolutionary position comes to appear little short of pathological. Yet, despite all his Philistinism, he has never been able to reconcile himself completely and permanently to capitalism. His scores of books indicate how very uncomfortable he is between the horns of that dilemma.

July 3, 1934

The State of Britain

General Buntop's Miracle, and Other Stories,
    by Martin Armstrong
The Woman Who Had Imagination, by H. E. Bates
Defy the Foul Fiend, by John Collier
Full Flavour, by Doris Leslie
Spinner of the Years, by Phyllis Bentley
Love on the Dole, by Walter Greenwood

Mr. Armstrong's stories are all neatly constructed, and some of them—*Mrs. Vaudrey's Journey,* for example—are adroit enough to be pleasant reading. They are of all kinds, from the crisp brutality of Saki to the whimsicality of Milne. When one tries to discover where Mr. Armstrong is in the variety of mood and method he displays, one suddenly realizes that he isn't there at all. He is on the outside, carefully manipulating his effects. This is art for entertainment's sake, pleasant to the taste and bad for the digestion.

The stories of H. E. Bates, on the other hand, run to the slice-of-life type, and they are both sensitive and honest. There are some fine, vigorous portraits of old men, and there are excellent descriptions. The title story, *The Woman Who Had Imagination,* is delicate and perceptive. But Mr. Bates cuts his slices of life rather thin. He deliberately isolates his little scenes so that he can dwell on them. Herman Melville said that you need a great theme to write a great book. I am afraid that Mr. Bates, for all his talent, would not know a great theme if he saw one.

Great themes are not necessarily rare, but in the bourgeois world today they are seldom utilized. Pseudo-great themes, however, are since the success of *Anthony Adverse,* the order of the day, and it appears, with the arrival of Collier's Willoughby Corbo to join Linklater's Magnus Merriman, that England is to have her share of boisterous heroes. The hero of *Defy the Foul Fiend* is, one is pleased to note, a little more human than Anthony or Magnus, but he goes through a series of amorous adventures, described in what Mr. Collier probably hopes is a Rabelaisian manner. Like Anthony and Magnus, Willoughby is a sound conservative at heart, and in the end he settles down as a good imitation of a landed gentleman. This seems to be a reliable formula for pleasing the solid bourgeois: give him plenty of vicarious adventure, and then assure him that he, in his cautious quest for security, was right all the time.

Doris Leslie has chosen for *Full Flavour* a theme that usage, especially British usage, has consecrated as great, the story of a family. The central character is Catherine Ducrox, who inherits and runs and makes a success of a London cigar store, disastrously marries an artist and successfully marries a tobacco magnate, loses her daughter in a tragic marriage, and sees her grandson fall in love with her old rival's granddaughter. In the background of all these domestic mishaps is the account of the tobacco business, told with some tenderness for the small shopkeeper who is conquered by the monopolies. Miss Leslie writes vigorously, makes skillful use of minor historical details, and keeps her characters alive. She seems, however, to have nothing important to say.

Full Flavour naturally reminds us of Phyllis Bentley's handling of a British family in *Inheritance*. Miss Bentley's family had more than a sentimental interest because it was directly involved in one of the great historic movements of the nineteenth century, the rise and fall of the textile industry, and the attendant struggles between capital and labor; and even Miss Bentley's incurable liberalism could not prevent her from grasping some of the implications of her material. *Spinner of the Years* is a much earlier novel, and it is obviously a piece of apprentice work. It is a study, careful to the point of tediousness, of the influences that shape the character of Imogen Armitage. The scene is the textile district, but textiles play no part in the story.

Walter Greenwood has looked for his theme in the very center of the life of his times, and *Love on the Dole*, published more than a year ago in England, is, despite many an amateurish touch, a strong and moving novel. It seems to me, indeed, the finest novel of the depression I have read, quite as tender and human as *Little Man, What Now?* but free from mawkish sentimentality and weak evasiveness. It is a story of people who, in the very best of times, live in rotten poverty, always in fear of unemployment, always in debt to the pawnshop, always in need of decent food and decent shelter. For such people the depression means bare survival on the dole, and the Means Test is a death sentence.

The novel tells of Harry Hardcastle, eagerly leaving school to serve his apprenticeship in a machine shop, and turned out in the end to make room for another generation of schoolboys on apprentices' wages. For him love means fugitive meetings to avoid the bestialities of his girl's parents; it means bitter quarrels while the futile search for a job goes on; it means forced marriage and survival in rat-ridden rooms on his wife's wages. His sister Sally is in love with Larry Meath, a worker for the Labor Party who is killed in a demonstration against the Means Test. Sally, becoming the mistress of a successful bookie, brings a measure of prosperity to her family and Harry's, but they know, and the author knows, how uncertain, as well as how exceptional, their good fortune is.

"The time is ripe, and rotten ripe for change; then let it come," the author quotes from Lowell, and from Rosa Luxemburg: "What we are witnessing . . . is a whole world sinking." *Love on the Dole* successfully shows a world in decay. But Greenwood's awareness of the need for change far outruns his perception of the forces that make change possible and inevitable. Larry Meath, the only conscious rebel in the book, is a more or less typical educated British workman, bitterly dissatisfied with his lot, eager for a socialist state, but limited to a futile faith in education and reform. Greenwood himself, as his portrayal of the demonstration shows, scarcely goes farther than Larry. In itself, therefore, the book is pessimistic, for the only forces of revolt it describes are obviously inadequate to combat the enormous evil it portrays. But we must remember that such a book is not read in a vacuum. Taken alone, it is incomplete, but the reader may supply for himself what the book lacks. Disgust with the existing order is never enough, but it may be the beginning of wisdom, both for the author and for his readers.

September 4, 1934

Greenwood's Second Novel

The Time Is Ripe, by Walter Greenwood

In most forms, but particularly in the novel, the proletarian literature of Great Britain has lagged far behind that of the United States. It is therefore both surprising and gratifying to find in one season two excellent revolutionary novels by English authors. One of these, Ralph Bates' *Lean Men,* Edwin Seaver has already reviewed in *The New Masses*—and very justly praised. The other is Walter Greenwood's *The Time Is Ripe.*

This is Greenwood's second novel. His first, *Love on the Dole,* might legitimately be regarded as the best novel of the depression that has appeared in any country. It is not the most harrowing, and it is one of the least militant, but it is uncommonly rich and full and many-sided. It shows how the depression affects the entire lives of its victims, how it degrades and stultifies and tortures them. And, if it fails to do more than hint that only through organized fight can workers, employed and unemployed alike, put an end to this horror, it permits no other conclusion.

The Time Is Ripe is also a novel of the depression, and especially of the latest device English capitalism has employed to protect its profits, the means test. In its depiction of Joe Shuttleworth, jobless coal miner, of Mrs. Shuttleworth, of their son Jack and his wife Meg, of the neighbors, Mrs. Evans, Mrs. Nattle, Mrs. Dorbell, and the others, it is as unmistakably genuine and as richly alive as its predecessor. Shuttleworth, summoned before the board that administers the means test, is brow-beaten and robbed of the pitiful dole that has kept him and his family alive. It is no wonder that he loses his reason and waits daily before the abandoned coal-pits to be the first in line when they open up. It is no wonder that he is taken to the insane ward of the workhouse hospital to die. But a younger generation is left to find a way to life instead of death.

What lies behind all this? In *Love on the Dole,* Greenwood did not try to say, contenting himself with showing the effects of the depression. In *The Time Is Ripe,* however, he has dealt with causes as well. The novel tells two stories, Edgar Hargraves' as well as Joe

Shuttleworth's. Hargraves is merely a haberdasher with social and political ambitions until his aunt's considerable fortune falls into his hands. Then he becomes, in rapid succession and with a discreet outlay of cash, president of the social service center, councillor, and mayor, with a title not far distant. He helps administer the means test, in the interests of the taxpayers and the landlords. Incidentally, he also robs the taxpayers, to line his own purse. The petty shopkeeper who once harassed his domestic help has become a great man with the privilege of torturing the poor. If Joe Shuttleworth is not class-conscious, Edgar Hargraves is, and he uses his power with unfailing consistency on behalf of his class and his pocketbook.

By placing these two stories together and showing at a hundred points how intimately the fortunes of the Hargraves and the Shuttleworths are related, Greenwood completes his pictures of depression-ridden England. His picture of the working class is never idealized or romantic; he does not forget the Mrs. Nattles, the poor who scrape along by robbing their companions in poverty. But he makes the reader conscious on every page, of the enormous latent capacities of the proletariat, that capitalism stifles and seeks to destroy. And, on the other hand, he depicts, with much restraint and remarkably little bitterness, the insatiable greed and the appalling narrowness and emptiness of the shopkeeping and industrial bourgeoisie.

Mr. Greenwood is now, we are told, a city councillor in Salford, the scene of his two novels. He is, I presume, a member of the British Labor Party. One wonders what will become of him. Obviously his political and literary careers are not unrelated. He cannot sell out the workers in the Salford city council and serve them in his books. It is encouraging to note that he can refer to Communism without apology, shudder, or denunciation, but more significant is the quality of experience that has made his books distinguished. It is hard to believe that a person who has seen so clearly and felt so deeply the exploitation of the workers could betray them, either in politics or in literature. And if Greenwood does not go backward, he must go forward. He has the ability to go a long way.

April 2, 1935

Life, Liberalism And Revolution

Abinger Harvest, by E. M. Forster

Last year, speaking at the International Congress of Writers in Paris, E. M. Forster said: "As for my politics, you will have guessed that I am not a fascist—fascism does evil that evil may come. And you may have guessed that I am not a Communist, though perhaps I might be one if I was a younger and a braver man, for in Communism I can see hope. It does many things which I think evil, but I know that it intends good."

In this typically cautious and yet candid way Mr. Forster was expressing a conviction that had long been growing in him. As early as 1920, in an essay on the British character, he wrote: "The supremacy of the middle classes is probably ending. What new elements the working class will introduce one cannot say." In 1925, in a fine, indignant attack on middle-class snobbishness, he spoke of "the instrument of a new dawn." And in 1934 he wrote, "No political creed except Communism offers an intelligent man any hope."

In his 1934 essay Forster went on, just as he did in his 1935 speech, to say that he was too old for Communism, but his reservations interest us less than his affirmations. Who can imagine any of his literary contemporaries going so far? Not Lytton Strachey, for example, or Clive Bell, his friends at Cambridge. Shudder as they might at middle-class vulgarity, they never stopped to ask themselves if there was hope in the working class. Not Virginia Woolf, whose novels Forster's more than a little resemble. In the pursuit of Life with a capital L, she has fluttered farther and farther from life as the majority of Englishmen know how to spell it. Not D. H. Lawrence, another writer to whom Forster is akin. Though, unlike Forster, Lawrence was born in the working class, he turned his back on it, and found death instead of the Life he so rhapsodically sought.

Yet Forster, in his early novels, was no more directly concerned with social problems than Lawrence or Mrs. Woolf. They and he alike belonged to the group that broke away sharply from the tradition of Wells, Shaw, Galsworthy, and Bennett. None of the situations he portrayed pointed to the need for parliamentary reform. Each of the four novels published between 1905 and 1910 deals with the problem of the survival of vitality in an individual situated in a hostile environment. The central character is usually a person of the middle class, a person sensitive enough to feel that the conventions of that class are murderous and yet too timid or too gentle to break away from them. For this person vitality is represented by a member of a different class—not, I hasten to say, a class-conscious worker, but rather some apparently good-for-nothing vagabond, carefree, irresponsible, but alive—Gino in *Where Angels Fear to Tread,* Stephen in *The Longest Journey,* George Emerson (who does not quite fit the pattern) in *A Room With a View,* and Leonard Best in *Howard's End.* It is the conflict between convention and vitality that provides the drama in each novel, and both convention and vitality are shown, for the most part, as if they had little to do with social conditions.

This seems a far cry from Communism until we remember that the Communist Party is, in Lincoln Steffens' phrase, the party of the poets. The contradictions of capitalism, one may say, are such that the full expression of human potentialities demands the creation of a new economic order. If a man values highly enough the possibilities of human life, and if he sees clearly enough what is required for their realization, he is forced to be a revolutionary. It is the second "if" that makes the trouble: most literary men value life, but few of them understand it. D. H. Lawrence took a small segment of experience, called it Life, and forgot everything else. Mr. Forster might have made the same mistake, but he didn't.

A Passage to India, the only novel Forster has written since *Howard's End* appeared in 1910, shows he is a serious liberal. That is, he really does try to see all sides of a problem. It is not necessary to ignore the weaknesses of liberalism to see that liberalism and the passion for life make a valuable combination. Liberalism alone results in a paralysis of action, and often, indeed, is little more than an excuse for inactivity. A sensitive awareness of human potentialities, on the other hand, can, without intellectual guidance, end in the empty glorification of one's personal preference, i.e., one's more or less unconscious class prejudices. But when these qualities re-enforce each other, the result is a definite propulsion towards revolution.

All these tendencies are fully illustrated in *Abinger Harvest,* a collection of essays written over more than thirty years. I have already quoted from some of the essays in the first part, called "The Present," and the others show much the same awareness of the nature and causes of bourgeois decline. The second section, "Books," with essays on Ibsen, Eliot, Proust, Lewis, and others, displays Mr. Forster as the very shrewd and balanced critic that, from *Aspects of the Novel,* we already know him to be. "The Past," with re-creations of scenes from the lives of Voltaire, Gibbon, Coleridge and Keats, demonstrates that Forster can play the game of Lytton Strachey and Mrs. Woolf, and, if only by virtue of unpretentiousness, beat them at it. "The East" contains a series of notes, mostly pretty marginal, on the theme of *A Passage to India.* The final section is a pageant written about Abinger, the village in which Mr. Forster lives.

It is, all told, an interesting book and one very much to the author's credit. It makes the reader wish that Mr. Forster were as well known and as widely read as he deserves to be. And at the same time it makes the reader wonder why he isn't a first-rate novelist. For he isn't, though in time it will be recognized that he came closer to the mark than many of his much more celebrated contemporaries. Perhaps it is not a good thing for a novelist to be balanced too precariously between classes.

July 7, 1936

Samson as Symbol

Eyeless in Gaza, by Aldous Huxley

Aldous Huxley, despite his reputation for wit and sophistication, has always been as serious a truthseeker as his grandfather and as implacable a moralist as the greater Huxley's contemporaries. Obviously he could not be satisfied forever with brilliant attacks on false values; sooner or later he had to make the enunciation of what he regarded as true values his chief concern. Foreshadowed in *Point Counter Point,* his adoption of the role of preceptor and prophet began with *Brave New World*. *Eyeless in Gaza* is a further revelation of prophetic doctrine.

Brave New World was an irritating book. No one could deny that its picture of a utopia of mechanical perfection, mass thinking, and universal boredom was amusing as well as disgusting. What irritated the reader was that Huxley drew this picture with the express purpose of discouraging attempts at social improvement. On the title page he quoted from Nicholas Berdyaev: "Utopias are realizable. Life marches toward utopias. And perhaps a new age is beginning, an age in which the intellectuals and the cultivated class will dream of ways of avoiding utopias and returning to a non-utopian society, less 'perfect' and more free." The duty of the intellectual, it appeared, is to try to check all efforts at creating an ordered society lest the horrors of *Brave New World* result. Even if the dangers had not been largely imaginary, one would still have objected to Huxley's emphasis: he said nothing about trying to bring the social improvements without incurring the dangers; rather than take any risks, he would simply preserve the *status quo*. More than that, he loudly insisted on the right to suffer. That Aldous Huxley might have his make-believe sufferings, the millions and millions of the exploited were to be kept in the real and indescribable miseries of the capitalist system. The egoism of this thesis could not fail to sicken a sensitive reader.

Eyeless in Gaza proceeds a step beyond *Brave New World*, and therefore deserves close scrutiny. Looking at it as a novel, one is strongly reminded that Mr. Huxley is an essayist. One of the favorable things to be said about his novels is that they contain his best essays, but good essays do not make good novels, and perhaps Mr. Huxley's novels, as novels, are not very good. Each has a central figure that is obviously autobiographical and quite persuasive. The other characters, even when they are as memorable as Rampion, Burlap, Illidge, or Spandrell, are close to being caricatures. There is something slightly synthetic about Huxley's novels, and one of the symptons is the shameless way in which he plagiarizes himself, using again and again types, scenes and situations that please him. Of course he is very skillful in concealing the weaknesses of his creative powers, but one feels he is a first-rate essayist who has raised himself by his own bootstraps to the level of novelist, and done an extraordinarily good job at it.

Perhaps that is why he is seldom satisfied to tell a straightforward story in a straightforward way, why he resorts to technical ingenuities in construction that distract the reader's attention from lapses in his understanding of character. *Eyeless in Gaza,* for example, moves erratically in time as *Point Counter Point* does in space. One episode is in 1932, the next in 1902, the next in 1934, the next in 1912, and so on throughout the book. The theory of this procedure is suggested when the leading character, Anthony Beavis, is reminded by kissing his mistress of playing in a chalk-pit twenty years before. "Somewhere in the mind," he says to himself, "a lunatic shuffled a pack of snapshots and dealt them out at random, shuffled once more and dealt them out in different order, again and again, indefinitely. There was no chronology. The idiot remembered no distinction between before and after. The pit was as real and vivid as the gallery. That ten years separated flints from Gaugins was a fact, not given, but discoverable only on second thoughts by the calculating intellect. The thirty-five years of his conscious life made themselves immediately known to him as a chaos—a pack of snapshots in the hands of a lunatic."

This is the theory: chronology is unreal, and Huxley will have none of it. I doubt that the theory is sound, and I am sure that his method of presentation does not reflect the movement of the human mind—as, for example, Proust's method of presentation does. All the device does, it seems to me, is to lend to the novel an element of novelty that amuses a lively intellect. It is rather fun because you always know what is going to happen, and you take pleasure in figuring out the course of events. Moreover, the method permits the author to arrive almost simultaneously at a series of climaxes that were considerably separated in time, juxtaposing crucial events in Anthony Beavis's life and enabling you to compare them. But these, after all, are minor advantages, and one wonders why Huxley thought they were worth the effort involved for author and reader.

The method's weakness is suggested by the fact that the reader, in order to think about the book at all, has to stop and make a chronological reconstruction of the events. So reconstructed, this series of episodes in the life of Anthony Beavis is easily summarized. The son of an arid philologist, he lost his mother when he was eleven. In school and college he fell alternately under the influence of his bullying, snobbish, conventional schoolmates and of an idealistic, high-principled boy called Brian Foxe. After graduation, he had an affair with an older woman, Mary Amberley, who encouraged the pose of cynicism. Her influence helped him to hurt Brian Foxe, hurt him to such an extent that his friend committed suicide. Later Anthony dignified his cynicism into a *Weltanschauung,* making it the basis of a career as sociologist. Still later, while carrying on his career and his philandering, he was shocked by a sudden break with his mistress, Helen, the daughter of the now ruined Mary Amberley. This led to his going with a friend to Mexico, where he met Dr. Miller, the man who changed his life.

Though less startling than either *Antic Hay* or *Point Counter Point, Eyeless in Gaza* does portray, and often with stinging sharpness, elements of emptiness and decay in contemporary civilization. We feel the incurable triviality of Anthony's father, the grasping sentimentality of Mrs. Foxe, the gruesome irresponsibility of Mary Amberley, the total impotence of Hugh Ledwidge, the painful pride of Mark Staithes. But the breakdown of capitalist civilization is most clearly reflected, as one would expect, in Anthony Beavis. Three things emphasize Anthony's failure: Brian Foxe's suicide, the collapse of his relationship with Helen, and the futility of his sociology. They are related, for all three grow out of the defects of his character. In condemning these defects of character, Huxley is condemning not only Anthony's past but his own as well. "He himself, Anthony went on to think, he himself had chosen to regard the whole process as either pointless or a practical joke. *Yes,* chosen. For it had been an act of the will. If it were all nonsense or a joke, then he was at liberty to read his books and exercise his talents, for sarcastic comment; there was no reason why he shouldn't sleep with any presentable woman who was ready to sleep with him. If it weren't nonsense, if there were some significance, then he could no longer live irresponsibly. There were duties towards himself and others and the nature of things. Duties with whose fulfillment the sleeping and the indiscriminate reading and the habit of detached irony would interfere. He had chosen to think it nonsense, and nonsense for more than twenty years the thing had seemed to be."

Huxley thus clearly recognizes that cynicism is a defense, not merely of a state of mind, but of actual concrete privileges. He sees that, if one believes the future is hopeless, it is because one does not want to do the things and make the sacrifices that would substitute good for evil. So far, he registers a clear intellectual advance. But when he comes to consider how evil can be overcome, he shows how far he still is from clarity of thought. He examines the two traditional methods of overcoming evil, social reconstruction, which means Communism, and individual reconstruction, which means religion. He rejects the former and accepts the latter.

His examination of Communism, at least so far as this novel is concerned, is both superficial and unfair. The statement that Mark Staithes is a Communist is a libel on the Communist Party of Great Britain. Helen is no more representative. Only Giesebrecht, the German refugee, is a conceivable Communist, and he scarcely figures in the story. It is safe to say that Huxley does not know Communists, and it is doubtful if he knows Communism. The converted Anthony makes three points against Communism. First, he raises the usual objection about ends justifying means, as if it were ever possible to judge means apart from ends. Second, he says that Communism rests on hatred, forgetting that it is capitalism that creates hatred, and that Communism, at its worst, harnesses hatred to constructive ends and, at its best, gives men understanding enough to transcend it. Finally, he argues that it is a fallacy to assume that better social conditions make better people.

This last point is vital. Rejecting Communism, Huxley is forced to adopt the position that progress can come only through changes in the individual's heart, soul, mind, personality—whatever you want to call it. How convincing, one first asks, does he make the actual visualization of this process in the novel? In Mexico Anthony meets Dr. Miller. Miller appears on the scene with his mouth full of phrases reminiscent of both Bernarr Macfadden and Frank Buchman. Here, one thinks, is the perfect opportunity for Huxley's satire. But no, to our amazement, Huxley takes Miller perfectly seriously, and asks us to. This blather about constipation and right posture and vegetarianism and love and peace succeeded, we are asked to believe, in changing the life of Anthony Beavis. It might almost be the perfect Huxleyan joke.

And we can say little more for the presentation of Miller's ideas in Anthony's journal, which is scattered through the book. If you love people, they will love you, and, if they love you, they will be better people, and war and exploitation will vanish. All this is justified on the basis of what seems old-fashioned Emersonian transcendentalism, decorated with a few figures of speech from modern science.

Impossible as it is to discuss adequately at this point the relative merits of social and individual reconstruction, it may be pointed out that three thousand years of preaching the latter has accomplished singularly little. Social reconstruction, however, has worked. Huxley pokes fun at the Webbs for believing that more tractors will make better persons, but the Webbs have actually seen, in the U.S.S.R., that social reconstruction does mean individual reconstruction. We have, moreover, far more evidence than the relatively brief experience of the Soviet Union can give. All through history social conditions have changed, and the changes have altered human beings. There are no other terms in which one can understand history. What Communism does is to use the knowledge that comes from history so that man can cooperate with social forces in shaping his own destiny.

It is necessary to deal thus flatly with Huxley's ideas because they are all that matters very much. As a novel, as a picture of human beings and a particular society, *Eyeless in Gaza* is inferior to *Point Counter Point*. As a sample of Huxley's thinking, it marks an advance over the earlier novel because it shows that he is now seriously concerned with the problem of making a better world. But on the other hand, the methods of reconstruction he proposes seem to me quite demonstrably wrong.

His title comes from *Samson Agonistes:*

> Promise was that I
> Should Israel from Philistian yoke deliver;
> Ask for this great deliverer now, and find him
> Eyeless in Gaza at the mill with slaves,
> Himself in bonds under Philistian yoke;
> Yet stay, let me not rashly call in doubt
> Divine Prediction; what if all foretold
> Had been fulfilled but through mine own default,
> Whom have I to complain of but myself?

Yet Samson, it may be remembered, fulfilled the prophecy and delivered Israel, not by converting the Philistines to some mystical doctrine of love and peace, but by pulling down the temple on their heads. It was a crude method, but it redeemed Samson's self-respect, and it did dispose of the Philistines.

July 21, 1936

A Novel of Spain

The Olive Field, by Ralph Bates

Unlike Ralph Bates's first novel, *Lean Men,* which has a not altogether credible English revolutionary as hero, *The Olive Field* deals solely with the people of Spain. The result is undeniably a book much more unified in tone than its predecessor. Francis Charing brought into *Lean Men* countless echoes of recent British literature, the novels of the bright young men, the religio-sexual obscurities of the D. H. Lawrence school, the Marxism-cum-mysticism of Middleton Murry and his ilk. There is none of that in *The Olive Field.* Bates takes the mysticism of Robledo and even the mysticism of Father Soriano more seriously than he needs to, but at least their notions grow out of the soil that is the novel's scene and are not transported from a foreign land. *Lean Men* is, as its subtitle states, "an episode in a life," the life of a wayward member of the British intelligentsia. *The Olive Field* is a novel of Spain.

It is, whatever Spaniards might think of it, a novel that completely convinces the outsider. Most of the action takes place in a little village, Los Olivares de Don Fadrique, in the southernmost part of Spain. Don Fadrique, the principal landowner, is more interested in sixteenth-century music than in agriculture or politics. He is quietly incompetent, a vestigial survival from the feudal past. His major-domo, on the other hand, Indalecio Argote, brutal though he is in the exploitation of the peasants, loves the olives and is a master of agricultural lore. But the story is principally concerned, not with Fadrique and Argote, nor with the priests, the worldly Martinez and the ascetic Soriano, but with the workers: the Caro family, the Robledo family, the Perez family— Diego Mudarra, Acorin, Molinos, and a score of others.

For nearly four hundred pages we see these people going about their tasks, and we come to know them and their village. Every phase of olive-culture is described with affectionate intimacy. The festivals are presented, not merely as picturesque pageants but also as occasions of strife between the faithful and those workers who have broken with the church. There are anarchist meetings, lively gatherings of friends, the gossip of neighbors, the games of the children. Here is the many-sided life of agricultural Spain in the early years of the Republic.

The plot is simple. Joaquin Caro and Diego Mudarra are both olive workers and left anarchists, and they are close friends. After Mudarra seduces Caro's fiancée, they are estranged and only partly reconciled. They are chosen by the anarchists to blow up a reservoir, but Caro cannot consent to the useless destruction of crops. This begins his disillusionment with anarchism and he turns toward communism. Mudarra is arrested, tortured, and imprisoned. Caro marries Lucia, who has given birth to Mudarra's child, and they go to Asturias, where Caro works first as a miner and then in a warehouse, and becomes active in the Communist Party. Mudarra comes there after his release from prison, and he and Caro become involved in the Asturian uprising of 1934. Mudarra is captured and killed. Caro and Lucia escape, to return to Los Olivares and their work and their struggle for the revolution.

The way this story is told invites criticism. In the first 400 pages, devoted to life in Los Olivares, Bates often becomes so absorbed in details that he loses his sense of proportion, expanding minor incidents and merely sketching major ones. For page after page the story stands still to permit some bit of interesting but irrelevant description. Bates seems unable to keep hold of all the threads of his narrative, and characters weave in and out of the story inexplicably. Then suddenly the leading figures are picked up and deposited in Asturias, as if the author were determined to introduce the uprising at all costs. And, worse than that, he abruptly abandons his leisurely gait, apparently alarmed at the length of the book, and races ahead with a speed as bewildering as his earlier meanderings, until the uprising is reached, and he can settle down to a climax that, in itself at least, is magnificent.

It would be idle to try to deny that the book would be far better if it were free from these faults of construction. They seem, moreover, quite unnecessary, the sort of weakness that careful revision could readily have eliminated. But it will not do to exaggerate their importance. E. M. Forster says that if a novel bounces you into a sense of life, it is good. That *The Olive Field* does. One remarkable thing about the book is that the reader is never conscious of the fact that an Englishman is writing it. A Spaniard, as I have intimated, might well be aware of lapses of knowledge or insight, but there are none of the tell-tale touches of condescension or surprise. Always one is inside the life of Los Olivares.

At the present moment, with the future of Spain of such passionate concern to every revolutionary, one cannot read *The Olive Field* without emotion, for in the book one feels the driving force of the revolution. Bates does not show the workers as fighting simply for bread. His workers are complex human beings, capable of joy in their tasks, in their sports, in their loves. They are fighting not merely for the means of keeping alive but for the rich, abundant life of which they are worthy. In the olive fields, in the mines, or on the barricades, they are the builders of a new world. To know them as one does in this novel is to have confidence in that world.

August 18, 1936

D. H. Lawrence as Messiah

Phoenix: The Posthumous Papers of D. H. Lawrence. With an introduction by Edward D. McDonald

There has been a great garnering of scraps since D. H. Lawrence died, but this is the real thing—more than eight hundred pages of articles and reviews, some of the most important hitherto unpublished. It makes one suddenly aware of Lawrence's productivity. During the twenty years of his literary life, years when he was never in good health, he wrote twelve novels, four plays, some twelve books of short stories, six or seven volumes of studies and essays, four travel books, several hundred poems and enough essays to fill this volume and more—for there is also the posthumous *Assorted Articles*. Add his half-dozen translations and his voluminous correspondence, and you have a record which, though I suppose it is not comparable to that of H. G. Wells or E. Phillips Oppenheim, makes most authors seem inarticulate. One must remember, furthermore, that Lawrence often wrote his novels two and three times, something, I am sure, Mr. Wells has never done.

More important, *Phoenix*, which represents all the twenty writing years, makes us fully aware of Lawrence's multiplicity—a fairer word, perhaps, than inconsistency. Like **Whitman, he was** unashamed of contradicting himself, for he knew he contained multitudes. In this collection there are statements that flatly contradict each other, not because Lawrence's mind was changing and he repudiated earlier beliefs, but because either his solar or his cardiac plexus happened to register differently on different occasions. Moreover, "Phoenix" reveals a different Lawrence from that of the novels or the poems or the letters. With all the inconsistencies of statement, there is a sort of homogeneity in the volume, the result of the fact that most of its contents were written with the definite purpose of instruction. Though a few essays are purely descriptive, the book primarily presents its author as thinker. This is the Lawrence of *Fantasia of the Unconscious,* not the Lawrence of *Sons and Lovers* or *Look! We Have Come Through!*

Although the thinker is not the best or the most important Lawrence, there are fine essays and fine passages of essays in this book. The "nature and poetical pieces," as Mr. McDonald classifies them, are for the most part excellent, and so are many of the travel articles. Much of the criticism is good, especially the sardonic reviews of Stuart Sherman, H. G. Wells, Cunninghame Graham and Carl Van Vechten. Even the long essay on Hardy, which contains much pretentious philosophizing, often comments soundly on the novels. Indeed, in every essay, not excepting those grouped under "ethics, psychology, philosophy," there is fine eloquence and a certain amount of sense of a rather startling kind.

But there is also a great deal of nonsense. I know of no other applicable term when Lawrence starts talking about "the eternal systole-diastole of the universe," "affective centers," "dynamic consciousness," "polarized center," "pristine conscious-force," "the two dark poles of vital being," or "the flashing centers of volition in the fierce proud backbone." What he says about heredity is nonsense, this business about our grandmothers' dreams, or his Mesopotamian self, or the influence of his "dark-faced, bronze-voiced father far back in the resinous ages."

Almost everything he writes about races is nonsense, whether his theme is Germans and Latins or "the great aboriginal spirit the Americans must recognize again, recognize and embrace." His social views are just as preposterous, his disposing of all economic problems by saying it is cowardly to worry about money, his lumping together of capitalism and socialism, neither of which he understood, his perfectly serious proposal to end war by abolishing guns while keeping spears and swords to preserve the benefits of the martial spirit. Some of this corresponds, no doubt, to realizations of more or less important truths, but it is none the less nonsense. And it is objectionable and dangerous because Lawrence tried to give his perceptions and his prejudices a scientific form at the same time that he hated science and repudiated it whenever it contradicted his "intuition."

Lawrence has been compared to both Whitman and Blake, but, at least as a thinker, he most resembles Carlyle. Like Carlyle, he lost touch with the class of his origin, and yet was never at peace with the middle class. Like Carlyle, he hated democracy: the average man, he writes, "demands somebody to bow down to." Like Carlyle, he praised the martial spirit—which somehow had nothing to do with the damnable World War—and condemned soft humanitarianism. Like Carlyle, he regarded self-consciousness as the source of most evil, and if on one occasion he specifically repudiated the gospel of work, because it seemed to encourage the greedy accumulation he disliked, on another he wrote, "Work is, or should be, our heavenly bread of activity, contact and consciousness." Most important of all, he joined Carlyle in condemning science and the human reason in general. Carlyle, says Louis Cazamian, "denounced as a danger and a disease every conquest that clear thinking and clear consciousness have made over the activities which are instinctive." So did Lawrence, and he found, as Carlyle did, plenty of disciples.

This is not the place to say all that could be said in praise of Lawrence's greatness as novelist and poet or in admiration of those qualities in the man which make themselves felt in his letters and which so obviously impressed his associates. We are concerned with him here in his Messianic role. It ought, certainly, to be said that much of what he attacked deserved to be destroyed, but we have to ask where the weight of his influence falls. I refuse to abandon any great writer to the fascists, and I have no doubt that Mr. McDonald is right in saying Lawrence would have condemned Hitler—though there is precious little condemnation of Mussolini. But it seems perfectly clear that such thinking as is revealed in *Phoenix* gives encouragement to the fascist mind.

October 28, 1936

In Quest of Integration

Sherston's Progress, by Siegfried Sassoon

Siegfried Sassoon has already told in *Memoirs of an Infantry Officer* about his one-man revolt against the war. Deciding that the war was futile and unjust, he announced this fact to his superiors, and awaited the consequences. Since he was an officer and a gentleman, it was naturally assumed that he was suffering from some mental disorder, and he was sent to a hospital for the shell-shocked.

Sherston's Progress, the third volume in his slightly fictionalized autobiography, tells what happened. He fell into the hands of W. H. R. Rivers, a psychiatrist who immediately won his respect. Under Rivers's influence, Sassoon—or Sherston, as he calls himself in the book,—determined to go back to the trenches. If the masses of men were fighting and dying, there was only one way for him to preserve his sanity and self-respect: he must fight and die too. Discharged from the hospital, he was sent to Ireland and thence to Egypt and Palestine. But with the German advance of the spring of 1918, his regiment was recalled to France, and he again went into action. His service was of short duration, however, for he was wounded, through his own recklessness and the over-zealousness of one of his men, and was sent home to England.

In this volume, as in its predecessors, one is impressed by Sassoon's effort to be honest. He knows that his revolt, looked at from the outside, came to a miserable anti-climax. From one point of view, he realizes, his decision may be regarded as cowardly. On the other hand, it was not an easy decision to carry out, and, with a careful avoidance of over-emphasis he describes some of his bad moments. His diary, especially as it describes his weeks in France, is a touching record, a record all the more poignant for its reticence.

One is also impressed, again as in the other volumes, by Sassoon's poetic gifts, his powers of description and evocation. These are best displayed in the section on his experiences in Ireland, for his life was then more nearly normal, and he writes with gusto of the Mister and his other fox-hunting companions. But there are effective scenes in the account of hospital life, especially the story of his having tea

with an astronomer instead of waiting for the medical board, and the
diary contains many memorable passages.

The great importance of the book, however, lies, it seems to me,
in the implications of Sassoon's cure. From the point of view of Rivers,
Sassoon was certainly a sick man when he arrived at the hospital:
though it is normal for a man to risk being killed in war, it is not normal for him to expose himself, in cold blood, to the danger of being
killed by a firing squad. Rivers's job was to restore Sassoon to nor-
mality. He succeeded, and Sassoon went back to the trenches.

This, I think, is the way in which psychiatry almost invariably—
though not necessarily—functions. So far as the maladjusted Sassoon
was concerned, integration was possible either in terms of revolt or
in terms of conformity. There were opponents of the war whose sanity
even Rivers could not have questioned. They were integrated because
they understood why the war was fought, knew what they were doing,
and were conscious of fellowship with their comrades throughout the
world. Rivers might have guided Sassoon to that kind of integration,
but even to suggest the possibility is ludicrous.

From his own point of view, no doubt, Rivers was right, but I
think Sassoon was tricked. When he was in the hospital with his
wound, he thought, "How could I begin my life all over again when
I had no conviction about anything except that the War was a dirty
trick which had been played on me and my generation?" Then Rivers
appeared: "He did not tell me that I had done my best to justify his
belief in me. He merely made me feel that he took all that for granted,
and now we must go on to something better still. And this was the
beginning of the new life toward which he had shown me the way."
What has "the new life" been for Sassoon and his generation? Perhaps
he will write more volumes of his memoirs to tell us, but I think we
already know the answer.

Standing Room Only, by Walter Greenwood

Walter Greenwood wrote two novels, of which the earlier and
better, *Love on the Dole*, was made into a play by Mr. Greenwood
and somebody-or-other. Somebody-or-other, I assume, was a good
play doctor, and the result of his labors was a combination of moving
scenes from the novel and sure-fire hokum. This combination was a
great success in London, and didn't do too badly in New York.

Standing Room Only is obviously the outcome of Mr. Greenwood's excursion into the theatrical world. That is, its material comes from that experience. So, perhaps, do the vices of this uncommonly shoddy piece of work. A local boy, Henry Ormerod, writes a play. It is taken in hand by a stock-character producer, who hires a stock-character director, very cynical, and a stock-character star, very beautiful, and finds a stock-character angel, very vulgar but good-hearted. The beautiful star, strangely enough, is seduced by the wealth of the vulgar angel. The manager falls in love with the play doctor, who falls in love with the director. Henry—who, by the way, has a stock-character mother, very grimly sensible, and a stock-character father, very drunken—is caught by the local girl. She might be described as a stock-character local girl.

This, from an author who was making some contribution to British literature of working-class life, is an insult. There are some bad moments in both *Love on the Dole* and *The Time Is Ripe*, but their worst is better than the best in *Standing Room Only*. We had better assume, in all charity, that Mr. Greenwood has had a temporary lapse, and try to forget about it.

November 10, 1936

The British Are Coming

The backwardness of revolutionary literature in England has long been apparent. It is true that, three years ago, we were startled by the appearance of a group of brilliant young poets who pledged their allegiance to revolutionary principles. But a few poets do not make a literary movement. Moreover, though no one can deny the originality and the technical skill of Auden, Spender, and Lewis, soberer judgment does suggest that their work expresses a not particularly representative type of revolutionary impulse. To us in America, who are used to seeing revolutionary writers take an active part in the revolutionary struggle, the apparent isolation of these three writers from the working-class movement is an ominous sign. One cannot feel sure of either their future development or their influence on revolutionary poetry.

The development of the crisis of capitalism usually produces, on the one hand, a tense excitement among a section of the intellectuals of a country and, on the other, a preoccupation with working-class lives and an expression of working-class attitudes. Auden, Spender, and Lewis have eloquently recorded the intellectual ferment, but the literature of the working class has been slow in appearing. There is, indeed, Harold Heslop, who has militantly expressed the Communist point of view in such novels as *Last Cage Down,* but Heslop is not an altogether prepossessing writer. The only British novelist of working-class life who is at all familiar to Americans is James Hanley. In *Ebb and Flood,* in parts of *Boy* and *Stoker Bush,* and especially in *The Furys,* Hanley has described with knowledge and power the lives and characters of sailors and waterfront workers. Hanley knows how the working class lives, but he seemingly has little interest in why it lives as it does. My objection to Hanley is not that he is not an avowed revolutionary, but that he refuses to make the intellectual effort that his art demands. The effort would probably make a revolutionary of him; it would certainly make him a better writer.

My reservations about Hanley, which are intensified by his most recent book, *The Secret Journey,* do not keep me from recognizing that, like the three poets, he has a real place in British revolutionary literature. The truth is that one can always find faults in any writer. The revolution expresses itself through the imaginations of many men, not through the imagination of a single genius. What we are looking for in Great Britain is a body of revolutionary literature, and that is what we are beginning to get.

Three recent novels indicate what is happening. Ralph Bates's *The Olive Field,* a considerably better book than his *Lean Men,* shows that he is one writer who knows working-class life—that of Spain, as it happens—and is not afraid of revolutionary passion. Naomi Mitchison, in *We Have Been Warned,* brings to the examination of contemporary life the candor and unconventionality that made *Cloud Cuckoo Land* and *The Corn King and the Spring Queen* so superior to other historical novels, and to these virtues she adds a militancy that is more important than her political confusion. *Daugh-*

ters of Albion, by Alec Brown, is based upon a shrewd and thoroughly Marxist analysis of the breakdown of bourgeois society. It is almost Dreiserian in its freedom from literary graces, but it reaches the imagination because of the author's dogged determination to get at the truth. All three books are badly constructed—irritatingly so— but all of them are alive.

Another significant phenomenon is the appearance of *New Writing,* a semi-annual anthology edited by John Lehmann, who recently contributed to *International Literature* a valuable essay on British revolutionary poetry. *New Writing* is not limited to British literature; Egon Erwin Kisch, Anna Seghers, André Chamson, and other Continental writers are in the first number, and America is to be represented in the second. The anthology is not specifically revolutionary, but its pages are not open to "writers of reactionary or fascist sentiments."

It is noteworthy that Lehmann and his associates are interested in gathering together for British readers some of the best work of the international revolutionary movement. It is also important that an outlet is being given for British writers of revolutionary or anti-fascist tendencies. Of the writers I have mentioned, only Bates and Spender are represented, and Alec Brown as a translator. The most notable contribution, it seems to me, is the story by Christopher Isherwood, who wrote a bizarre but memorable book, *The Strange Case of Mr. Norris,* and who collaborated with W. H. Auden in writing *The Dog Beneath the Skin.* His picture of Germany is as immediate as a news report and yet achieves a deeply tragic effect through its understatement. For me it establishes beyond any question Isherwood's importance as a revolutionary writer.

Among the other British contributors, Edward Upward, William Plomer, and John Hampson, all of whom contributed to *New Country,* and Gore Graham, who is apparently the youngest of the writers represented, seem to me clearly capable of first-rate revolutionary fiction. (Plomer and Hampson have written novels, unpublished, so far as I know, in this country.) Upward, like Isherwood, has the same kind of mind as Auden and Spender. Hampson and Graham write out of immediate knowledge of the working class.

There is more variety in American revolutionary literature, and I think we have the superior writers, but there is a British revolutionary literature that can be read and enjoyed and respected. Perhaps the time is not far off when we shall have to admit that we have been equaled if not outdistanced.

December 15, 1936

English Men of Letters

Aspects of Wilde, by Vincent O'Sullivan
Rodeo, by R. B. Cunninghame Graham
  (edited by A. F. Tschiffely)
Autobiography of G. K. Chesterton
Swinnerton: An Autobiography

In a brief and disorganized and overpriced book, Mr. O'Sullivan gives us his recollections of Oscar Wilde and his views on Wilde's works. Neither the recollections nor the views are especially important, though the former do serve to counteract some of the fantastic gossip about Wilde's last years. If there is anything valuable in Mr. O'Sullivan's comments, it is his reminder that Wilde was, before his trial, a popular writer. The usual conception of Wilde as the isolated æsthete is false; he had an unusual sense of what the public wanted, and he made the most of it. He was the leader of a revolt, but the ground had been thoroughly prepared by better men, and he sniped away at the bourgeoisie without much danger to himself. (Of course the bourgeoisie took a cowardly revenge, but that is another story.)

A great deal has been written about Oscar Wilde, and Mr. O'Sullivan's book fills a small space on a big shelf. Very little has been written about Cunninghame Graham—a rather amateurish biography was published a few years ago—and yet his life, if not his work, has more interest than Wilde's. The son of an old Scottish family, he was elected to Parliament in 1886 as an advanced Liberal, and immediately began a crusade for unpopular causes. When, in 1887, various Socialist meetings were broken up, he protested in Parliament and in public gatherings. He and John Burns were among the fifty men arrested at a Trafalgar Square demonstration, and he was given two months in prison. He was active for a time in Keir Hardie's Scottish Labor Party, but he withdrew from politics in 1892, and most of the remainder of his life—he died last January at the age of eighty-four—was spent adventurously in South America, Spain, and Morocco.

Cunninghame Graham was the author of twenty-five or thirty biographies, histories, and collections of short stories. He has never, I think, been widely read in this country, and Mr. Tschiffely has prepared *Rodeo* with the purpose of winning for him the following that Tschiffely—in common with many critics—thinks he deserves. *Rodeo* contains nearly fifty stories and sketches, half of them dealing with South America, and the other half with Spain, Africa, and Scotland. They reflect almost all the aspects of the author's adventurous life, but there is not a word to indicate that he was for five years a member of Parliament. There is a brief sketch of his experiences in prison, but nothing to tell why he was imprisoned.

Mr. Tschiffely's selection is representative: Cunninghame Graham's political experiences left no mark on his writing. The sketches in *Rodeo* do, however, help us to understand why this Scottish gentleman was at one time a fighter for the working class. In the first place, he always had a strong sympathy for the underdog. Call it *noblesse oblige* if you will; at least it led him to get his head cracked in a London riot. In the second place, he hated the spirit of commercialism. Part of this hatred came from a contempt for all kinds of meanness; part of it was a gentleman's distaste for "trade." These two emotions appear again and again in *Rodeo*, and they help to give the volume its tone.

Nevertheless, I confess that most of Cunninghame Graham's work seems to me rather slight and distinctly marginal. His descriptions are written with precision and distinction, but he always seems to be a detached spectator. His subjects are naturally remote from us, and they seem just as remote when he has finished with them. In his philosophical discussions, which are frequent, he vacillates between an aristocratic scorn for the masses and a rather puzzled belief that most people would be all right if they had a chance. That seems to me the key to his life and his writing. Hating commercialism, he put his trust for a time in the working class, but, when there were no immediate results, he turned to the pre-capitalist life of the pampas. British literature was, I think, the loser.

Graham was born in 1852, Wilde in 1856, Chesterton in 1874, and Swinnerton in 1884. According to the usual classifications, Wilde and Graham belonged to the nineties, Chesterton was an Edwardian, and Swinnerton is a Georgian. Meaningless as such classifications are, it remains true that there are certain resemblances between Wilde and Graham, who reacted in not wholly dissimilar ways to the same phenomena, whereas Chesterton clearly belonged to the period of Wells and Shaw. Indeed, as time goes on, it seems more and more possible to define Chesterton in terms of his contemporaries: he was so determined to disagree with the Fabian-Liberal school of thought that his own thinking was very largely conditioned by theirs.

His autobiography is in most ways a disappointing volume. Largely a recapitulation of ideas to which he has devoted his several score of volumes, it does not do what ideological biographies ought to do: it does not illuminate the origins of those ideas. There are some interesting accounts of his earlier years and a few amusing anecdotes of his contemporaries, but for the most part the book is just more Chesterton.

Chesterton's major literary asset was his mastery of the half-truth, which is what is meant by the Chesterton paradox. A simple example will show what I have in mind. He talks rather amusingly about those persons who want "to improve the drama." "To talk of helping 'the drama,'" he says, "sounds to me like helping the typewriter or the printing press. It seems, to my simple mind, to depend a good deal on what comes out of it." Now those who do talk about helping the drama do so, of course, because the production of plays requires an elaborate, specialized, and expensive machinery. They do not expect that the creation of this machinery will in itself result in good plays, but it is common sense to recognize that good plays are more likely to be written if there is some chance of their being produced.

Paradoxes on precisely this level are generously sprinkled throughout the book. They range from the contention that, despite the jokes about simple-minded curates, clergymen are really very intelligent persons, to the contention that socialism and imperialism are pretty much the same thing because both believe in "unification and centralization on a large scale." The juiciest exhibition, however, of Chesterton's mode of reasoning is his theory that the pacifists caused the world war. The logic runs this way: many pacifists were rich Quakers; the government has to conciliate rich men; therefore the government could not take a firm stand against Germany; therefore Germany challenged Great Britain; therefore the pacifists caused the war, Q.E.D.

It would be foolish to prolong this discussion of the Chestertonian half-truth. The best thing to be said about the *Autobiography* is that it contains almost all of Chesterton and makes the reading of his earlier books practically unnecessary. One wishes, however, that it explained why a mind as brilliant as his spent itself in futile gestures.

If Chesterton's autobiography is an extreme example of concern with ideas, Swinnerton's illustrates with equal completeness the anecdotal type of autobiography. The result is that it rather closely parallels his book of literary history, *The Georgian Scene,* but is, if anything, more informative and perhaps more usefully critical. After the chapters on his boyhood and early publishing experiences, the chapter headings are little more than lists of names: Bennett, Wells, Mackenzie, Murry, Mansfield, Galsworthy, Monkhouse, Tomlinson, Maugham, Walpole, Forster, Sassoon, Huxley, and dozens of others. About each of these, Swinnerton tells anecdotes, often shrewdly revelatory, making his book valuable for anyone interested in British literature of the past thirty years.

Moreover, despite all his material about other people, it is undeniable that a pretty clear picture of Swinnerton himself emerges. He is not a first-rate novelist—he feels, I am glad to say, that *Nocturne* has been overrated—and, if I can judge from his book on Gissing and from *The Georgian Scene,* he is not a first-rate critic. But he is and always has been a man of common sense, a man who accepted the world as he found it but reserved the right of private judgment, a man who remained on good terms with everyone, but, I suspect, on intimate terms with very few. (Reviewers have commented on his extreme friendliness; a deeper truth, I believe, lies in his comment on one of his cats—"I loved him more than I have loved most human beings.") It is somehow a tribute to his integrity and essential simplicity, as well as a revelation of his limitations, that he can end his book, quite seriously and without cant, by quoting in full the ten commandments.

Swinnerton, like his much greater contemporary, Arnold Bennett, was a self-made man of letters. He had no special training for his career and perhaps, unlike Bennett, no great aptitude for it. One has no sense, as one has with Wilde and Cunninghame Graham and possibly Chesterton, that under happier circumstances he might have been a much more distinguished writer. On the contrary, he seems to belong to his period, and, on many sides, to represent it at its best. One comes to regard him with the tolerant friendliness with which he regarded most of his contemporaries, and that is presumably all he would ask.

December 29, 1936

Kipling's Last Book

Something of Myself, by Rudyard Kipling

This is in a way a good book, a better book than might have been expected. It is unpretentious and fragmentary, and because of that fact the author keeps within limits that include his virtues and exclude many of his faults. It shows Kipling's personal modesty, his sense of humor, and his devotion to his craft. Its power of evoking a scene equals that of his best work, and the style has the originality and precision of phrase that once won him the praise of so exacting a critic as Henry James.

It is well that Kipling's last book should exhibit his talents, for it is easy to forget that fifty years ago his first books were being acclaimed, not merely by James, but by almost every English man of letters. The young man who was born in India, suffered in a British lodging house, passed triumphantly through the ordeal of the United Services College, and for seven years performed heroic tasks on Indian newspapers, seemed, in the late eighties, a genius of the first order. We who think of Kipling chiefly as the high priest of imperialism, and are inclined to regard a taste for his work as something to be outgrown with maturity, find it difficult to understand the impression that his earliest work made. That work has its virtues, certainly, but the trouble is that, whereas his contemporaries were startled, quite naturally, by the possibilities of the man who could do such work at twenty-four or twenty-five, we know all too well what it led to.

There was, it seems, a point in Kipling's career when he might have developed in either of two directions. He might have continued as the shrewd observer he had shown himself to be in his short stories of India, or he might have become, as he actually did, the spokesman of a cause—the cause of the Empire, as opposed both to "little Englandism" and to other empires. Why he chose the latter course this book does not greatly help us to understand. (He does point out, in precisely this connection, that both his grandfathers were Wesleyan ministers.) But we can vaguely discern the process. His early work did, without his having particularly aimed at that result, perform a useful function in the new phase of imperialism that brought England out of the depression of the eighties: it helped to make the under-privileged members of English society feel that they had a share in the empire. He assumed the role of high priest largely by accident, and then, of course, his prejudices and upbringing led him to continue in it.

It may seem, to some superficial critics, a paradox for a Marxist to reproach Kipling for being, as these critics would say, a propagandist rather than an artist. No career, as a matter of fact, could illustrate better than his what Marxists really believe about the literary processes. The Marxist never wants an author to impose a set of ideas upon his observations. The Marxist, on the contrary, believes that honest observation must lead an author to recognition of some part at least of the truth—the revolutionary truth—about our civilization. What he objects to is any shrinking away from the truth, any willingness to compromise with bourgeois prejudices. Kipling, in becoming the bard of imperialism, was delivering himself over to his prejudices, and his powers as an artist were consequently stultified.

It is the elimination of much of the familiar preaching that makes *Something of Myself* less irritating and more readable than most of Kipling's later work. But there are glimpses enough of the imperial evangelist—in his account of his friendship with Rhodes, in his hatred of Irish, Jews, and Americans, even in his strictures on dressing for dinner. And time and again one catches hints of the process by which the imperialist stifled the genius in Kipling. One comes to understand, too, the loving, patient craftsmanship with which rather pathetically, he tried to compensate for the narrowness of his sympathies and the distortion of his vision. One comes to feel that it was only as a crafts-man that he really grew up, that his values were always those of an adolescent. That is, of course, why his following is chiefly among adolescents. It was, this book reminds us, a heavy price to pay.

March 30, 1937

Revaluing Ford Madox Ford

Great Trade Route, by Ford Madox Ford
Portraits From Life, by Ford Madox Ford

Nearly ten years ago, I read Ford Madox Ford's *The Good Soldier*, and was so impressed with its virtuosity that I went through a good many of the sixty-odd books he had published up to that time, and a little later wrote an article called "Ford Madox Ford—A Ne-glected Contemporary." It did seem to me extraordinary that so little attention had been paid to the author of *The Good Soldier* and the Christopher Tietjens tetralogy, who had also been Joseph Conrad's collaborator and the editor of the impressive *English Review*.

Rereading my article, I am relieved to find that I did not com-mit myself to anything silly. Indeed, most of what I said in 1930 I could endorse today. But if I were writing the article now, which would scarcely seem worth doing, I confess, my emphasis would be a little different. I do think that Ford began his career with unusual talents, and I would argue that he might have become a first-rate novelist. But I doubt, however, if he has been underestimated. What-ever his potentialities, he has written an unforgivable number of trivial books. The war tetralogy, though it has some memorable scenes—the Duchemin breakfast still sticks in my mind—is, from volume to volume, increasingly diffuse. And as for *The Good Soldier*, it is, as I wrote in 1930, "remarkable for its sustained inventiveness and its sound, unfaltering progress," but I fear I must recant any assertion that it is "not merely a *tour de force*."

The explanation of my recalling an article published some years ago in an obscure periodical—*The Bookman,* to be exact—is, I suppose, the natural desire of a writer to keep his record as orderly and coherent as possible. But there is some justification for my making this review a kind of appendix to that article. The three books by Mr. Ford that recent months have brought us—*Collected Poems* was published in the fall—are all reworkings of material that has previously been used in one or another of his publications, now perhaps eighty in number. One is, of course, frankly a collection. The second combines in a familiar pattern some new experiences with many old ideas. The third, as we shall see, contains scarcely anything that has not appeared in earlier books. This habit of repetition, which Mr. Ford developed early, forces the reviewer to refer his latest books* to their predecessors, and thus invites speculation upon his entire career.

Great Trade Route is a travel book, and was preceded not only by several books on England and France, but also by at least two on the United States. It differs from these predecessors by being more loosely organized and by being more political in its emphasis. Mr. Ford pretends that civilization has always followed the fortieth parallel, and he describes a trip to New York and thence into the South. The method is associative, and the author rambles widely in space and time, slipping from anecdote to anecdote and from impression to impression. Therefore, although it is based upon a trip to the United States that has taken place since he wrote *New York Is Not America,* the volume introduces some of the material of that book and of other books as well. The method of presentation, incidentally, makes it difficult to read, and classes it with the not inconsiderable number of dull books that Mr. Ford has written.

If *Great Trade Route* is worth reading at all, it is because of the political views it expresses. These, too, have been previously stated, or at least adumbrated; but Mr. Ford, like everyone else, has grown more politically conscious in the past six or seven years, and he feels it incumbent upon him to take a position. He is against imperialism, war, and economic injustice. These evils he proposes to abolish by encouraging small producers and doing away with mass production. This somehow is to be brought about by general change of heart, which, in turn, is largely to be accomplished by the arts. He calls himself a Quietist Anarchist, and expresses sympathy with the aims of the Confederate agrarians.

Surely it would be pointless to underline the futility of his program, but I might allow myself the luxury of touching on one issue that is very close to Mr. Ford's heart, the issue of food. He rails against canned vegetables and refrigerated meat, and praises the diet of the small producer who grows his own food. I live in a community of small producers, and I know how many months of the year they subsist on pork and potatoes. It is true that my home is north of the fortieth parallel, and therefore in a region that Mr. Ford would apparently like to see abandoned to lower forms of life, but the fact is that millions of people do live in this region, and I am not sure that dwellers on the great trade route—to use his fanciful name—are much better off. Modern methods of refrigeration and transportation have made possible for almost the entire country a more varied and better balanced diet than home production could ever achieve. What comfortably well-off persons in New York City now have, everyone could have—but not by going back to the soil.

We pass from Mr. Ford as gourmet, traveler, and political philosopher to Mr. Ford as literary critic and friend of the great. *Portraits from Life* contains essays on James, Conrad, Hardy, Wells, Crane, Lawrence, Galsworthy, Turgenev, Hudson, Dreiser, and Swinburne. Mr. Ford has written small books on James and Conrad and a study of the novel, and at least three volumes of reminiscences, and from this it can be imagined how little in *Portraits from Life* is new. Even *Great Trade Route* contains some of the anecdotes that are used in the other book, and I wager that not even Mr. Ford knows how many times they have served his purposes. Apparently he was urged by Mr. Palmer of the *Mercury,* to whom the book is dedicated, to do the series, and he obligingly raked over the ashes, hoping to find embers enough to make the pot boil once more.

There are some good stories in *Portraits from Life,* if you happen not to have met them on one of their earlier appearances, and there are a few critical comments of real shrewdness, but what chiefly impresses the reader is that Ford knew all these great men more or less intimately, and was accepted by them more or less as an equal. They, too, must for a time have regarded him as, at least potentially, a major writer.

What happened to Ford Madox Ford, born Hueffer? A precocious youth, growing up in a literary household, he appeared in print long before he had anything to say. He was facile and something of a rebel, and, in the æsthetic nineties, he justified both his facility and his nonconformity by the familiar device of the art-for-art's-sake dogma. Later he defended this dogma by maintaining that art for art's sake was also art for society's sake. ("This civilization of ours . . . can only be saved by a change of heart . . . a change that can only be brought about . . . by the artist.") Meanwhile, egotism and a kind of effervescent energy kept him producing book after book, books shaped by personal whims and literary fashions. His emotions were fundamentally decent, I think, but, as you can readily see if you compare him with the men he writes about, he had no intellectual center. Their philosophies were often inarticulate—more so than his—but they knew, deep down, where they were going, and he never did—and still doesn't.

So it happens that Ford has written many bad books, and a few good books that aren't quite good enough, and a number of old books under new titles. In *Portraits from Life,* he talks about authors who have been ruined by a Cause, and undoubtedly authors have been ruined by a Cause. It seems to me, however, that their ruins are more impressive than Mr. Ford's.

April 27, 1937

Dicken's Indictment of Victorian Society

Charles Dickens: The Progress of a Radical, by T. A. Jackson

To certain academic critics—e.g., George Saintsbury—Dickens' concern with social problems was a deplorable blemish on his work. Forster, in the official biography, made as little as he could of the novelist's powerful discontent with society. Walter Crotch and G. K. Chesterton suggested that he was concerned only with specific evils, not with the social structure. Even George Gissing, who said some very sensible things, reduced Dickens' social views to Christian charity. It has remained for T. A. Jackson not only to remind us that Dickens was a Radical in the political sense but also to prove that his social radicalism was far-reaching and persistent.

Unfortunately, Mr. Jackson has not presented his thesis in the most persuasive form, for he has adopted an expository method that results in repetition and confusion. He devotes his first one hundred pages to what he calls "Dickens' Development in General," setting forth Dickens' major ideas in their relation to the time in which he lived, and illustrating the various points from the various novels. In the next section, "Dickens' Work Considered in Detail," he reviews all the novels in chronological order, giving long and rather confusing outlines of each, and necessarily duplicating to a considerable extent what he has previously said. And his concluding section, "Dickens' Outlook as a Whole," goes over much the same ground.

If the result is not altogether easy reading, the conclusions are nonetheless important. Everyone knows that Dickens considered himself a Radical. The Radicals wanted to push on, after the Reform Bill of 1832, to the further extension of the suffrage and the establishment of their ideal of democracy. After 1848, however, the Radicals, as well as the Chartists and the Communists, seemed to have been defeated, not only in England but throughout Europe. The triumph of reaction in England went hand in hand with prosperity, for England was so far advanced industrially that the free-trade policy of being the workshop of the world could succeed. Minor reforms were adopted, but the democratic drive petered out.

In the years after the Great Exhibition of 1851 most of the Radicals lapsed into luke-warm liberalism, and it is usually held that Dickens was one of them. Jackson shows that this is not true. He divides Dickens' work into three periods: before 1842, between 1842 and 1850, after 1850. In the first period, he maintains, Dickens was a typical petty-bourgeois Radical—optimistic, confident of accomplishing certain specific reforms as steps to true democracy, opposed to the physical-force Chartists, inclined to rely on the benevolence of employers rather than on the action of the working class. The second period—which I think Mr. Jackson is less successful in characterizing—marked a kind of transition, the loss of facile optimism. The last period exhibited distress over the triumph of reaction, combined with intense hatred of the reactionaries. Though he did not see how change was to be accomplished, Dickens' sense of the need for change, according to Jackson, was so strong that "with a little outside aid it might easily have emerged as positive Socialism or Communism."

Most critics would agree with what Jackson says about the novels Dickens wrote before 1850, but they would quarrel with his comments on the third period. The novels of this period are *Bleak House, Hard Times, Little Dorrit, A Tale of Two Cities, Great Expectations,* and *Our Mutual Friend. Bleak House,* Mr. Jackson points out, is an attack not only on the law but also on vested interests in general. *Hard Times* satirizes and denounces the Manchester school of economics. *Little Dorrit* describes the injustices of society—the suffering of the poor and the success of the callous rich. *A Tale of Two Cities,* by showing how injustice once led to revolution, is a warning to the ruling classes. *Great Expectations* and *Our Mutual Friend* exhibit the folly and stupidity of the Victorian bourgeoisie.

Hostile critics would, I am afraid, have some basis for maintaining that, in treating these novels, Jackson has exaggerated Dickens' revolutionary tendencies, for he overlooks some passages that do not fit his thesis. For example, in speaking of *Hard Times,* perhaps Dickens' most explicit novel, he dismisses the treatment of the union organizer as a kind of inexplicable lapse. But it is an integral part of the conception of the book. Note the chapter in which Stephen, who has been ostracized by the workmen because he will not join the union, talks with Bounderby, his employer. Bounderby criticizes the organizer, and Stephen replies: "I'm as sorry as you, sir, when the people's leaders is bad. They take such as offers. Haply, 'tis not the smallest of their misfortunes when they can get no better." And Stephen ends the interview by urging that employers take an intelligent interest in their workmen.

Jackson admits that Dickens had earlier placed his faith in employers of good will, but insists that he outgrew this attitude after 1842. It seems to me clear that he never grew beyond it. In *A Tale of Two Cities* Dickens is arguing, as Carlyle argued in *The French Revolution,* that the revolution was a punishment visited upon the upper classes because of their failure to serve the interests of the masses. Indeed, I see no evidence that Dickens ever outgrew Carlyle's influence. He never emphasized the purely reactionary side of Carlyle's doctrines, as Carlyle himself came to do, and he remained closer to the masses of the people, but he believed to the end that salvation must come from the top down.

Yet, for all this, there is a fundamental truth in Jackson's study. He says at the end: "It is no doubt true that Dickens never fully realized the cumulative force of his own indictment of bourgeois society. Hence he did not draw the theoretical conclusions that, to us, seem to have been staring him in the face." My only quarrel with Jackson is that he sometimes attributes those "theoretical conclusions" to Dickens when he has no basis for doing so. But the indictment of bourgeois society is there, and it is very much to Jackson's credit that he has given a clearer account of it than we have ever had before. That indictment has been obscured by the critics, but, as Jackson says, the people have not failed to recognize Dickens as their spokesman.

One merit of the book is that Jackson has kept his attention sharply focused on Dickens' novels, which he has obviously read and re-read with understanding and affection. He says all that needs to be said about the social background, but he never forgets that Dickens is his theme. Perhaps the literary background deserved more attention, but a more detailed discussion of such writers as Carlyle, Ruskin, Mrs. Gaskell, and Kingsley would not have altered Jackson's conclusions. Other authors began, as Dickens did, with warm humanitarian ideals, but Dickens clung to them all his life, and, as Jackson makes clear, he could not be true to them without in some measure outgrowing them. In his feeling about contemporary society Dickens came amazingly close to being a revolutionist, and it is Jackson's distinction that he has established this point once and for all.

May 31, 1938

Studies of Reputations

The Writings of E. M. Forster, by Rose Macaulay
The Life of D. H. Lawrence, by Hugh Kingsmill

Both of these books are studies of reputations, but beyond that they have little in common. One might, indeed, say that Miss Macaulay's aim is to show why E. M. Forster does deserve his reputation, whereas Mr. Kingsmill wants to prove that D. H. Lawrence doesn't deserve his. Neither, it may be pointed out at once, succeeds.

Mr. Forster published the first of his five novels in 1905 and the fifth in 1924. In spite, however, of his long silences, he has a curiously strong position in the affections of a not inconsiderable number of readers and in the opinions of his fellow-craftsmen. The work he has done commands respect, and, furthermore, even at nearly sixty, he gives the sense of impressive possibilities. More than twenty years ago one knew what to expect from Wells, say, or Galsworthy or Bennett. One still does not know what to expect from Mr. Forster.

That is Miss Macaulay's theme, and it is a worthy one. Her treatment of it, unfortunately, is less commendable. As she treats each of Forster's books in turn, mingling summaries and comments, one notes with pleasure how good the summaries are, but the comments are marked with a coyness that is almost paralyzing. Even her shrewder observations do not seem to get her anywhere. We gather that she likes the five novels Forster has written, and wishes he would write another. That is where she starts, and that, to all intents and purposes, is where she finishes.

Aimlessness is not one of the vices with which Mr. Kingsmill can be charged. His professed purpose is to take all the many books that have been written about Lawrence and reduce the facts to a clear pattern. Actually there is, behind the smooth pretense of impartiality, as deadly a hatred as has made itself felt in recent criticism. Mr. Kingsmill's violence of feeling can be compared only with that which inspired Malcolm Muggeridge's attack on Samuel Butler, and it may be worth noting that Messrs. Muggeridge and Kingsmill have at times been collaborators. Kingsmill has written some amusing, if malicious, books, notably his biography of Frank Harris, and he might have done good work in puncturing the Lawrence legend—

if he had not been so determined to demolish Lawrence himself.

Regarding Lawrence as both dangerous and contemptible, he attributes his viciousness to two qualities: his sexual incompetence and his materialism. By no means clear when he talks of Lawrence's psychological peculiarities, he becomes little less than asinine when he discusses "will" and "spirit." In any case, however, one cannot take his psychological and philosophical excursions seriously, for he obviously has no interest in objective analysis. Always he attributes to Lawrence the worst motives imaginable, and he conducts his whole argument with the aid of innuendo.

Only the idolatrous few will deny that Kingsmill is occasionally correct. The picture of Lawrence and his followers that emerges from the memoirs of the latter is, to put it mildly, disillusioning. Oscar Wilde once said, "Every great man nowadays has his disciples, and it is always Judas who writes the biography." Lawrence's apostolic band seems to have been composed almost equally of Judases and jackasses, both articulate, and between them they not only have provided plenty of material for a Kingsmill but have intensified the doubts of more dispassionate students. Yet, when one grants all of Lawrence's weaknesses, the frequency with which he transcended them becomes the more remarkable. He was often a fool and sometimes, in his muddled way, a dangerous reactionary, but to say merely that is not, as Kingsmill would like us to believe, to do Lawrence justice.

Compared with Kingsmill's book, Miss Macaulay's seems innocuous and almost commendable. Yet, if its inadequacies are not so shocking, they are nonetheless regrettable. Both Lawrence and Forster deserve better books. Vastly dissimilar in temperament, they have certain similarities in outlook—compare, for example, *Where Angels Fear to Tread* and *The Lost Girl*—that ought not to be ignored. Both of them say something significant about and for our times. What it is Mr. Kingsmill has not tried to ask, and Miss Macaulay has indulged only in random surmises.

November 8, 1938

A Writer in Action

Sirocco, by Ralph Bates

In this moment of Spain's agony, in this moment of dedication to unceasing struggle, Ralph Bates' *Sirocco and Other Stories* appears as appropriately as *The Olive Field* did, in the first month of the rebellion. As *The Olive Field,* written before the electoral success of the People's Front, helped us to understand that democratic victory and the peril in which it stood, so *Sirocco* moves with the spirit of the people's battle. Bates gives us here the invincible Spain.

Though most of its stories concern revolution and war, and though it is certainly born of the long struggle of loyalist Spain, *Sirocco* is an impressively impartial book. I can find in it no trace of bitterness. The earlier stories show the exploitation of the peasants, as the later give us glimpses of fascist cruelty, but Bates never piles up an indictment or even underscores an accusation. He has consciously avoided sensationalism, even when sensationalism would be absolutely truthful. He is looking for something in the lives of the Spanish people more fundamental than their sufferings, and for something deeper in the revolutionary movement than the mere righting of wrongs.

I wonder if a lesser writer than Bates could afford to give such an impression of impartiality, and if a writer who had not fought in Spain would dare to do it. Bates does not have to prove his partisanship in books. His years in the Spanish labor movement and months in the Spanish army have taught the world where he stands. When, as in "The Yoke," he portrays fascists, he does not have to hate them and make a show of his hatred, for he has given proof of his resistance to them and their ways. He has won the right to understand them and even to pity them a little. Pity is dangerous only when it weakens the will, and who does not know that the will of Ralph Bates cannot be weakened?

Sirocco suggests, as Malraux's *Man's Hope* has already suggested, that in our time great literature is most likely to be given us by writers who have learned to act or by men of action who have learned to write. The problem of the writer is always to find a vantage point from which he can see clearly, and today that vantage point seems to be in the midst of the battle. On the surface it appears that Bates and Malraux can write so well of the Spanish war because they know what they are talking about, and to a certain extent that is true. But they have gained a psychological advantage as well by their participation. They know what they believe because they have put their beliefs to the test, and they do not have to argue about them. They have no need for apologetics or polemics. They can let experience speak for itself, for their kind of experience—and perhaps only their kind of experience today—speaks convincingly.

In other ways, of course, they are quite unlike. Malraux is interested in the revolutionary spirit, whether he finds it in China, in Germany, or in Spain, for he sees that spirit as the noblest and truest manifestation of human nature in the contemporary world. Bates, on the other hand, looks for the roots of the revolutionary movement, the basic human aspirations out of which it springs. The difference is suggested in their attitudes towards comradeship. To Malraux it is a difficult and infinitely valuable achievement. Bates finds it just as valuable, but sees it as quite natural, something that has been made difficult, perhaps, but that can be and should be easy. Malraux finds in revolution a flowering of the human spirit. Bates sees in the daily lives of simple people the possibilities that sanctify revolt.

For Malraux the revolutionary spirit transcends national boundaries. Bates would not deny this, but he is always concerned with its appearance in a particular locality. "A good revolutionary," says Andreu in the title story, "must have a sense of locality; I mean that he should know and love the country he works in, the *little* country. The valley he tills, he must sing in it and listen to its peculiar echoes; the village whose gardens he tends, he must be concerned not only for its material welfare, but its decorum, its dignity; he should resent vulgarization of its tales, of its music, or even of the cry of its night watchmen. He must, in fishing a coast, know more than the reefs, the depths of the sea's bottom, and the mysterious currents, but the habits of mind and the hearts of the men who fish there. By such a love a man may be lifted above mere obstinacy in opinion, or dry, crackling fanaticism, and revolutionary passion will not be egotism with him. For him, revolutionary creation will be the unfolding and the nourishing, the bringing to perfection, of what good the past has created, or as near to perfection as carters, weavers, melon growers, and fishers can hope to arrive."

Bates found his little country in Spain many years ago. He could have found it as well, I think, in Mexico or the United States or even in his native England. His impulse is always to identify himself with men in their daily lives, and his success in this gives his tales their beauty. Malraux went to Spain because there was the revolution. Bates was in Spain, and as soon as the civil war began fought side by side with his people. And he writes about them as he fought beside them, without self-consciousness and with complete integrity.

His tales are mostly of fishermen and peasants, of how a boat was launched or a field planted, of how a prostitute longed for her home or a woman died in childbirth. Of the three long stories, one tells about a revolutionary hiding away in a Catalonian village, the second describes a Catholic doctor in Franco's territory, the third is the tale of an undisciplined scout in the Pyrenees. Bates knows them all, knows them intimately, and his knowledge is a marvel. In "43rd Division," for example, the account of Pere's climbing the mountain is a fine piece of writing, so tense that it becomes almost unbearable, but even more remarkable is the utter rightness of what goes on in the man as he carries on his single-handed campaign. This is the work of a great artist, and of a man who has seen much and been no small part of what he has seen.

Bates, as even my brief quotation shows, is not a careful writer. On the good side, it may be pointed out that he suffers from none of the inhibitions that have so many of his contemporaries tied up in knots. He knows what he wants to say, and says it without embarrassment or difficulty. On the other hand, though he often writes with great beauty, he sometimes writes awkwardly or even obscurely. It would be pointless, however, to recommend critical revision. What one feels, watching the growth of his work, is that he will mend his faults in his own way. His flow, which—fortunately and amazingly in this age of crabbed and stammering authorship—does not diminish, does become purer.

I could go on, exploring this aspect and that of Bates's work, but I should always come back to the man himself. I went to meet him for the first time in a railroad station, and asked how I should recognize him. A friend said, "Watch for the man who looks least like a novelist and least like an officer in the International Brigade, and that will be Ralph." It was. And as, in the days that followed, to the author and the soldier was added the musician, the student of Joyce and Proust, the labor organizer, the authority on art, and, above all else, the warmhearted companion, the wonder grew. But at the heart of every new manifestation of Ralph Bates was his devotion to the cause for which he had fought in Spain and was ready to fight for anywhere in the world. And at the heart of that devotion was the wisest understanding of men and the sincerest participation in their hopes I have ever met. These are the qualities of *Sirocco*.

February 14, 1939

V

EUROPEAN WRITERS

Hicks did not review much continental fiction. For this reason I have grouped this diverse collection of writers under one heading. Ilya Ehrenbourg and Mikhail Sholokhov were Soviet writers of differing talents and concerns. The essay on Marcel Proust is the most significant piece in this section.

Sean O'Faolain, an Irish writer, has been placed in this section although some may feel he should have been included with the British writers. Despite some indebtedness, Irish literature has its own traditions and variations and should be considered apart. O'Faolain, unfortunately, has not lived up to the promise of some of his early stories.

A Nest of Reviewers

A Nest of Simple Folk, by Sean O'Faolain

The chorus of praise for Sean O'Faolain's *A Nest of Simple Folk* has been extraordinary, especially when one considers what the reviewers have praised and what they have not. Perhaps the most amazing review of all was J. Donald Adams' in the Sunday Times. Mr. Adams ended his little piece with the inspired suggestion that Marxist critics ought to read O'Faolain's book in order to realize that their talk about proletarian literature was misguided. This, as Robert Cantwell has pointed out, would be magnificently impudent if it were not so obviously stupid, for O'Faolain, in Cantwell's phrase, "is nothing if he is not a poet of the revolution."

Cantwell is, of course, quite right, and it is illuminating to ponder on the insensitivity or the prejudice that led to the reviewers' failure to perceive or unwillingness to admit this simple fact. The novel is primarily the story of Leo Foxe-Donnel, but it is also the story of three generations of the Irish and of three attempts at revolt. In the first part Leo, ruined financially and morally by his family's desire to ape the British squirarchy, throws himself into the Fenian movement of 1867. Jailed for ten years, he is finally released and enjoys for a time, during the era of Parnell, a taste of public esteem. But hard times come, and, after a vain struggle against eviction, he loses his estate—to his avaricious brother—and goes to Rathkeale. Once more he joins the movement of revolt, this time in alliance with his illegitimate son, Johno, is betrayed by his nephew, Johnny Hussey, a policeman, and spends five years in jail. Again he moves, this time to Dublin; again he is drawn into rebellion; again he is betrayed; and he dies on Easter Monday, 1916.

This is by no means all the story, but it is unmistakably the novel's central theme. Built around this theme are many effective evocations of Irish character and Irish life. Leo shares the first part with his mother, and the opening scene, in which she forces her dying husband to write his will, is perhaps the finest in the book. The whole of Book I, with its portrayal of the struggle between English and Irish, between town and city, between the old gentry and the new capitalistic landlords, is an admirable example of the way in which complex social forces may be revealed in the attitudes and actions of such simple folk as the book deals with. In the second and third parts Leo divides the reader's interest with Johnny Hussey, who is from one point of view an admirable and substantial supporter of law and order, and from another—which is obviously O'Faolain's—a blackguard and a spy. Superficially, the victory on that bloody Monday is with Sergeant Hussey, but his son turns in disgust against him just as the book ends. Thus the revolutionary motif, furnishing the novel's climax, gives it its unity.

Cantwell is fully justified in calling this a revolutionary novel, but I think he has not been careful enough—either in his Sean O'Faolain review or in his recent article on Joyce—to distinguish among revolutionary traditions and aims. Today the vital revolutionary force in Ireland is the radicalized working class, which has been repeatedly betrayed by the bourgeois nationalists. O'Faolain's sympathies, however, seem to lie with the nineteenth century form of nationalism. Perhaps that is why he is so much more successful in Book I in evoking the actual social forces that are expressed in Leo Foxe-Donnel's actions. In '67 the agrarian nationalist movement was, as Marx pointed out, truly revolutionary, and O'Faolain not only reveals the bases of that movement but effectively recreates the emotions that attended it. He is nowhere near so successful in his accounts of later revolts, and his characters move merely on the margin, so far as the readers can judge, of the 1916 rebellion.

It seems to me that the reviewers, Cantwell among them, have exaggerated the values for O'Faolain of the literary tradition of which he is heir. The peculiar position of Irish writers, poised, as it were, between two languages, has made them uncommonly conscious of linguistic problems. Ever since Synge returned from his exile, the authors of Ireland have been trying to invent a language of their own. Not unnaturally this effort has resulted in a deepening of sensibility as well as an improvement of expression. But too often this sensibility has been operative only under rather special circumstances. It has resulted in the amazingly complete expression of certain kinds of experience, but these experiences have often been relatively unimportant. The worst example of misdirected sensibility is Francis Stuart, but Joyce is not wholly free from guilt, and O'Faolain illustrates how easily such delicacy can degenerate into mere decorative facility. Cantwell, it is true, points out the dangers of such a gift for creating atmosphere, but he seems unaware of the extent to which the virtues and defects of O'Faolain's style spring from the same sources.

Thus we come back to Mr. Adams of the *Times*. There are two questions I should like to raise. First, are any of the genuine virtues of *A Nest of Simple Folk* incompatible with a thoroughly (i.e., a Marxian, a Communist) revolutionary attitude? The answer is no. The variety of scenes and characters, the sureness of characterization, the effectiveness of the human revelation of social forces, all these are virtues that would be hailed by the Marxian critics, who have repeatedly lamented the absence of such qualities in various proletarian novels. The second question is this: are there any virtues lacking in *A Nest of Simple Folk* that a truly revolutionary attitude might have supplied? The two preceding paragraphs suggest the answer: a clearer and more sustained understanding of the play of social forces and a more determined avoidance of mere embroidery would make this the great novel that the critics call it; and these are precisely the virtues with which Communism could endow an author.

February 6, 1934

Men of Iron

Out of Chaos, by Ilya Ehrenbourg

Ehrenbourg begins: "The men possessed the will and the despair—they held out. The animals retreated." Construction at Kuznetsk was commencing: "Men came from all the four corners of the land. . . . In Moscow this was called the Five-Year Plan. Moscow planned, and Moscow did not budge. . . . Over the country railway engines strained to the bursting point. An anguished whistle issued from their breasts: do what they could, they could never keep pace with man. . . . Two hundred and twenty thousand men were engaged on the construction work there. Day and night workmen built barracks, but of these there were never sufficient . . . Men lived as in a war. They blasted stones, felled trees, and stood up to their waist in icy water, fortifying the dam . . . Fly-by-nights came to the construction works. They received boots and coat, and decamped for another construction works. . . . The road-paving brigade smashed the record. . . . On April fourth the fires in the first blast-furnace were lighted."

At the end Ehrenbourg writes: "From Kuznetsk men went to Mondy-Bash. From Mondy-Bash some pushed on to Temir-Tau, others went to Telbess. Men were plentiful in the land and the taiga yielded a few yards every day." These men spoke of the civilization and quiet of Kuznetsk. They fought in spring to hold back the rivers. May Day came, and Shukhaiev spoke: "We must remember the words of Lenin: Lenin said that iron was the chief foundation of our civilization. We must see to it that the Kuznetsk Giant is adequately supplied with our Siberian ore." The veteran Samushkin "faltered his sentences, stammered, mopped his forehead with his sleeve. But he spoke with feeling, and the workers listened to him." He concluded, "With such men we shall get iron, too, because they are stronger than iron. As an old Red irregular, I say to you that now I can die in peace, because, comrades, we have real men."

The fight against chaos is Ehrenbourg's theme, and the molding of character in that fight. Among the many who come to Kuznetsk is Kolka, a bored youth from Sverdlovsk. Kolka becomes a leader, a fighter. He becomes a man, with a brain and a will. Volodia Safonov, on the other hand, attends classes in Tomsk and writes in his notebook: "If I had lived a hundred years ago I should have been perfectly adjusted. I should have despised men as I do now. But they could have been creatures of my own species. It is impossible, of course, to despise the bees or the rain." He, too, goes to Kuznetsk, chiefly because he is in love with Irina, who has left Tomsk to teach the children of the Kuznetsk workers. But Irina is in love with Kolka. Volodia's nihilism leads Tolia Kuzmin to sabotage. Volodia goes home and hangs himself.

There are other characters in abundance—too many, some critics will say. But Ehrenbourg is not writing about the eternal triangle; he is concerned with men and women under the first Five-Year Plan. He does not isolate Kolka, Irina, and Volodia; on every side other lives touch theirs. And all these lives are being shaped by such a revolution as the world has never seen before. There is chaos in the book, just as there is chaos in the Russia Ehrenbourg describes, but out of the chaos order is coming. It is Ehrenbourg's ability to recognize the forces that are creating order that gives his book its unity. Confused and undirected as the various lives he portrays seem, they have a historic meaning that he perceives and communicates to his readers.

His achievement is all the more striking because he insists on treating his characters in terms of their intimate personal problems. His book is less objective than Kataev's *Time, Forward!* and is therefore not so stirring but more memorable. What particularly impresses one is the realization that, though personal problems obviously exist in the Soviet Union, they are essentially new problems. In Irina's love for Kolka there are factors that could not exist in a capitalist country. Varia's unhappiness, when Glotov leaves her, is a very real unhappiness, but it is complicated—and alleviated—by emotions and attitudes that only the revolution could have made possible. Even Volodia, though his antecedents are recognizable enough, is by no means a character out of Dostoyevsky; his *Weltschmerz* has a peculiar tinge, for he is not only a misfit but also a misfit in a world in which misfits have become anachronistic.

Other writers have suggested some of the new qualities of life in the Soviet Union, but they have taken them so much for granted that they have failed to make them clear. Ehrenbourg, perhaps because he has spent so much time outside of Russia, has managed to communicate to western readers his understanding. This alone would make his novel one of the most important, for us, that the Soviet Union has produced.

June 5, 1934

Proust And The Proletariat

The Remembrance of Things Past, by Marcel Proust

The Remembrance of Things Past has recently been issued in a very impressive and satisfying new format by Random House. Among bourgeois critics there seems general agreement that Proust is the greatest of modern writers, and Marxian critics will, I think, concede that in literature he is the supreme contemporary representative of his class. Will Proust be read after the revolution? The question invites more than idle speculation, for the answer depends on our view of his value today.

We should, first of all, be prepared to assert that it would be neither surprising nor particularly shocking if Proust was to be forgotten. After all, many men have passed into oblivion who were hailed as geniuses in their own age and by their own class. For that matter, many writers of the past whom we still honor as great masters actually survive because of their positions in textbooks and college curricula and not because of any widespread appetite for their works. The histories are full of names that are only names to all but the professional scholars, and even the scholars read the books with a minimum of enthusiasm. No one can expect that Proust will live forever, and his day may be briefer than his admirers suppose.

If Proust does survive, it will not be for the reasons that his admirers give. They speak, for example, of his revelation of fundamental truths of human nature. But Proust himself, more than any other writer I can think of, explicitly repudiates such a claim. It is the very essence of his view of human character that it is changing and that even our understanding of it is relative to our own interests. I do not mean that he even dimly perceives the Marxian conception of class division, but he is quite well aware of the fact that what his people do and say, and even the way they feel, is conditioned by particular circumstances. And, indeed, without Proust's recognition of this fact, we should be driven by common sense to admit it. Who could maintain that most persons in love are like Swann and the narrator, to whose love affairs so much of the work is devoted? Who could regard either Robert de Santi-Loup or the Baron de Charlus as representative of anything but a particular small class? There are books, it is true, that superficially seem to refute Marxian theory by appearing to portray Man, rather than men of different classes, but *The Remembrance of Things Past* is not one of them.

Nor do I think it can be more successfully maintained that it is Proust's philosophy that gives his work its value. That philosophy, when it is specifically stated in the last volume, *The Past Recovered*, is seen to rest upon a curiously mystical conception of time. It is a philosophy that has a special appeal to artists, for it ingeniously affirms that the artist's reconstruction of past experience is the only reality; but even artists cannot, except under rare circumstances, live by it. It is obviously both the product and the defense of Proust's peculiar way of life, of the detachment that was dictated by his disease, made possible by his private income, and dignified by his art. The sudden emergence of the past into the present, provoked by the right kind of stimulus, is not a rare occurrence, and most of us have had Proustian memories, but even his most devoted disciples fight a little shy of the elaborate philosophy he based on this simple experience.

No, we turn to Proust for the picture he gives us of the life led by certain kinds of people in a particular period of history. *The Remembrance of Things Past* is not like the ordinary novel of social life, the novel of Dickens or Thackeray, of Balzac or Zola, of Howells or James, but it does exactly the same sort of thing. Proust has found a way of showing us his characters from many points of view instead of only one. We see Mme. Verdurin, for example, not only in several stages of her career but also as she appeared to several different persons. We know more about his people than we know about people in most novels. He probes deeply, and he looks at them from all sides. But what we are chiefly aware of is that, taken together, all these varied revelations of a great variety of persons form a picture, an extraordinarily full and detailed picture, of a certain society.

And the most important thing about this society is that it is in decay. There is a great deal of evidence to show that Proust was a snob, that he placed an almost ludicrously high value on his associations with the aristocracy. But, as not infrequently happens, the writer was better than the man. He was sometimes deceived by the false standards of the class with which he tried to identify himself, but by and large he saw through its pretenses. Not only are his aristocrats personally unattractive; they are ineffectual and most of them stupid.

Even those whom he treats with most tenderness, the Duchesse de Guermantes, for example, or Robert de Saint-Loup, constantly betray weaknesses, and the aristocrat whom he portrays in most detail, Charlus, is by turns hideous and ridiculous in his decadence. The characters who come from "the people," though in no sense class-conscious, are all stronger and finer than the Guermantes and their kind. And at the end of the work the complete collapse of the aristocracy is symbolized in the nauseating corruption of Charlus and in the rise of the petty-bourgeois social-climber, Mme. Verdurin, to the rank of Princesse de Guermantes.

It is true that Proust gives us no idea of the causes of this collapse. We never see how the aristocracy is linked to French industry and finance by marriages and investments. We discover neither how the aristocracy is being swallowed by monopoly capitalism nor by what methods it has preserved itself as long as it has. Though the esthetes will howl at the suggestion, I believe that the *The Remembrance of Things Past* would be a greater work if Proust had followed the Guermantes out of the salons and bedrooms into the fields and factories that support them. He has told only part of the story, and it is a very important part that is left untold.

But what he has done, he has done superbly well. Thanks to an independent income and certain more or less accidental acquaintanceships, he was permitted to see the aristocracy at the closest possible range. At the same time, and despite his snobbish longings, he was detached from this class by family position, by race, by his illness, and by the seriousness with which he took his literary functions. Detachment from a decadent class is a virtue when it brings freedom from the artifices and illusions with which that class consoles and deceives itself. Proust was in that sense detached from the class that he made his theme, and that is why he saw as much as he did.

All this will, I believe, be understood even more clearly in a post-revolutionary society than it is today, and *The Remembrance of Things Past* will be valued as a unique record of a kind of life that is fortunately extinct. Other kinds of insight than Proust's will be recognized as necessary to a complete understanding of that life, but his extraordinary sensitivity to certain sorts of experience will be appreciated. I do not think he will be chosen as a model by Communist writers; they will see too clearly that his methods are indissolubly part of an attitude towards art and life that they could not possibly recapture and certainly would not want to. But there will be readers who will want to participate in the life of the bygone age, that they better understand their own age and themselves, and they will read Proust with enjoyment and profit, though not, I suspect, without moments of acute disgust.

Today, however, I should hesitate to recommend *The Remembrance of Things Past* to a mechanic or a longshoreman or a farmer. Not only does the reading of the work take time that might better be devoted to Marx and Lenin; it requires a kind of preparation that, in our society, workers can seldom have; and it serves a function that is not immediately important for the worker. But for the revolutionary intellectual Proust seems to me required reading. It is important, not for its deadening mysticism, not for its caressing style, not for its fascinating technique, but for its revelation of the decadence of the society that has nurtured the intellectual and that still, in all probability, holds him with a hundred ties. He cannot break with bourgeois society unless he wholly understands it, and that Proust, with all his ignorance and inadequacy, helps him to do.

November 20, 1934

Not All of Briffault

Europa, by Robert Briffault

Although there is an "I" in this story, he serves no apparent purpose, and it seems clear that Julian Bern, the central character, is nearer to Mr. Briffault than is the inconspicuous and unimportant narrator. It is through Bern's eyes that the reader sees Europe from the beginning of the century to the outbreak of the war. Brought up in Italy, given a year at a British public school, trained in biology at Cambridge, Bern breaks away from the traditions of the English ruling class. Shedding one illusion after another, he comes to realize that European civilization is ready for collapse, and he sees vaguely that the hope of the future lies with the working class. But, though he is inspired by the sincerity and clarity of such working-class leaders as Jean Jaures, Tom Mann and Karl Liebknecht, and though he identifies himself momentarily with a group of striking coal miners in England, he cannot cross the class barrier. In August, 1914, he stands ready to join the German radicals in their anticipated struggle against war, but the socialist vote for war credits disillusions him and he takes flight with his mistress.

The story of Bern's education is told against a background of cosmopolitan upper-class life, the amusements, vices and intrigues of aristocrats of twenty nations. In beautifully-documented detail Briffault shows us the bankruptcy of the ruling class. The steady procession through the pages of *Europa* of people with titles naturally suggests *The Remembrance of Things Past*. It is a good deal to ask of any novel that it bear comparison with Proust's masterpiece, but the contrast is illuminating. Briffault is a Marxist and understands the causes of European decay far better than Proust ever did, but he is vastly less successful in making the reader aware of that decay as an actual process. It is true that Proust is working on a larger scale and has single scenes—for example the Verdurins' party in *The Captive* —that are almost half as long as *Europa,* but the difference is not merely one of length. One of Proust's briefest scenes makes us more conscious of the manifestations of social rottenness than the whole of Briffault's novel.

It is symptomatic that there is not a single character in *Europa,* not even Julian Bern, who makes a sharp impression as a human being. The Italian, Russian, French, German and British nobles seem curiously alike. Probably, as a matter of fact, they were; but it is Proust's peculiar virtue that he exhibits the bankruptcy of his aristocrats not only in the more superficial qualities that they have in common, but also in the elusive traits that distinguish one from another. Briffault lacks this sense of character, and he lacks as well, though there are brilliant bits of description, Proust's startling awareness of places. He has not, in short, the sensibilities of a poet.

Yet *Europa* is a book with virtues of its own, virtues that must be called, with no sense of disparagement, journalistic. I vastly prefer Mr. Briffault's informed, intelligent journalism to the wretched soul-searching and the secondhand sensibilities of most of the "poetic" novelists. The sense of journalism is, of course, enhanced by the introduction of historical personages, from Nietzsche to Mussolini, **D. H. Lawrence** and Henry James. But it is not merely these informal glimpses of the great that make one feel that this is a piece of immensely clever reporting; the whole spectacle of international aristocratic society is set down with the quick assurance of a man who knows news values. Good journalism is by no means to be despised in the novel, and the journalism in *Europa* is so good that it raises it far above most of the novels of the year. I can think of only one recent novel that is comparable to *Europa* on its own grounds, and that is Leo Lania's *Land of Promise,* which is just as skillfully journalistic but reveals a much less informed and active intellect.

I wonder, however, in spite of my admiration for *Europa,* if the novel is the form that best employs Briffault's talents. In *Redder Than the Rose,* which Briffault reviewed so shrewdly in the *New Masses,* Robert Forsythe has a suggestive discussion of the novel. He points out that there are a number of first-rate autobiographies that might have been bad novels and innumerable mediocre novels that could have been first-rate autobiographies. The essay, however, is not primarily a plea for autobiography, but a call for a new form that will permit the full utilization of all of an author's resources.

Europa is completely a case in point. I was struck, for example, by the banality of the dialogue and the general lack of stylistic distinction. I have always thought of Briffault as a brilliant writer, but I caught only flashes of his brilliance in *Europa.* Glancing at the new edition of *Breakdown,* I discovered the explanation. Briffault is a rhetorician, a master of eloquent exposition and argumentation. Would it not have been infinitely better if he had handled the material in *Europa*—material out of his own experience that it was very important to record—in a form that would have permitted him to use his rhetorical skill instead of cramping himself by employing conventional narrative and dialogue? More important, would it not have been better if he could have utilized his vast intellectual equipment? He is an eminent scientist, one of the few Marxists in the western world whose Marxism has a scientific foundation. (Reading *Anti-Dühring,* one realizes how important that is.) How much of his scientific Marxist insight he had to shut out of *Europa* because the novel-form had no place for it!

These are somewhat ungracious reflections on an exciting and illuminating novel. I hope they will deter no one from reading *Europa.*

If much of Briffault is omitted, there is enough of the man in the book to make it rewarding reading. But all of Briffault is not here, and if the novel will not contain all of a Briffault, then, within limits of course, Forsythe is right—"Down with the novel!"

September 10, 1935

An Epic of Collectivization

Seeds of Tomorrow, by Mikhail Sholokhov

Seeds of Tomorrow is one of the novels that make us realize how life is being changed in the Soviet Union. Karl Radek has hailed it as vastly superior to its predecessor, *And Quiet Flows the Don.* The majority of American critics, it is safe to predict, will not like it anywhere near so well. The truth is, I suspect, that generations of Russian novelists had prepared us to appreciate *And Quiet Flows the Don,* which innumerable critics compared—quite justly—with Tolstoy's *War and Peace. Seeds of Tomorrow,* however, deals with the new Russia, which we find harder to understand. It is, as Radek calls it, the epic of collectivization, a subject about which most of us know vastly little. In the Soviet Union, on the other hand, every detail of Sholokhov's novel is fresh and significant and comprehensible.

One gathers from Radek's article, published in *Literature of the Peoples of the U.S.S.R.,* a special number of Voks Illustrated Almanac, that the critics of the Soviet Union were a little impatient with *And Quiet Flows the Don.* They recognized the power of this vast panorama of the Cossacks in war, peace and revolution, but its events seemed a little remote from them. The Soviet world was changing so rapidly that they and perhaps the vast majority of readers were less interested in the decade from 1910 to 1920 than they were in the new decade that was beginning, the nineteen-thirties.

Sholokhov, though probably he knew well enough why it was necessary for him, as an artist, to tell the story of life in which he had his own roots, could see the critics' point. He, too, was aware of the importance of the battle for collectivization and of its potentialities as a literary theme. Like other Soviet authors, he refused to accept the dictum that only what is dead can come to life in art. He wanted to portray the present and influence the future. But he was wise enough not to try any short-cuts. "Some of our writers," Radek states, "unable to fix on their canvas the stormy flow of events, have tried to grasp life by means of the photograph or by superficial essays. Sholokhov took another course: he gave a large canvas of the great struggle for collectivization in richly profound artistic imagery."

That is the significance of *Seeds of Tomorrow*. Sholokhov realized, on the one hand, that a novel of collectivization could be built only out of what he knew and felt and understood, what, in short, he had assimilated. And, on the other hand, he realized that distortion and falsification would be quite as disastrous to the effectiveness of his book in the campaign for collectivization as they would to its literary merit. He had to immerse himself in the life he was describing so completely that the book would have the accuracy of an expert diagnosis and at the same time would be the concretely realistic story of living human beings.

The novel is laid in the village of Gremyachy Log in the Don Valley in the year 1930. The central character is Davidov, an ex-sailor and a machinist in the Putilov works, who is sent to Gremyachy by the Communist Party to expedite collectivization. His task is nothing less than to change the peasant psychology that centuries have shaped. Not only do the kulaks fight collectivization with every resource they have; even the poorest peasants, those who know how much they will gain from the kolkhoz, have to struggle against their own impulses. There is Kondrat Maidannikov, for example, a loyal supporter of the collective farm, who admits to Davidov that it breaks his heart to let his cattle become part of the common stock. And then there are the extremists, men like Nagulnov, fine, idealistic revolutionaries who are so eager that they antagonize everyone and endanger the whole enterprise. Against all this Davidov has to struggle. Davidov is no superman, but he has unlimited courage and persistence and at the end, though most of his problems are yet to be solved, the reader is confident that he will win.

The more one makes the effort to immerse oneself in the novel, the more plausible it seems that the Soviet critics are right in regarding

Seeds of Tomorrow as a better book than *And Quiet Flows the Don*. The people are just as human and the incidents just as dramatic—the slaughtering of the livestock, Nagulnov's trial, the raid on the granary and Davidov's ploughing. *And Quiet Flows the Don* is one of the strong, simple novels that deal with the stark realities of life and death. But so, one comes to realize, is *Seeds of Tomorrow*. The conditions under which men live and die are different and much less familiar, but there is magnificent strength here and the strength is being used for the sake of the future.

Every sensitive writer feels the pressure that his age exerts upon him. No writer is free: he can run away, but only by paying a price. In an era of rapid and conscious change, pressure becomes more explicit; it is not something that the writer vaguely feels but something definite and clear-cut. Under such pressure lesser talents crumble: writers adopt easy devices, become mere photographers or political teachers. But such pressure cannot damage a great talent; in fact, it makes it flourish. That is what has happened to Sholokhov. *And Quiet Flows the Don* showed that he belonged with the great Russian writers of the past. *Seeds of Tomorrow* shows that he belongs with the great Russian writers of the future. The past could not have nourished him indefinitely, but the future can.

November 26, 1935

Looking Backward

Bird Alone, by Sean O'Faolain

Not only is *Bird Alone* inferior to *A Nest of Simple Folk;* it is inferior in a disturbing way. O'Faolain's first novel painted on a broad canvas the national revolutionary movement in Ireland. It was romantic and tinged with a vague regret for the past, but it was nevertheless alive. *Bird Alone* is weak in conception and elegiac in tone. Shrewd critics might have predicted, after reading *A Nest of*

Simple Folk, that nostalgia was O'Faolain's great danger, but they could scarcely have anticipated so purely nostalgic a novel as this. When a writer does not see the past clearly, one always suspects it is because he is refusing to look squarely at the present. So many writers have succumbed to preoccupation with a fancied past, a past arbitrarily reshaped to meet subjective needs, that we are justified in feeling alarm for O'Faolain's future.

This is not to say that the young Irishman has lost his power of evocation. There are extraordinarily fine scenes in *Bird Alone:* the visit of Corney's grandfather to his school; the arrival of the news of Parnell's death; the call on the Condoorums; the trip to London to see Christy in prison. Over the streets and houses of Cork O'Faolain lingers with a fondness that is truly touching.

But the memorable scenes and the poetic richness of the style emphasize the weakness of the conception. The theme is the isolation of an individual from the life of his contemporaries through the collapse of his patriotic hopes, the loss of his religious faith, and the death of his mistress. The destruction of revolutionary dreams because of the failure of Parnell is the most movingly presented of these three motifs, but even here one feels that the Parnell episode is arbitrarily separated from Irish revolutionary history. Corney's religious disillusionment is barely sketched. And the death of Elsie is curiously unconvincing. In the end the reader does not much care what happens to Corney Crone, for Corney has about as much organic relationship to the exquisite scenes written around him as a dummy in a shop window has to the beautiful clothes it is used to exhibit.

The cruelest comment one can make on *Bird Alone* is to suggest that it be compared with *A Portrait of the Artist as a Young Man.* Twenty years ago James Joyce, looking at the Ireland of his boyhood, understood it, judged it, and made his plans for the future. Today O'Faolain looks at approximately the same Ireland—and sighs, and sighs.

September 29, 1936

VI

REVIEW AND COMMENT

In 1934 Hicks began contributing a regular column for the *New Masses* entitled "Review and Comment." Most of the pieces in this column were book reviews of a topical nature. Many, perhaps most, of the books discussed here were relevant to the issues of the middle 1930s but have not endured well. Hicks from time to time used the column to attack writers who were then favorite targets of the Party, John Chamberlain and Max Eastman for example. He also reviewed several books on Marxism in which his perspective was rather orthodox and dogmatic, if not intolerant. It is in these pieces, perhaps, that the messianic spirit of the Left in the 1930s is best (or worst) typified.

I have included in this section some essays and reviews that appeared either before the column or under strictly review format but which in form and content belong in this grouping, such as the lengthy attack Hicks made on the *New York Times Book Review* in October 1934 and a critique of *The Nation* he wrote in December 1937.

The section concludes with a long verse poem Hicks completed in April 1938, "Revolution in Bohemia." It is a delightfully malicious satire.

Of The World Revolution

International Literature, Moscow, 1933. Numbers 1–4

In the third year of publication *International Literature* (originally *Literature of the World Revolution*) gives many indications of realizing the purposes designed for it at the Kharkov conference of the International Union of Revolutionary Writers. Always indispensable because it was the only international organ of proletarian literature, the magazine has within the last year come closer to doing justice to the extent, the power, and the distinction of that literature. Its improvement is significant and satisfying because here we have the concrete manifestation of the international spirit of the revolutionary movement in its cultural expressions.

Each of the four issues published in 1933 has been arranged according to the same pattern: a section devoted to fiction, a section devoted to Soviet life, a section devoted to articles and criticism, and a section containing letters from writers, autobiographies of writers and news of the literary world. In the fiction section Russian writers have, not unnaturally, been predominant. In the course of the year *International Literature* has published extracts from works by Boris Pilnyak, N. Ognyov, L. Kassil and A. Fadayev, as well as stories by I. Babel, R. Fraierman and others. We welcome these examples of what Soviet writers are doing, for they help us to understand both the Russian scene and the progress of literature under the dictatorship of the proletariat. Certain of this material stands up very well under the ordeal of translation not only into another language but also into another world. Pilnyak's *O. K.* is inevitably interesting because it displays the reactions of his brilliant mind to our own country, but the extracts from Ognyov's *Three Dimensions* and Kassil's *Shvambrania,* which deals with Russian situations, are equally readable, and, indeed, they make one eager for the complete novels. On the other hand, certain stories have dealt so exclusively with conditions unfamiliar to us that is has been almost impossible to follow them and quite impossible to perceive their literary merits. One hopes that, in the future, the editors will bear in mind the difficulties of reading certain sorts of fiction across the barriers of language, race, and, more important, economic conditions.

The literature of other countries has not been neglected. The United States has been rather well represented with stories by Agnes Smedley, Walter Snow, Jack Conroy, and Marvin Klein, poems by Joseph Kalar, a sketch by Norman Macleod, part of Dos Passos' new play, *Fortune Heights* and letters from a good many other writers. Sketches and poems by Louis Aragon, an extract from a novel by Leon Moussinac, and a brief excerpt from Rolland's new novel speak for France; a story by Harold Heslop for England; a story by Bela Illes for Hungary; a story by F. Hayashi for Japan; and a story by Maria Gresshoner for Germany. American artists have also fared well; there have been drawings by Fred Ellis, Hugo Gellert, and Louis Lozowick. In the most recent issue Helios Gomez, a Spanish artist of the proletariat, has several drawings.

In criticism the Russians have been most active. There have been general articles by Lunacharsky, Lifschitz, and Dinamov, articles that touch on fundamental problems of Marxian esthetics. There have also been articles on particular writers: Ivasheva on Lionel Britten, Filatova on Langston Hughes, and Dinamov on Sherwood Anderson. These articles, together with Ellistratova's discussion of Italian literature under Fascism, illustrate the variety of approaches that are possible within the general framework of Marxian principles. Perhaps the most interesting and valuable critical material, however, may be found in the various letters on literary questions by Marx and Engels that have appeared with comments by F. Schiller.

The only complaint I have to make against *International Literature* is that, as yet, countries other than the Soviet Union and the United States have not been adequately represented. It seems to me that the best work that appears in the proletarian magazines of each country should be reprinted in *International Literature*. To make room for this additional material, it might be well to omit from the English edition all work by English and American authors, from the French edition all material by French authors, and so on. After all, most of the readers of the magazine must know what is going on in their respective countries, and in each of these countries there are periodicals eager to publish work of merit. What we in America want to know is what Russian, French, German, South American, Japanese and Chinese proletarian writers are doing, and *International Literature* is almost our only way of finding out. It might also be possible to omit some of the material on Soviet life, for, interesting as the various articles in this department have been, it is not difficult for us to learn about the Soviet Union from other sources.

Whatever the possibilities for improvement, however, *International Literature* is indispensable for everyone who is seriously interested in proletarian culture. And certainly, there is no reason not to expect improvements when each issue of 1933 has been better than its predecessors. On many grounds this progress is gratifying, but readers of the *New Masses* will feel particular satisfaction in being able to attribute no inconsiderable part of it to Walt Carmon.

January 9, 1934

A Study in Hangovers

Reflections on the End of an Era, by Reinhold Niebuhr
The Necessity of Communism, by John Middleton Murry

Perhaps I ought to beg Dr. Niebuhr's pardon for coupling his book with Middleton Murry's *The Necessity of Communism,* which is the culminating achievement of a long and singularly asinine career. But I am afraid that Dr. Niebuhr, before many years have passed, will find himself in even worse company. Both books show that, for a considerable number of intellectuals, the great choice today is between some private conception of revolution and the Communism of the Communist Party. And these private conceptions have a way of leading to very strange alliances.

But let us see what Dr. Niebuhr's private conception is. It includes much with which we shall not disagree. Dr. Niebuhr recognizes not only the evils of capitalism but also its instability. He perceives the reality and immediacy of the class struggle, and he believes that that struggle will culminate in a violent conflict, provoked by the unwillingness of the ruling class to surrender its privileges. In the revolutionary conflict the proletariat, he believes, must ultimately triumph. Though he stresses and even exaggerates the peculiarities of the American situation, he does not regard America as an exception to the general rule of class struggle and proletarian victory. Moreover, while praising liberalism for its virtues, he clearly sees the futility of the liberals, the weaknesses of their theories, and the dangers of their mode of conduct in time of crisis. Finally, he understands the nature of bourgeois individualism and the paradoxical way in which it results in standardization.

So far, so good! But Dr. Niebuhr remains what he calls an orthodox Christian, and he therefore urges an alliance of Christianity and Marxism. Orthodoxy, he maintains, will contribute to the revolutionary movement a saving sense of the sanctity of the individual soul, a mitigation of the proletarian desire for revenge, an attitude of tolerance towards the genuine values of bourgeois society, and a check upon utopian illusions. Orthodoxy, for Dr. Niebuhr, means simply a sense of conscious purpose in the universe. The only evidence rience of grace, by which he means "the apprehension of the absolute he offers for this supernaturalistic dualism, as he calls it, is the expe- from the perspective of the relative." "If it is recognized or believed," he says, "that the moral imagination conceives ideals for life which history in any immediate or even in any conceivable form is unable to realize a dualistic world-view will emerge."

It may be pointed out that most persons who call themselves orthodox Christians would deny Dr. Niebuhr's right to that title and would class him among the very liberals he condemns. Historically Christianity, both Catholic and Protestant, rests upon its claim to provide a way of salvation for the individual soul, and the orthodox will accept no substitute. Moreover, the orthodox might well insist that the ethical imagination is a good deal less substantial base for religion than divine revelation. Both orthodox Christians and materialists would be aware that the jump Dr. Niebuhr asks us to take is a longer one than the quickness with which he makes the leap might indicate. Unless all simpler explanations of the ethical imagination fail, we are not compelled to resort to a dualistic theory; and simpler explanations of man's capacity for wanting more than he has—or even can have—are available.

But it would be foolish to waste space in refuting theories that have been refuted time after time. What interests us is the practical bearing of Dr. Niebuhr's attempt to synthesize Marxism and Christianity. First of all, he denies the scientific character of Marxism, offering as evidence certain unscientific statements by certain Marxists. (By this method how easy it would be to prove that physics is not a science!) He exaggerates the terrorism of the Russian Bolsheviks and the possible terrorism of Communists in other countries. He flirts with nationalism, and he advocates alliances with farmers and with the middle class on terms that would make impossible the very ideals he advocates. Finally, in the interests of this Christo-Marxist synthesis, he attacks, in speeches and articles and to some extent in this book, the Communist Party, not only as it functions in the United States but also as it functions in Germany and Russia.

We know, then, where Dr. Niebuhr stands. All things considered, he has come a long way. The best part of his book, moreover, his demolition of liberalism, will hit particularly hard the very people who are likely to read it. At the same time we must recognize that his talk about a sense of grace is, in its practical effect, only one more excuse for preferring the forces of reaction to the forces of revolution. When one remembers that Dr. Niebuhr, who seems to find more evil in the organized church than he does in the Communist Party, nevertheless remains affiliated with the former while he pours scorn on the latter, it is not surprising that he prefers a united front with Woll and La Guardia to a united front with Communists.

Niebuhr at least has sense enough to recognize that what he is doing is combining certain elements of Marxism with certain religious theories, but Murry insists that his is the simon-pure word of Karl Marx. What he has really done is to add Marx to a pantheon that already included Jesus, Keats, and D. H. Lawrence, and the best that can be said for him is that he has not distorted Marx's teachings much more vulgarly and preposterously than he had previously distorted the teachings of the others. Our own "national Communists" will be pleased to note Mr. Murry's reason for arguing that Communism in England must be English Communism: "The simple form taken by this instinctive feeling of the impossibility of Russian Communism in England is that the Englishman is too 'decent' to allow such inhuman horrors to be perpetrated." Remembering the long record of British imperialism, one is reminded by Murry's words of the last scene in *Point Counter Point,* and one can only repeat with Huxley, "Of such is the Kingdom of Heaven."

Mr. Murry wants to be both a revolutionary and a sentimental middle-class Britisher; Dr. Niebuhr wants to be both a revolutionary and an orthodox Christian. It is not difficult to understand such folly, and one could lightly dismiss it if it were an isolated phenomenon. But unfortunately the doctrines of such well-intentioned gentlemen prove very useful to other gentlemen who are neither so well-intentioned nor so naive. Already these brands of religious Communism, non-Marxian Communism, pacifist Communism, nationalist Communism, and the like are tolerated by sections of the capitalist press that attack bitterly and unscrupulously the Communist Party. Tolerance will yield to encouragement, no doubt, as the revolutionary movement grows, and capitalists, fearing only the Communism of the Communist Party, eagerly avail themselves of their last line of defense.

                                                                            March 13, 1934

White Guards on Parade

The contention of this article is that the *New York Times* Book Review, Section Five of the *Times'* Sunday issue, carries on a consistent campaign against the Soviet Union, against Communism and Communists, and against revolutionary literature. I shall show that all books on Russia are reviewed by persons opposed to the Soviet government, and that every pro-Soviet book is damned and every anti-Soviet book praised. I shall show that Section Five never delivers a thoroughgoing attack against any one but Communists, being relatively friendly to Socialists, Czarists, and Fascists. I shall show, finally, that Section Five has constituted itself a bulwark against the growing strength of revolutionary American literature, always attacking its principles, usually attacking and always deprecating the works of revolutionary writers, and frantically seeking for other literary schools to oppose to the revolutionary movement.

Readers of the *New Masses,* though they may be surprised to realize how consistently Section Five has followed these policies, will certainly not be surprised to learn that it is prejudiced. There may even be some who, admitting the bias of the *Times,* will defend it on the ground that the *New Masses* is also biased. Certainly the *New Masses* has never given a book to a reviewer who was known to be either anti-Soviet or pro-Fascist. Certainly most *New Masses'* reviewers are Communists or Communist sympathizers. Certainly *New Masses'* critics, though they rigorously analyze the work of revolutionary writers, are in complete sympathy with their principles.

But there is a significant difference between the *New Masses* and Section Five. The *New Masses* has adopted a certain position, and every issue explains what that position is and why it has been adopted. Section Five, on the other hand, claims to have no position. It is supposed to be the great impartial review of books. It must be remembered that no other American magazine devoted to literature has so wide a circulation, or carries so much advertising, or influences so many book-buyers. Section Five pretends to take its responsibilities seriously. It pretends to give the news about books, to select the facts that potential purchasers need to know. It does not try to be a critical journal. No one reads Section Five for sharp analyses or careful evaluations. No one reads Section Five for the stimulus that is provided by the shrewd, careful expression of a critical philosophy. People read Section Five to find out what the new books are about.

Look at any representative issue of the *Times.* On the front page, let us say, is a long review by Percy Hutchinson of some mediocre British novel. Mr. Hutchinson, with great seriousness, takes twelve or thirteen hundred words to tell the story, and then concludes with a few trite generalizations and a sentence or two of praise for the publishers to quote. On page two P. W. Wilson learnedly, but quite uncritically, gives a resumé of some conventional historical or religious work. On page three William MacDonald or Walter Littlefield discusses some recent work on politics or international affairs, or perhaps R. L. Duffus tackles a book on American culture. Any one of these reviewers can be depended upon to tell accurately what the book in hand contains—unless it happens to be by a Communist— and the publisher can rely on all of them not to expose any of the book's shortcomings. Page four is likely to be devoted to a couple of travel books, and *Times* reviewers are always enthusiastic about travel. Scattered about on these pages are two or three shorter reviews: perhaps Percy Hutchinson judiciously acclaiming a conventional poet, perhaps Rose C. Feld describing a sociological volume. The shorter fiction reviews ordinarily begin on page six, and here Section Five impartiality is beautiful and never-failing. Column after column is devoted to sheer trash. There is never excessive praise, of course, but there is never dismissal. The reviewer may, to save his self-respect, hint that the book is a vulgar product for *hoi polloi*, but almost invariably such an heretical suggestion is counteracted by at least a line that will sound well in the advertisements.

It is against this background that the *Times'* treatment of Russian and revolutionary books must be studied. In dealing with bad or mediocre books, Section Five is grandly impartial. You can imagine the instructions to reviewers: "This is a newspaper, not a journal of opinion. Of course you don't have to praise a bad book, but you don't have to say it's bad. Give the facts and let the reader decide. You can criticize minor points, but let's not have any of this silly Menckenian denunciation. And if it is a good book, say so." I don't suppose any such instructions have ever been issued, but I am sure that no reviewer would last long on the *Times* who failed to follow the general spirit of them so far as the average run of books is concerned. And I am equally sure that no reviewer would last long who did not follow these instructions if the book assigned him happened to belong to any of the categories that fall within the province of this article.

The Last White Line

Section Five boasts a considerable staff of authorities on Russia and Russian literature. Who and what they are will subsequently be made clear. It was to one of these authorities, apparently, that the editor handed Maurice Hindus' *The Great Offensive* when it appeared last fall (Nov. 12, 1933). This reviewer, who remained anonymous, was somewhat smarter than most of his fellow-experts: He kept up the appearance of impartiality. He even seemed to praise the book, but he took care to contradict or minimize every favorable statement that Hindus made about the agricultural situation.

When, a little later, the Stratford Company of Boston issued Chapin Huntington's *The Homesick Million: Russia-out-of-Russia*, a book that most papers and magazines reviewed briefly or not at all, the Times gave it the better part of page four. "A Vivid Story of the

Emigré Groups Around the World That Valiantly Carry On," read the subtitle of the review (Jan. 14, 1934). Mr. A. M. Nikolaieff, the reviewer, is one of several mysterious Times experts. I know nothing about him except that he is such an authority on the Imperial Army that he was given two columns (Aug. 26, 1934) to describe a very unimportant Russian book, published in Paris, in praise of General Yudenitch. In Mr. Nikolaieff's hands Mr. Huntington's glorification of the White Guard became a "vivid and illuminating account," which "grasped the epic proportions and historic weight." Mr. Huntington, it seems, "possessed the rare advantage of knowing pre-revolutionary Russia," and his book is a "fine achievement." Nikolaieff quotes with approval Mr. Huntington's statements that the emigrés represent "an incalculable loss for Russia" and that "modern Russian literature has been transplanted abroad bodily," and he closes with warm words in praise of the author's "thorough knowledge and impartiality."

Knowledge and impartiality are, of course, qualities that the editor of Section Five and his associates strongly approve. When Newsholme and Kingsbury's *Red Medicine* appeared, to be widely hailed as the best informed and most judicial treatment of the subject, Section Five assigned the book neither to a leading American physician nor to a well-known writer on Russia. Instead, it discovered another of its unique authorities, Dr. Henry A. Koiransky. Dr. Koiransky's page review (January 21, 1934) is by no means the usual summary. The first seven paragraphs are devoted to an attack on the professional standing, general intelligence, and personal honesty of the two authors. The next four paragraphs assert the excellence of medicine under the Czar. The next three attack the book's account of the present situation, offering in refutation a letter from "the late Dr. L. O., a brilliant bacteriologist." The two concluding paragraphs sum up: the book is "misleading in the extreme to the uninformed reader."

Messrs. Nikolaieff and Koiransky are good snipers, but the heavy artillery must be brought up when the enemy appears in force. When Fanina Halle's *Women in Soviet Russia* was published, it was assigned to Manya Gordon. Manya Gordon, White Russian, is the wife of Simeon Strunsky. Simeon Strunsky, of the editorial staff of the *Times,* occasionally joins the Section Five anti-Soviet squad, but he has his own post of duty, "Topics of the Times," on the editorial page, and here he concocts some of the brightest bits of anti-Soviet slander that find their way into print. The editor, therefore, was keeping things right in the family when he gave the book to Manya Gordon Strunsky. Mrs. Strunsky, you can be sure, did not write the conventional summary. More than half her review (February 18, 1934) was devoted to the thesis that all the real achievements of feminine emancipation in Russia were the work of the Kerensky regime and that the Bolsheviks had merely utilized, when they had not destroyed, these accomplishments.

Another mainstay of Section Five is a Socialist by the name of Joseph Shaplen, who was assigned Allan Monkhouse's *Moscow, 1911–1933*. "Mr. Monkhouse," said Shaplen, "tells of this 'frame-up' with the calmness and judiciousness of a man who knows himself to be innocent." (March 4, 1934.) But not content with blanket praise of Monkhouse, Shaplen went on to devote three paragraphs to the Menshevik trial, paragraphs filled with vituperation of the Soviet Union. It is instructive to compare the review by Shaplen, Socialist, with the review by Bruce Lockhart, ex-spy, in the *Saturday Review of Literature* (Feb. 17, 1934.) Mr. Lockhart, it seems, was less impressed by Mr. Monkhouse's "calmness and judiciousness":

It is, however, on the subject of the trial that Mr. Monkhouse is most disappointing. His account of his arrest is graphic enough, but on the trial itself he throws no new light. He takes the official view that it was an Ogpu "frame-up" to divert attention from the constant breakdowns of machinery due to Russian incompetence. He praises the British officials whose grasp of the situation frustrated the efforts of the Ogpu "to bring the frame-up trial to a conclusion which would have been more satisfactory to their own prestige."

This is balderdash, and it is hard to believe that Mr. Monkhouse can subscribe to this story with a whole conscience. Even in England it is painfully obvious to the dullest intellect that the Ogpu finished the trial to their entire satisfaction, and that, as far as the honors of propaganda were concerned, the Bolsheviks scooped the lot. . . .

On the trial Mr. Monkhouse is therefore unsatisfactory. I cannot resist the feeling that he would have written a better book if he had not been and was not still in the employ of his firm.

The publication of Kerensky's *Crucifixion of Liberty* was a god-given opportunity for Section Five, and it had to be handled by the master of slander, Simeon Strunsky. His review was proudly flaunted on the first page (March 18, 1934.) Strunsky understands perfectly the technique of hiding savage hatred in the cloak of *Times* impartiality! "So much water—and blood—has run under the Russian bridges that Lenin's responsibility before his native land is now an academic question," and "Whether or not Lenin is the spiritual father of Fascism and Hitlerism is a question that concerns only the historian." Such admirably dispassionate statements merely adorn a review whose real purpose is to glorify pre-revolutionary Russia. "When it is shown," he writes, ". . . that in the decade between 1905 and the outbreak of the World War, a decade of comparative freedom, Russia advanced industrially by leaps and bounds, we have an answer to the argument that dictatorship is the only road to economic progress." Kerensky himself could profitably sit at the feet of Strunsky and learn from him how to malign Soviet Russia.

Books favorable to Russia are not reviewed on page one. Unless they provide material for a Manya Gordon or a Koiransky, they are tucked away on page fifteen, where, in the issue of April 22, you will find another expert, John Cournos, disposing in two columns of Sherwood Eddy's *Russia Today*, Alexander Wicksteed's *My Russian Neighbors,* and Leonard Elmhirst's *Trip to Russia.* Mr. Cournos strikes the proper note by speaking of the fashion for "sentimental travelers to return to rhapsodize over the proletariat, Lenin's tomb and the great experiment." About half the review is devoted to Eddy's book, but not to the chapters in praise of Russia. It is the criticism of Marx and the Soviets that Mr. Cournos dwells on. Mr. Wicksteed is rebuked for providing less material for Section Five; he is, says Mr. Cournos, "less troubled in his conscience by such doubts as possess the author of *Russia Today.*" Cournos does well, however, with what he can find: Wicksteed "makes no effort to conceal the lack of liberty" and "does not think that the inhuman treatment of the so-called kulaks was a commendable affair." Unfortunately for Mr. Cournos, Wicksteed unequivocally praises the Soviet achievement in industry and agriculture, but Mr. Cournos is ready with his own counterstatement. Wicksteed thinks the Russians will become intellectual leaders of the world, "a statement," Mr. Cournos comments, "one can scarcely accept seriously." Wicksteed is hopeful about the future of Russia, but "the reviewer, in any case, does not agree with him."

"The reviewer, in any case, does not agree." There, in Mr. Cournos' own nutshell, is the policy of Section Five with regard to any book that even mildly praises any aspect of life in the U.S.S.R. The reviewers, you observe, are not persons who have recently studied Soviet Russia. You would scarcely expect to find Ella Winter or Corliss Lamont or Mrs. Alice W. Field in Section Five, but you might expect the reviewers to be on the level of Walter Duranty or Harold Denny. But no, Section Five invariably assigns books on the Soviet Union to emigrés and their sympathizers. It is, as a matter of fact, the principal organ of the White Guard in America.

The Politics of Art

It is a little too much to expect of the emigrés and renegades of Section Five that they should maintain as close a watch over Soviet literature as they do over political studies. But, in view of their professed enthusiasm for a free and non-political art, they do exceedingly well. There was, it is true, a review of Kataev's *Time, Forward!* by Peter Monro Jack (November 5, 1933) that bestowed praise almost without qualification. One feels confident, however, that such a mistake will never happen again.

The editor of Section Five made a serious error in not assigning *Time, Forward!* to his principal expert on Soviet literature, Alexander Nazaroff. Mr. Nazaroff, if he had seen fit to praise the book at all, would have known how to make his praise an instrument for the condemning of the Soviets and all their works. Mr. Nazaroff, for example, found Gladkov's *Energy* "a happy exception" to the "general rule" that "the so-called 'industrialization novels' " are "beyond the pale of that which deserves the name of literature." It is one of the few books, "amid the mass of propaganda that pours from the Soviet presses," that have "an interest independent of the gospel according to Marx and Lenin." (Dec. 17, 1933.)

Mr. Nazaroff found Ehrenbourg's *Out of Chaos* (June 3, 1934) similarly exceptional. (Mr. Nazaroff apparently believes not only that it is the exception that proves the rule, but also that the more exceptions, the better the rule is proved.) *"Out of Chaos,"* he says, "belongs in that class of literature which, in Moscow, is termed 'production novels.' Soviet writers have long since evolved a rigid formula for such novels. . . . As it is known, since the introduction of the Five-Year Plan, the Communist party has been virtually forcing writers to turn out that kind of stuff. Needless to say, most of the 'production literature' is hopeless trash. Obligatory pathos over the 'building of socialism' has emasculated even some of the best Soviet authors." Ehrenbourg, it happens, is "one of the felicitous exceptions." "Mr. Ehrenbourg," Nazaroff continues, "does not shut his eyes to the dark side of Russia's life. . . . And yet (it is here that the obligatory didactic element common to all production novels lies) the author stresses time and again that this—and this alone— is 'real life.'" (Mr. Nazaroff wields a wicked quotation mark.) "Some of his heroes," the analysis continues, "pronounce long and bombastic speeches on socialism and the 'new life.' . . . Do such speeches outweigh the hideous reality which Mr. Ehrenbourg himself has painted? No. Artistically, the latter are more convincing than the former."

Mr. Nazaroff, you perceive, is nothing if not an esthetician. The struggles of Kolka and his comrade shock-workers are not heroic; they are merely hideous. There is nothing, according to him, in the book that shows the satisfactions and the achievements of these heroes; there are merely "long and bombastic speeches." Having thus misrepresented the novel, he can render judgment. What he means is, "I thoroughly enjoyed every indication of the hardships of the Russian workers, for such indications nourished my hope that socialist construction will fail, and I deliberately ignored all evidence of success, for the possibility of success is too painful to contemplate." Being an esthetician, he puts it, "Artistically, the latter are more convincing than the former."

But Mr. Nazaroff's esthetics is not so rigorously logical as it might be. Reviewing *And Quiet Flows the Don* (July 15, 1934), he neglected to point out how, in a country where "the Communist party has been virtually forcing writers to turn out" production literature, Sholokhov has somehow managed to finish a trilogy that has nothing to do with construction. And there is a further mystery that Mr. Nazaroff neglects to explain. "The Soviet critics have justly pointed out that, for instance, Bunchuk, a Communist officer carrying on propaganda among the Cossack troops at the front . . . is a sheer abstraction. . . . The Soviet critics are right in that, too, the White officers figuring in the novel are far more alive than those just mentioned pasteboard figures." Mr. Nazaroff finds consolation in the book, you see, even though he is painfully obliged to agree with Soviet critics. But he also says, "It has sold more than 1,000,000 copies in Russia and Soviet critics have praised it to the skies (this in a country where libraries buy books and critics form their judgment by order of the ruling party.)" The Soviet critics, according to Mr. Nazaroff, were

smart enough to see that the book was not effective propaganda for
Communism, and yet, though they could easily have buried the novel
and presumably sent Sholokhov to Siberia, they praised it to the skies,
and horsewhipped a million people into buying copies.

Mr. Nazaroff, though he is the principal medium through which
Section Five permits its million or more readers to learn about Soviet
literature, seems far more at home with the achievements of the
emigrés than with what is happening in Russia today. Perhaps the
brightest moment in what must be a rather dreary life came last fall
when Ivan Bunin was awarded the Nobel prize. Mr. Nazaroff immediately composed a long article, fully setting forth the reasons for
his passionate admiration of the emigré. Bunin, he observes, "never
conceals the profound contempt with which he regards the authors
of 'the great Soviet experiment.' . . . Indeed, those who, in the interpretation of other people's psychology can see only selfish motives
may ascribe Bunin's anti-Sovietism to his 'class feeling.' Only those,
however, who know him very little can accept this explanation. He
loves Russia—both the noble and the peasant Russia alike—too organically to look with bland complacence at its transformation into a
laboratory for experimentation. . . . To him Sovietization means only
the bestialization of Russia."

Of course Nazaroff felt warmly about Bunin's *The Well of Days*
(February 25, 1934), and predicted that it would survive "not only
in the Russian, but also in world literature, as an example of con-
summate and highly original art." Other reviewers, you may recall,
were not so enthusiastic. Indeed, Nazaroff's enthusiasm was matched
only by the lush and almost inarticulate rejoicings of Eveline S. (Mrs.
J. Donald) Adams in the *Saturday Review* (Feb. 17, 1934).

Bunin is, of course, the great consolation of the White Guard of
Section Five, and Nazaroff wrote of him once more with tenderness
in the issue of August 19; but there are others. John Cournos, for
example, found much cause for satisfaction in Nicholas Berdyaev's
The End of Our Time (Oct. 29, 1933), and Mr. Nazaroff devoted
several columns (May 20, 1934) to V. Sirin. And there is the anti-
Soviet literature of other countries. Kuhnelt-Leddihn's trashy melodrama of Catholic espionage in Russia, *The Gates of Hell*, is, according to an anonymous reviewer (July 22, 1934), "a remarkable production," "an inspired clerical tract against atheism," and "a considerable achievement." And another anonymous reviewer (March

11, 1934) contemplated calmly another bit of melodramatic tripe, James Hilton's *Without Armor,* and could find no ground for criticism except that it was not rabid enough in its depiction of the revolutionary period, "the most abysmal chaos into which humanity has ever plunged itself."

The Art of Politics

The beauties of *Times* impartially became apparent when we leave the subject of the Soviet Union. Look, for example, at William MacDonald's review of Spengler's *The Hour of Decision,* a very long review on the front page (Feb. 11, 1934). Mr. MacDonald gives a detailed summary, without a word of criticism or objection. Presumably so ardent a liberal, a former member of the staff of *The Nation,* is brutally shocked by the coarse reactionary diatribe, but he preserves the judicial calm appropriate to Section Five.

But look at Mr. MacDonald's review of John Strachey's *Menace of Fascism* (Oct. 1, 1933). Again we find a long and careful summary, but somehow Strachey's errors demand, as Herr Spengler's do not, a paragraph of correction:

Mr. Strachey's book will perhaps afford some comfort to those who still affect to believe that a socialized state, in the uncompromising form in which he visualizes it, is the ideal to which a civilized society should aspire, but it will not deeply stir anyone else. . . . There is no sufficient ground for assuming that a corporative state means the degradation of the workers, and none at all for thinking that a proletarian dictatorship would be more terrible or beneficent than the dictatorship of a relatively small governing group.

The *Times* also managed to find an impartial reviewer for Hitler's *My Battle.* Ex-ambassador James W. Gerard appears (Oct. 8, 1933) as the goddess of justice, and carefully holds the scales in which he weighs the good and the bad of the Hitler regime:

Hitler is doing much for Germany; his unification of the Germans, his destruction of communism, his training of the young, his creation of a Spartan State animated by patriotism, his curbing of parliamentary government so unsuited to the German character, his protection of the right of private property are all good; and after all, what the Germans do in their own territory is their own business, except for one thing—the persecution and practical expulsion of the Jews.

Mr. Gerard's efforts are neatly complemented by Walter Littlefield's review of *Hitler Over Europe* (July 22, 1934). Headlines help
the reader to approach the review in the correct frame of mind: "A
Violent Vision of Hitlerism Spreading Over Europe," and " 'Ernst
Henri's' Panicky Volume Holds out the Offer of Communism as the
Only Possible Alternative." The review coyly begins, "The torch
which Stalin was expediently suffering to become an ember has now
been snatched from his grasp and blown into a terrifying flame." It
ends,

> The phrase "Socialist revolution" will deceive none who has read his
> book. I have abundantly indicated, here and elsewhere, that the case of
> Germany is rather more psychopathic than political. With due considera-
> tion for his erudite communistic propaganda, this also seems to be the case
> of Ernst Henri. This said, we freely admit his unusual gift for furnishing
> entertainment—just as we do that of the late Freiherr von Munchausen.

What *Times* impartiality can rise to, when Fascism is concerned,
becomes fully apparent in Dino Ferrari's review of Fausto Pitigliani's
The Italian Corporative State (May 13, 1934). Mr. Ferrari, who is
Section Five's expert on Italian literature and Italian affairs, is a
pleasant running-mate for the Czarists and renegades. The review
begins:

> If dubious Communists, along with sensation-mongers, could be
> induced to see "things" as they are instead of through red lenses, no doubt
> many foolish statements and half-truths would be spared us—such as Mr.
> John Strachey's astonishing assertion, in his biased review of the English
> edition of Signor Pitigliani's book in The Nation (Oct. 18, 1933) that the
> "Italian Corporative State" exists only on "paper."
> Up to a certain point, Mr. Strachey's contention may be valid. Ob-
> viously a new order of society cannot be created overnight. Even the most
> rabid disciples of Marx and Lenin must admit that, at least in practice,
> whatever good there may be in Marxian theory, the Soviets' moguls have
> not been averse to a bit of political back-sliding. . . .
> The truth of the matter would seem to be that the Italian Corporative
> State has probably gone further in matching theory with practice, and
> with infinitely less bungling and human suffering, than the Soviets' counter-
> part or any other revolutionary movement in history. Who knows but
> future events may prove the modified syndicalism of Sorel and the social
> realism of Pareto right, and windy dialectics—just what they are?

Although I have tried, in quoting from the *Times,* not to emphasize the obvious, I think it wise to call attention to such phrases

as "dubious Communists," "sensation-mongers," "Soviets' moguls," and "windy dialectics." Mr. Ferrari's review is precisely the kind of review that Section Five is supposed to avoid. In the first place, it is an open avowal of Fascism. In the second place, it is an irrelevant and vituperatively personal attack upon a writer. In the third place, there is not one word of evidence in the whole review to show that the Italian Corporative State does exist anywhere but on paper; we merely have Mr. Ferrari's word for it that Pitigliani's book is "an impartial, thorough exposition." It is a review that, I believe, no other magazine in America, except those openly espousing Italian Fascism, would have printed.

A White Guard by Marriage

Although I have no illusions about the nature and role of capitalist newspapers, including the *Times,* I think it is perfectly obvious that the policy of Section Five with regard to Russia is more insidious and vicious than that of the *Times'* news columns. What is the ultimate cause of this I do not know. I do know that the *Times* was once as rabid in its news columns as it is now in its literary supplement. It may be that, once the *New Republic* (Aug. 4, 1920) had exposed the crimes of the *Times,* a simple policy of misinformation was bound to defeat its own ends. To restore confidence it was essential to print news dispatches that were at least plausible, even though that meant making them occasionally favorable. Then, with a reputation established for reliability, it was possible to carry on a·subtler campaign of misrepresentation and slander, under the guise of esthetic impartiality, in the book review section.

If some such policy determines the nature of Section Five, which one assumes is not merely the result of the prejudices of the particular man who edits it, the fitness of the editor for his role is unmistakable. James Donald Adams, who is forty-three years old, graduated from Harvard in 1913. After a brief period as a teacher in the West, he became a reporter, and, except for an interval during the war, has worked on newspapers ever since. After working in various provincial cities, he joined the staff of the *New York Sun and Herald* in 1920. In 1924 he became assistant editor and in 1925 editor of Section Five. The only other important information concerning him that can be found in *Who's Who* is that in 1921 he married Eveline Georgievna Simeon "of Petrograd, Russia."

The effect on a naturally reactionary temperament of marriage to a Russian emigré is something to think about. One can readily see the Adams household becoming the center of the intellectual White Guards of New York City. The Nazaroffs, the Koiranskys, and the Nikolaieffs rub elbows with the renegade Strunskys and the Socialist Shaplens, perhaps against a background of grand dukes and generals. Mr. Adams, possibly aided by instructions from above, possibly merely persuaded by the company he keeps, begins to see his duty clear. And Section Five becomes the major instrument in the United States of anti-Soviet propaganda.

During the greater part of his decade with Section Five Mr. Adams has done his part by his judicious choice of reviewers. There is nothing, after all, to indicate any particular equipment on his part for criticism. He was hired, presumably, as a reporter and editor, not as a critic. But within the last year—perhaps because of a reduction in the Section Five budget—he has been writing more reviews, and evidently he has begun to fancy himself as an authority on literature.

The more Mr. Adams writes, the more fantastic it seems that he should be editing a literary review with a circulation of three-quarters of a million. He reached his highest point to date on the front page of the issue of May 20. Instead of entrusting *Escape from the Soviets* and *Winter in Moscow* to Strunsky or Shaplen or Nazaroff—any one of whom is considerably more adept in the subtler forms of slander—he took on the job himself. The result has been analyzed by Joseph Freeman in *The New Masses* for June 5, and there is nothing for me to add. Mr. Adams has surely been made an honorary member of all the White Guard societies there are, and no doubt Mrs. Adams is very happy that her husband has made good.

But Mr. Adams does not limit himself to anti-Soviet propaganda. He has also set himself up as the last great bulwark of rugged individualism. When the *Saturday Review of Literature* wanted someone to answer Bernard Smith's discussion of the critics of the middle generation, J. Donald Adams was chosen to champion the lost cause. In the course of his article he wrote a paragraph that I think remains unparalleled for sheer effrontery and complete disregard of even bourgeois standards of decency:

For some of us the philosophy of communism has no appeal because it is a negative philosophy, rooted in hatred, because it holds up a cowardly way of life as the good life. Its most emphasized promise to its adherents is the promise of material security. Is security the most precious prize for which human beings may strive? Is the quest of it the utmost measure of man's courage and aspiration? And is its attainment worth the sacrifice of those satisfactions which can sometimes be had only at the price of insecurity? It is a poor half-loaf the Marxists offer us, nor have we yet reached the point where they can tell us that half a loaf is better than none.

If some self-reliant anarchist, living in Thoreauvian solitude and poverty, uttered such words, I should disagree, but I should respect him. When Mr. Adams, living on a fat salary paid him for his ingenuity in catching publishers' advertising, says them, contempt seems an inadequate emotion. I should like to know what price, in terms of insecurity, Mr. Adams has ever paid for his satisfactions.

Imagine it; Mr. Adams sits smug and happy in his *Times* office or his White Guard home, and talks to Communists about cowardice and security.

This is the man who proposes to stem the tide of revolutionary literature. His article in the *Saturday Review* and his review of the two anti-Soviet books had at least the merit of being open attacks. Back-stabbing methods are more natural to him. He waited, for example, two months before reviewing my book, *The Great Tradition*, and then devoted to it less space than the *Times* ordinarily devotes to a novel by Elinor Glyn (Nov. 19, 1933). In his review of *The Mother* (Jan. 14, 1934) he introduced a line about "the difference between Mrs. Buck and a proletarian critic being that Mrs. Buck sees with two eyes instead of one with a blinder over it." He interrupted his review of *The Unpossessed* (May 20, 1934) to say: "Russian intellectuals, Miss Slesinger, no longer exist as such; the remnants are scattered over the world or concentrated in the penal camps of Siberia and the Arctic." The next week, reviewing *The Lost Generation,* he took the opportunity to lecture Malcolm Cowley:

What is it the workers have won in Russia: the right to be slaves in a regimented State, to enjoy a standard of living below that they enjoyed before the war? And the intellectuals—Mr. Cowley can learn, if he will, what they have won from Tatiana Tchernavin's *Escape from the Soviets,* reviewed in these columns last Sunday. And he can learn what writers in particular have won from Max Eastman's *Artists in Uniform.*

A little later he cries: "Come out of your dream, Mr. Cowley; all but
a fraction of the human race was born to be led, as Lenin well knew."
And, to clinch the argument, he concludes, after quoting a poem by
Cowley: "The man who can write lines as good as these should not
be wasting himself in the promotion of class warfare and its concomi-
tant hatreds."

Almost everything Mr. Adams says is, if you can forget his venomous intentions, rather funny; but he is most comical when he thinks
he has found some positive literary achievement to oppose to the
solid growth of the literature of revolution. A young man named Paul
Engle, to be specific, has written a book of very sophomoric and imita-
tive verse called *American Song*. This little volume, simply because
it is nationalistic and "affirmative" and non-revolutionary, sent Mr.
Adams off in spasms (July 29, 1934). He proclaimed it "a heartening
book," and could recall no other "piece of writing of equal compass
in which there is so strong a distillation of all that has gone into the
making of the American land and the American people." In the course
of the review Mr. Adams hinted that he had up his sleeve other poets
of equal calibre, and we are eagerly waiting for him to produce them.

Stark Young's *So Red the Rose* also pleased Mr. Adams (Aug.
5, 1934). As he indicated in his address at a literary conference in the
South last year, he has a great admiration for the Southern aristocracy, though his own origins are urban, and presumably he would
have liked to marry a Virginia belle if he had not had the good fortune
to meet a young lady from "Petrograd, Russia," In reviewing Mr.
Young's book, he contrived to bring his two loves face to face:

> One is struck again, in reading this novel, by the many and deep-cut
> parallels which exist between the culture of the planter aristocracy of the
> Old South and that of the landed families of Imperial Russia. . . . Both
> built something precious out of "a great human wrong," something that
> almost removed life from the easy material plane on which it rested.
> Wiser men, perhaps, will find a better base on which to build.

The quotation marks around "a great human wrong" seem to me the
finest accomplishment of Section Five impartiality.

Class War in Times Square

Even aside from the White Guard, Mr. Adams has an able staff
of assistants, who do not need such an article as this to tell them how

to write the kind of reviews that are fit to print in Section Five. There is, for example, Harold Strauss, who wrote the review of Robert Cantwell's *Land of Plenty* (April 29, 1934). Please recall once more the hundreds of mediocre novels that *Times* reviewers, Mr. Strauss included, review with that perfect impartiality that refuses to distinguish good from bad. Then look at the treatment *Land of Plenty* received. Mr. Strauss began by charging that Cantwell rewrote *Laugh and Lie Down* at the request of his publishers, a charge that according to Cantwell, Strauss knew was false. This accusation, however, was merely introductory to a more serious one, that Cantwell had written *Land of Plenty* to please "a minority bloc of our critics." "That none of the characters emerge as human beings," Mr. Strauss summed up, "is the direct result of Cantwell's service to the Marxists and their essentially non-literary purpose." The word "service" is important, for Strauss subsequently, under fire from Cantwell, pretended he had said only that Cantwell "was subject to influences which no man of letters can wholly escape today."

Mr. Strauss acquitted himself so well in his review of *Land of Plenty* that he was given an important assignment, Max Eastman's *Artists in Uniform* (May 13, 1934). Though Mr. Strauss knows no Russian, and has never given any evidence of familiarity even with the Soviet literature that exists in translation, he did not hesitate, despite an elaborate pretense of explaining Eastman's biases, to accept and endorse everything Eastman says about the Russian literary situation. His chief concern, however, was to make the best possible use of the weapon with which Eastman had so kindly provided him:

> At this moment there is a certain radical snobbism in the air which dictates the writing of proletarian novels and poetry upon aspiring intellectuals. There is, as yet, despite Granville Hicks, Edmund Wilson and Malcolm Cowley, no systematic regimentation of American writers. But there are certain critics, to whom large space in print is available, whose interests are more economic, or at least social, than literary. By their mere ballyhoo of the least worthy "proletarian novel," they are urging young writers uncritically toward a barren tendentious technique.
>
> Into this mass of misdirected purpose Eastman has plunged with wit, intelligence, and good common sense.

Other reviewers are also deeply concerned with the dangers of "radical snobbism." In the issue of October 29, 1933, for example, we find R. L. Duffus seizing upon and praising the passages in Orton's

America in Search of Culture that attack Marxian criticism, and Peter Monro Jack hailing the anti-Communist chapters of Hazlitt's *Anatomy of Criticism.* Mr. Jack is also, by the way, an authority on Soviet literature. He ended his review of the Reavey and Slocum anthology (April 22, 1934) by saying: "Much more important than any such statement is the tolerance now being granted writers. Literacy is recognized as being important to literature; at the least as important as political convictions; and it is realized that good fiction is something other than an ordered report—and sometimes an ordered whitewashing—of Soviet conditions." Apparently Mr. Jack had not received the latest revelations from Max Eastman. Apparently also he did not recall that *Time, Forward!* which he praised in the issue of November 5, was written at the height of the "oppression."

As for Mr. Duffus, he has perfect manners and a suave style. Observe, for example, his review of *In All Countries* (May 6, 1934). John Dos Passos is, of course, too successful an author to be flatly damned. So Mr. Duffus jocosely begins: "Mr. John Dos Passos ... seems to have been animated by two impulses: a profound sympathy for the oppressed and a hatred for hyphens." He toys with Dos Passos' strange compounds for a time, and then he goes on to say one or two nice things about the book. But he sums up: "Mr. Dos Passos, in short, is a radical and these sketches are primarily radical propaganda. . . . His intellectual dice are loaded. . . . He sees the world through doctrinal spectacles." With the same suavity he points out (June 24, 1934) that Malraux's *Man's Fate* is not revolutionary, and makes the best of his opportunity to deliver himself on the subject of proletarian literature, which, he finds, is unfortunately making progress in these parlous times.

No Section Five reviewer would think of praising a revolutionary novel without insisting that it was exceptional. Margaret Wallace, for example, felt safe in commending Jack Conroy's *The Disinherited* (Nov. 26, 1933) after she had devoted a paragraph to proving it was not propaganda. And even Louis Kronenberger, though his praise of *The Shadow Before* (March 18, 1934) was warm enough, found it necessary to imply that all other strike novels were clumsy distortions: "For if this book openly protests, if by being partisan it is also in a sense propagandist, it achieves its effect, not through clumsy wish-fulfillments, violent invective and perfervid exhortation, but through an honest and convincing portrayal of people and events."

Mr. Adams, one would say, knows what he wants, and so do his reviewers. Of course Section Five reviewers do not follow a "rigid formula" like the poor Soviet critics, nor "form their judgments by order of the ruling party," but they do manage to achieve a striking homogeneity of opinion none the less. In the issue of February 25, 1934, for example, an issue in which there is commendation for such novels as G. B. Stern's *Summer's Play,* Anne Green's *Fools Rush In,* and Ethel Turner's *One Way Ticket,* there happen to be six reviews that touch on Communism. An anonymous reviewer wholeheartedly and unqualifiedly damns Arnold Armstrong's *Parched Earth.* Jane Spence Southron begins her review of Marvin Sutton's *Children of Eve* by saying, "Here is a proletarian novel entirely free from bias, animus, or exaggeration," by which she means that it is non-revolutionary and hence confused and inconclusive and hence to be praised. An anonymous reviewer, perhaps Percy Hutchinson, who by actual count has praised more books of bad poetry than any other living human being, dismisses Robert Gessner's *Upsurge* in sixty lines, more than half of them facetious. Harold Strauss, reviewing *On the Shore,* says Halper is too honest to be a Marxist. And Rose Field, who thought (March 25, 1934) *Rebel America* must be fair because Lillian Symes attacks Communism, says Horace Davis, in *Labor and Steel,* "evaluates life in terms of one dimension."

All in all, Section Five contrives to be astonishingly consistent. There are few lapses. *The Cannery Boat,* a collection of Japanese revolutionary short stories, produces the usual diatribe against proletarian literature (Dec. 3, 1933); Traven's *The Death Ship* is described (Apr. 29, 1934) as "original" but "preposterous"; and Guy Endore's *Babouk* is anonymously characterized (Sept. 9, 1934) as "a somewhat hysterical piece of special pleading." Owen Lattimore condescendingly praises Agnes Smedley's *Chinese Destinies* because it deals with a little-known subject, but he says the author "lacks insight" and her book "is a long way from the whole truth" (Dec. 10, 1933). And he refers to it later (June 24, 1934) to say that it is "weakened by the shrillness of zealotry." The same reviewer finds less fault with General Yakhontoff's *The Chinese Soviets* (Aug. 19, 1934); but the review is captioned, on the strength of a few minor corrections, "General Yakhontoff's Survey of the Chinese Soviets Is a Useful if Not Completely Reliable Guide to the Situation."

It is instructive to observe how different from the treatment of

Communist books is the handling of Socialist volumes. Hillquit's autobiography produces a eulogy from Joseph P. Pollard (Apr. 22, 1934).
Norman Thomas' *The Choice Before Us,* according to Louis Rich
(Apr. 1, 1934), is "a clear and persuasive statement." Joseph Shaplen
objects to G. D. H. Cole's revision of Marx only because it does not
go far enough in the direction of Kautsky and Bernstein (June 3,
1934).

The reason for this attitude towards Socialism becomes altogether clear in Simeon Strunsky's review of *Socialism, Fascism, Communism,* a volume of which Shaplen was one of the editors. "Half a
dozen writers," says Strunsky, "join with Kautsky in a symposium on
the problems which beset socialism and the Socialist parties in the face
of formidable competition from Fascism on the right and Communism
on the left. We hear nothing of the much older competition between
socialism and capitalism. Events have brought the two together as
allies in defense of democratic government and civil liberty." The
lion and the lamb have lain down together—with the usual results
for the lamb.

Counter-Attack

The case has been stated and proven up to the hilt. And now,
what can we do about it?

We can present these facts to every reader of Section Five we
can reach. We can say, "You read the *Times* literary supplement on
the assumption that it gives you an unbiased summary of the new
books. You see what the facts are. Section Five is the organ of the
White Guard; it apologizes for Fascism; it discriminates against every
writer suspected of having revolutionary sympathies. Its editor, moreover, is as incompetent as he is dishonest, and most of his reviewers
are second-rate as well as biased. You are being cheated, and it is
your duty to protest. You ought not to expect too much from any
capitalist journal, but there is no reason why you should submit to
the falsehoods and prejudices of a little clique of Czarist emigrés.
The *Herald Tribune* Books, for example, prints an honest review now
and then, and why shouldn't Section Five? Let the editors of the
Times know that you demand a change."

To such a protest from readers there could easily be added a protest from publishers. At the moment many companies are publishing revolutionary books, not because they have gone left but because they know a market when they see one. These publishers are being hurt by Section Five where they can be hurt—in their pocketbooks. At present they are too timid to buck the prejudices of Adams and his anti-red squad, but they would be delighted to support a public protest. After all, we do not have Fascism in his country; even Section Five can carry on its campaign only under the guise of defending liberty and democracy; Mr. Adams might well be given an opportunity to enjoy the satisfactions of insecurity.

But our strongest weapon is simply the exposure of Section Five's duplicity and viciousness.

Once even a few thousand of its readers realize how utterly and unscrupulously undependable it is, it will be forced to change its tactics, and the White Guard will have to do their sniping from some other fortress.

October 2, 1934

A High Talent for Straddling

It occurs to me that perhaps John Chamberlain has had his feelings hurt because I devoted so much space last week to the book reviews in the Sunday *Times* and said nothing about his contributions in the daily issues. I confess that I should scarcely have suspected that daily book reviewers had any feelings if Lewis Gannett had not remonstrated with me for calling him "perennially unscrupulous." I hadn't, I must insist, thought I was saying anything Mr. Gannett didn't know.

But if it's too late to do anything about Mr. Gannett, at least I can fix things up with Mr. Chamberlain. I can assure him, in the first place, that his reviews are a great deal better, from any point of view, than any that have appeared in Section Five since he left its staff, and, in the second place, that his column is considerably superior to the columns in the other New York dailies. This, as Chamberlain will probably feel, is not recklessly high praise. It means little more than that he reads most of the books he reviews, that he has some intelligence, and that he is not obscenely subservient to the interests of the owners of the paper.

If, however, I credit Mr. Chamberlain with a certain commendable independence of spirit, it is not to be supposed that I regard him as exactly foolhardy. On the contrary, I detect, from day to day, considerable evidence of a high talent for straddling. He very rarely, for example, puts in a good word for Marx without underlining the obvious by saying that he is not "a hook-line-and-sinker Marxist." He cannot, apparently, praise a revolutionary novel without attacking "the American RAPP." So confirmed has the habit become of neatly balancing a gesture to the left with a gesture to the right that he occasionally speaks almost warmly of Fascism, to which he is certainly opposed.

The intellectual habits he is forming were never better revealed than in the ambiguity—oh, very humorous, of course, even arch—of the beginning of his recent review of *Fontamara*. But more distressing was the review he wrote last spring of *Escape from the Soviets*. His skepticism, which makes him so superior to "hook-line-and-sinker Marxists," does not, I gather, operate with a Tatiana Tchernavin. But what bothered me far more than his swallowing Tatiana's story was his taking the occasion to ask how, in view of the Ogpu persecution in Russia, Communists could protest against the framing of Tom Mooney and the Scottsboro boys. The theoretical question is, of course, one that a liberal might be expected to raise, but its practical implications are nonetheless disturbing. The remark obviously provides a beautiful excuse for those borderline intellectuals whose consciences are just a little touched by the Mooney and Scottsboro cases, but who don't want to have to do anything about them. If that crack deprived the Scottsboro boys of five dollars—and I suspect it had far more effect than that—John Chamberlain ought to go to work in sackcloth and ashes.

This is, in case you have forgotten, the same John Chamberlain who, last February, signed an open letter to the Communist Party that contained this sentence: "We who write this letter watch with sympathy the struggles of militant labor and aid such struggles." It may be, of course, that Mr. Chamberlain, in aiding the struggles of militant labor, follows the Biblical injunction. If so, it must keep his left hand pretty busy, making up in private for what his right hand does in public.

But let us turn to the more pleasant subject of literary theory. Way back last fall Mr. Chamberlain said that my book urged the novelists, by implication, "to go into the shop and mine, to visit the farm and the railroad yard, to wait in the breadline and to sit with sparrow-bright eyes upon the park bench." I have, as a matter of fact, never said or implied that there was any particular subject the novelist must write about. What I do believe is that the novelist must understand the fundamental movements of his own age and know how the particular sector of life he chooses is related to them. What seems to me important is not the novelist's material, but his attitude towards it.

I begin to suspect that Mr. Chamberlain really objects to the revolutionary attitude in literature, but doesn't like to say so. Recently, commenting on Scott Fitzgerald's introduction to the Modern Library edition of *The Great Gatsby,* he said, "What has made Fitzgerald mad, evidently, is the Leftist tendency to chastise an author for choosing literary material which is 'such as to preclude all dealing with mature persons in a mature world.'" Did Mr. Chamberlain hasten to point out that, even if Left critics do insist that novels must deal with the working class—and, once more, they do not!—that scarcely precludes dealing with mature persons? No, he promptly remarked, "I know just how Fitzgerald feels." This makes me a little dizzy, for, if the characters of *Tender Is the Night* are mature and the characters of *The Shadow Before* and *The Land of Plenty* are not then I, even if I am a college graduate, as Mr. Chamberlain once kindly pointed out, don't know what the word means. It strikes me that it is Mr. Fitzgerald who is stifling literature by limiting it to a few narrow themes, and Mr. Chamberlain appears to be aiding and abetting him.

The problem is simply whether the novelist is to take the old, outworn, decadent bourgeois attitudes towards his material or is to adopt the fresh, clear, forward-looking attitudes of the revolutionary movement. Where John Chamberlain really stands was suggested by his review last June of *Man's Fate.* He commented upon Trotsky's characterization of Malraux as an individualist and pessimist, and said, "Of course, it is because Malraux is what he is that he is a novelist, not a prophet and historian." And he ended, "Malraux belongs, not to any temporary classification such as 'proletarian novelist,' but to the company of Conrad and Hardy, men who realize that life in any society is hemmed about by death."

There is no reason that I can see why a man who thinks literature must be individualistic and pessimistic should even pretend to be more than fashionably interested in the work of revolutionary writers. All that we can ask is that Mr. Chamberlain give us his real reasons for his opinions. All we can object to is his attacking men of straw instead of confronting fundamental issues. Why should he pretend to be opposing only the excesses of what he pleasantly calls "an American RAPP" when what he really objects to are the basic assumptions and ultimate aims of Marxist criticism?

This American RAPP, incidentally, seems to be coming in for a good deal of attention. According to Chamberlain, *The Foundry* is a good novel because Halper ignored this RAPP. (According to James Burnham, on the other hand, it is a bad novel because Halper was subservient to RAPP.) I wish Mr. Chamberlain would be a bit more explicit about the character and whereabouts of this dread organization. There are Left critics, of course, and each of them, not unlike critics of other schools, thinks his opinions are right and hopes they will be followed. But Mr. Chamberlain, I imagine, draws his conception of RAPP from Max Eastman, and hence visualizes some sort of literary inquisition, with the power of enforcing its decrees. I can only ask if, when he read *Authors' Field Day* in *The New Masses* last July, he saw any evidence of fear or docility on the part of the revolutionary novelists.

If John Chamberlain wants to come out openly as a somewhat cynical liberal in politics and a middle-of-the-road eclectic in esthetics, it would be fun to debate with him; but so long as he persists in suggesting that he is not only a friend of militant labor, but also a kind of Marxist and a critic of Left sympathies, it is hard to get anywhere without clearing the ground of the corpses of all the men of straw he has so valiantly slain.

October 9, 1934

The Urbanity of Mr. Krutch

In *The Nation* a month or two ago Mr. Joseph Wood Krutch wrote a series of four articles under the general title, "Was Europe a Success?" I am glad Mr. Krutch wrote these articles. For three or four years he has been sniping at Communism and the Marxist critics in his reviews of books and plays, and it was about time that he got down to fundamentals.

Thanks to Mr. Krutch's strange manner of generalizing about Europe, the reader is not likely to discover at once what his basic principles are, but close scrutiny reveals them. The revolution, he says, threatens to destroy not merely capitalism but "a way of life and a heritage of philosophy and art" and "the very sensibilities and forms of thought which made that heritage possible." Specifically, the revolution threatens individualism, freedom, and disinterestedness. Therefore, he concludes, the intellectual has "a stake in capitalism."

I do not doubt that the revolution will destroy a great deal that Mr. Krutch cherishes. If he wants to argue that such writers as Joyce and Proust, for example, could not possibly be developed in a proletarian society, I for one will not disagree with him. He happens to like a great deal in contemporary literature that I think is either definitely decadent and bad or else superfluous. He will miss it when it is gone, and I do not suppose the appearance of other qualities— which I regard as better and more important—will console him.

I can readily see why Mr. Krutch is unhappy at the prospect of the destruction of this culture of his, but I wonder how he intends to preserve it. He apparently has the strange idea that he can preserve it by defending capitalism. This culture did, it is true, develop in close association with the rise of capitalism, but I doubt if the capitalist system as such has nourished culture. A large proportion, perhaps a majority, of the artists of the past century have said or given the impression that their work was accomplished in spite of, not because of, capitalists and the capitalist system. From Shelley and Byron to Shaw and Wells, from Thoreau and Melville to Lewis and Dreiser, writers have testified that the values on which business is founded are utterly opposed to those on which culture rests.

Yet, Mr. Krutch may say, art has flourished under capitalism.

There has been art, certainly, and very good art, but it is a byproduct. Though individual capitalists have occasionally patronized the arts, capitalists as a class have been brutally indifferent to them. The culture Mr. Krutch enjoys and the values he adheres to have not been created by the capitalist class nor even fostered by it. The best one can say is that capitalism has tolerated them.

What will happen if it becomes definitely to the interest of the capitalist class not to tolerate this culture and these arts? The question is not an academic one, for the thing has already happened. Monopoly capitalism, threatened by destruction as the depression grows worse, has not hesitated to destroy everything that might hamper its exploitation of the workers. This last desperate stand on the part of capitalism is called Fascism, and even Mr. Krutch seems to suspect that Fascism is not precisely favorable to culture. What has happened to the artists and scientists of Germany we all know. In Italy, where Fascism has had a longer and less tumultuous history, there has, according to an article in *Current History* last spring, been no considerable achievement in any of the arts. Mr. Krutch and his kind may have a stake in capitalism as it is at present operating in America. Will he maintain that they are going to have a stake in Fascism?

The difficulty is, of course, in convincing Mr. Krutch that Fascism is certain to come in this country unless revolution intervenes. The task is more, I suspect, than I could accomplish even if I had unlimited space at my disposal. I very much wish, however, that he would take the time to read and ponder over Palme Dutt's *Fascism and Social Revolution.* A year or so ago he got round to reading the *Communist Manifesto,* and it is time that he continued his education. He would not find in Dutt's book any brilliant generalizations about European man and the nature of civilization, but he would find an extraordinarily lucid argument, beautifully documented. When he finished it, I should like to ask him if he still thought Fascism could be avoided by non-revolutionary means.

And in the meantime, I should like to inquire what Mr. Krutch, who will, I suppose, admit that Fascism is at least a possibility in the United States, is doing to prevent its triumph. If Fascism comes, culture, freedom, individualism, detachment, urbanity, and all the other good things of the civilized life will disappear. Mr. Krutch might devote to the combatting of Fascism at least a portion of the energy he spends in fighting Communism.

It may be possible to convince Mr. Krutch that in the long run he has no stake in capitalism; I doubt if it will ever be possible to convince him that he has a stake in Communism. But I trust that many of the intellectuals he is addressing are not quite so concerned as he with remaining urbane and detached and civilized in the midst of the kind of struggle that is now going on. I hope they are capable of looking at the Soviet Union, not with malicious joy at every evidence that it is not a Utopia, but with interest and sympathy. They will see though that bourgeois culture is very much alive. If, for example, they will read even hostile reports of the recent congress of writers in Moscow, they will discover that large masses of the Russian people are deeply concerned with what their artists are doing. No American writer today has so large or so keenly attentive an audience as any one of a score of Russian writers has. Russian literature may be dull and mediocre according to Mr. Krutch's standards, but he can scarcely deny that it has deep roots in the interests and hopes of millions of people. I am well aware, of course, that he would prefer the appreciation of a chosen few to that of multitudes of workers and farmers, but I have too much respect for American intellectuals to believe that he is wholly representative.

As for disinterestedness, freedom, and the sacredness of the individual, one question is indeed, as Krutch says, whether they have ever existed. For the vast majority they never have. Moreover, even for the minority they have existed only within limits. Mr. Krutch is free to do the things he wants to do because he does not want to do any of the things that are prohibited. He knows well enough, however, that there are many things he would not be free to write in the Nation or to say in an American college, and many things that he would not be free to do in New York City. He is satisfied with the treatment his individuality has received because he is not conscious of the forces that have moulded it. He is more disinterested, as he says, than S. Stanwood Mencken, but the limits of that disinterestedness are perfectly obvious to the revolutionary reader of his articles.

Under the dictatorship of the proletariat Mr. Krutch would have less freedom than he has now, but other people would have more. He would be painfully aware of the forces impinging upon his individuality because they would be forces exerted by a class hostile to his, but millions of people would have for the first time in their lives and, indeed, in the history of their class an opportunity to expand and grow. The awareness of individuality will presumably diminish in a collective society, but the opportunities for the realization of individual potentialities will, for the majority, enormously increase. During the period of the dictatorship conscious partisanship will no doubt be the rule, but in a classless society the freedom of the mind from the pull of economic interests will at last become a human possibility.

Communists, according to Mr. Krutch, "are full of an intense and burning hatred for that urbanity, detachment, and sense of fair play which make thinking amiable." I had not supposed amiability to be the principal requisite in thinking; accuracy and effectiveness, I should have said, are more important. Mr. Krutch's essays are no doubt amiable and urbane, but they are neither detached nor fair. Is it, for example, precisely fair, in view of the diversified achievements of Russia in science and all the arts, to say that the tendency of Communism is "to reduce all intellectual life to a state where it is concerned with nothing except essentially theological debates concerning the meaning of dialectical materialism"? Is it detached to grasp at every bit of slander about the Soviet Union and to disregard the steady progress that is being made there in every field of activity?

Not all the intellectuals who read his articles will, I believe, accept his thesis that he has all the virtues on his side and that on the Communist side are only dogmatism, harshness and intolerance. Mr. Krutch has his own variety of dogmatism and intolerance and even, beneath the mask of urbanity, his own brand of harshness too. Communists may be dogmatic, harsh, and intolerant; perhaps they have need to be; but that is not all they are. If intellectuals are looking for courage and honesty and impatience with cant and intolerance of injustice, they will not find them on Mr. Krutch's side.

October 23, 1934

H. L. Mencken and Robert Herrick

Those of us who are interested in proletarian literature cannot fail to be pleased with the increasing attention that is paid to the subject in the bourgeois press. Two recent discussions are particularly enlightening, though for different reasons. One is Robert Herrick's *Writers in the Jungle* in the New Republic for October 17. The other is H. L. Mencken's *Illuminators of the Abyss* in the October 6 issue of the *Saturday Review of Literature.*

The editors of the *Saturday Review* have provided an uncommonly suitable setting for Mr. Mencken's dissertation. The issue of October 6 marks the tenth anniversary of the founding of the magazine, and the editors are apparently overwhelmed by the fact that, in this land of freedom, progress, and culture, a literary weekly has survived for a decade. Invited comments from twenty-six men and women of letters signalize this achievement. They range from the dismal taciturnity of Theodore Dreiser, who thinks it is probably a pretty good magazine, but almost never reads it, to the lush enthusiasm of the author of *Anthony Adverse.* They range also from the warmth of Christian Gauss, who congratulates the editors on having kept their heads in a "literary reign of terror," to the embarrassment of Michael Gold, who detects "a faint aura of Wall Street."

Most of the letters dwell on the fairness of the magazine. Sinclair Lewis is impressed with this, and Oswald Garrison Villard and Booth Tarkington and William Harlan Hale. The editors, too, it is obvious, are fairly well satisfied with themselves on this point. Dr. Canby modestly refers to the possession of this virtue in his editorial, and William Rose Benet disposes of Mike Gold's allegations with the information that editorial salaries are far from plutocratic. Surely it would be an unreasonable critic who could remain unconvinced by such testimony. But what of Mr. Mencken's article, which is given the leading position in this issue of issues?

Can we reconstruct the mental processes of the editors of the *Saturday Review?* Perhaps they realized that the rise of a proletarian literature is the most important cultural event of the past decade and saw that it was the obvious subject for the principal article of their anniversary issue. Their problem was then to discover the person best fitted to deal with this theme. The author should, one would say, have an understanding of economics, know all American work that lays claim to being proletarian, be aware of the operations of the proletarian dictatorship in the Soviet Union, and enjoy the respect of informed persons as a critic of insight and integrity. With these criteria in mind, they looked around and picked out—H. L. Mencken.

Perhaps I am wrong; perhaps that is not the way it was done; I insist, however, that that is how it should have been done. The Review's reputation for fairness and the editors' sense of responsibility to their readers demanded it. If they merely sought the somewhat bedimmed glory of Mr. Mencken's name, they were betraying their readers. If they wanted at all costs an attack on proletarian literature, what can be said of their claims to fairness?

But if they really considered what qualifications a writer on proletarian literature should have, why did they choose Mr. Mencken? His knowledge of economics is on a level with Herbert Hoover's, with whose views he substantially agrees. If he has ever read one proletarian novel, short story, or poem, there is not the slightest evidence of it in this article. What he knows about Russia he learned from reading, for review purposes, half a dozen discredited collections of scandals and lies. As for his standing as a critic—well, a man can't live on the strength of having discovered Theodore Dreiser.

Mr. Mencken's ideas about proletarian literature can be summarized even more briefly than Mike Gold summarized them in the *Daily Worker* for October 17. Gold generously listed nine points. I can discover only five: proletarian literature is dull; its novelists and poets have turned in disappointment to the revolution because they couldn't make the grade of the Cosmopolitan; its critics are "young men with a disinclination for steady jobs" and a desire to attract attention by shocking people; it relies on banal indecency; it is a fad, which started two or three years ago and will end in a year or two.

That is all he says, absolutely all. It is unnecessary to refute him, for he offers no evidence. And it would be futile to abuse him. The Sage of Baltimore, bereft of the following he once had, is naturally turning to unprincipled slander and violent denunciation in the vain attempt to recapture a little of the acclaim that formerly rewarded his every word. But he has lost his old flair for vituperation, and his style, which once ranked him near the top of living American humorists, has become labored and sluggish. The old dog can't learn new tricks, and he seems a little senile in his performance of the old ones. We have nothing to be concerned about, though it does seem to me that Dr. Canby and his colleagues might have the matter a little on their consciences.

The sad collapse of Mr. Mencken makes the vitality of Robert Herrick seem almost miraculous, for Mr. Herrick, after all, was writing novels when the Sage was in grammar school. Never so widely acclaimed as other muckraking novelists, he went on, year after year, piecing together his record of American life in the era of monopoly capitalism. He has not always seen clearly, but he has never deliberately shut his eyes, and, as the *New Republic* piece shows, they are still open. The article is an intelligent and sympathetic account of certain proletarian novels, notably *The Disinherited, The Shadow Before, The Land of Plenty,* and *The Foundry.* Mr. Herrick understands very well what the authors of these books are trying to do and why they want to do it. So far as I know, there is no other discussion of proletarian literature by a critic uncommitted to revolution so consistently perceptive and so nearly just.

There is one contention of Mr. Herrick's with which I would quarrel. He says that these novelists do not show that employers are as much "conditioned" as workers. The proletarian novelist should, he tells us, be guided by "a tragic conviction that the social system is writing its own doom, and his part is merely to record the steps." "The creative writer at least," he concludes, "is not under the compulsion of political exigencies, of expediency or partisanship. He is free—it is his supreme function to exercise such freedom—to rise beyond the turmoil and the strife, to see *all* the human elements in the social complex."

We know, of course, that the social system is writing its own doom, but only in the sense that it is creating the forces that will overthrow it. Capitalism will collapse only when it is destroyed. This is not some mechanical process that the writer can study from the outside; it is a conflict of active forces, and the writer is part of one force or the other. The writer cannot rise beyond the turmoil, for it is all-inclusive. He can no more be outside the class struggle than he can be outside the operations of the law of gravitation. He can, of course, vacillate, lending his strength now to this side and now to that, but that is a very different thing from the objectivity Mr. Herrick desires.

The impossibility of impartiality does not mean that the author cannot see all the human elements; it merely means that he must see them from one point of view or the other. Perhaps Herrick is right in saying that as yet proletarian novelists have not portrayed fully enough the lives and minds of the employers. They ought, certainly, to do so, for they can give the reality of the class struggle in no other way. But from what point of view shall they examine these elements? Take MacMahon in *The Land of Plenty*, for example. Cantwell may not reveal him fully enough, but any further revelation would be valueless unless it were from the same point of view. Even if he were to show MacMahon as he appears to men of his own class, he would have to evaluate the judgment of that class in terms of the attitudes of the working class. And after all the essential truth about MacMahon is that he is mean and narrow in his relations with his employes, as any employer has to be, and his meanness and narrowness carry over into his domestic life. Cantwell sees this essential truth because he looks at MacMahon through the eyes of the workers. He could not see it in any other way.

The great weakness of Mr. Herrick's own novels is, I believe, that he has sincerely striven for this impartiality he recommends to others, and it happens to be an illusion. Jumping from one side of the barricades to the other does not conduce to power of conviction, singleness of purpose, and unity of conception—virtues to be found in most great literature. But my recognition of his faults is accompanied by admiration for his virtues, and my quarrel with his theories does not diminish my respect for the man. I cordially recommend his article to the attention of the editors of the *Saturday Review of Literature*.

October 30, 1934

The Vigorous Abandon of Max Eastman's Mind

In her article on "Communism and Romanticism" in the *New Masses* for Sepember 25 Genevieve Taggard said a number of exceedingly shrewd things about the romantic temperament and its dangers for the revolutionary movement. It seemed to me that her chief fault was too lenient a treatment of the humanist or, as she called it, classicist position. We have even less in common with the humanists than we have with the romanticists. Perhaps all that we share with them is an understanding of the complete decadence of the romantic movement, and even there we differ since, as Miss Taggard's article shows, we can appreciate the historic importance and genuine virtues of the founders of the movement at the same time that we recognize the sterility of their present-day followers.

In her diagnosis of the romantic nature Miss Taggard said: "This godlike type, this poet who is a law unto himself, who is above life, in his opinion, and above material limitation, this person who pretends to be free of human limitations and free of the need to accomplish realities with his fellows, can only feed his audience with the fiction of personality, the decay of those convictions that once fought for a free market, free competition, laissez-faire, and all the rest of it." "Is there any room in Communism," she inquired, "for the eternal rebel, the Shelleyesque protagonist, the ethereal creature who flies forever in an azure mist away from reality?"

Reading these and similar lines, I thought of various romanticists of the present day, and of what has happened to them. I thought of the poems, pretty little things, about love and spring and love, that Max Eastman used to write at the very time that he was editing the *Masses* and the *Liberator*. I remembered his novel, *Venture,* in which the class struggle somehow gets lost in the lustrous light of feminine eyes and in the meanderings of a Nietzschean businessman. I recalled his recantation at the second *Masses* trial, which Miss Taggard herself has described in her preface to *May Days.* And I thought of him crusading today on behalf of the downtrodden artists of Russia, still the eternal rebel, flying in an azure mist.

These thoughts have recurred to me as I read *Art and the Life of Action.* The book contains two or three book reviews and some travel sketches, but it is interesting chiefly because of the long essay that gives it its title. This essay I have examined with as much objectivity as I could muster, trying to read it as if it were by an unknown writer and not by the author of *Artists in Uniform*. It is a notable statement of the esthetics of romanticism in an age of revolution.

Much of the essay is concerned with describing the various uses attributed to art in the past. For some strange reason, according to Mr. Eastman, men have been unwilling to accept art as its own justification, and they have therefore invoked certain sanctions for it, such as magic, religion, education, and the like. These sanctions, he argues, are no longer valid. It is now seen that art exists "for its own sake and because of the pure desire to have and focus and intensify experience," and only "the dupes of practicality, those joyless adults who can never have been children," will ignore this fact. The "major and defining purpose" of artists is "to live life and communicate it," and they must resist any effort to control the "vivid life and vigorous abandon of a poet's mind."

This notion that art is somehow set apart from the rest of life is not, of course, peculiar to Mr. Eastman. Nevertheless, as his own analysis shows, it has not been and is not the prevailing view. The fact that there have been scores of different conceptions of the function of art is taken by him to indicate that art has no function. It would seem to me, on the other hand, to demonstrate that the majority of men in all times have been aware of the profound and far-reaching influences of art. What they have all expressed, in their various ways, is the conviction that art does something.

Mr. Eastman will say, I suppose, that in his view too art does something: it focuses and intensifies experience, and that is enough. But experience, whenever he speaks of it in this essay, is always treated as if it were made up of isolated, independent experiences. It is a good thing, he says, to heighten the consciousness of any person, and of course this is true; but actually to heighten a person's consciousness of some thing or some event involves the awakening of a perception of the relations of that thing or event to other things or events. Science, says Mr. Eastman, conceives things in their relations, art in their qualities. What qualities are or can be apart from their relations he does not bother to state.

Exactly what is the quality of wine apart from the eye, nose, palate, and brain of the drinker? And from immediate relations such as these one is inevitably carried to more involved relations: the consequences of the wine in the drinker's mood, the responses of his companions to his mood, the effect of their intercourse on their action. The writer cannot reveal all the innumerable relations that define any given experience, but he must portray some of them if he is to be articulate—even Mr. Eastman admits that "pure" realization is "perhaps" impossible—and by and large the further he pursues his revelation, the more impressive it will be.

It is because art is concerned with relations, and not with some abstraction called "qualities," that it refuses to stay cooped up in the little compartment to which Mr. Eastman relegates it. The artist's perception of relations comes sooner or later to have some effect on our own perceptions. His perception is neither identical with nor yet a substitute for the perception of the scientist. On the one hand it is not limited to the scientist's terms; on the other it is not excluded from using them. (One of the founders of romanticism, William Wordsworth, saw the fallacy of Mr. Eastman's romantic barrier between science and art.) The artist's perception is, of course, more like that of everyday life than that of the laboratory, though at its best it has something of both.

What the artist does to us and for us by setting forth his particular vision of life is not easy to define. He alters, in some degree or other, our modes of seeing and feeling. Thus he changes our response to events, and this in turn affects our actions. I. A. Richards, in *Principles of Literary Criticism,* gives an account of the process that seems to me largely sound as far as it goes. Mr. Eastman does not like Richards' account, partly, it appears, because it bears some resemblance to Bukharin's. Both Richards and Bukharin recognize that a work of art changes us, and that it is necessary for the critic to ask what the change has been and whether it is desirable. They naturally differ on what is desirable.

But Eastman will have none of this. Science, he says, does all the serious work, and science and art are incompatible. It is a splendid idea, for him, for it establishes the complete irresponsibility of the artist. "There is no clearer line of demarcation among human types," he states, "than that between the artist and the man of action." "The art for art's sake formula," we are told, "however meagre as a program, was unimpeachable as a statement of fact." "Artists," he inevitably concludes, "should not only refuse to join a practical organization, but should do so with a reliant pride capable of resisting any attempts upon the part of such an organization to direct their work." He admits, reluctantly, that "art's heroic ages have been those in which it was not conscious of itself as art at all, but was a devoted service to some great aim." He believes, however, that this evidence of artistic backwardness can be outgrown. The artist must learn to devote himself in solitary splendor to pure experience.

Of course Mr. Eastman rejects the Marxian conception of the class basis of art, for that, since he pretends to be a revolutionary, would interfere with his romantic irresponsibility. As evidence that art is neutral he cites the Rockefellers' appreciation of Rivera's frescoes. He argues that, just as both proletarians and bourgeois "drink tea or coffee and reject a dose of mustard," so there are "works of art, and elements of art, irrelevant to the class struggle." Of course there are, but the question is whether these irrelevant elements have any importance, or even can be understood, apart from the elements that are decidedly relevant to the class struggle. Only such "art" as one finds in Mr. Eastman's insipid verses is content to limit itself to the drinking of tea and coffee.

From beginning to end, *Art and the Life of Action* expresses the stalest kind of romanticism, precisely the kind Miss Taggard eloquently attacked. But it will, I suppose, serve its purpose, and will receive fulsome praise from the capitalist press, which was so delighted by the author's *Artists in Uniform*. The little phrases about revolution will not trouble even J. Donald Adams, who may be stupid but knows an ally when he sees one.

November 6, 1934

It Still Goes On

Dr. Harry Elmer Barnes of the *World-Telegram* has been reading church history and has discovered a resemblance between the psychology of the early Christians and that of contributors to the *New Masses*. The comparison, which is not altogether original, is based on the violence that Dr. Barnes detects in the polemics of both the Christians and the Communists. I wonder if he has forgotten his own controversies on the subject of war guilt, especially the campaign that, with all the zeal of an Athanasius or a Tertullian, he carried on against Bernadotte Schmitt. Most people, as a matter of fact, get a little excited when what they regard as fundamental issues are at stake, and it is hard to see what is gained by dragging the Book of Jude into the discussion.

Moreover, Dr. Barnes' illustrations of the *New Masses'* apostolic fervor are rather strangely selected. He says, for example, "One prominent writer in this journal assaulted the reviewers in the *New York Times* Sunday Literary section as 'White Guards,' assigned to assassinate any books favorable to Soviet Russia." I am very glad that he read my article on Section Five; I only wish he would read Section Five. In the issues that have appeared since my article was published he could have found a good deal of evidence to support my "assault."

In the issue of September 30, for example, was Alexander Nazaroff's review of the Countess Tolstoy's *I Worked for the Soviets.* Mr. Nazaroff felt that the book lacked "the gripping drama" of his favorite reading, the "unforgettable" *Escape from the Soviets,* but "in the deep sincerity and truthfulness, in the conviction which her story carries, and in the darkness which the picture unfolded by her presents, Alexandra Lvovna's book fully equals the work of her predecessors." Readers of Section Five learned that the Countess, with "no trace of rancor in her tone" and "without bitterness," describes the prison-like atmosphere of the Soviet Union, the wrecking of Russia's educational system, the pregnancy of fourteen-year-old schoolgirls, and the eagerness of the peasants to turn their guns on the Kremlin. The book, to put it briefly, is a powerful piece of evidence in the trial of the Soviet Union at the bar of "the conscience of the civilized world."

In the issue of October 14, Section Five's mysterious expert on Russia, A. M. Nikolaieff, appeared in a new role, as authority on China, reviewing Agnes Smedley's *China's Red Army Marches,* which he did not like. In the issue of October 21, J. Donald Adams lent his solemn approval to Chamberlain's *Russia's Iron Age.* In the issue of October 28, Mr. Nazaroff—back on page 22, it is true, and with several qualifying phrases—wrote at length and with some satisfaction on Boris Kamyshansky's *I Am a Cossack.*

It still goes on, but Dr. Barnes does not see it. His comment on my article is: "Whether the charge is correct or not, certainly it is only fair to recall that, after the famous exposure of the news published on Russia in the *Times* which was brought out by Walter Lippmann in the *New Republic,* the *Times* has published more valuable and authentic material on Russia than has appeared anywhere else in the English-speaking world." I do not know whether he means that my article may be as fruitful as Mr. Lippmann's or that I ought to have given the *Times* credit for its Russian news, but let him have the benefit of the doubt. The important thing is that scholarly phrase, "whether this charge is correct or not." Nothing, of course, about the pages of evidence the article contained. Nothing to indicate that the learned doctor has ever read Section Five. Just a good academic bit of hedging.

But note how, when he has occasion to praise the *Times,* this blushing modesty vanishes. The *Times* "has published more valuable and authentic material on Russia than has appeared anywhere else in the English-speaking world." Why he qualifies his statement with "English-speaking" I cannot understand.

In general I have the impression that my article on Section Five, "whether the charge is correct or not," does not wholly meet with Dr. Barnes' disapproval, for he continues: "But when this critic sails into the *Times* reviewer, John Chamberlain, and denounces him as a weak 'straddler,' this is a little too much. Mr. Chamberlain is known best for his book, *Farewell to Reform,* which is a very critical summary of American progressivism and liberalism in the last generation and a forthright relinquishment of any hope in reformist programs." But I did not criticize Chamberlain on the ground that he was a reformist. On the contrary, it is precisely because he pretends to be more than a liberal that he may legitimately be attacked for straddling. If he wrote under some such title as "The Liberal Viewpoint," as Dr. Barnes used to do, straddling would be natural and unexceptionable.

And John Chamberlain's straddling, like Section Five's White Guardism, still goes on. There was a pleasant example in his review of Max Eastman's *Art and the Life of Action* in the *Times* for October 29. "Granville Hicks," he wrote, "and others who drop frequently into the habit of applying mechanical moralistic criteria to literature might read the first half of Mr. Eastman's book with profit; but others should be warned that Eastman, in his willingness to make out a case against his enemies, overlooks facts that might do his thesis damage." I shall start worrying about my "mechanical moralistic criteria" if Mr. Chamberlain will take the trouble to show me what they are and when and how I have applied them, but for the moment I am concerned with his introducing these criteria to balance the mild rebuke he administers to Max Eastman. A slap on my wrist, a slap on Mr. Eastman's, and everyone is happy.

Dr. Barnes' third example of patristic fervor in the *New Masses* is S. Snedden's review of *Challenge to the New Deal,* which he finds "even more reminiscent of the diatribes of the old heresies." He quotes two sentences: "It has been a matter of note that some of the cleverest and most influential enemies of the working-class have been prepared for their careers by a taste at the Marxian spring. The 'little knowledge' of these renegades has indeed turned out to be a dangerous thing— for the masses." He neglects to quote Snedden's next sentence: "It was as 'Marxists' that MacDonald, Mussolini, Briand, and Pilsudski learned to know the nature of capitalist society and were thus equipped to advance themselves in it." That, it appears to me, is a simple statement of fact.

But Dr. Barnes insists that the contributors to *Challenge to the New Deal* are "brilliant left-wing specialists on American civilization today," and that is that. The reviewer should not have pointed out that certain essays are very good, others sadly confused, and others dangerously suggestive of Fascism. Such discrimination, according to Dr. Barnes, gives aid and comfort to capitalism: "So long as the American radicals stick to backstabbing in their own ranks as the great indoor sport the American Bourbons can sit pretty with few grounds for fear."

It would be nice if we could be one big happy family, as Dr. Barnes wants us to be. Unity in the radical movement is enormously important, and I suspect that Communists realize its importance quite as well as the *World-Telegram's* expert on the history of world civilization. But we happen to believe that unity on the terms, let us say, of Mussolini or MacDonald or even Selden Rodman or A. J. Muste would defeat the purposes for which we and, theoretically at least, all radicals are striving. Dr. Barnes thinks we are wrong, but that can scarcely prevent us from showing, as forcefully and as clearly as possible, why we are right.

The growth of a revolutionary movement is a strange thing. Primarily created by economic forces, it receives its apparent stimuli from all sorts of sources. Even Dr. Barnes may help to make a revolutionary now and then. I know one young man who became interested in the Communist Party, which he subsequently joined, as a result, so far as he could tell, of reading "The Liberal Viewpoint."

But he would not have become a Communist if Communists had refrained from criticizing Barnes and his ideas; he would have stayed right where Barnes is. The sharpening of the class struggle goes on day by day. It is no longer enough to be vaguely against capitalism; it is necessary to be clearly and wholeheartedly for revolution. Those who stand resolutely and openly for the existing order cannot be influenced and need not be exposed. Exposure is for those who conceal hostility under a guise of impartiality, and criticism for those who divert the energies of the revolutionary movement into unprofitable channels. If this is the spirit of the Book of Jude, so much the better for the Book of Jude.

November 13, 1934

Our Magazines and Their Functions

In the current issue of the *Partisan Review* Jerre Mangione criticizes *Leftward,* the organ of the John Reed Club of Boston, for trying to be "the *New Masses* of New England," and suggests that the editors had better try to find a particular function that no other magazine is performing.

This seems to be good common sense. The revolutionary movement, with its terrific tasks, has neither manpower nor money to waste. There are scores and scores of revolutionary magazines, appearing weekly, monthly, bimonthly, and quarterly, and serving a great variety of purposes. The maintenance of these magazines is not easy. There have to be constant drives for funds, and both editors and contributors make incalculable sacrifices. All this is justified only if each magazine is making some specific contribution to the revolutionary cause.

I think it quite possible that there is room for re-organization in the revolutionary press as a whole, but let us look for the moment only at the literary magazines. There are more than a dozen of them. In a sense this is fine, for it shows how widely the revolutionary movement is appealing to the writers of the nation. I hope that, as the movement grows, it will be possible to support all of these and many more. But we must always be sure—and especially now, when our resources are so inadequate—that the effort expended is accomplishing the most that it can possibly accomplish.

One thing I think we have to take for granted, and that is that the *New Masses* ought to be given every opportunity to perform the task that has been set for it. This may sound immodest, but there is no sense in mincing words. The *New Masses* is the principal organ of the revolutionary cultural movement. It reaches not only most of the revolutionary writers and artists themselves; it reaches their proper audience, the militant workers and large sections of disillusioned and actually or potentially petty bourgeois. It ought to represent the very best that the revolutionary movement can produce in fiction, poetry, reportage, criticism, and political and economic analysis. And it ought to be so provided with funds that it can be brought to the attention of the thousands and thousands of proletarians, white-collar workers, and professional men and women who are ready to listen to what it has to say.

Practically this means that no work should appear in other revolutionary magazines that could be effectively used in the *New Masses*. It means, also, that money ought to be spent in making the *New Masses* a better magazine rather than in publishing other magazines unless it is clear that these magazines are performing functions that the *New Masses* cannot perform. This assumes, of course, that the editors of the *New Masses* are making the best possible use of the opportunities they have. By and large I believe this to be true. If it is not true, then the thing to do is to improve the *New Masses*, not to start another magazine.

At the risk of stepping on a number of corns I should like to be quite specific. Last spring a magazine called the *Monthly Review* was started, and I believe that four issues in all appeared. The purpose of this magazine, as I understand it, was to reach sections of the middle-class that are not yet ready for the *New Masses*. Unfortunately, however, the contents of the magazine were very badly adapted to this purpose. There were a few articles that might have made the right kind of appeal, but they could hardly have offset the effect of the rest of the contents. Certain articles were of a highly technical and perhaps even sectarian nature, and could have only the most limited appeal. Others were on an exceedingly low intellectual and literary level, and served only to bring the revolutionary movement into dispute. Still others merely duplicated the *New Masses*.

Now the *Monthly Review* obviously lost money, and I believe that those who supplied the funds would have been glad, if they had understood the situation, to have had them used, as they easily might have been, to better advantage. Moreover, the magazine took the time and energy of a number of highly trained men, whose usefulness to the revolutionary cause is beyond question.

On the other hand, *New Theatre* has quickly and unmistakably made a place for itself. There is certainly no other journal that provides adequate space for the detailed discussion of the particular problems of the revolutionary drama and for the careful analysis in revolutionary terms of the bourgeois stage. The only questions are whether there is a need for such analysis and discussion and whether there is an audience for them. The answer to the first question is obvious; the answer to the second has been triumphantly provided by the rapid growth in the circulation of *New Theatre*.

When we turn to the John Reed Club magazines, we have a different situation. The usual purpose of such a magazine is to provide an outlet for the literary productions of the club's members. This is important. Writers not only want to see their work in print; they need to. Publication seems an essential part of the process of learning to write, and these magazines are, potentially at least, instruments in the development of a new generation of revolutionary writers. The material they publish is often unsuitable for a magazine that reaches a large, varied, and partly hostile audience, but it has interest and value for readers in a particular area. Moreover, the publication of such a magazine has value as a collective enterprise.

There is, however, one of the John Reed Club magazines that does not exist for the encouragement of the less mature members of the club. This is the *Partisan Review*, published by the John Reed Club of New York City. In each of the five issues that have appeared a large proportion of the contributions has come from writers who are not members of the club. Practically all the contributors, moreover, are well-established writers, who have no difficulty in publishing their work elsewhere.

The *Partisan Review* is obviously in a category by itself. Let us look at the current issue. Nearly one-half of it is devoted to book reviews. All of the reviews are competent, and some are very good, but I do not think that on the average they are superior to the reviews in the *New Masses*, in which the same books have been or will be reviewed. It is good to be able to compare the views of two Marxist critics, but I doubt if the value is great enough to justify, under present circumstances, the publication of two magazines. As for the other contributions, they are all on a high level, and there are one or two of them that probably could not have been printed elsewhere and that deserve to be read. On the whole, however, relatively little is accomplished that would not or could not be accomplished by other magazines.

The same criticism applies in the main to the four previous issues of the *Partisan Review*. Reckoning roughly, I should say that only about one-fifth of the total number of pages of Volume I of the magazine have been used to what I would call good advantage. And now the editors announce that in 1935 each issue will have ninety-six, instead of sixty-four, pages.

It seems to me that, if the *Partisan Review* is not to be the organ of the John Reed Club of New York City, it ought to be primarily devoted to long, theoretical critical essays. We have *Dynamo* for poetry and *Blast* and *Anvil* for short stories. The *New Masses* publishes some critical essays, but it cannot print many and it cannot assume that its readers are in general interested in esthetic theory. There is a need for fundamental consideration of both the theoretical and the practical problems of proletarian culture, and the *Partisan Review* could fruitfully devote itself to this field. What I am interested in, and all I am interested in, is the effective utilization of our forces.

As I have already indicated, I think that *Dynamo* is valuable; it has printed good poems, and I doubt if all these poems would have been published elsewhere. Perhaps, however, its functions should be taken over by the *Partisan Review*. There might be a special poetry section edited by the present editors of *Dynamo*. As for *Anvil* and *Blast,* there is a place for one magazine devoted to proletarian short stories, and possibly—though I am not so sure of it—for two. Both magazines have printed first-rate stories, and one magazine that printed the best of both would be very effective.

All of this is likely to sound a little arbitrary to some people. The idea has always been that anybody who had a little money and could pry a little more out of his friends had not merely a right but a duty to start a magazine. These magazines, as a rule, died painlessly and soon, and other magazines took their places. But such Bohemian individualism and irresponsibility are entirely incompatible with the serious tasks of revolution and the intelligent discipline of revolutionaries. The question of effective reorganization of the revolutionary cultural press is obviously not to be settled on the basis of any one person's opinions; but someone has to start the discussion that might lead to such re-organization, and that is what I have tried to do.

December 18, 1934

Another Authority on Marxism

Mr. John Chamberlain has returned to the subject of proletarian literature in his review of John Strachey's *Literature and Dialectical Materialism.* Very few of his comments are sound, and several are unfair. Since I want to devote myself this week to another authority on Marxism, I cannot discuss Chamberlain's misguided efforts to refute Strachey's analysis of Hemingway, MacLeish, *et al.* I must, however, comment on his response to my invitation to produce examples of my application of "mechanical, moralistic criteria." This is what he offers:

When Robert Cantwell wrote *The Land of Plenty,* Mr. Hicks lamented that the novel did not contain a ringing assurance that the working class is bound to triumph. But Mr. Cantwell at the time he was completing his novel, happened to be depressed at what he regarded as the sinister outcome of a number of strikes under the N.R.A. His depressed feeling, quite naturally, was reflected in his novel. And the value of the novel, from a radical's point of view, is that it is a key to a state of mind and a state of society. If Mr. Cantwell had faked the proletarian equivalent of a happy ending, he would have been misleading his readers. Mr. Hicks should not, I submit, have lectured Cantwell for failing to rally the morale of the troops.

What I said and all I said is:

The book gives the reader the mental atmosphere of a factory as no other novel does that I have read, and it shows in its essentials the unconquerable militancy of the workers. In the second part of the book, especially at the very end, Cantwell relies too much on obliqueness, and the heroism of the embattled workers is a little obscured. As a result *The Land of Plenty* fails to sweep the reader along, as William Rollins' *The Shadow Before* does, to high resolve and a sense of ultimate triumph. There remains, however, a feeling that one has been in contact with people and with forces that cannot be ignored.

Now where is the lament and where is the lecture? Cantwell has himself admitted that the ending was confused. I merely pointed out that, if it had been clearer, the book would have said more effectively what he wanted to say.

Despite Dr. Harry Elmer Barnes' second plea for an era of good feeling, I still believe that it is our friends who need watching. Lewis

Gannett dismissed Strachey's book as nonsense. John Chamberlain took it seriously and devoted his whole column to it. The comparison is, obviously, all in Chamberlain's favor. Yet Gannett's dismissal will do the book no particular harm, whereas Chamberlain's confused and misleading comments are bound to create misunderstanding and make the growth of proletarian literature more difficult.

Exactly the same comment has to be made about the two articles that the *Saturday Review of Literature* has published. Mencken's article was a disgraceful performance, and I still think Dr. Canby ought to be ashamed of having published so shoddy an essay. But Mencken so completely exposed himself that his article was almost as much of a boon to Communists as Herbert Hoover's *Challenge to Liberty* was to the Democrats. Louis Adamic, however, writing in the *Saturday Review* for December 1, comes forward as a sympathizer with militant labor and a friend to radical authors. His piece at least has elements of plausibility, and what I regard as its errors are all too likely to be accepted by the unwary.

Mr. Adamic's thesis is that "the overwhelming majority of the American working class does not read books and serious, purposeful magazines." This is his conclusion, "based on a year's study among hundreds of workers throughout the United States." He offers the statement as if it would startle his readers, especially the radicals. But we knew it all the time. Times are changing a good deal more rapidly than Mr. Adamic will admit, and I suspect that a different kind of sampling would have got different results, but circulation figures alone would be enough to show that the number of workers that read revolutionary novels is relatively small.

If what Adamic has to say is news to any proletarian novelists, I hope they will profit by it. But I am much less interested in his account of the reading habits of the average worker than I am in his generalizations on proletarian literature. For, despite the modest title, "What the Proletariat Reads," the essay not only offers a good deal of advice to authors but ventures into the field of theory.

The essay begins by summarizing Trotsky's familiar argument that proletarian culture is impossible, since under capitalism and the dictatorship alike the proletariat is too busy to produce an authentic art, and by the time leisure has been achieved a classless society will have been established. Unfortunately for Trotsky and Adamic, art has been flourishing for seventeen years in the Soviet Union. It is not a classless art, any more than the Soviet Union is a classless society; it is the art of the class in power, the proletariat. And even in capitalist countries a considerable body of art has developed that one cannot possibly call bourgeois and certainly is not classless. Mr. Adamic recognizes this in practice by discussing several examples in his essay.

Even a casual analysis of cultural processes will reveal the fallacy in Trotsky's assertions. During the period of capitalist decline, a growing number of proletarians realize that their economic interests are opposed to those of the bourgeoisie, then that their political interests are opposed, and finally that their cultural interests are opposed. Bourgeois books do not portray life as they see it, do not deal with the problems that seem to them important, do not express their attitudes. Despite all the hardships of their class in a capitalist society, certain of them attempt to write about life in their own terms. They are joined by members of the middle class, usually the lower middle class, who realize that capitalism is doomed and that the future lies with the workers. These revolutionary intellectuals, identifying themselves, perhaps never completely but in important respects, with the proletariat, express essentially the same attitude as their proletarian allies. Together these two groups lay the foundation for a literature that is fundamentally different from that of the dominant class.

This point we have already reached in the United States. Russia, of course, is far ahead of us. Even in the period of greatest struggle against class enemies, Soviet writers were at work, and today, with the establishment of higher standards of living and the achievement of greater leisure, the Soviet Union is the scene of far greater cultural activity than can be found in any capitalist country. The authors of the USSR are not only given every opportunity to write; their books are sold in editions of hundreds of thousands, and are read and discussed by millions of workers. The culture of the Soviet Union rests, not on the whims of a leisured minority, but on the fundamental interests and ever-expanding desires of the creative masses. No culture in history has had so firm a foundation.

But culture in the USSR is still a class culture. The proletariat must remain militantly class-conscious so long as its enemies survive at home and abroad, and its literature reflects this class-consciousness. When the proletariat is the only class, it will cease to be conscious of itself as a class. The classless society will not be achieved by manifesto; it will be a slow and imperceptible growth. Literature will respond to every phase of this transition, and proletarian literature will gradually become the literature of a classless society. Proletarian culture will not last as long as bourgeois culture has lasted, but it is the only possible bridge between bourgeois and classless culture. It is bound to exist because it is the expression of a class that is, during a considerable period of time, conscious of itself as distinct from other classes. Moreover, it has a role to play in the creation of attitudes that are essential to the final evolution of a classless society.

If this is true, it is meaningless for Adamic to say, "All proletarian literature is intended to be propaganda," for it is not propaganda in any sense that bourgeois literature is not. If the expression of a particular attitude towards the world is propaganda, then the term applies to all literature. The aim of the proletarian author is the aim of any author: he wants to write about representative persons and significant events in such a way as to bring out what he believes to be the truth about them.

Out of his vast misunderstanding of proletarian literature Mr. Adamic attempts to lay down a series of rules. There should be no individual villains, he says. Every Marxist knows, of course, that there are no villains, but he also knows that there are people who do villainous things, who are regarded as villains by their opponents, and who have to be treated as villains. Again, he says that the proletarian novel "must not be about the proletariat alone, as if it existed in a kind of semi-vacuum." I trust the critics will observe that this time it is a non-Marxist who is telling writers what they should write about —something Marxist critics don't do but are accused of doing. It may suit the purposes of the writer to deal with both the workers and the bosses or it may not. Halper was right in devoting so much attention to the bosses in *The Foundry,* and Jack Conroy, who was writing *The Disinherited* from the point of view of a particular worker, was right in including only as much of the bosses as that worker would see. Yet Larry Donovan does not exist in a vacuum.

All this suggests to me that Mr. Adamic is trying hard to make a case against proletarian literature and has raked together all the arguments he can borrow or invent. This impression is confirmed when I read, "Most of the proletarian writing so far, as I have said, has not been overburdened with truth. Much of it, with its lies and exaggerations, is downright counter-revolutionary in character." This is a serious charge and ought to be backed with a little evidence. The only specific case of misrepresentation Adamic mentions is in Catherine Brody's *Nobody Starves,* which is a sentimental, humanitarian novel with no suggestion of revolutionary understanding. Of course there are unconvincing portrayals of character and implausible descriptions of events in certain proletarian novels, but I am convinced that under-statement is more characteristic of revolutionary fiction than exaggeration. If Mr. Adamic wanted to object to certain passages, I—and, I am sure, the authors—would listen with interest even when we could not agree, but this indictment of most of proletarian literature as "lies" is unpleasantly reminiscent of the Mencken article.

The shrewdness of some people is extraordinary. Certain followers of Trotsky loudly proclaim that they are more revolutionary than the Communists. Yet *The Nation* and other liberal periodicals, which will not have a Communist as contributor and which are not in any sense sympathetic to revolution, constantly print the reviews and articles of the Trotskyites. Mr. Adamic is also deeply concerned about the revolution and worries because the proletarian authors tell counter-revolutionary lies. Yet the very unrevolutionary Dr. Canby—who also, it may be noted, admires Eastman's latest book—employs Adamic to write the *Saturday Review's* article on proletarian literature. And I must say that Adamic, pointing out that the whole idea of proletarian literature is stupid and conveying the impression that most proletarian writers are fools or rascals or both, didn't let Dr. Canby down.

December 25, 1934

Revolutionary Literature of 1934

It has been a good year, an exceptionally good year, a year to put the Menckens, Hazlitts and Soskins on the defensive. Before 1934 it required some understanding of literary and social processes to recognize the promise of revolutionary literature, but now even a daily book reviewer has to blindfold his eyes to ignore its achievements and its potentialities.

The drama has made the most startling advance. The amorphous rebelliousness of the New Playwrights has yielded to the strong, clearcut, revolutionary intelligence and discipline of the Theatre Union, depending for its support not on the whims of dilettantes but on the eager enthusiasm of workers and their organizations. Founded in 1933, the Theatre Union not merely achieved popular backing in 1934, but demonstrated maturity in authorship, directing, and acting. The eloquent but confused *Peace on Earth* was followed by *Stevedore*, rich in its conception of character, firmly integrated in construction and method, and revolutionary in its understanding of social forces. Melodrama the bourgeois critics called it, unable to deny the effectiveness of Peters' and Sklar's writing and Blankfort's directing, but they could point to no distortion of character or event for the sake of sensation. The term was their unconscious tribute to an alive and exciting play.

Aside from the Theatre Union plays, we have John Wexley's *They Shall Not Die,* a kind of experiment in dramatic journalism, most effective when it follows most closely the actual events of the Scottsboro case, least effective in its invented scenes. It might have been a better play if it had been written for the Theatre Union rather than the Theatre Guild. A dramatist cannot rise very far above the intellectual level of his audience, and the Guild audience is, in matters such as the Scottsboro case, singularly ignorant. Yet Wexley made it a moving play, and the enlightened spectators knew that he understood the true issues.

Nineteen thirty-four has also brought the publication of books of plays by John Dos Passos and John Howard Lawson. Neither author has wholly escaped from the mannerisms of the New Playwrights era, but the former's *Fortune Heights* and the latter's *Gentlewoman* show not only talent but growing clarity. Melvin Levy's *Gold Eagle Guy*, which I have not seen, has divided critical opinion. Samuel Ornitz's *In New Kentucky*, soon to be produced, is, if one can judge from the first act published in the *New Masses* last spring, a forceful and authentic portrayal of working-class life. Finally, we must note the activity of the workers' theatres and the progress of dramatic criticism in the thriving magazine, *New Theatre*.

The poets, I think, are getting away from the kind of obscurity that marred the work of so many of them. Robert Gessner's *Upsurge* is direct enough, and taken as a whole it gives a sense of the urgency and irresistibility of the revolutionary movement, though taken line by line it is disappointingly diffuse. Isidor Schneider's poems in *Comrade-Mister*, on the other hand, are firm and strong, and a second reading finds them more impressive than a first. He has sacrificed none of the originality and profundity that distinguished his earlier work, and he has added to them strength and clarity.

It is impossible, of course, to mention all the poetry, even all the good poetry, that has appeared in the periodicals. I remember particularly Alfred Hayes' *Van der Lubbe's Head* and his May Day Poem, Alfred Kreymborg's *America, America*, Stanley Burnshaw's parody of T. S. Eliot, and Kenneth Patchen's poem on Joe Hill.

Two revolutionary poets that seem to me to have developed materially in 1934 are Kenneth Fearing and Edwin Rolfe. The latter's *Unit Assignment* in the *New Republic*, is an excellent example of clarity achieved not by oversimplification but by the extension and integration of the poet's experience It is richly personal and full of sharp poetic perception and at the same time broad in appeal and free from literary echoes.

A definitive list of good short stories is as impossible as a definitive list of good poems. The work of Meridel Le Sueur, Louis Mamet, Erskine Caldwell, Alfred Morang, Fred Miller, and William Carlos Williams is particularly memorable, but there are many others whose stories deserve examination. My general criticism of proletarian short story writers is that they limit themselves too persistently to incidents of suffering or frustration. These are well adapted, of course, to the short story form, and there is every reason for portraying the cruelty and barrenness of life under capitalism, but there are other subjects as worthy of attention, and the danger of monotony could easily be avoided.

Two collections of short stories deserve at least a word. James Farrell's *Calico Shoes and Other Stories* is open to the same general criticism as his *Young Manhood of Studs Lonigan*, of which I shall speak later. No one, however, can deny the gruesome horror of such stories as *The Scarecrow* and *Just Boys* or the pathos of *Honey, We'll Be Brave*. Langston Hughes' *Not Without Laughter* was more disappointing than *Calico Shoes* because I had expected more. After the militant clarity of some of Hughes' poems, the confusion of most of his stories—his emphasis on situations and events that the revolutionary must regard as of only secondary importance—was something of a shock.

Criticism has to be discussed in terms of the revolutionary journals. Week after week the *New Masses* has reviewed books in all fields written from all points of view. Often the reviews have not been so good as they should be, but on the whole they have cogently and intelligently applied Marxist principles. The reviews here and in other revolutionary periodicals have made Marxist criticism a force in the literary world. It is worth observing also that the best reviews that have appeared in any non-revolutionary publication in 1934 have been written by a fellow-traveler, Malcolm Cowley.

The revolutionary novels deserve detailed consideration, because they have attracted so much attention, and they lend themselves to it. Here are the novels published in 1934 by avowed revolutionaries or close sympathizers: *Parched Earth*, by Arnold B. Armstrong; *The Shadow Before*, by William Rollins, Jr. *The Last Pioneers*, by Melvin Levy; *The Land of Plenty*, by Robert Cantwell; *The Great One*, by Henry Hart; *The Death Ship*, by B. Traven; *The Young Manhood of Studs Lonigan*, by James Farrell; *Slow Vision*, by Maxwell Bodenheim; *A House on a Street*, by Dale Curran; *The Foundry*, by Albert Halper; *Those Who Perish*, by Edward Dahlberg; *The Death and Birth of David Markand*, by Waldo Frank; *Babouk*, by Guy Endore; *The Executioner Waits*, by Josephine Herbst; and *You Can't Sleep Here*, by Edward Newhouse.

Some of the novels are revolutionary only in a rather broad sense of the word. Tess Slesinger recognizes the sterility of bourgeois culture, apparently sympathizes with the revolutionary movement, and has sense enough to prefer real revolutionaries, but doesn't know any well enough to put them in her book, *The Unpossessed*. She is herself rather too close to the futile chattering about revolution she satirizes, and her New Yorkerish wise-cracking becomes tiresome. Like Albert Halper, when he wrote *Union Square,* she tries to satirize the neurotic fringe before she has acquired the knowledge of the essential revolutionary movement that would make it possible to see the fringe in true perspective. Yet her talent is unmistakable, and even though her novel is as much a symptom as it is a portrayal of the fringe psychosis, sincerity manifests itself above the wise-cracking. One can hope she will follow the path of Halper.

James Farrell's position cannot be questioned as Tess Slesinger's can; everyone knows where he stands. But *The Young Manhood of Studs Lonigan* pretty much disregards the insight Marxism can give into the psychology of the petty bourgeois. Lonigan, a potential gangster, is interpreted chiefly in terms of sex urges and religious influences, which are not to be ignored but, taken by themselves, offer inadequate explanations. Farrell's novel comes to seem a mere transcript of observations, almost without proportion or emphasis. Despite the fact that he has written three novels and a book of short stories, I have a curious sense that Farrell is still in a preparatory stage. He has extraordinary powers of observation and a remarkable memory, but his sense of human values is distorted. That he will develop into a clear and powerful writer I do not doubt, but I sometimes wish he would hurry up.

Guy Endore's *Babouk* is an historical novel, and the very idea of an historical novel written from a Marxist point of view is exciting. Many scenes in *Babouk* are memorable, and it is a magnificent indictment of one of the cruellest phases of human exploitation. As in many historical novels, however, the documentation is so profuse in some portions that the story stands still. Moreover, as Eugene Gordon pointed out in his review, Endore, especially in his eloquent and challenging last chapter, treats the race issue as if it were a simple conflict between black and white.

All three of these novels are important to the revolutionary movement because of their authors' varied abilities. Tess Slesinger's wit, James Farrell's precision, Guy Endore's gift for research and for imaginative re-creation of the past—these are qualities that ought to enrich revolutionary literature. At present, however, these writers seem to stand a little apart from the struggle. It is not merely that they deal with marginal themes; they deal with them in a marginal fashion. Greater unity in their work, better proportioning, and a sharper, truer emphasis can come only through deeper understanding, and that is something Communism can give them.

I have said many times that the Marxist critic should not attempt to prescribe the subject-matter of revolutionary novels. It is the author's attitude that counts, not his theme. But I believe that there can be no greater test of an author's powers than an attempt to face the central issues of his time where they are most sharply raised. I want to turn, therefore, from the three marginal novels I have just considered to *The Shadow Before, The Land of Plenty,* and *The Foundry.* Merely writing about a factory does not make a good book, but any author who attempts to depict the class struggle in its most acute form deserves respectful consideration.

Both *The Shadow Before* and *The Land of Plenty* have been so widely—and so deservedly—praised that I shall take their virtues for granted and speak chiefly of their faults. It was pointed out to me by a labor organizer that *The Shadow Before,* by transferring details of the Gastonia strike to a New England setting, portrayed a situation that is true to neither section. This, I am afraid, indicates the great weakness of the book: it is to a certain extent synthetic. I feel, for example, that the neuroticism of Mrs. Thayer and her daughter, though possible enough, is not representative. The book does not give an accurate cross-section of the various classes in a mill town. Rollins did not know enough to do what he so ambitiously attempted. He had to fit together fragments of knowledge. Even the method, which owes a good deal to Dos Passos, does not always have an organic relationship to the material. One can say all this and still grant the effectiveness of the book, which, through the author's accurate insight into certain fundamental issues and his warm sympathy, transcends in general its particular weaknesses, and rises to a stirring and altogether convincing climax.

The first part of Cantwell's *Land of Plenty* has none of the faults of *The Shadow Before,* and I rank it as the finest piece of imaginative writing the revolutionary movement in America has produced. The second half, however, is less satisfying, and for reasons akin to those that explain the imperfections of Rollins' novel. Cantwell gave a frank account of his difficulties in a letter to the *New Masses* last summer: he simply did not know how such a situation as he had portrayed would work itself out in real life, and he deliberately blurred and confused the ending to conceal his ignorance.

This is clearly a case in which half a loaf is a great deal better than none, and Cantwell deserves to be praised for what he accomplished, rather than censured for what he failed to do. But both *The Land of Plenty* and *The Shadow Before* make it plain that a revolutionary novelist has to have a very exact knowledge. Lafcadio Hearn pointed out many years ago that a magnificent novel might be written about Wall Street, but that no novelist ever got a chance to know enough to write it. The labor movement is quite as complicated as Wall Street, and when a first-rate novel, first rate from start to finish, is written about it, its author will have to be more than an observer of the class struggle.

For that reason Halper may have been very wise in limiting himself as he did in *The Foundry*. *The Foundry* is less good than the first half of *The Land of Plenty;* it depends on the rather heavy-handed amassing of details instead of such shrewd and sound selection as Cantwell practises. Yet Halper—like Dreiser, whom he so strikingly resembles—gets his effects. Even a good deal of bad writing, and the choice of details that are merely picturesque, rather than revealing, cannot do more than slightly blur Halper's picture. We see the men and the bosses, and we feel the struggle that goes on between them even in this relatively peaceful shop. It is probably true that a less cautious writer would not have stopped where Halper did, just at the point at which Heitman's predictions of an intensified struggle are coming true, but it was better for Halper to stop there, to recognize his limitations, than to plunge into depths from which he could not extricate himself.

The Novel and the Middle Class

As I have said, no Marxist insists that revolutionary novels must deal with the working class, and yet it is rather striking that the three novels I have been discussing are relatively successful, whereas two novels that deal with the upper middle class are generally unsatisfactory. Melvin Levy's *The Last Pioneers* somehow bogs down in the picturesque details of the careers of the enterprising rascals he portrays. Henry Hart's *The Great One* is, page by page, a better book, but it is limited in much the same way. His theme is that the life of his hero, Bayard Stuart, a powerful politician modeled after Boise Penrose, is tragic in Stuart's own terms. To maintain this, he must convince us that Stuart really wanted to be a reformer, and he does not succeed in doing so. Stuart, as Edwin Seaver pointed out in his review, is a success according to his own standards, and to show him as anything else one must apply other standards and demonstrate their relevance. Hart does see that Stuart is the victim of forces that are greater than he, but he does not make us believe either that his hero would be conscious of this or that it would seem to him so hearteningly tragic. The portrayal of a member of the ruling class in such a way as both to make him a human being and to show his social role is a problem still to be solved.

More of our novelists have written about the lower middle class than have written of any other group in society. This is natural because it is the class to which most of them belong. Dale Curran's *A House on a Street* has been unduly neglected. It is an intelligent example of the "conversion" novel, and I am sure that Curran has correctly described the steps by which so many declassed bourgeois have been led to ally themselves with the militant working class. The novel is a model of precision and restraint. Unfortunately, however, it has the vice that often goes with those virtues; it is rather thin and over-intellectualized. The reader rationally accepts the development Curran portrays; he is not swept along by it.

Edward Dahlberg has come much closer to making us feel the upheavals that shake the lower middle class in times of crisis. Indeed, my principal criticism of *Those Who Perish* is that it exaggerates the neuroticism of the petty bourgeoisie. A secondary criticism is that Dahlberg is still guilty, though less often, of the mannerisms that spoiled his earlier novels for me. I agree with James Farrell that one of the principal duties of the revolutionary writer is to break through bourgeois clichés, the persistence of which inhibit the functioning of a new kind of sensibility, and perhaps it is inevitable that a pioneer in this task should give an impression of artificiality and strain. But I believe that Dahlberg, even now, occasionally makes the mistake of measuring the effectiveness of metaphors by their difference from conventional figures of speech, not by their precision in terms of his sensibility.

Important as the point is, I do not want to dwell on it too much, lest I give a false impression of *Those Who Perish*. As a matter of fact, the reader is only rarely bothered by inept figures of speech and most of the time is held fast by the devastating accuracy of Dahlberg's revelation.

But both Dahlberg's book and Curran's seem limited in comparison with Josephine Herbst's *The Executioner Waits,* the best, I think of all revolutionary novels dealing with the middle class. The flaws I found in its predecessor, *Pity Is Not Enough,* do not exist in this book. Those of us who come from the middle class can see ourselves and our fathers and mothers in Miss Herbst's novel. The people in *The Executioner Waits* are representative of millions of Americans, and yet they are sharply and unmistakably individuals. They are living human beings, eagerly pursuing their own ends, and yet they are the instruments of great impersonal forces. The reader never thinks of Miss Herbst as imposing Marxist conceptions on the material of the novel; these conceptions inevitably emerge from the substance of her story. She has almost perfectly integrated her intimate knowledge of the kind of person with whom her life has been spent with the broader insight given by the study of economic change and by familiarity with other classes. Her style, though growing naturally out of the careful commonplaces of the prose of her early work, has become beautifully flexible. When we are asked what we mean by talking about Marxist novels of the middle class, we can now point to *The Executioner Waits.*

What Josephine Herbst has succeeded in doing is what Arnold B. Armstrong failed to achieve in *Parched Earth.* There is a certain disparity between Armstrong's knowledge of social tendencies and his understanding of human beings, and as a result his novel is at times schematic. This effect is heightened, I am now inclined to think, by his attempt to make his characters symbolic. Fortunately, the symbolism, though it provided hostile critics with a point of attack, is less important than the straightforward portrayal of life in a representative American town, with its workers, its business men, and the boss. Only at the end is the symbolism prominent, and there it is justified by the dramatic impressiveness of the idea of revolution that is portrayed. Aside from the symbolism, however, the novel is marred by the author's reliance on superficial details for the characterization of minor persons in the story. This weakness is made particularly palpable when Armstrong's methods are contrasted with Miss Herbst's complete and unfailing insight into even the least of her characters.

Maxwell Bodenheim's *Slow Vision* also suffers from superficiality. There is a mass of details here, but many of these details do not serve to bring us any closer to the hero and heroine. Moreover, the novel is weakened—and this is strange in view of Bodenheim's long experience as a writer—by a great deal of direct exposition. To some extent these defects are offset by the author's intimate knowledge of the kind of lives he is describing, and there are many authentic episodes, but on the whole the book is disappointing.

Both Bodenheim and Edward Newhouse have written about the direct effects of the depression, and it seems to me that the younger author has done much the better job. *You Can't Sleep Here* is a slighter book than *The Executioner Waits,* but it has the same firmness of touch. The hard-boiled journalistic style falters now and then and becomes a mere mannerism, but for the most part it is admirably sustained. And it does what Newhouse wants it to do. He knows how to use understatement, and the last scene, when the dwellers in Hooverville are defending their homes, is, for all its simplicity, shot through with revolutionary implications. Newhouse is completely free from the kind of self-consciousness that so often enters into revolutionary writing. His heroine, as several critics have pointed out, is an idea rather than a person, but his hero is entirely real, and the hero's development from passive sympathy with the revolutionary cause to active Communism is flawlessly natural.

I have left to the next-to-the-last the most difficult book on the list to talk about, Waldo Frank's *Death and Birth of David Markand.* The emphasis Frank places in this book on personal salvation seems to me both historically and psychologically false. That is, I do not believe that such experiences as Markand's are in any sense representative, nor can I believe that they are necessary either for the individual's development or for the growth of the revolutionary movement. Yet I regard *The Death and Birth of David Markand* as an important book, and I think it has been given singularly shoddy treatment by the reviewers in the capitalist press. For one thing, even if what goes on inside Markand's mind seems unreal, what goes on in the world about him is real enough. I am not impressed by the scenes in which Markand alternately finds and loses his soul, but I am impressed by such scenes as those in the Kansas speakeasy, the offices of the Farmers' Guild paper, and the Kentucky mining town. And even at its worst, the novel is significant as the expression of Frank's mind. Wrongheaded as he seems to me to be, I honor him for his persistence and his honesty. The *Death and Birth of David Markand* is a novel into which a man has, with infinite pains, poured the whole of himself. Novels of that sort are too rare to be ignored.

Frank dedicates the book to "the American worker who will understand." My pedagogical training makes me wonder if the absence of a comma after "worker" is intentional. I doubt if many American workers will understand the book—or read it, for that matter. If Frank is interested in the kind of novel workers do understand and read, I recommend B. Traven's *The Death Ship* to him. For a good many reasons American workers have never heard of Traven, but hundreds of thousands of European workers read his novels. For all that he is better known abroad than in this country, he is an American, and I think we should hasten to claim his work an an important addition to our proletarian literature. Traven is unspoiled; he is a worker first of all and only incidentally a writer. His book does not hew to the Party line, but he knows what the class struggle is because he has fought in it. I hope we are going to have more of his books in this country.

It has been a year of enormous gains. New writers have appeared. Sympathizers have drawn closer to the movement. Accepted revolutionary writers have surpassed themselves. Despite the dread terrors of the American RAPP (which can be discovered only in certain Times Square imaginations), there is variety here, in theme and method, as well as vitality. Such vitality can be found nowhere else in American literature in 1934. It has not been a good year for the enemies of the revolutionary movement. If the works I have discussed were left out of account, it would prove a singularly empty year for American letters. And novels by Thomas Boyd, Myra Page, James Steele, and Tillie Lerner are already announced for the spring of 1935!

January 1, 1935

A Test for Critics

Mr. Joseph Wood Krutch's book, *Was Europe a Success?* is a crucial document in the long controversy between the literary right and the literary left. Although it seems to me of relatively little intrinsic importance, it has become, as intrinsically unimportant books sometimes do, the center of a tremendously important debate. Inasmuch as I have already discussed the articles incorporated in this volume (the *New Masses*, Oct. 23, 1934), and inasmuch as the book itself is to be reviewed in these pages, I shall limit myself to a few comments on the debate that the book has aroused.

In the first place, the fact that Mr. Krutch wrote the book is a beautiful confirmation of one of the principal Marxist theses, that literature and politics cannot be separated. Mr. Krutch has not been one of the more prominent defenders of the art-for-art's-sake position, but he has frequently accused Marxists of introducing extraneous considerations into their criticism. Now he himself admits that his literary theories rest upon certain assumptions about the nature of society, and these assumptions he hastens to defend.

His defense is shrewd enough to make a good deal of trouble for his fellow-liberals. When John Chamberlain reviewed the book he did more than straddle; he vaulted from side to side of the fence—and not with the greatest of ease. "Such, more or less, is Mr. Krutch's position. And yet, though I am in essential agreement with this position, there is just enough in the astigmatic radical's case against Mr. Krutch to make chastisement plausible." "Because some radical critics lack humor, or are dull and portentous, or see bogies where there are no bogies, or are scared of missing the party line, it does not follow that virtue is all in one camp and vice wholly in the other." Mr. Chamberlain even says a good word for the *New Masses*. The review ought to make everyone happy except those who want to know where Chamberlain stands.

But if Mr. Krutch did not succeed in making John Chamberlain reveal his position, he did bring Dr. Harry Elmer Barnes into the open. Dr. Barnes says that he believes capitalism is finished; he sympathizes with the revolutionary movement; when he rebukes the radicals, it is always, as I have previously noted, in the interests of radicalism. Now, however, we know what radicalism means to Dr. Barnes; it means the views of Joseph Wood Krutch. *Was Europe a Success?* is not a defense of liberalism, Dr. Barnes tells us in his review in *The Nation* for January 23; Mr. Krutch "comes far closer to writing a brief for civilized radicalism."

On this particular point I should like to quote from Malcolm Cowley's review in the *New Republic* for January 9. I have the greatest respect for Cowley as a critic, and, though he sometimes seems to me to oversimplify literary problems, he is almost always clear on political issues. Cowley says, "Mr. Krutch has aimed at Communism and has overshot his mark. In effect, his argument is a defense of inequality and injustice on the ground that the suffering of the masses makes possible the culture and disinterestedness of those who rule over them. In effect, it strikes at the base of the whole humanitarian tradition. . . . He has not one word to say against the philosophy of the fascist leaders. This of course does not mean that Mr. Krutch accepts their philosophy or hopes to see it put into effect. He is a liberal and a humanitarian; he sincerely hates all dictatorships, but his arguments have carried him into a strategically weak position. . . . He does not agree with Maurras and Mussolini, but he no longer has a logical base from which to combat them."

I should like to go on and quote what Cowley has to say about Krutch's method of handling history. Dr. Barnes is by way of being an historian; he has just completed no less a task than a history of world civilization. Yet he has nothing whatsoever to say in criticism of Krutch's bizarre generalizations about Europe. There are two perfectly clear questions: To what extent and on what terms did the values Krutch attributes to "Europe" really exist? How can these values be preserved today? The very essence of the Marxian analysis is the assertion that, even if these values did exist, they are now threatened by the decay of the system that Mr. Krutch identifies with "Europe." Dr. Barnes, as an historian, might have been expected to examine Krutch's assumptions; as a soi-disant radical, he was under obligation to question his conclusions. He does neither of these things.

What Dr. Barnes does do is to dodge. "Perhaps," he says, "the best way of resolving the dilemma is to regard Dr. Krutch as writing not so much a refutation of, or direct attack upon, the basic principles of economic radicalism as a most powerful and engaging argument for better intellectual manners and sounder esthetic values on the part of contemporary radicals." At this point there is nothing to do, rudeness or no rudeness, but guffaw. Mr. Krutch is trying to attack the whole basis of Communism, and, as Cowley points out in the sentences I have quoted, he goes beyond that and undermines the very foundations of liberalism.

This question of manners seems to bother Dr. Barnes considerably. "Urbanity," says he, "has appealed to me as the highest of human virtues." Looking back on Dr. Barnes' record, I am pleased to report that he does not practice what he preaches. For myself, I think urbanity is probably a very nice thing—in its place. I am very glad, however, that Lenin and not Montaigne—Dr. Barnes' ideal man—happened to be the leader in Petrograd in November, 1917.

Dr. Barnes says, "It is becoming ever more evident that capitalism neither can nor will feed its sheep. It begins to look as though revolution, though not necessarily a bloody one, is the sole way in which the economic requirements of a civilized society can be assured." But revolutionaries must be gentlemen; otherwise they will offend "those who count." Dr. Barnes is quite right; gentlemanly revolutionaries will never offend "those who count" because they will never seriously threaten their power. The rules of the game are very nicely drawn up so that the people on top will always win; the good doctors help out by shouting to the people on the bottom, "You must abide by the rules."

A singularly bright light is thrown on Mr. Krutch's liberalism by the correspondence with Roger Baldwin published in the same issue of *The Nation* as the Barnes review. Mr. Krutch sent a check to the Civil Liberties Union, accompanying it with a letter in which he said, "I would be happier if I were convinced that the majority of members really believed in civil liberties as such." Mr. Baldwin replied very reasonably, justifying his personal support of the dictatorship in the Soviet Union. I think it would have been more logical—though very rude, and especially to a contributor—for him to have inquired how Krutch had ever demonstrated his belief in civil liberties.

In regard to civil liberties, the radical maintains, it seems to me, a perfectly tenable position. We live under a supposedly democratic government that guarantees certain civil rights. Every teacher in this state has had to take an oath to support the constitutions of state and country. So long as he keeps his side of the bargain, he has every right to demand that the government keep its side. The Marxist knows,

of course, that the government is not the impartial instrument that it
pretends to be, but there is certainly nothing illogical in his insisting
that the pretended principles be adhered to. He knows that ultimately
issues are determined, not by abstract principles, but by the application of force, and he knows that only mass pressure can save the victims of class "justice." At the same time, however, he would be foolish
to disregard the legal and theoretical weapon, and he very properly
demands that all those who believe in civil liberties as absolute rights
join with him in the struggle.

Mr. Krutch is one of those who believe in freedom at all times
and for all persons. But what does he do about it? Did he take an
active part in the fight for Sacco and Vanzetti, for Tom Mooney, for
the Scottsboro boys? I am putting myself entirely on Krutch's own
ground. If a person believes in civil liberties, he does not put himself
on record and let it go at that; he goes out and fights. If Mr. Krutch
has ever done anything on behalf of civil liberty, beyond giving a little
money to Roger Baldwin, I have yet to hear of it.

Mr. Krutch says that Communists are "full of an intense and
burning hatred for that urbanity, detachment, and fair play which
liberals pretend, at least, to admire." I am sorry that that is how it
looks to Mr. Krutch, but I think I can explain to him why he gets that
impression. Let us take a concrete example, the San Francisco general strike. The longshoremen were striking for exceedingly reasonable
demands. They were attacked by police, militia, vigilantes, college
boys, gangsters. The press lied about them with the utmost ferocity.
A. F. of L. officials did their best to sell them out. There was no pretense of maintaining liberties in the San Francisco strike. There never
is when profits are seriously threatened.

What did Mr. Krutch do for the strikers? Did he write even one
letter of protest to Governor Merriam? Did he contribute five cents
to a relief fund? I imagine not. And now he comes along, and he says
to militant workers, "You ought to be urbane." He says to Communists and radicals in general. "The trouble with you is that you don't
work for civil liberty for everybody, but merely for the workers." He
says to every Communist intellectual, "You ought to be detached and
see both sides of this matter."

And then he is surprised because the answer is a resounding
razzberry, and he shouts that we're all boors. No, Mr. Krutch, we don't
hate urbanity, detachment and a sense of fair play. We think we care a

lot more for them than you do because we're working to establish a society in which they would be possible—as they are not possible, for you or for us, in our present society. We do, however, feel a good deal of resentment, if not hatred, for persons who, in the name of urbanity, detachment and a sense of fair play, tolerate the most outrageous abuses of the rights they pretend to believe in, use the language of liberalism to defend reaction, and spend their time in attacking Communism.

February 5, 1935

Educating the Middle Class

The Coming Struggle for Power, by John Strachey

Although Strachey's book is, I hope, familiar to all readers of the *New Masses,* it may not be amiss to make some general comment on the book and on Strachey's position in the revolutionary movement, as well as to discuss the material that has been added since the first edition. *The Coming Struggle for Power,* though it was published only a little more than two years ago, is already, as its appearance in the Modern Library indicates, something of a classic and its author, thanks partly to the actions of the United States Government, is a very conspicuous figure. Both deserve our attention.

First of all, then, there is a special introduction in which Strachey discusses the question of force and violence raised by his arrest last March. The discussion is conducted with such logic and good sense that it would be worth buying the book just to read it. Strachey makes three points. First, this is actually a world of violence: "Whatever the Communists are preaching, other people are here and now practicing a constant use of violent methods for attaining their ends." Second, to predict that the transfer of power will take place through the use of force is not the same as advocating force. Third, this prediction rests on a recognition of the fact that capitalists do not hesitate to destroy democratic institutions to preserve their power and therefore, "for the workers to pledge themselves in no circumstances to use force in the struggle to abolish this system would make the abolition of capitalism forever impossible."

There is also included in this volume the note that Strachey wrote in April, 1934, for the second edition of the book. One year after the inauguration of the New Deal, he predicted that either it would lead at once to inflation or, if that was temporarily avoided, would result in an increase of the profits of the great corporations without diminishing mass unemployment. Its collapse, he stated, would be followed by an intensification of reaction. Since its prophecies have been fulfilled, the note is now chiefly interesting as an exhibition of Marxist logic. As such, it would make valuable reading for those who blame Mr. Roosevelt or think that any other policy he could have adopted, under capitalism, would have been more successful.

Between these two notes lies the book itself. Its sale has been one of the noteworthy literary phenomena of recent years. No book that makes so many demands on its readers has had a comparable circulation. Quite apart from its Communism, which automatically deprived it of the ballyhoo by which best-sellers are ordinarily launched, its sheer solidity ought to have frightened away a public that regards the works of Stuart Chase, Walter B. Pitkin, Will Durant and Ernest Dimnet as heavy reading. And yet there it was, week after week, in the best-seller columns and this is its third edition.

Part of the explanation is, obviously, the fact that Strachey had something to say and a large section of the middle class, to which he was primarily addressing himself, has been educated by the depression so that it is beginning to recognize the difference between intelligence and nonsense. But a good deal, after all, has to be attributed to the way Strachey said it. I refer not to the lucidity of his exposition or the brilliance of his phraseology, though these are important, but to his whole method of writing the book. "Many of these pages," he wrote in his original preface, "contain evidence of the road along which I have traveled. Indeed, the reader will see at once that the argument of this book follows the course of its author's transition from old views to new." It is, in other words, the story of how a very alert middle-class mind arrived at Communism and middle-class Americans have read it, some with the joy of self-discovery and others with fear and trembling.

The depression forced Strachey to explore the origin and nature

of capitalism. He discovered that capitalist economists, whether orthodox or heretical, made assumptions that he could not accept and failed
to answer questions that he knew to be urgent. Only Marxian economics, so scorned by the academicians, provided a convincing analysis. This analysis led Strachey to the conviction that capitalism was
doomed and his opinion was strengthened by a survey of capitalist
culture. Religion, science and literature, as he carefully showed in
his book, all pointed to the decay of the system. And on the continent,
especially in Italy and Germany, he saw the form that capitalism took
in its final stages, fascism. His own experience in Labor Party politics
showed him that the social democratic method of attacking capitalism,
fascism, imperialism and war was futile. There was no alternative but
Communism.

The greatness of *The Coming Struggle for Power* lies in the
knowledge, eloquence and logic with which it sets forth the case against
capitalism and for Communism. The significance of John Strachey—
and he is a significant figure in the English-speaking world today—
lies in his readiness to accept his own conclusions. Of course he has
many assets; his erudition, his candor, his wit and, at least in America,
his name, his manner and his accent. But the important thing is that
he has placed all his talents at the service of the revolution. The
movement has been cursed by intellectuals of a certain sort, such as
Hook and Eastman in this country, who wouldn't play if they couldn't
be generals and like J. Middleton Murry in England, who insisted
on bringing with him into the revolutionary camp all the rubbish that
twenty years of slovenly thinking had accumulated. Strachey has
never sought eminence as political leader or as theoretician, has never
exaggerated the importance of what he was doing, has never tried to
impose his views upon other Communists. He has accepted his role
as interpreter, as apostle to the middle class. He is doing a superb job.

The three books that Strachey has written since *The Coming
Struggle for Power,* elaborate portions of that work. *The Menace of
Fascism,* though it has been in large measure superseded, as Strachey
realizes, by Dutt's *Fascism and Social Revolution,* was the first clear
presentation to the general public of the Marxist analysis of Hitler's
rise to power. *Literature and Dialectical Materialism* applies to American authors the methods employed in the dissection of Shaw, Wells,
Huxley and Lawrence. *The Nature of Capitalist Crisis* is much the
most important of the three, for it shows the further education of the

author in Marxian economics and offers an admirable introduction to the study of *Capital*. All three of these books not only enlarge upon and clarify the arguments of *The Coming Struggle for Power* but completely confirm its conclusions.

There is one other section of the book that I wish Strachey would elaborate, the last section, that devoted to the nature of Communism and the outlook for the future. Although the Communist objection to purely utopian speculation is unquestionably wise, there is much that might legitimately be said about life under Communism and to say it would bring conviction to wavering sections of the middle class. When Strachey was here last spring, he was thinking of doing precisely this, of showing what Communism would mean to England and America. I hope he is going to do it, for there is no one better fitted for the task.

October 22, 1935

Some Books of the Month

The book of the month that has most interested me is Ralph Fox's *The Novel and the People,* which combines in almost ideal proportions breadth of sympathy and clarity of analysis. No one could call the study sectarian, and yet it is free from the kind of wishy-washiness that, in the name of broad-mindedness, praises all writers of the past indiscriminately. Fox saw in the novel one of the great achievements of bourgeois culture, an achievement that still has incalculable importance for the future. The growth of the novel, however, was checked by the rottenness of capitalism, and it is only in a socialist society that its potentialities can be realized. So his argument runs, sustained by an intimate knowledge of French and English literature and by fine insight into the creative process. If anyone needs to be reminded how talented a comrade was lost when Ralph Fox died in Spain, *The Novel and the People* will serve as a poignant memorial to the vigor of his mind and the firmness of his revolutionary spirit.

Another book that comes to us from England and from a fighter for Spanish democracy is Ralph Bates's *Rainbow Fish*. And at last Bates is beginning to attract the attention that some of us said he deserved when his first novel, *Lean Men,* appeared. It can, of course, surprise no reader of the *New Masses* to discover that it is *Rainbow Fish,* which is in no overt sense a revolutionary novel, that wins the applause of the old-line reviewers. The critics have been discerning enough all along to see that Bates is a man of talent, but many of them were just a little loath to praise such a book as *The Olive Field. Rainbow Fish,* however, is safe, and the reviewers can let themselves go and salve their consciences.

Yet true conservatives, if they were really astute, could take little pleasure in Bates's new novel. Though I confess that it seems to me less important than *Lean Men* or *The Olive Field,* and though certainly it makes no direct assault on the capitalist system, many of its virtues grow out of the author's revolutionary convictions. Its deep sympathy with the poor fugitives who are its central characters, and its profound understanding of the forces that have made them what they are, reveal, as Jack Conroy has said, the qualities that sent Ralph Bates into the loyalist army. At the same time, the structure of the novel shows a technical advance over Bates's earlier work.

Applause in certain quarters for *Rainbow Fish* reminds us that bourgeois critics often have a blind spot when they approach a novel dealing with the class struggle. How many critics have had spasms of ecstasy on reading John Steinbeck's *Of Mice and Men* who could not find a good word to say for *In Dubious Battle!* Recently the curious functioning of certain of these minds has been exposed in their reviews of Josephine Johnson's *Jordanstown.* Except for Edith Walton's fine review in the Sunday *Times,* the book has fared badly indeed—for reasons anyone can guess. Though I admit that there is something to be said against the book, as well as much to be said for it, it does seem to me clear that it has all the virtues of *Now In November,* and at the same time, as Miss Walton pointed out, it is free from the nostalgic qualities that seemed a little ominous in the earlier book. Yet the critics have not praised *Jordanstown!*

Look at Bernard DeVoto's review in the *Saturday Review of Literature* for April 3. According to Mr. DeVoto, Miss Johnson has "forsaken her instinctive best in order to pursue an idea," she "has been glad to sacrifice the artist to the human being," and "she has chosen to abandon what only she can do in order to do what she is not best fitted to do." He fills two columns with expressions such as this, and then concludes: "The loss of a first-rate psychological novelist is too high a price to pay for a second-rate sociological novelist, or even a first-rate one." Just how a psychological novel is distinguished from a sociological one, or why the former is inherently superior to the latter, or in what way *Jordanstown* is less psychological than *Now in November,* Mr. DeVoto does not tell us. The point seems to be that the earlier novel deals with the "depths and dark places of the soul," whereas the latter deals with "the disinherited . . . with their suffering, their fellowship, their exploitation and betrayal, and their efforts to help themselves." The former is art; the latter is journalism and second-rate sociology.

I have no doubt that Mr. DeVoto is sincere; he could not otherwise have written so eloquently confused a review. What is one to conclude? Simply that non-literary judgments get in Mr. DeVoto's way when he tries to criticize such a book as *Jordanstown.* Even the most practised critic cannot always command his passions and his prejudices when he reviews a book. If, let us say, one had been in a terribly tragic automobile accident, could one read with perfect objectivity an account of a collision? Would not all sorts of emotions be set up that would come between one and the printed page? So it is, I believe, with Mr. DeVoto and many other critics when they read books about the class struggle. The subject is so distressing that the book in question has on them the effect of a bad book. Therefore, in all sincerity, they condemn it, and find whatever reasons they can to justify their doing so.

DeVoto and his kind are constantly expressing their scorn for Marxist criticism, but I think we do not have to worry much. Despite the assertions, repeated again and again during the past five years, that Marxism would turn out to be another fad, the general principles and methods known as Marxist continue to win the respect of critics who have demonstrated their understanding of literature and of the American scene. Several years ago T. K. Whipple wrote a book called *Spokesmen,* not in any sense, I think, a Marxist book, but a book full of insight and very shrewd, as time has proved, in it predictions. Now, in a recent issue of the *New Republic,* in a commentary on that magazine's series of revaluations, Professor Whipple arrives, by his own route and with many fresh perceptions, at essentially the conclusions Marxists have been advancing as long as there have been Marxists. He is not just repeating; he not only confirms but also strengthens; thus Marxist criticism grows.

Speaking of the *Saturday Review,* I recall that several weeks ago Dr. Canby was inspired to write an editorial by a telegram from the Western Writers' Congress. The Congress objected because the chapter on the U.S.S.R. in *We Cover the World* (reviewed by Hy Kravif in this issue) was to be written by William Henry Chamberlin, "notorious for anti-Soviet bias." This, said Dr. Canby, is condemning a book in advance. And so it was. But, as it happened, John Gunther, three weeks later, reviewing *I Cover the World* in Dr. Canby's magazine, asked, "And why not at least one friendly word from someone who is today in the Soviet Union?" In other words, the Western Writers' Congress, though it had not seen Mr. Chamberlin's chapter, was quite right in anticipating anti-Soviet bias. Dr. Canby, who holds that revolutionaries have closed minds, does not seem to realize that there are persons on his side of the fence whose reactions are fairly dependable. When lines are sharply drawn, you don't have to wait until you've been socked in the jaw before taking your hands out of your pockets.

Among the predictable characters of our day, the safest bet of all is Isabel Paterson. On April 18 she said, for the third or fourth time, that you could put no dependence on the Webbs because they were not disinterested. "They had spent their lives advocating certain theories....Their lives, their reputations were staked on those theories. . . . So the theories were put in effect in Russia. . . . Is it likely that the Webbs would admit they were all wrong, and didn't work out as guaranteed?" Somebody, you see, told Mrs. Paterson that the Webbs were Socialists. She simply doesn't know that all their lives they have opposed the theories of Marx and Lenin, the theories on which the Soviet Union is founded. She doesn't know, and doesn't want to know, that the Webbs quarreled with the labor theory of value, and with the whole Marxian theory of economics, staunchly upheld gradualism and parliamentary democracy, condemned the dictatorship of the proletariat. She doesn't know that the Webbs were Fabian Socialists, and that fabianism is considerably closer to Lloyd George's pre-war liberal program and to the New Deal than it is to Bolshevism. Saying that the Webbs must have been prejudiced in favor of the U.S.S.R. because they were Socialists is like saying that Bible-belt Methodists must be prejudiced in favor of the Pope because they are Christians. But the ignorance of Isabel Paterson is probably invincible, and little can be done about the prejudices of a DeVoto. The most one can say is that it may be useful to place their more flagrant absurdities on record.

May 18, 1937

The Threat of Frustration

Robert Cantwell, in reviewing some book—I forget what—commented on the picture it gave of literary frustration. "This," he said bitterly, "is the great tradition in American literature."

We may well think so. For nearly forty years literary criticism has been preoccupied with the frustrations of American authors. Puritanism, we were first told, was the cause of failure. Then Van Wyck Brooks looked more carefully and indicated our money-centered culture. Finally the Marxists have talked about frustration in terms of the contradictions and the decline of capitalist civilization.

We may quarrel about the explanation, but we cannot dispute the fact. Can anyone say that Mark Twain, Henry James, Hamlin Garland, Frank Norris, Upton Sinclair, and Jack London accomplished a quarter of what they had it in them to do? Look at the eighteenth-century British novelists, Richardson, Fielding, and Smollett; look at Scott and Jane Austen; look even at Dickens, Thackeray, and George Eliot. It does not matter whether you admire their work or not. The only thing to notice is that there is no marked discrepancy between their potentialities and their achievements. They did as much as, by any reasonable standards, one could expect. We cannot say the same for American writers of the late nineteenth and early twentieth centuries.

Nor can we take more satisfaction in what has been called the middle generation. A group of critics in the *New Republic* has recently been examining the writers of this generation. Perhaps certain critics have exaggerated the degree of frustration, or attributed it to the wrong causes, but on the whole the series carries conviction. And note that the younger critics are not attacking the aims of the older writers, as one generation so often attacks the aims of its predecessor; their recurring complaint is that the writers who dominated American letters between 1910 and 1930 have not realized their aims, have not lived up to their promise. Frustration is the theme.

If one tenth of what has been said about frustration is accurate, it is obvious that no body of writers, such as the National Writers' Congress, ought to convene without placing upon its agenda what would appear to be the all-important topic for American authors. If the majority of our predecessors have been baffled and defeated, what reason have we for supposing we will escape the same end? And, more practically, what do we propose to do to frustrate the menace of frustration?

American writers cannot face the future without facing this problem. Each of us desires to do his job well. Each believes that he has certain talents, and, whether they are major or minor, he wants to use them. Each of us sees something about American life, something that seems to us true and unseen by others, and we want to communicate what we see. To be a minor writer is not necessarily a tragedy, but it is tragic to be a minor writer when one has major gifts. It is tragic to be driven to suicide or silence or hack work. It is tragic to fumble one's way from imperfect book to imperfect book, and it is tragic to achieve perfecion by dtescending to trivialities. It is tragic to be driven inward into hard smugness, and it is tragic to dissipate one's powers in gushes of sentimentality. Vast museums of horrible examples have been assembled for our benefit; can we learn anything from them?

We face the future, hoping—perhaps unreasonably in view of what we know about the past—that we can persuade it to let us do our work. What kind of future is it likely to be? What will the next decade or two bring?

First of all, it is apparent that we are now in a period of partial recovery. This recovery we largely owe to the fear of war, for which the countries of Europe are preparing, not only by building up their armies, navies, and air forces, but also by amassing great piles of foodstuffs and war supplies. Our own government is, less frantically, making the same preparations. The industrial machine is being set to work again, partly in order to fill the actual demands created by military programs, partly because American finance is speculating on future demands.

No great knowledge of economics is needed to predict, in a rough way, the course that recovery will follow. If war in Europe is postponed, the familiar cycle will be gone through, probably more rapidly than in the past. If the postponement of war is accompanied by the diminution of war preparations, this in itself might bring about a collapse. Even, however, if war buying continues, or if industrial enterprise is sufficiently strong to withstand the effect of a sharp reduction in military business, the collapse will nevertheless come, probably accompanied by ruinous inflation.

Few persons, I suspect, are optimistic enough to believe that peace will outlast the business cycle. Few persons doubt that the next two or three years will bring the beginning of war. The first effect of war, since we can assume that we will not participate at the outset, will be to stimulate American business. In the event of our remaining neutral, this would postpone, but at the same time would intensify, the inevitable depression. Far more likely, however, is our participation, with results that those of us who can remember 1917, 1918, and 1919 have little difficulty in imagining.

Either depression or participation in war would result in Reaction. Because big business has frequently yielded to the C.I.O., we are not to suppose that business men have fallen in love with unionism. On the contrary, the necessity for making concessions has intensified their fear and their hatred. There are signs enough that they are eagerly awaiting the day when they can begin a campaign of reprisal. Already there are American capitalists who feel that only fascism can protect their profits, and either depression or war will bring, in one form or another, an attempt at a fascist coup.

What the next few years—or it may be only the next few months—offer us is a breathing spell, quite literally that, an opportunity to get our breath and brace ourselves for the impact of fascism. The victory of fascism is not inevitable. A year or so ago it was fashionable to say privately that fascism was bound to win in the United States. Now we know better. We know that there are great forces that can be brought into the struggle to preserve and extend democratic rights, forces that the power of reactionary capitalism cannot withstand. The only question is whether these forces can be led into action quickly enough.

This, then, is the future the American writer faces. Shall we deceive ourselves? It is not going to be a comfortable period for human beings. It is going to be a damned uncomfortable time for writers. It will not be easy in such a period for us to do the work we can and ought to do. Frustration waits, I fear, around many corners, and only good men—and good women—will survive.

Let us, so far as we can, draw up a program for survival.

We might, first of all, examine one or two paths, that, I trust, none of us is likely to take. So firmly fixed is the tradition of protest in American literature that no writer is apt to say baldly, "Go to, now, I will be a reactionary." But there are writers who, under the guise of defending established authority, let us say, or some sort of religious dogma, will take the reactionary side. Other writers, by some sort of hocus-pocus, will be able to convince themselves that loyalty to democracy requires them to defend the special privileges of the great capitalists. Still others, taking refuge in the doctrine of the aristocratic minority, nature's noblemen, will look with contempt upon the masses, and, in practice, by trying to restrain the masses, will lend their aid to Reaction.

I need not tell you that these writers are on one of the paths to frustration. We have seen some of the reactionary writers, and we know what they are doing to themselves. We have seen other men, better men, some of them with us in this Congress, turn back from the path of Reaction as if they had had a vision of death and caught the very stench of decay. Where, even in the confusion of present-day America, are the generous impulses, the broad sympathies, the seeing eye and the feeling heart? We know, and we know what kind of literature is created when these qualities are absent. We do not have to wait to see our reactionary writers follow their predecessors, the fascist writers of Germany and the fascist writers of Italy and the Gadarene swine, in the suicidal plunge into the sea of brutality and lies.

There can be no temptation for us here; but what of the author who tells us politics is none of his—or our—business? The writer must see and record, he says, and keep himself aloof—and particularly in times such as these. How persuasive this is! We do want to do our work, and we know that our work requires concentration—requires indeed, a degree of aloofness. Political activities take time; political

passions make it difficult to see clearly; political thinking may interfere with the writer's special kind of thought.

The only trouble with this program of aloofness is that it will
not work. It will not work, in the first place, because, while we calmly
go about our literary labors, the forces of fascism are sedulously
creating a world in which such labors cannot be carried on. Try to
be aloof while storm-troopers' clubs are beating upon your skull!

In the second place, and more important, aloofness is not hu-
manly workable in such a period as ours. Why is it that Robinson
Jeffers, Robert Frost, Edna Millay, and all the other devotees of the
ivory tower suddenly sally forth now and again and mount soap-
boxes? It is because no sensitive, alert, broadly sympathetic human
being—no artist, in short—can remain permanently indifferent to
the injustices of our world and to the threat of organized injustice in
a fascist world. You cannot stand aloof from the issues of today and
remain a whole man. There are those, it is true, who become eunuchs
willingly for the sake of the Kingdom of Art, but I do not know that
they attain it.

We are, I take it, writers who have rejected both of these paths.
We will not aid Reaction, and we will neither try to stand aloof nor
confine our participation in the struggle to confused, ineffectual sallies
from ivory towers that have become strangely prison-like. We are
agreed on two propositions: we are against war and fascism, and we
believe that the writer must participate, as a human being and as a
writer, in the fight against the twin evils. These are the solid and
sufficient bases of our own united front.

The immediate question is, of course: what can we do? We ought
to discuss first, perhaps, some practical problems of the united front.
These practical problems may seem to you unworthy of consideration
in a paper that began with the rather grandiose aim of discussing the
dangers of literary frustration in the coming years, but it is on our ability to solve just such problems that our survival depends. Take, for instance, the eminently practical problem of division of time. It is equally
our duty to do some good writing and to try, by our writing and by
whatever other means are possible, to make the world a place in which
good writing can be done. It is not easy to do either of these things;
it is almost impossibly difficult to do both of them together.

Yet do them we must. I do not need to talk to you about the
calls for help that reach us all: will you speak here? won't you con-

tribute to that? please send a letter of protest to so-and-so; be sure to attend this meeting. For God's sake, you cry, let me do my work! Yes, that's right, you must do your work, if it's worth doing—and only you can decide that. But at the same time you must help. There are causes more important than your work. There are causes that can be served by sacrificing not your work, but your leisure. Where is the line to be drawn? I cannot tell you. Nobody can tell you. You must decide for yourself. And heaven help you if you decide wrong!

There is another, a related but a subtler problem. Writers, in common with other intellectuals, find themselves brought by the fight again fascism into association with great mass movements, labor unions, political parties, and organizations of other types. Now the role of the intellectual in the labor movement is a difficult one, as much unhappy experience has shown. There is, for example, the writer who goes to the labor movement with the conviction of his own transcendent wisdom. In his own mind he is the gracious representative of the intellectual nobility, offering himself to the people as their leader. And it often happens that the people are flattered. See, the great So-and-so has come among us. But the great So-and-so is not content to be flattered as a leader; he must exercise leadership. And the people, quickly discovering that he is less fitted to lead a labor movement than the bootblack on the corner, refuse to follow him. Thereupon he discovers that the party, the union, or other organization to which he has offered himself is not only ungrateful but stupid, incompetent, and evil. He becomes the simon-pure friend of labor who criticizes any particular labor policy for the anti-labor press.

There are other and less disastrous types. There is the perfectionist, the man who approaches the labor movement with a starry look in his eyes, and is sent scurrying back to his hermit's cell when he discovers that workers are human. There is the man who commits himself to downright radicalism, and then, finding that he is unwilling to pay the price, tries to save his face by insisting that radicalism is at fault. There is the fence-sitter, the man who is always in favor of the labor movement in general but always opposed, on the soundest theoretical grounds of course, to any policy that requires him to act.

These are types of frustration. And, on the other hand, there is the writer who allows himself to be absorbed by an organization. Absorption can be either physical or intellectual. Physical absorption is at least dignified, and may sometimes be the better way. Intellectual absorption is always bad. No writer can afford to let a party or a union do his thinking for him. He may properly act in unison with his group, but the only kind of thinking that is fit for his books is his own.

More and more, writers will be called upon to take an active part in the labor movement, and the writer must learn to subordinate his personality while maintaining his integrity. As with the simpler problem of time and energy, the individual must draw the line, and it is not easy to do.

We come closer than our predecessors to understanding the world, not because we are brighter, but because the issues have become sharper. And we have, as many earlier writers have had, a sense of belonging to America. In the masses who are marching with us we have companions and we have a potential, if not yet actual, audience.

Problems that our predecessors found insoluble are solved for us, and I believe that the problems that do face us, real as they are, are less difficult. In the past it has often been the writers we feel to have been the most talented who were the most terribly frustrated. I have a feeling that will not be true for our generation. Lesser writers may be overcome by difficulties such as I have described. Our major writers will not.

I believe that here, in this audience, are men and women who, during the next five or ten or fifteen years, will do work as fine as the best in American literature. They will know how to draw strength, not only out of the struggle in which we are all engaged, but also out of the very difficulties I have set before you. They will be with us in the struggle, perhaps leaders, perhaps not, but always dependable, always striking the blow they are fitted to strike, and they will express the spirit of our struggle, though they may never write directly about it. Their books will march in step with the marching feet of millions, and they will be great as the tasks of these coming years are great. And perhaps in some future day men, reading their books, will understand this period as we cannot understand it, and will see in it, not an uncomfortable breathing-spell, filled with torturing decisions and hazardously complex problems, but a stirring preface to a glorious era.

June 15, 1937

Today's Labor Leaders

Men Who Lead Labor, by Bruce Minton and John Stuart

The most important news in the book world this fall is the appearance of good books at twenty-five and thirty-five cents apiece. At last a publisher has had nerve enough to break through the hidebound traditions of the business. Books at two and a half, three, and four dollars have long been an anomaly. Prices have stayed high, in spite of constantly improving methods of production, simply because publishers have preferred the safe method of selling to fewer people and getting a larger profit on each book. Now *Modern Age* has dared to try to break through the really ridiculously small circle of book-buyers. This company is pricing books for the millions, with faith that the millions, will buy.

And it is highly encouraging to find on *Modern Age's* first list such a book as *Men Who Lead Labor.* Readers of the *New Masses* know its authors: Bruce Minton, for some time an editor, has written many articles on labor struggles, and John Stuart, formerly editor of *Health and Hygiene,* has also contributed to this magazine. Both of them are now in Spain, and soon will be reporting to us on their observations.

Men Who Lead Labor is the story behind the stories you read every day in your newspapers, and it tells you what you need to know to understand the day-to-day accounts. It is about leaders, but leaders as Marxists understand them, that is, as men who represent groups and forces. The book does not underestimate the reactionary influence of William Green as an individual or the progressive influence of John L. Lewis, but it does not reduce their actions to idiosyncrasies and whims. It shows what these men and others stand for, and why they are succeeding or failing.

It is, therefore, a history and an interpretation of the American labor movement. We all know what kind of man William Green is, and the question is why a man of that particular caliber happens to be president of the A. F. of L. We know that Lewis was once a reactionary, and we want to know why he is now a progressive. We are all acquainted with the Heywood Broun of the Algonquin Club; how was he transformed into the fighting president of the Newspaper Guild?

Before Edward McGrady was called to higher things, he was always appearing in the headlines as the administration's trouble-shooter; what were his qualifications for the job, and why were his traits useful to Madame Perkins?

These are the questions that *Men Who Lead Labor* answers. It tells you how the craft unions developed, how racketeering came into the picture, what the C.I.O. is trying to do. It tells you what the government has and has not done for labor. It tells you about the predicament of the middle-classes, the position of the Negro, the history of the sit-down strike, the use of labor spies, and the rise of vigilantism. It describes the San Francisco general strike and gives you the background of the present situation in the maritime unions.

The chapters of the book are devoted to Green, Hutcheson, McGrady, Lewis, Broun, A. Philip Randolph, Harry Bridges, and a group of leaders in such C.I.O. unions as the United Rubber Workers, the United Automobile Workers, the I.L.G.W.U., the Amalgamated, and the United Textile Workers. The book gives you a sense of the personality of each of these men, tells you a lot you never knew about their past, and fits them into the pattern of today's struggles. This is no psychoanalytic rigmarole, but a straight story that makes sense. You will not find out much about their complexes, their love life, their taste in dress, or their views on Wally Windsor, but you will see them as real persons and understand where their power comes from.

If there is a fault in the book, it is at least a fault on the right side. Minton and Stuart have loaded some of their pages pretty heavily with information about the labor movement. I wish, for example, that there were not that solid block of facts about white-collar workers in the chapter on Broun. I wish A. Philip Randolph had not been forced to carry a burden of data about the Negroes, other racial minorities, working women, and child labor. I know the facts are important, but I believe that, if Minton and Stuart had looked a little more steadily at Broun and Randolph, and told their stories a little more carefully, they would have made the information they convey even more significant. I wish, in other words, that the exposition of economic conditions were always as firmly integrated with biographical material as it is in the article on Bridges. That is a fine job that does not sacrifice either the man or the movement but makes each help to interpret the other.

I hesitate to complain about the Broun and Randolph chapters, not only because the others are so good, but also because I may be wrong. Certainly there are thousands of people in this country who want just the information that is in *Men Who Lead Labor,* and they are very foolish if they don't spend thirty-five cents to get it. But if I am right, it is worth saying. We need first-rate labor reporters, and Minton and Stuart are so well on the way that even minor faults are worth paying attention to.

September 21, 1937

A 'Nation' Divided

The Nation recently celebrated the twentieth anniversary of the Soviet Union with an editorial, an article, and a book review. The article, by Maxwell S. Stewart, commented upon the industrial growth of the U.S.S.R., the rise in living standards, the progress in agriculture, "the extension of protection against the risks of modern society," the increase in democratic rights and civil liberties, and the beneficent role of the Soviet Union in world affairs. The editorial hailed Russia as the bulwark of western civilization against the onslaught of fascist barbarism. The book review talked about starvation, torture, slave psychology, the correctness of "Trotsky's thesis of the impossibility of building socialism in one country," and the movement of the U.S.S.R. "in the direction of fascism."

To casual readers of the *Nation* this difference of opinion may seem surprising but not significant. To the regular reader, however, it will seem very significant—and not in the least surprising. Some four years ago the book-review section seceded from the rest of the magazine, and it still exists in a state of rebellion. On the whole, the *Nation* has been a liberal magazine, providing a forum for the various points of view the editors regarded as progressive. It has published articles for and against the Soviet Union, for and against the people's front in France, for and against the loyalist government in Spain, for and against the Communist Party. From our point of view, it has often been open to criticism, but it has taken the right side on many issues, and it has always tried to be fair.

The book-review section, on the other hand, has taken the wrong side on most issues, and it has not been fair. About what is the right and what the wrong side there can be infinite argument. About the lack of fairness there can be no argument at all. The bias of the *Nation's* book-review section can be proved.

Let us look, for example, at recent books on the Soviet Union. What is generally conceded to be the most important of recent studies, the Webbs' *Soviet Communism,* was given by the *Nation* to Abram Harris. Of the quality of the review, Louis Fischer, the *Nation's* own Moscow correspondent, has said all that needs saying. "He uses the review," Mr. Fischer wrote in a letter to the editors, "to air his own threadbare, shopworn, and uninteresting prejudices against the Soviet Union, which, I think, he has never seen. . . . What I miss is an evaluation of the service which the Webbs have performed in giving us a rich, comprehensive account of the workings of the Soviet system. . . . Where the Webbs fall down miserably—in their criticism of the Third International—Harris finds them 'more realistic.' "

Albert Rhys Williams's *The Soviets* and Anna Louise Strong's *The New Soviet Constitution* have not, so far as I can discover, been reviewed at all. On the other hand, when André Gide reported unfavorably on his visit to the U.S.S.R., the *Nation* could not wait for the book to be translated and published in this country, but brought out immediately a special and laudatory article by M. E. Ravage, its Paris correspondent.

And now, in this issue with the article and editorial commemorating the twentieth anniversary of the Soviets, we find a three-page review by Edmund Wilson. Seven books were given to Mr. Wilson, two of them pro-Soviet, five opposed. One of the pro-Soviet books, Dr. Gantt's *Medical Review of Soviet Russia* (issued in the United States as *Russian Medicine*) is judiciously described as containing some important facts. The other, which is dismissed in a contemptuous paragraph, is Lion Feuchtwanger's *Moscow, 1937,* published four months ago. Feuchtwanger, you know, was impressed by what he saw in the U.S.S.R., and therefore his book—instead of being hailed in a special article—is belatedly and maliciously reviewed by Mr. Wilson. The five anti-Soviet books, according to Mr. Wilson, "fill in a picture as appalling as it is convincing."

Within the past year, so far as I can discover, only one book on the Soviet Union was assigned to a pro-Soviet reviewer. That was Trotsky's *The Revolution Betrayed,* which was given to Louis Fischer —and also to Ben Stolberg. Repeatedly enemies of the Soviet Union have been allowed to voice their opinions, to damn books like the Webbs' and Feuchtwanger's, to praise books like André Gide's, Eugene Lyons's, and Victor Serge's. When, however, Trotsky's book is criticized by Louis Fischer, his criticism is paired with a fulsome eulogy by Stolberg!

Nor is it only with books on the Soviet Union that the bias becomes apparent. In 1936 Earl Browder, general secretary of the Communist Party, published a book called *What Is Communism?* The *Nation* assigned it to Louis M. Hacker. From any point of view, the choice was not a happy one, for Mr. Hacker, as a historian, concentrated his attention on Browder's discussion of the American past, and thus devoted most of his review to one chapter out of Browder's twenty-one. But, apart from the question of proportions and the relevance of the review, the significant point is that the literary editor of the *Nation* knew in advance that Mr. Hacker's review would be a bitter denunciation of the Communist Party and all its works.

James S. Allen's *The Negro Question in the United States* was assigned to Sterling D. Spero, whose quarrel with the position Mr. Allen takes was familiar to most well-informed persons. Maurice Thorez's *France Today* and Ralph Fox's *France Faces the Future* were reviewed by Suzanne LaFollette, who had hitherto not been known as an authority on either France or politics, but who, as a disciple, at least so far as the people's front is concerned, of Leon Trotsky, could be depended on to attack the Communist International and to question the integrity of Fox and Thorez. *Spain in Revolt,* by Harry Gannes and Theodore Repard, was given to Anita Brenner, who devoted her entire review—entitled "Let's Call It Fiction"—to attacking the authors and denouncing the people's front in Spain.

During the same period, I hasten to say, five books that are, in various ways, sympathetic to the views of the Communist Party were given favorable reviews: my *John Reed,* Spivak's *Europe Under the Terror,* Anna Rochester's *Rulers of America,* Joseph Freeman's *An American Testament,* and Angelo Herndon's *Let Me Live,* reviewed by Max Lerner, Frederick L. Schuman, George Marshall, Louis Kronenberger, and Horace Gregory. So far as I can disengage myself from the political convictions that are involved in my estimate of all the books, and the personal prejudices involved in my estimate of one, I think the reviews were, from the liberal point of view that the *Nation* is supposed to represent, more adequate than the reviews by Hacker, Spero, Miss LaFollette, and Miss Brenner. I also think it is worth pointing out that these books do not raise very sharply the issues at stake between the Communist Party and the Trotskyites. Finally, it is obvious that not one of the five reviewers can be regarded as a spokesman of the Communist Party, and some of them are, as a matter of fact, critical of its policies. However, I want it on the record that these five books received favorable reviews in the *Nation*.

Does this disprove my charge that the literary section of the *Nation* is biased? I am afraid not. It only indicates that the bias does not operate all the time—perhaps because it would be too easily discovered if it did. I have spoken of the way books on the Soviet Union have been reviewed, books on the policies of the Communist Party in the United States, books on the people's front in France, a book in defense of the loyalist government of Spain. I have said that the *Nation* neglected two important books on the U.S.S.R., and I might add that it also failed to review Dutt's *World Politics* and William Z. Foster's *From Bryan to Stalin*.

But what reveals the bias of the literary section beyond any question is that the Communist Party is never allowed to speak for itself. It is at least four years since there appeared in the *Nation* a review by a person who could by any stretch of the imagination be regarded as the party's spokesman. A few sympathizers have reviewed for the magazine, it is true, but for the most part books far removed from the struggle over communism. Books opposed to the Communist Party have been given to reviewers opposed to the Communist Party. Who reviewed James Rorty's *Where Life Is Better?* Anita Brenner. Who reviewed Charles Rumford Walker's *American City?* James Rorty. Who reviewed Fred Beal's *Proletarian Journey?* Rorty reviewed it, and then Edmund Wilson reviewed it again. Did it occur to the literary editor that, in the interests of the forum principle, Beal's book might be given to someone who held different opinions of the Soviet Union? No, it was reviewed twice, and both times by persons who, everyone knew, would endorse Beal's attack.

When Mr. Wilson's *Travels in Two Democracies* appeared, it

was conceivable that *Nation* readers might be interested in hearing the other side, but the book was reviewed by Margaret Marshall. Philip Rahv was given Céline's *Mea Culpa,* and, though he could not praise the book, he took the occasion to approve Céline's disapproval of "the present Soviet leaders." Sidney Hook disagreed with Albert Weisbord's *Conquest of Power,* but he used his review to attack "the opportunist leadership of the Communist Party."

It becomes perfectly apparent that the policy of the book section of the *Nation* is not the policy of an open forum. I can remember a time when Communists were asked to review for the *Nation,* but that has not happened since the end of 1933, when Joseph Wood Krutch became literary editor. With his arrival, the Communists went out and the anti-Communists came in. Anita Brenner attacked Hugo Gellert's *Capital.* Edna Kenton praised Tchernavin's *Escape from the Soviets.* Reinhold Niebuhr was given a page in which to praise the pamphlet, *Socialism's New Beginning.* James Burnham devoted a review of Palme Dutt's *Fascism and Social Revolution* to the thesis that "acceptance of the line of the Communist International means political blindness."

Meanwhile it became reasonably certain that any left-wing novel would be damned in the *Nation.* Cool indifference or forthright condemnation met Albert Halper's *The Foundry,* Josephine Herbst's *The Executioner Waits,* Waldo Frank's *Death and Birth of David Markand,* Edward Newhouse's *You Can't Sleep Here,* Thomas Boyd's *In Time of Peace,* Erskine Caldwell's *Kneel to the Rising Sun,* Clara Weatherwax's *Marching, Marching!* and Isidor Schneider's *From the Kingdom of Necessity.* Nobody argues that they are all masterpieces, but the unanimity of Mr. Krutch's reviewers is a little suspicious. Only last spring he handed three left-wing novels to James T. Farrell for exactly the kind of strong arm job for which Mr. Farrell is notorious.

During these four years Mr. Krutch's own war against communism has been conducted in his dramatic criticism, in essays on literature, and even in political articles. No Communist has been allowed to talk back. When Mr. Krutch's series of articles, *Was Europe a Success?,* was published in book form, it was assigned, not to a Communist, but to Harry Elmer Barnes, a Scripps-Howard liberal. And Mr. Krutch has protected his friends: parts of Farrell's *A Note on Literary Criticism* had appeared in the *Nation,* and therefore the policy of the good controversy would have suggested that the book's reviewer should be chosen from the many critics Farrell attacked, but it was given to Edmund Wilson, who was chiefly concerned to add a few criticisms of the Marxists that Farrell had been unable to think of.

Dr. Krutch's anti-Communist obsession reached its height when he joined the American Committee for the Defense of Trotsky. Criticized for his action, Mr. Krutch insisted that his interest in Trotsky "was exclusively an interest in fair play." To most of us that interest had seemed quite dormant during the past decade, as one case after another of injustice failed to rouse him to protest. Nevertheless, no one suspected him of being a Trotskyite. We merely felt that he joined the Trotsky Committee for the sake of attacking the Communist Party, just as, for three years, he had been using only too eager Trotskyist reviewers to attack Communist books.

Dr. Krutch has given up the literary editorship to return to the academic life, but the situation on the magazine does not seem to have improved under his successor, Margaret Marshall. Those who were present at the second American Writers' Congress will recall a little group of individuals whose purpose in attending seemed to be to prevent the congress from accomplishing the ends for which it was convened. Chief among the disrupters were Dwight MacDonald, Mary McCarthy, Philip Rahv, and William Phillips. All of them have been contributing to the *Nation,* and it is apparent that Miss Marshall, in her new position, counts on this little coterie, in addition to the larger group of enemies of the Communist Party assembled by her predecessor.

In the relatively short time since Dr. Krutch's retirement, Rahv has been the most active, and it is interesting to trace his career. Prior to the Writers' Congress, his attacks on communism had been cautious. After the congress, reviewing Ostrovski's *The Making of a Hero,* he virtually announced his open anti-communist campaign with a characteristically cheap innuendo: "Marxists, being fond of discerning contradictions in the social process, ought to apply their analytic prowess to investigating the discrepancy between the prodigious dimensions and meanings of the October revolution and the feeble records of it recently produced on its home grounds by writers seemingly most devoted to its progress."

Mr. Rahv's next gesture was a review, pretentious and sneering and rather childish, of a book of short stories by Leane Zugsmith. It was quite inevitable that Miss Marshall should assign him Walter Duranty's *One Life, One Kopeck* and Robert Briffault's *Europe in Limbo*, and equally inevitable that he should seize upon literary weaknesses, not unrecognized by other reviewers, to prosecute his attack on communism and the Soviet Union. To date, however, his most revealing review is that of Ilf and Petrov's *Little Golden America*, which gives the impression—wholly false, it is needless to say—that the Soviet humorists were so impressed by American machines that they failed to say a word in criticism of the capitalist system that controls those machines.

Miss Marshall's reliance upon this particular turncoat, despite his general incompetence as a literary critic and his peculiar unfitness to review books on the Soviet Union, does not promise well for her regime as literary editor. It seems possible, indeed, that, even more fully than Dr. Krutch, she will make the book section of the *Nation* an organ of the Trotskyites. I do not care whether these persons call themselves Trotskyites or not. I know that they are opposed to the Communist Party, to the Soviet Union, and to the people's front, and that they use exactly the same arguments as Trotsky uses. They are united, I suspect, by a common hatred rather than by a positive policy, but that does not alter the role they play.

It appears to me that readers of the *Nation* are being deceived. The *New Masses* takes a definite position, and its book-review section is edited according to a stated policy. By no means are all the contributors Communists, but it is not our intention to publish reviews by persons who are hostile to the Soviet Union or are unwilling to work in the people's front against fascism. The *Nation* has no such clear-cut policy. In the body of the magazine, as I have said, it tries to be fair. In the book section, however, it discriminates against one point of view and favors another. And this is never stated.

I presume that most readers of the *Nation* are what we call, not very precisely these days, liberals. I suspect that many of them are friendly to the Soviet Union and would not willingly aid its enemies. Almost all, certainly, are opposed to fascism and are eager to find effective ways of fighting it. They know that the people's front is the strongest barrier against fascism and at the same time a positive force for progress. I should like to convince these people that, all questions of sincerity to one side, the Trotskyites do in effect injure the Soviet Union and hamper the fight against fascism. I think that, if they happened to belong to trade unions or other organizations in which Trotskyites were active, they would see this for themselves.

But even if these liberal *Nation* readers do not share my opinions, I wonder if they really like the fare that is being served them. Do they subscribe to the *Nation* to listen to the notions of a little clique of anti-Communists, or do they want the opinions of representative authorities? Have they not the right to demand that, in its books reviews as elsewhere, the *Nation* should follow the principles it avows? And should they not, if necessary, take steps to enforce their demands?

December 7, 1937

Revolution in Bohemia

I

In 1923 young Halstead Weeks,
    The product and the pride of Saint Tim's school,
Denounced in ringing tones the Bolsheviks
    And proved that Bob LaFollette was their tool.
His mother felt the tears run down her cheeks,
    His banker-papa growled, "The boy's no fool."
Young Halstead got a watch for graduation
And old Saint Tim's a sizeable donation.

II

At Yale he learned from Phelps that *V.V.'s Eyes*
    And *Peter Pan* were modern works of art;
From Keller that the man of enterprise
    Serves God and country in the busy mart;
From good Dean Brown that one should not tell lies
    Nor masturbate nor scorn the pure at heart.
And if he'd made a single freshman team
He'd have fulfilled his father's every dream.

III

But even Yale had students in those years
    Who laughed at Phelps, and Halstead got the habit.
Not only did he imitate their sneers
    But when they praised a book was quick to grab it.
He read *This Side of Paradise* with tears
    And turned to *Jurgen, Sister Carrie, Babbitt.*
He read the prefaced plays of Bernard Shaw
And grew ashamed of his pot-bellied Paw.

IV

He read *Of Human Bondage, Dorian Gray,*
    Three Soldiers, In Our Time, The Enormous Room,
Ulysses, Rainbow, Mrs. Dalloway,
    Remembrance of Things Past, In Nero's Tomb,
The Magic Mountain, Tamar, Antic Hay,
    The Dial, Transatlantic, Exile, Broom.
Now where could youth with such distinguished taste land
Except among the lovers of *The Wasteland?*

V

He wrote an essay, keenly analytic,
    But possibly a little bit obscure,
Entitling Eliot the perfect critic
    And just as pure as poet could be pure,
Insisting that he was not parasitic,
    Although he borrowed widely to be sure.
The Lit had snubbed him, so he snubbed *The Lit,*
And tried *The Bark & Blare,* which published it.

VI

So Halstead Weeks emerged with his diploma,
    A published essay, and a great ambition.
But papa had not missed the strong aroma
    Of art and uncommercial erudition.
Commencement night he woke Hal from his coma
    And let him see the world of competition,
In which, he said, the boy could take his place
Or else—alternatives Hal could not face.

VII

And, lo, the brave new world of Silent Cal,
    Where Jesus was in business and in Rotary,
Where Socialists derided *Capital*,
    Where Ford was prophet and Filene his votary,
Where high-hat Hoover fought brown-derby Al,
    Where Babbitt had his cult and More his coterie—
It welcomed Halstead to its busy breast.
It gave him work, in short—at Pa's request.

VIII

The little cash that Pa had one time sunk
    In Biggs and Boggs now justified his hopes.
To gild the cabbage and perfume the skunk
    Was their concern, and they taught Hal the ropes.
He thought them boors, they counted him a lunk
    But set him writing ads for lesser soaps.
He cursed his lot and damned the silly stuff,
But—give him credit—wrote it well enough.

IX

When Halstead took the job he planned to spend
    His lonely nights composing stern critiques,
In which he would expound, condemn, defend
    The modern poets and their new techniques,
But somehow found it easier to lend
    His presence at the better Village speaks.
When he sat down to write the spirit balked,
But galloped like a racehorse when he talked.

X

A year went by. His bosses were impressed
    By what he'd written; friends by what he'd not.
In many Village hangouts they confessed
    That Halstead's bolt and Halstead both were shot.
But he could speak as glibly as the best
    Of syntax, values, cadences, and plot.
And he had found a girl and was impassioned—
A circumstance that some friends called old-fashioned.

XI

The time has come when we must talk of sex—
    A lively subject if there's lots of data.
But Hal's affair was not at all complex,
    Although he spouted Freudian dogmata.
The truth's so simple it is bound to vex:
    He liked to sleep with his inamorata.
And she, somewhat experienced, found Hal
Quite adequate though not phenomenal.

XII

He pleased his pa, his boss, his lady fair,
    But still he knew that there was something wrong.
And then one night he met young Clifton Hare,
    Who scorned superbly all the vulgar throng,
Who, by request, had left *The Bark & Blare*,
    Who talked with soft insistence all night long,
Who said at last, "We could, we might, I mean—
My friend, why don't we start a magazine?"

XIII

The seed was sown and promptly was manured
    By Halstead's father, who was riding high
And, feeling Halstead must by now be cured,
    Was not averse to giving him a try.
The magazine's existence was assured
    By adding to the board Erasmus Bly,
A Harvard lad whom Clifton recommended—
His insight faulty but his income splendid.

XIV

Their secret nightly meetings brought them fame;
    The Village wondered; Hal's Elaine grew pale.
They chose an office, tried to choose a name.
    Hal, wanting *Icarus,* could not prevail;
Hare urged *Return,* and Bly proposed *The Flame.*
    They argued till their arguments grew stale.
"In the beginning," Halstead said. . . . He halted
In wild amaze. "The word!" they cried, exalted.

XV

The Word it was—a name at least prophetic
    As Hal and his confreres abruptly found.
The bare announcement served as an emetic,
    Producing both the fury and the sound.
Dick Blackmur wrote on mysteries esthetic.
    A dozen letters came from Ezra Pound
(You know the endless way that Ezra runs on)
And manifestoes streamed from Gorham Munson.

XVI

They got from Waldo Frank some little gems,
    Incomprehensible but truly great;
From Gertrude Stein some scrambled apothegms;
    Confederate laments from Allen Tate.
Hal wrote on e. e. cummings' roots and stems,
    And Clifton barked and blared a hymn of hate.
Chicago's tough guy reached into his barrel
And let them have an early James T. Farrell.

XVII

In one short year *The Word* became the voice
    Of D. H. Lawrence and the vibrant male,
Of polylingual antics à la Joyce,
    Of Herman Melville and the great White Whale,
Of Irving Babbitt and the human choice,
    Of Oswald Spengler and the dismal wail.
And at the end the issue that was seething
Was Buchmanism versus Gurdjieff breathing.

XVIII

I say the end. Our epic's reached the day
    When Wall Street crashed and Halstead's Pa crashed too.
Then Biggs and Boggs reduced employees' pay,
    And little Bly announced that he was through.
Next Hal's Elaine went home to Troy to stay,
    Discharged from Constable's without ado.
Thus died *The Word* that dark and fateful winter,
And no one minded much except the printer.

XIX

But Biggs and Boggs somehow survived the storm,
    And Hal survived it too, with paychecks shrinking.
His solitary life resumed the norm
    Of noisy talk and not so quiet drinking.
He had some new ideas on style and form,
    And loved to tell his friends what he was thinking.
But they, he found, were less than fascinated.
In fact, they told him frankly he was dated.

XX

Do not suppose that Hal submitted tamely
    To all the current talk of politics.
He struggled to defend his thesis, namely
    That art and economics do not mix.
But though he marshaled all his reasons gamely,
    It did no good to kick against the pricks.
We are but human, and you must not ask us
Why we see visions going to Damascus.

XXI

Conversion's dangers are an ancient story,
    And Hal's was not a stable constitution.
He felt the working class was full of glory,
    And hated all the ruling-class pollution.
The reckoning, he ventured, would be gory;
    He hoped to see the day of retribution.
He found the works of Sidney Hook sublime,
And planned to read Karl Marx when he had time.

XXII

He nearly signed a Foster proclamation
    And did say Norman Thomas was a dub;
He almost joined the Harlan delegation
    And gave the Hunger Marchers dimes for grub;
He wrote some letters full of indignation;
    He visited at times the John Reed Club;
And, as he said to some insulting smarty,
Was practically a member of the Party.

XXIII

He'd gladly join—in this he would insist—
    But that the leadership was so naïve.
The opportunities the Party missed
    Were bound to make a thoughtful Marxist grieve.
He did not like to seem a dogmatist,
    But there were errors one could scarce conceive.
How can a party grow if it disdains
The wisdom of the nation's finest brains?

XXIV

And after all his field was literary,
    And one must work wherever one is able.
No task, perhaps, was quite so necessary
    As purifying that Augean stable,
That realm of vulgar thought and crude vagary,
    That vast confusion like the storied Babel,
That gloomy sink, that bottomless abysm
Which sometimes passed for Marxian criticism.

XXV

Now Dr. Krutch—long may his tribe decrease—
    Had likewise felt the Marxists needed purging,
And meeting Hal one night proposed a piece,
    A task to which Hal needed little urging.
He sat him down and let his soul release
    The bitter, bitter truths that came a-surging.
Esthetic ruin faced the working classes
But for Hal's brave exposure of the *Masses*.

XXVI

The day the piece appeared Hal got a note
    From Calverton, whose praises knew no measure.
He asked if Hal would kindly let him quote
    A certain passage that he called a treasure.
To publish the next essay that Hal wrote
    Would give him, furthermore, the greatest pleasure.
The *Modern Monthly* craved a contribution
From such a loyal friend of revolution.

XXVII

Hal wrote the piece and made a date for lunch.
　　V. F. brought friends and there was conversation.
Hal soon was meeting weekly with the bunch,
　　And taking pleasure in their commendation,
Since he and they most dearly loved to crunch
　　Upon a ripe and juicy reputation.
They praised no one but Trotsky, that great mind,
For whom they wrote petitions, which Hal signed.

XXVIII

The *Masses* staff had viewed with some tranquillity
　　Hal's literary gestures of defiance,
But it announced its utter inability
　　To overlook his Trotskyist alliance.
It pointed out the touch of imbecility
　　In Calverton's demands and his compliance.
The *Masses* said in simple white and black
His friends were knaves and he was just a jack.

XXIX

Hal might have been dismayed, but noble Max,
　　With many shakings of his great white mane,
Convinced him Stalin paid for these attacks.
　　(And had not Eastman once seen Trotsky plain?)
Hal answered with the gang supplying cracks.
　　(It was the same old Trotskyist refrain.)
He signed his name upon the dotted line,
And thought the document extremely fine.

XXX

His ego had enough to feed upon,
　　And skillful flattery had turned his head,
But bad was bound to turn to worse anon,
　　For he had got a girl, a super-Red,
Who used "amalgam," even "epigone,"
　　And other words that she had learned in bed.
(She had, as folks say, lived, and spent her nights
With half the city's leading Trotskyites.)

XXXI

With her to help his Marxian passions flare,
    He called, at home, at work, for blood to flow.
But Biggs and Boggs, he found, did not much care
    So long as he denounced the C.I.O.
Nor were his words too much for Pa to bear
    Since he called Roosevelt a so-and-so.
And Catholics rejoiced when he'd explain
How Stalin had betrayed The Cause in Spain.

XXXII

The magazines discovered he existed,
    Books, Common Sense, the *Saturday Review.*
Paul Palmer, double-faced if not two-fisted,
    Presided at his *Mercury* debut.
Amazingly the *Forum's* Leach enlisted
    In this crusade to save the world anew.
Hal wrote "I Left the Party in the Lurch"
For *Harper's,* though he'd always loathed research.

XXXIII

He mingled with the city's cognoscenti,
    Was mentioned more than once by I.M.P.,
Had drinks with Sinclair Lewis, and had plenty,
    Was introduced to Lippmann at a tea.
The boy went places and where'er he went he
    Said Communism served the bourgeoisie.
And cocktail drinkers up and down the city
Agreed with him the sell-out was a pity.

XXXIV

But renegades have never been a rarity
    And Halstead's little boom was not to last.
He soon perceived the growing popularity
    Of Eugene Lyons, knew his day was past.
His girl perceived it too, with perfect clarity
    And wrote a note that left poor Hal aghast.
Poor Hal, indeed, in view of his ambitions:
He'd nothing left to do but sign petitions.

XXXV

In time he could not quiet the conviction
    That even Trotskyites might be a bore,
And though steadfastly vaunting his addiction
    To revolution, wondered more and more
If Marx's teachings were not all a fiction
    And human nature rotten at the core.
He'd gladly die upon the barricades,
But proletarians were pampered jades.

XXXVI

Increasingly he felt his noble soul
    In books alone could find its rightful place.
Let others struggle toward a social goal
    And seek to save the worthless human race.
He'd watch the tide of angry passion roll
    While he communed with wisdom face to face.
He wrote a piece, describing his decision
As if the gods had granted him a vision.

XXXVII

The article appeared in the *Atlantic,*
    For Sedgwick liked it, as one might suppose.
Had he not made a pilgrimage romantic,
    Toured rebel Spain in spats, defied its foes?
Had he not told with raptures corybantic
    How Franco saved the Spaniards from their woes?
Of course he felt with Hal that art must be
From taint of propaganda ever free.

XXXVIII

Our story's wandered to its sad conclusion.
    No need to chronicle Hal's small success;
No need to tear away each fond illusion;
    No need to note his growing snobbishness;
No need to castigate his vast confusion:
    We know too well how such affairs progress.
The time would come for haughty jeers at pickets
And voting straight reactionary tickets.

XXXIX

The Lippmanns and the Thompsons and the Lyons,
　　They have their brief if somewhat gaudy day.
The Eastmans and their literary scions
　　Proceed to find and fatten on their prey.
The Franks seek vainly for Spinozan Zions,
　　Nor lose their little egos by the way.
And men like Halstead lapse predictably
Into pretentious mediocrity.

XL

In '38 an older Halstead Weeks,
　　Alumni orator at Saint Tim's School,
Denounced in ringing tones the Bolsheviks,
　　And proved that John L. Lewis was their tool.
He also said nice things about the Greeks.
　　(The students thought the speech was so much drool.)
His honorarium was slight, I fear,
But trustees hinted at a job next year.

April 12, 1938

VII

SOME MONUMENTS

The essay "The Legend of John Reed," is particularly noteworthy. Reed, the poet and bohemian radical, had been America's first martyr for Communism. In 1914 he had traveled to Mexico as a journalist to cover the revolution in progress there. Two years later he was in Europe writing about the war on the eastern front. The February revolution brought Reed to Petrograd and he stayed to witness the Bolshevik seizure of power in October. His eyewitness account quickly became a classic: *Ten Days That Shook the World*. Reed returned to New York where he helped to create the American Communist Party. In 1920 he was back in Russia doing propaganda work for the Third International when he contracted typhus and died. Reed's ashes are preserved in an urn in the Kremlin wall.

Reed was an energetic and romantic figure for the Communist movement who the leaders were anxious to exploit. Late in 1929 the Party had launched a series of John Reed clubs with the aim of inspiring "proletarian" writers.

A committee of Harvard University leftist alumni suggested that Hicks write Reed's biography. *John Reed: The Making of a Revolutionary* appeared in 1936 and was acclaimed by *Current History* as one of the "ten distinguished nonfiction books" of the year. It is probably the book for which Granville Hicks is best known today.

Thomas Boyd, Communist

A year ago a letter appeared in Percy Hammond's column in *The Herald Tribune*, accusing him of having defended capitalism and war in his review of a play by George Middleton. The letter concluded:

> In the next World War, for which American capitalism is busily preparing, the basic conditions will be the same as in the last. Workers will be herded in by the draft. White-collar youths, unable to find another place in a society which has no better use for them, will eagerly enlist. Bankers will pyramid their riches by huge flotations. Some millions of men will be turned into foul cadavers. . . . Others will be patched with gut and silver where bone and sinew have been shot away. And in the end the industrialists of some country—England, Japan or America— will have gained a little larger markets for the things their workers produce but are paid so little they are unable to buy. There will be immense profits for the capitalists, death and misery for the clerks and workers. All this is clear. What I want to know is, where do you come in?

Thomas Boyd, who in this letter made public for the first time his newly formulated conclusions about capitalism, had every right to speak on the subject of war. Enlisting in the Marine Corps when he was eighteen years old, he saw service at Belleau Wood, Soissons, and St. Mihiel. He emerged from the war with the Croix de Guerre and with a body racked by poison gas.

When he was only twenty-four, Boyd wrote the story of the war as he had seen it. His novel, *Through the Wheat*, is, I hold, the most convincing portrayal of the World War by an American writer and the most devastating indictment of the war machine. Even hostile critics admitted that Boyd's characters were representative American soldiers and that this depiction of trench warfare was exact and unexaggerated.

Written in the very simplest style, depending on the cumulative effect of a series of unadorned descriptions, the novel overwhelms the reader with the terrifying reality of war. This is the final passage:

> On the drab earth, beaten lifeless by carnage and corruption, drab bodies lay, oozing thin streams of pink blood, which formed dark, mysterious little pools by their sides. Jaws were slack—dark, objectionable little caverns in pallid faces. Some men still moaned, or, in a tone into which discouragement had crept, called for help.
>
> Each body was alone, drawn apart from its companions by its separate and incommunicable misery.

Hicks tramped on through the field, dimly sensing the dead, the odors, the scene. He found his rifle where he had thrown it. As he picked it up, the ridge swarmed with small gray figures, ever growing nearer. He turned and walked toward his platoon. The breath from his nostrils felt cool. He raised his chin a little. The action seemed to draw his feet from the earth. No longer did anything matter, neither the bayonets, the bullets, the barbed wire, the dead, nor the living. The soul of Hicks was numb.

Though this ending is as coldly pessimistic as anything could well be, the reader somehow feels in the whole book a power of protest that almost succeeds in translating the defeat into victory. And it is true, of course, that Thomas Boyd had not surrendered to despair. A full decade intervened between the publication of *Through the Wheat* and his avowal of Communism. It was a decade, for Boyd, of varied activities, blind stumblings, false starts. But never at any time did he enroll in the lost generation. He refused to be lost, he would not adopt an easy, comfortable, prosperous pessimism. And never for one moment did he cease to hate war or to try to find a way to end war.

The results of that decade, so far as his writing was concerned, were not wholly satisfactory. He wrote a book of short articles, only one or two of which approximate the intensity of *Through the Wheat*. His historical novels are certainly inferior to his war novel. The three biographies he wrote are shrewd, well-informed, more than competent studies of unconventional Americans: Simon Girty, Anthony Wayne, Harry Lee.

It would be pleasant to say that Boyd was a great writer, but it would not be quite true. His work, taken as a whole, entitles him to a perfectly respectable place among American novelists and biographers of the twenties. He had, moreover, written one novel, *Through the Wheat*, that very clearly suggested latent greatness. But nothing that he did beween 1923 and 1935 measured up to the standard he had set.

I knew Boyd only after he became a Communist, but it is not difficult to imagine what he was like in the ten years before. He has, as a matter of fact, given many hints in his new novel, soon to be published, *In Times of Peace*. It is the continuation of the story of William Hicks, the central character of *Through the Wheat*, and it tells of restlessness, dreams of success, and frustration in the mad bourgeois world of the Coolidge era. It ends with Hicks among the unemployed, battered down by ruthless police as he stands in line for a job. But this time the soul of Hicks is not numb: he knows now whom he is fighting and why, and he goes to take his place in the ranks of the militant working class.

More than once I have heard Boyd say, "I was a Communist all the time, but I didn't have sense enough to know it." He was always aware, and perhaps most clearly at times of personal success and financial well-being, that contemporary society was rotten. Even if he had not been able to use his eyes, the memory of the war would have shown him the viciousness of capitalism and the instability of what is called civilization. But why society was rotten and what could be done about it, he did not know. It took the years of crisis to teach him.

When Boyd did realize that he was a Communist, he wanted to act. He was living in Woodstock, Vermont, a small country town with a few writers and artists. He talked, of course, and his talk was fruitful, but conversational Communism was not enough. He wrote for *Fight,* and he volunteered to do reviews for the *New Masses.* Then, when a unit of the Communist Party was formed in one of Vermont's few industrial cities, he joined. Last summer members of the party told him that he was the only person available as candidate for governor. Obtaining signatures and speaking throughout the state meant the postponement of work he was eager to do, but he accepted the responsibility, and thousands of Vermonters realized for the first time that Communism was a reality and Communists human beings.

When the campaign was over, he went back to writing, and finished the two books on which he had been working. They were the first books he had written since he became a Communist, and he was naturally interested in giving expression to the new attitude he had developed and to the fresh insight that he felt he had acquired. I have read the novel, *In Times of Peace,* and part of the biography of John Fitch. It would be less than honest to say that I was wholly satisfied with the novel. It was a story that Boyd had to get out of his system, and it is certainly an interesting and an illuminating book. But I think it is fairly clear that it is the work of a man in a period of transition. It does not represent the complete integration that I feel Boyd had achieved only within the last few months of his life. It is not quite the book that the author of *Through the Wheat* should, once he had become a Communist, have written. The biography, so far as

I can judge from the fragment I read, comes closer to satisfying achievement. The treatment is Marxist throughout, and this poor, exploited inventor of the steamboat—one of the innumerable inventors who have been robbed of both profit and fame—takes on significance as a symbolic figure in the development of American capitalism.

I am afraid that so restrained an analysis of Boyd's work conceals both the admiration I felt for him and the confidence I had in his future. It would be pleasanter for me to throw critical reservations out the window and write in unbounded praise. But it is precisely the greatest tragedy of his premature death that he died without having given a clear indication of the literary achievement that, if he had lived, would have been his.

Boyd was certainly a born rebel. His contempt for bourgeois convention was deep-seated, and it found constant expression in word and action. He had been, I gather, quite capable of breaking rules for the sake of having them broken and shocking people for the sake of seeing them shocked. This rebelliousness was at first largely blind, but it was one of the qualities that impelled him toward Communism. And when he fully understood what made contemporary society so detestable and what had to be done to change it, boisterous protest gave way to serious, laborious activity in the revolutionary movement. It took 1,500 signatures to put the Communist Party on the ballot in Vermont, and Boyd secured the larger part of them himself by persistent, wearisome, house-to-house and farm-to-farm canvassing. He submitted to the routine of committee meetings; he delivered speeches, which he very much disliked to do; he spent long hours driving over the state to take care of minor details of the campaign. And he did all this with extraordinary vigor. Even when he was most serious, his high spirits simply brushed aside any suggestion of pompous solemnity. All his energy, so long dissipated in futile revolt, poured itself into his new-found tasks.

Twice in the course of the Vermont campaign I heard him speak. He was not a good speaker, nervous and at a loss for words. And yet his speaking was always effective, for the whole force of the man drove home his stumbling but perfectly sound analysis of capitalist decay. One of the meetings at which I heard him speak was attended largely by middle-class people, and the other was attended entirely by workers. He spoke much better at the second meeting. And I understood why when I saw how completely the workers—many of them granite cutters—accepted him as one of themselves. He obviously thought and felt almost entirely from the workers' point of view, and they responded to this quality in him.

Boyd signed the call for the Writers' Congress, and I have no doubt that he would have played an important part in it. He had the qualities of which revolutionary writers are made. His books, whatever their faults, prove it. His record in Vermont proves it. In terms of achievement and even more in terms of potentialities, the loss to the revolutionary movement is beyond measurement.

February 12, 1935

Two Jeffersonian Poets

Vachel Lindsay, by Edgar Lee Masters

Mr. Masters has written a confused, careless, badly-proportioned book, but an important one for the student of American culture. He understands Lindsay because he is so much like him. Both of them were unmistakably and even self-consciously of the Middle West. Both came into prominence with the pre-war poetry renaissance. Both hated industrialism as a system of production and the machine as a factor in American life. Both were Jeffersonian democrats in their political thinking. To a great extent, Masters has only had to look into himself to understand Lindsay.

Insofar as they differed, it was largely because Masters was more rational, building his distaste for big business into a defense of southern agrarianism and the doctrine of states' rights. Lindsay, on the other hand, was illogical enough to glorify Lincoln, whom Masters recognizes as the instrument of the northern industrialists in their destruction of Jeffersonian values. Lindsay was a good deal like the average middle-class American, resenting large-scale monopoly capitalism when he was conscious of its evils but never really doubting or even examining its premises. He called himself at one time a Socialist

("Come let us vote against our human nature"), but it was only because the word signified a distaste for the status quo and a devotion to
non-commercial principles. His ideal was a nation of small towns,
rather like his own Springfield but more beautiful and more hospitable
to poets.

The strength of Lindsay's poetry came from the fact that he
genuinely represented an important section of the American people,
even in his prejudices, which were numerous. He made no attempt to
isolate himself from American life; on the contrary, he sought to be a
poet of the people, meaning, naturally, middle-class people. He concerned himself with the highest ideals of his class, which he expressed
with passion and often with beauty. "General William Booth Enters
Heaven," "Old, Old, Old Andrew Jackson," "The Eagle That is Forgotten," "The Virginians Are Coming Again" and "Factory Windows
Are Always Broken" are moving poems.

But the middle class had very little place for poetry of any kind,
and the ideals that Lindsay expressed were cherished in memory only.
They belonged to the great days of Jefferson and Jackson, not to the
days of Roosevelt and Wilson. The middle class was made up for the
most part of smug, avaricious people on the way up or frightened,
avaricious people on the way down. The former would pay to see
Lindsay go through his stunts on the platform, but they did not respond
to his poetry. The latter were too worried to bother about him or any
other poet.

Lindsay was a poet who needed a responsive audience. If he
could have felt that his work was needed, he would have grown in
confidence and power. As it was, he turned more and more to his
infantile poetry-games, and finally he committed suicide. There were,
as Masters shows, many psychological factors in his ultimate collapse,
but it was the lack of external support that made his inner weaknesses
fatal.

This is not, needless to say, Masters' interpretation, though he
gives plenty of evidence for it. And even he, individualist that he is,
realizes that Lindsay's suicide was a social tragedy. Something could
have been done, he says, but all he can suggest is that some of the
useless rich might have given Lindsay a subsidy.

A subsidy would have helped, but that was not primarily what
was needed. As has been said, Lindsay, like other poets but perhaps to
an uncommon degree, needed an audience. He also needed under-

standing. All his life he wandered about in a haze of unrealizable ideals. The ideals had once been splendid and they still had a certain meaning, but he could not reinterpret them for his age because he did not understand it. He was bound within the intellectual confines of his class. He could not grow; so he deteriorated—and died.

December 24, 1935

More Light on Mark Twain's Ordeal

Mark Twain's Notebook, edited by Albert Bigelow Paine

In his column in *The Daily Worker,* Mike Gold recently claimed Mark Twain as "one of ours," as a forerunner of the revolutionary movement in American literature. If one remembers the deadly attacks on imperialism, race persecution and militarism in "To the Person Sitting in Darkness," "War Prayer," and "The United States of Lyncherdom," the claim seems not unreasonable, for few writers have denounced capitalism more bitterly than Mark Twain did on one or two occasions.

But Mark Twain, as the *Notebook* shows, was a long way from being revolutionary. He was, indeed, in most respects a typical petty bourgeois of the late nineteenth century. It has been often pointed out that he was frantically eager to make a lot of money. The *Notebook* is full of reference to inventions, patents, investments and securities, and Mr. Paine says that he has eliminated many of the records of money-making schemes because they were so dull. If one can judge from his journals, Clemens was never so deeply interested in any of his books as he was in Paige's typesetter, and it is worth noting that, in listing the advantages of this machine he mentions the fact that it does not belong to a union. He was proud to have dinner with Andrew Carnegie and his gratitude to H. H. Rogers of Standard Oil was so strong that he damned to hell a man who wanted him to publish a book attacking Rogers' company.

Even in his moods of rebellion, Mark Twain was a petty bourgeois. The one political crusade in which he joined was the attack on monarchy: he wrote *A Connecticut Yankee in King Arthur's Court* and the *Notebook* is full of eloquent denunciation of kings and nobles. The American petty bourgeois had had reason to denounce monarchy a hundred years earlier, but the issue was not altogether pertinent in the United States of the eighteen-eighties. Moreover, as the *Notebook* reveals, Mark Twain, like many other good petty-bourgeois democrats, lost much of his anti-aristocratic bias when nobility started patting him on the head. The lack of enthusiasm with which he viewed a demonstration of the Berlin proletariat in 1892 contrasts unpleasantly with the warmth that enters into his description of his meeting with the emperor and, later, his meeting with a collection of princesses.

His other revolt was against organized religion, and there are many sharp and irreverent comments on churches in the *Notebook*. But it must be remembered that he dared publish few of these criticisms during his lifetime. His one strongly anti-religious books, *What Is Man?* went unpublished for many years and finally appeared anonymously. And *What Is Man?* shows how confused and uninformed his opposition to religion was. To a scientific materialist, it seems not only sophomoric but largely irrelevant to the real issues religion raises. One can only compare it to some of the early attacks of the less-informed bourgeois rationalists of the eighteenth century.

There are two passages in the *Notebook,* both written in the eighties, that make clear just how typical of his class Mark Twain was. "We Americans," one of them reads, "worship the almighty dollar. Well, it is a worthier god than Hereditary Privilege." The other is: "Instead of giving the people decent wages, church and gentry and nobility made them work for them for nothing, pauperized them, then fed them with alms and persuaded themselves that the alms-giving was the holiest work of God and the giver sure to go to heaven, whereas one good wage-giver was worth a million of them to the state." Aristocracy was always the villain in Mark Twain's mind and by contrast capitalist enterprise was the hero.

There is nothing very surprising about all this, but it is worth pointing out, not only because it ought to discourage extravagant claims, but also because it has a definite bearing on Mark Twain's literary development. Ever since Van Wyck Brooks published his *Ordeal of Mark Twain,* there has been a savage controversy, reaching its climax in Bernard De Voto's diatribes against Brooks. Brooks' thesis is that Mark Twain's life was a tragedy, that he had in him the potentialities of a very great writer and that these potentialities never came to fulfillment.

The evidence for this contention seems to me so overwhelming that I can only regard De Voto's venomous objections as a defense of the right of an author to be immature. No one denies Mark Twain's genius, least of all Van Wyck Brooks, but Brooks does say that Mark Twain never grew up and the facts support him. There is nothing finer in American literature than a few scattered chapters of *Tom Sawyer*, the first two-thirds of *Huckleberry Finn*, the first half of *Life on the Mississippi*, two or three episodes in *The Gilded Age*, certain passages in *Roughing It*, half-a-dozen short stories and a couple of essays. But what can be said for the Injun Joe episode in *Tom Sawyer*, the rescue of Jim in *Huckleberry Finn*, the melodrama of *The Gilded Age*, the sentimentality of *Joan of Arc*, the slap-stick of *The Connecticut Yankee*, the low spots of *Innocents Abroad*, the flat stretches of *Following the Equator* or the sophomoric bathos of *What Is Man?* And what can be said for a writer who never wrote a single book that was good from start to finish, that did not demand apologies for a third or a half of its contents? All that can be said is just what Brooks did say: Mark Twain was a genius who never grew up.

Where Brooks fails is in his explanation, which is idealistic in the bad sense. He does not take into account the effect on Mark Twain of the age in which he lived. And it is on that point that the evidence of the *Notebook* must be taken into account. We must remember that the world in which Samuel Clemens grew up was, to a great extent, actually a democratic world. In the Missouri of his boyhood, on the Mississippi River when he was a pilot and in Nevada and California of the sixties, class distinctions (except in so far as slavery was concerned) were few and easily overcome. It was only after he had come East, made his trip to the Holy Land, married the daughter of a wealthy man and settled down in Hartford, that he really saw the kind of exploitation that capitalist industrialism had brought about. His first thirty years were spent in a democracy; his last forty-five in a plutocracy. The plutocracy had grown out of the democracy; its seeds were in the ambitions of just such pioneer individualists as Samuel Clemens; but the democracy had existed.

This is significant. Mark Twain developed just as any man in his

environment might have been expected to. The national transition
from democracy to plutocracy corresponded to his own transition
from relative poverty to relative wealth. In his own way he belonged
to the gilded age. But he was not happy in it, for, though he approved
its values as a man, he could not approve them as a writer. Plutocratic
capitalism had nothing to give his imagination; he was not really at
home with it; as a writer he could not come to terms with it. That is
why, in his most successful books, he turned back to the Mississippi
Valley he had known as a boy and young man.

To a certain extent, then, Mike Gold is right: Mark Twain is, if
not exactly one of ours, then certainly not one of the enemy's. He belongs in the democratic tradition and to the extent that we are heirs
of that tradition we can claim him. His best work, though it is not
proletarian, is not incompatible with the proletarian spirit. His failures
belong to the bourgeoisie, which could not nourish him, could not
help him to grow up, could not give him any but pecuniary values. If
he could have continued to live in the near-democracy of the mid-
century West or if there had been a militant proletariat, the result
might have been different.

The fact that Mark Twain is the most popular of American writers may be interpreted in many ways, but I suspect that Newton Arvin's
explanation, presented in a *New Republic* article last June, is not far
from the truth. "He is read," Arvin said, "not because he makes experience more intelligible or enriches the imagination with the possibilities
of new experience, but because he cooperates with the desire to play
hooky." But Arvin, though correct in saying that Mark Twain has
provided his millions of readers with an escape from the complexities
of modern industrial civilization, fails to ask one important question:
escape to what? The answer is that he leads them not merely into the
personal past of individual boyhood but into the past of the nation, into
the era of democracy, when classes were pretty much limited to the
decadent old Continent and the effete East and effort and ambition
meant something. Ever since Appomattox, the masses of the petty
bourgeoisie and the more hopeful sections of the proletariat have been
looking backward. They have had their moments of irritation and disillusionment, just as Mark Twain had, but they have found consolation
in memories of the golden age of free competition and their most radical effort has been, as in the muckraking era, to try to restore it. Only
recently has the realization grown that the future alone can abolish

the evils of the present. The American people have had enough of looking backward; the heirs of Mark Twain must teach them to look ahead.

January 7, 1936

A Decade in Review

A Footnote to Folly, by Mary Heaton Vorse

It seems incredible that one woman could see and do so much in ten years. The book begins in 1912, with Mrs. Vorse reporting the Lawrence strike. After a trip to Europe, which included the suffrage convention at Budapest and a visit to Madame Montessori, she returned for the Paterson strike, the unemployment battles of the winter of 1913–14 and the aftermath of the Ludlow massacre. Back to Europe she went, attending the women's peace conference in Holland, sounding pubic opinion in Germany after the sinking of the Lusitania, witnessing the effects of war on the civilian population of Western Europe. In America she took part in the Mesabi Range strike and tried to help the persecuted objectors to war. After the armistice came England and Lloyd George, Paris and the peace conference, Italy with the workers in possession of the factories, the Second International, Berne, relief work in the Balkans, the smashing of the Hungarian Soviets and a putsch in Vienna. In the United States once more, she worked in the steel strike, organized shirt makers; took part in the fight for Sacco and Vanzetti and helped the victims of the Amalgamated lockout in New York. Then Russia, in 1921, and not merely the cities but far into the Ukraine. And finally, ten years after she had welcomed the strikers' children from Lawrence, she was assisting in the march of the children of political prisoners.

Only such an outline can suggest the scope of the book. "This is not a biography," Mrs. Vorse truthfully says. "It is a picture of the world as I saw it during an important moment of history." The reader is swept from one event to another, often protestingly. Mrs. Vorse will not linger. Always she presses ahead, sometimes saying, quite accurately, "A book could be written about this." *A Footnote to Folly* is sometimes breathtaking, but it is consistently illuminating.

It is illuminating because Mrs. Vorse has been not only a trained observer but also an active participant. In her quiet New England home she was taught not to be afraid of new ideas and to act on her convictions. The first ten years of her adult life brought her into contact with the labor movement, and, when she went to Lawrence in 1912, she was ready to learn what could be learned. "We knew now," she says of Joe O'Brien and herself after the strike, "where we belonged— on the side of the workers and not with the comfortable people among whom we were born." Everything else re-enforced that lesson.

The book begins with the children of the Lawrence strikers and ends with the children of the conscientious objectors and almost every episode tells of the suffering that curses childhood in a world of poverty and war. Today, Mrs. Vorse, looking at the depression, the amassing of armaments and especially fascism, sees how terribly childhood is menaced. "We still have a chance," she writes. "This philosophy of hate, of religious and racial intolerance, with its passionate urge towards war, is loose in the world. It is the enemy of democracy; it is the enemy of all the fruitful and spiritual sides of life. It is our responsibility, as individuals and as organizations, to resist this." But she knows that we cannot be content with defending the meager privileges we have; we must push on to a planned society.

A Footnote to Folly does not have—Mrs. Vorse did not try to give it—the leisurely, philosophical, introspective quality of *The Education of Henry Adams* or *The Autobiography of Lincoln Steffens.* It is a picture, a record, vivid and shrewd, of ten world-shaking years. It is a book that ought to be put in the hands of every complacent middle-class man and especially woman in the country. "Let us look carefully," she writes, "at this civilization which has caused the misery of countless children only to send them later to the slaughter of war. Let us weigh it and examine it. Let us not fear to look at its inequalities, its heights and depths. . . . Do we, whose children are safe at home instead of strolling the world, have no responsibility?" There is no one who has a better right to speak such words than Mary Heaton Vorse.

January 21, 1936

European Experiences, by Mabel Dodge Luhan

Mrs. Luhan has had a passion to know and to subjugate famous people and, being blessed with a good deal of energy and considerable cash, has usually succeeded in getting what she wanted. *European Experiences*, the second volume of her autobiography, describes the years in which she was living in Florence. She entertained, among many others, Gordon Craig, Eleanora Duse, Leo and Gertrude Stein, Jacques Émile Blanche, Paul and Muriel Draper, Stephen Haweis, John D. Herron and Jo Davidson. The names are worth giving because the list suggests the measure of the book's failure. Whenever she introduces a new celebrity, Mrs. Luhan begins with some lively description that rouses one's interests and hopes, but in the second paragraph the reader is right back to Mabel Dodge's melodramatic emotions and second-hand ideas. There is nothing in the book but Mabel, who appears to be such a dull and silly woman that one wonders how, in spite of her immense fortune, the celebrities ever were able to put up with her.

January 28, 1936

The Oneida Commune

A Yankee Saint, by Robert Allerton Parker

John Humphrey Noyes was an important part of the Utopian Socialist movement that developed in this country with the beginnings of industrialism. He established a colony at Oneida, New York, that was remarkably successful during the period of his leadership and he advanced, as an integral part of his communistic experiment, views on sexual morality that, when distinguished from his religious dogmas and his particular methods of birth control, are not without pertinence today.

Looked at today, Noyes, like the other Utopians of the thirties and forties, is a strangely paradoxical figure. His fanaticism is so apparent that one cannot blame his neighbors in Vermont for thinking him crazy. Moreover, those same neighbors, who, in their respectable, common sense, acquisitive way, went about the building up of capitalism, were actually, in the perspective of history, more progressive than he, for capitalism had to be developed to lay the foundation for a collective society. But one's sympathy is, none the less, with Noyes. He had idealism, courage and consistency and one admires him for the vigor with which he plagued the Philistines of his day.

This is a paradox that can only be resolved dialectically. The reformer who disregards the movement of social forces, who tries to build an ideal social system out of his own head, is always, from one point of view, slightly ridiculous. His isolation fosters abnormality and the hopelessness of his task makes him fanatical. But it does not follow that his ideas are contemptible or that his zeal is wasted. The ultimate victory is not with the Philistines, for there are forces working, however slowly, toward the ends the Utopian prematurely seeks to achieve. These forces, as they find expression in individual aspirations and mass movements, use the lessons of the Utopian reformer and are encouraged by his spirit. So Marx, founding scientific Socialism, profited by the visions as well as by the mistakes of Fourier and Owen and so we in this country turn back, with interest and not without admiration, to Brook Farm and Oneida.

Noyes, moreover, reactionary as his colonial scheme was in an age of advancing capitalism, was in other respects a progressive force. As Marx and Engels often pointed out, the bourgeois revolutions inspired in men's minds ideals that bourgeois society could not realize. The whole Utopian movement was an abortive effort to run ahead of history and realize those ideals at once. Doomed to failure as it was, the movement served to keep the ideals alive and helped to achieve intellectual if not social emancipation. By questioning the institution of private property, Noyes paved the way for the more realistic advocates of proletarian revolution. His views on sex illuminated the discrepancy between the romantic Victorian theory of love and the actual bourgeois practice. Even his religion, fantastic as it seems today, was a challenge to the organized church.

Parker does not offer this interpretation of Noyes; in fact, he offers no interpretation at all. His discussion of the Utopian experiment in general is superficial and even condescending and he treats Oneida less cavalierly only because of his pre-occupation with Noyes.

In the field of religion, though he has supposedly made a special study of mysticism, he varies between vagueness and the typical blindness of the modernist to the religious theories of the past. Only what he, in common with Havelock Ellis, regards as the up-to-dateness of Noyes' sexual morality receives due appreciation and this receives more than is due.

Fortunately, however, much more can be said about the biography. Nine-tenths of success in writing a pioneer biography such as this is getting the facts, which Parker has done, intelligently, patiently, accurately. He tells the story of John Humphrey Noyes as fully and as reliably as it can be told and, avoiding the obvious temptation of sensationalism, tells it with dignity. Thanks to the author's straightforward honesty, Noyes comes alive, and the reader can make his own interpretation.

February 4, 1936

Moody's Letters to Harriet

Letter to Harriet, by William Vaughn Moody
Edited with introduction and conclusion by Percy MacKaye

This book contains the letters that William Vaughn Moody wrote Harriet Converse Tilden, from the time he met her in 1901 to the time he married her in 1909, a year before his death. The letters have been affectionately annotated by Moody's friend, Percy MacKaye, who has also written a long and illuminating introduction. MacKaye tells how, in the first decade of the century, a group of poets attempted to raise the level of the American drama.

"Our aim," MacKaye writes, "was to cleanse the temple of Apollo, the stage, from the sins of Apollyon, the commercial speculation of Broadway. . . . To that cause, however, we dedicated ourselves not as religious, economic, or social reformers, but as poets." But, he goes on, the group was blind "to the truth that no one unit of society, such as the stage, can be healed without cleansing the whole organism."

Mr. MacKaye thus furnishes an accurate diagnosis of the failure of that gallant attempt with which the name of William Vaughn Moody is so closely associated. Yet he does not seem to realize that the failure of the group was twofold: they not only failed to destroy the commercialism of the theater; they also failed to write great drama. The second failure was related to the first. The esthetic self-righteousness—almost a kind of poetic snobbishness—with which they approached the theater was evidence that their roots did not go very deep into American life; and it was the lack of deep roots that vitiated their plays.

Needless to say, the times are to be blamed, not the poets. One feels in Moody's letters not merely poetic insight, but revolutionary aspiration. It is true that, in the strain of mysticism that runs through them, there is something foreign to the modern temper. There is also a kind of romanticism of expression that reminds us that the shadow of Victoria was still over America. But through these superficial qualities shines the spirit of the man, to waken our admiration.

Moody fell short of true poetic as of true dramatic greatness, but there was greatness in his character. His early death was a tragedy, but even more tragic was the stifling of what was really in the man.

February 25, 1936

Portrait of a Patroness

Movers and Shakers, by Mabel Dodge Luhan

Mabel Dodge came back to America, sobbing to her son, "It is *ugly* in America. We have left everything worth while behind us. America is all machinery and money-making and factories. It is ugly, ugly, ugly." She took an apartment and started buying old glass. She would catch its gleam from her speeding car, and "rush in and buy it, breathlessly impatient, eager to get back to the seclusion of the limousine." She "always hated shopping in America." Gradually the apartment took shape, and "seemed, at first, to do the thing I meant to have it do. It diminished New York, it made New York stay outside in the street." But "there was a peculiar instability in me. . . . From the moment I wakened and drank my coffee in the white bed, embraced by the silken curtains depicting reeds and roosters, the stirring within me began." "Alas!" she realized, "I couldn't live by things alone. . . . I had to have human beings in order to be myself."

So she summoned Hutchins Hapgood, Lincoln Steffens, Carl Van Vechten, Emma Goldman, and others, and created the salon at 23 Fifth Avenue. "I became a Species of Head Hunter, in fact. It was not dogs or glass I collected now, it was people. Important People." At her Evenings she "just let life express itself." She "stood apart, aloof and withdrawn, dressed in long, white dresses with maybe an emerald chiffon wrapped around me," but her influence was felt, and she gave her guests "a quite exciting sense of life."

The salon acquired a reputation, and Mabel Dodge became famous. She had successfully advertised Gertrude Stein, and the belief grew "that I had only to be in some way associated with a movement of any kind for it to be launched." Her "correspondence became enormous." Upton Sinclair, writing to her as "Dear Comrade," told her, "You need only come for half an hour, and the reporters will print anything you say. *Please!*" Max Eastman asked, "Will you take over the April or May number of the *Masses* magazine?" Walter Lippmann confided, "I spent last night at Oyster Bay with Roosevelt, and loved him more than ever."

But her great triumph was to conceive the idea of the Paterson textile-strike pageant. Big Bill Haywood was describing the inability of the Paterson strikers to get publicity, and, "in a small, shy voice," she said, "Why don't you bring the strike to New York and *show* it to the workers?" John Reed spoke up: "That's a great idea." And the thing was done.

While it was being done, John Reed fell in love with Mabel Dodge. How could he have helped it? She made it possible for him to stage the pageant: "I knew I was enabling Reed to do what he was doing. I knew he couldn't have done it without me. I felt that I was behind him, pouring all the power in the universe through myself to him." After the pageant was over, she took him to Italy, and, when they returned, they lived together at 23 Fifth Avenue. But it was not altogether satisfactory. For example: "I took my breakfast in bed, and he his at a little table by the bedside because I wanted him to. But he might as well have been gone from there for all he was with *me*. He drank coffee with the morning newspaper propped up before him, his honey-colored round eyes just popping over *'the news!'* Any kind of news as long as it had possibilities for thrill, for action, for excitement. Now newspapers have never meant anything to me."

Once he told Mrs. Dodge of talking with a prostitute, and "I threw myself on the floor and tried to faint." ("I had always tried to hold Reed to me so firmly that he could not pass the barrier of my will and take another woman.") Reed finally revolted and ran away. Mrs. Dodge fled to Hutchins Hapgood's home, and "flung myself on the bed and sobbed loudly. But no one heard me but that mother-in-law of Hutch's and so it was wasted." Reed came back, however, saying, "I can't live without you." Another time: "Reed published the articles in a book called *Insurgent Mexico*, and had two de luxe copies made, bound in red morocco, for his mother and me. He dedicated the book, however, to his mother, and this made me silently angry." (*Insurgent Mexico* is dedicated to Charles Townsend Copeland. *Tamburlaine*, which is dedicated to Reed's mother, was supposed, according to Max Eastman, to be dedicated to him. This is very confusing.)

After many vicissitudes, the affair ended, and Mrs. Dodge said good-bye, not only "to the gay, bombastic, and lovable boy," but also "to the Labor Movement, to Revolution, and to anarchy. . . . Instinctively I turned once more to Nature and Art and tried to live in them." Of course she had other friends. Walter Lippmann for instance—"I don't think Walter ever knew how strongly he figured in my fantasies." And Robert Edmond Jones—"I really dipped into Bobby's pool of life and drank." Once Jones had appendicitis, and she just shut her eyes and "sent my life to Bobby to save him." "That saved me," he told her afterwards.

She had other interests, too. For a time she took up Isadora Duncan, but, "after my disappointment over her when I found one couldn't do anything with her, I had not gone near Isadora again." Elizabeth Duncan, however, proved more tractable, and Mrs. Dodge set up a school for her: "I was always proud of the way I did that job at a distance. I thought out the whole thing, every detail of it, ordered it, and got it executed by letter." She had administrative ability.

Her friends appreciated her. Gertrude Stein wrote "Portrait of

Mabel Dodge." Andrew Dasburg painted a picture, "The Absence of Mabel Dodge," and Arthur Lee did a statue, "Adoration of Mabel Dodge." Donald Evans wrote, "You yourself are ineffable," and addressed her as "Dear Wonderful Person." Walter Lippmann wrote on the photograph of himself he gave her, "Mabel Dodge, maker of oases." Max Eastman said, "You have something strange, something mysterious about you." And Maurice Sterne "made a large number of drawings, some of them very fine, all of them of Mabel Dodge."

It was Sterne, of course, who stepped into Reed's shoes. Reed came back: "Once a man loved me, he said, he would never get over it." But she was through with all that, and Sterne was saying, "I didn't mean to fall in love with you—but there's something *compelling* in you!" Sterne was a challenge: he wanted to be a painter, and she knew he ought to be a sculptor. After a good deal of wrangling about this and other subjects, she said to him one morning, "Let's go and get married." They went.

What with one thing and another, hers was a life full of strain. She tried Christian Science for a while, but it "wore off." Then she discovered Emma Curtis Hopkins, who counseled "the effortless way" and taught faith in God. This was so successful that "I gradually impelled all my entourage to her quiet asylum. Bobby, Maurice, Nina, Elizabeth, Andrew, and others." At the same time Mrs. Dodge was going to Dr. Jelliffe, a psychiatrist who had theories about cancer being the result of hatred. She tried to get Maurice Sterne to go to him too, but he wouldn't; so "I made Bayard [Boyesen] go and try to get over his drinking." From Dr. Jelliffe she turned to A. A. Brill, who advised activity, and this was arranged by her friend Arthur Brisbane, who gave her a job doing a column for the Hearst papers. The real path to salvation, however, was opened when she had a vision of an Indian—"I was extremely psychic"—and started west.

Thus ends the third volume in the saga of Mabel Dodge. The most important, the most irritating, and the most readable of the three, it is a book to be recommended to every social historian. There is no comparable account of the destruction that can be wrought by money when it is in the hands of intelligence and determination. The picture of some of the principal artists and thinkers of the period crawling around this pretentious, grasping, officious woman is like a nightmare. Undoubtedly Mrs. Dodge's intellectual vigor and her personal charm attracted her victims, but it was her money that gave her power over them. In Soviet America the book ought to be made into a film called *Art Under Capitalism.*

November 24, 1936

An Astigmatic Anglophile

The Miracle of England, by André Maurois

In Great Britain, M. Maurois's book is called *A History of England.* Only on this side of the Atlantic, apparently, is England regarded as miraculous. Here, where we have been prepared by Hollywood, with its *Lives of a Bengal Lancer, Mutiny on the Bounty,* and *Lloyd's of London,* and by a pre-coronation press campaign that makes our great democratic newspapers appear more monarchist than T. S. Eliot, it naturally does seem as if God has taken a pretty personal interest in England, and the publishers chose the title accordingly.

It must be said at once that M. Maurois is considerably less lush than Hollywood or the New York *Sun.* Indeed, he sometimes seems to take no more than a proprietary pride in England; the country is, after all, his "field," and he must make the best of it. A much greater Frenchman, H. A. Taine, writing after the debacle of Sedan, was bewildered: Frenchmen were certainly more intelligent and more sensitive than Englishmen, but far less successful as a nation. In a mood of self-abasement, M. Taine paid lavish tribute to these amazing islanders. M. Maurois remains cooler. He gives the British full credit, to say the least, for their achievements, but "miracle" is a figure of speech.

For the rest, *The Miracle of England* is perfectly straightforward and commonplace historical writing, admirably lucid but otherwise no improvement on a number of its predecessors. One finds the usual pageant of kings and queens, prime ministers and generals, with the usual vague allusions to racial genius, and the usual unsatisfactory references to economic developments. M. Maurois, to take just one example, asks why England escaped a revolution in the early nineteenth century. Because of "the power of opinion," he answers, "which through the press, the jury system, and the workers' associations, imposed the necessary reforms on an oligarchic Parliament," because of "the lofty liberalism of the Whigs," and because of "the currents of evangelism, which made for a gentler morality and diverted men's passion into other courses." He has already shown how closely the Whig oligarchy was bound up with commerce and manufacture, but he apparently cannot connect this fact with the peaceful adoption of the first reform bill. He cannot see that "the lofty liberalism of the Whigs" was almost pure self-interest, that evangelical morality was middle-class morality, or that what checked the revolutionary movement in England was not the unsatisfactory compromise of the first reform bill, but the higher wages made possible by England's industrial priority.

Such blindness as this, though common enough, is perhaps more dangerous than the Anglophilia of Hollywood. It leads so astute a person as M. Maurois, for example, to assume that the rise of British capitalism has been uniquely free from bloodshed and that there must therefore be something unique about the British character. He mentions, but does not understand, the internecine wars that killed off the Norman aristocracy, the sufferings that resulted from the inclosures, the Protestant and Catholic martyrdoms of the sixteenth century, and the Puritan civil war. He never seems to consider how much of the bloodshed that attended the growth of British capitalism took place overseas, in the colonies, and he regards the agonies of the early decades of industrialism as a kind of accident, quite without revolutionary significance.

All this has to be said because, if one depends, as M. Maurois does, on "the kindly, disciplined, trusting, and tenacious character" of the British ruling class, one is likely, almost any morning now, to wake up with a headache. The ruling class in England is no worse than the ruling class in any other country, but perhaps it is shrewder, and certainly it is luckier, especially in its apologists.

June 1, 1937

The Legend of John Reed

The legend of John Reed, as it was handed on to members of the John Reed Clubs in the early thirties, was singularly sparing of details. Reed had gone to Harvard; he had been a Greenwich Village playboy; he had been a friend of Pancho Villa; he had been in Russia during the revolution and had written *Ten Days That Shook the World;* he had become a Communist, died in Moscow, and been buried beside the Kremlin.

That was all most of us knew, and in a sense all we needed to know. John Reed, long before 1930, was a symbol, and symbols do not need to be scrutinized too carefully. We—poets, novelists, critics, artists—felt the significance of the transformation of a man of letters into a man of revolutionary action. The exact steps by which the transformation had taken place did not seem to matter.

It is easy to see how Reed became a symbol. The warmth of his personality, his impulsiveness, his courage, the independence of his thought, and the freedom of his actions made an impression on his contemporaries that time could not wipe out. Talking with some two hundred persons who had known Reed, I realized how firm an impact he had made, even on the few acquaintances who disliked him and the many who disagreed with his ideas. It was inevitable that those who did share his beliefs should cherish the memory of their comrade. In the revolutionary movement, which has not always had time for thoughts of the past, John Reed's name lived.

Thus the memory of John Reed was affectionately passed on to a younger generation, whose imaginations were roused not only by the drama of his life but also, as Joseph Freeman has pointed out, by the tragedy of his death. Particularly for those Communists who came from the middle class he was the perfect symbol. He had broken the bonds of bourgeois convention and found his place in the final conflict. That it was quite literally and immediately final for him added to the glory of the legend.

Three or four years ago I began an attempt to find out what lay behind the symbol, and I discovered that Reed's life was more abundantly documented than might have been supposed. Not only had he written prolifically at every stage of his life from his sixteenth year on, not only had scores of friends preserved impressions and stories and letters, Reed himself had saved a great mass of notes, manuscripts, letters, clippings, and photographs. This restless wanderer, whose goings and comings had at first seemed so elusive, had, in one way or another, left an almost day-by-day record.

From this record, which John Stuart and I compiled, I learned that the legend was fully justified. Indeed, as Max Lerner wrote, it was no legend, but sober fact. Of course, one version of the legend was false—the version attributed to Communists by their enemies—but the "Soviet saint" was nothing but a product of the imaginations of Julian Street and other slanderers. The revolutionary movement never denied that Reed had been a playboy. Rather, it cherished the tales of college exploits and Greenwich Village pranks. But it insisted that, without losing his spontaneity and charm, he became a serious revolutionary. When his own eyes showed him the truth about capitalist civilization and the hope of the future, he acted courageously and effectively.

John Reed became a symbol because his life, the life he actually lived during his thirty-three years, was genuinely symbolic. This boy, born in one of Portland's proud houses fifty years ago, became, in Emerson's sense of the phrase, a representative man. The legend that grew up about him may have been meager, but it was not false. Not only the few facts known to admirers, but scores of apparently trivial details, were significant. Reed touched American life at many points, and every contact had its meaning for the student of America.

It was right, for example, that he should be the grandson of a pioneer, one of Oregon's first businessmen. It was right, too, that he should be the son of a Rooseveltian reformer, a businessman and wit who fought for good government side by side with Francis Heney and Lincoln Steffens. And it seems appropriate that his generation at Harvard should be one of the most brilliant in the college's history, so that he had as friends, in college and afterwards, such men as Robert Hallowell, Lee Simonson, Heywood Broun, Walter Lippmann, Robert Edmond Jones, Waldo Peirce, and a good many others whose names are famous today.

Either good fortune or good judgment brought Reed in touch from the first with whatever was vital in American life. He lived, for instance, in Greenwich Village when it was the center of an effective and necessary revolt against bourgeois standards in art and morals.

He was a poet, albeit a minor one, at a time when poetry was coming to life in America. He was a dramatist and, though his own plays were not first-rate, his faith in the drama helped to create the Provincetown Players.

Everyone who has written about the years just before the war has commented upon the vigor of the arts. Good work was done, but even more striking was the widespread feeling of great new possibilities, of a renaissance almost at hand. This upsurge in the arts was linked with a growing sense of the need for social change. The mingling of authors and labor leaders at Mabel Dodge's salon was not merely the result of the hostess's cleverness; literature and labor were feeling their way toward each other.

Of course John Reed went to Mabel Dodge's evenings at 23 Fifth Avenue, and naturally he contributed to the *Masses* when it was reorganized under Max Eastman's editorship. He was already a symbol of impetuous, rebellious, happy, generous youth. He was symbolic of this American upsurge, and he was to become symbolic of much more. That, when one thinks of what happened to most of Mabel Dodge's guests and to many of the *Masses* contributors, is what makes his story memorable. He was completely part of his times, and yet he transcended the limitations of his era and made himself one with the future.

His course was by no means straight; he traveled his own route, at his own pace, but he arrived at his destination, which is more than can be said of many of his contemporaries. And whatever he did seems to have some significance for us. We, who talk so much about literature and labor, cannot forget that his first contact with labor struggles resulted in a great creative effort, the Paterson pageant. His affection for Mexico and his zeal for the liberty of its people are echoed in many hearts today. The courage with which he fought against American participation in the World War can still hearten us as, twenty years later, we brace ourselves for the struggle against the war-makers.

It was Petrograd in the October days that set Reed clearly on his course. We cannot exaggerate the importance to him of actually seeing the revolution, but we must not forget what he saw with. He was not only a first-rate journalist; he was a man with a knowledge of the working class and its battles, with a profound hatred of war and a deep insight into the evils of capitalism. The apparent paralysis of the radical movement in the face of war had disillusioned him, but when he saw the proletariat in action, he understood and rejoiced.

We do well to observe how Reed conceived his role in the revolutionary movement. Thinking of himself as a poet and reporter, and dreaming to the end of the books he wanted to write, he had not the least desire to devote himself exclusively to agitation. But he was too astute not to realize that he could render a particular service and therefore had a special responsibility. As a famous journalist and an eye-witness of the revolution, he could speak to the American people in a way that radical labor leaders could not. He accepted his responsibility, and when it led, as inevitably it did, to more and more direct participation in the revolutionary movement, he did not flinch. He would have been glad if he could have performed his revolutionary duties through his poetry and his reporting, but he did the job that the moment demanded of him.

Karl Marx predicted that a certain number of bourgeois intellectuals would desert their own class and go over to the proletariat. History has proved him right. But still we do not understand why it is that certain intellectuals see the necessity for revolution and others do not. Lincoln Steffens said that Reed became a revolutionary because he was a poet, and I think he was right. Marx expected the recruits to be "those who have raised themselves to the level of comprehending theoretically the historical movement as a whole." Reed was little interested in theory, though he tried to be. But there is also the insight that comes from experience, the intense experience of the poet. That kind of insight Reed had, and, more than any other quality, it explains his career.

We make no mistake in holding to our conception of John Reed as the poet who became a revolutionary, for no other interpretation of his life is tenable. Since my biography of Reed appeared, Mabel Dodge Luhan, in her *Movers and Shakers*, has offered her interpretation. According to her, John Reed's life had one center—Mabel Dodge. It began when she met and ended when she left him. She not only had the idea of the Paterson pageant; she made it possible by "pouring all the power in the universe through myself into him." After the pageant they went to Italy together and became lovers. That thereafter she did for a time occupy Reed's attention is clear enough, but, as she laments, he still read the newspapers. He read the papers and worked on the *Masses*, and eventually he left her. She got him back, but he went to Mexico, with Mabel following him to the border. He returned, but left, and left again. In Paris, during the first months of the war, he fell in love with another woman. After his return, he and Mrs. Dodge were reconciled, but they soon separated—for good.

It is from this point on that Mrs. Dodge's distinctive interpretation takes shape. I doubt if it is true that, as she says, Reed constantly begged her to take him back, and I am certain that he did not marry Louise Bryant because he couldn't have Mabel. So much, however, can be forgiven injured vanity. But when she says that Reed went to Russia because it was "a chance to lose himself in a great upheaval," implying that it was frustrated love of her that made him a revolutionary, I cannot smile, for I find myself gagging a little.

Max Eastman, who, like Mrs. Luhan, refused to give me assistance when I was writing the biography, has also put forth an interpretation of Reed, and his is almost as egotistical as hers. He writes: "The simple fact is, and it is obvious from the documents, that Reed learned from me that there *is* such a thing—in the sense given to the term by the *Communist Manifesto*—as a revolutionary. He learned from me about the theory and tactic of class struggle." A conversation he had with Reed about the McNamara case was, he says, "the most angular moment in the process of John Reed's awakening to the revolutionary class struggle, a process in which it would be foolish to pretend I did not play a major part."

No one who feels, as I do, that Mr. Eastman is now badly in need of full credit for whatever good deeds he has done would want to deny that, in 1912 and 1913, when he met Reed, he was more advanced in knowledge of Marxist theory and had a healthy influence upon Reed. On the other hand, it is obvious to anyone who will study the facts that Reed became a revolutionary by a long process in which many persons had a share and in which events probably counted for more than persons. It is noteworthy that Reed's autobiographical essay, "Almost Thirty," speaks of Steffens, Haywood, Elizabeth Gurley Flynn, and others, but not of Eastman.

Having insisted that he made Reed a revolutionary, Eastman, being the sort of person he is, has to insist that he was a revolutionary of the Max Eastman 1937 model. To satisfy him, Reed must be more Trotskyist than Trotsky and repudiate the Third International at a time when Trotsky claimed to be its ardent supporter. Out of one of many of Louise Bryant's wild stories, bolstered by the assertions of persons who are grinding the same ax as Mr. Eastman himself, he paints the picture that suits his fancy. Reed, in the summer of 1920, was "shocked," "absolutely disgusted," "in a state of miserable revolt and inner wrath and turmoil." Finally the honest American told the dirty Russians what he thought of them. ("It was more like a war between Russia and America, as I heard about it," says Mr. Eastman, "than a 'disagreement about dual unionism.'") And then he died.

Mr. Eastman's attempt to recreate John Reed in his own image fails as completely as his attempt to feed his egotism by representing Reed as his disciple in the revolutionary movement. Mr. Eastman ought to read the articles that he himself published in the *Liberator*, the report on the second congress of the Communist International that Reed wrote for the *Communist*, and the official records of the speeches at the congress and at Baku. It is impossible, by any kind of juggling, to square Mr. Eastman's conception of Reed's last months with what, during those months, Reed said and wrote.

Mrs. Luhan's interpretation of Reed is motivated simply by vanity; Mr. Eastman's has vanity for one of its motives and for another his desire to capture Reed's memory for his own counter-revolutionary purposes. But Reed belongs to us. He belongs in a special sense to Communists, but also, as one non-Communist review of the biography pointed out, to all those who believe in a better social order. We know that, as the struggle intensifies, many will join us who now stand aloof. And for these, as for us, Reed is and will be a symbol.

It is in the nature of symbols to change a little with time, and, as I have tried to point out, Reed's life, because it was so rich and varied, lends itself to new emphasis. It might be well if, in this, the fiftieth year since his birth, we paid some attention to his attitudes toward the revolutionary movement. We might observe, for example, his utter contempt for prima donnas. Though he had a great capacity for self-dramatization, and relished those events that gave him the spotlight, it was impossible for him to place personal vanity above the revolution. In the left wing of the Socialist Party and in the Communist Labor Party his chief concern was to be useful, and he was as willing to do the Jimmy Higgins jobs as he was to take the star role in public. He would have scorned the sort of person who, if he is not glorified above all others and his tiniest whims catered to, discovers that the Communist Party is corrupt and Stalin an unspeakable villain. Reed's integrity was so completely beyond question that he never confused it with arrogance.

He was equally contemptuous of hair-splitting. Though his nature and training made him impatient of theory, he did make the intellectual effort necessary to master Marxism. He knew the importance of correctness and clarity in theoretical arguments. But he had a remarkable feeling for character, and he knew when a pretended concern for "correctness" masked cowardice or hostility. There were, even in his day, "super-Marxists" who emerged from their armchairs only when they saw a chance to obstruct revolutionary action, and he knew how to deal with them.

Toward persons who sincerely differed from him he could feel respect and even friendliness, the while he attacked their views with relentless vigor. But he had no use for the petty snipers, the persons who thrive on fault-finding. He saw weaknesses in the revolutionary movement, and he was glad to coöperate with anyone who would try to eliminate them, but he hated those whose interest in the faults was simply to justify their vanity and inactivity.

The significance of John Reed is far from being exhausted. As the revolutionary movement sends deeper and deeper roots into the American soil, it will find more and more in his life that is worth considering. I do not think John Reed would have liked to be a legend; he was too much alive for that. But, if he was to be remembered, he would have wanted to be thought of exactly as he was. It is our good fortune that, as he really was, he has more meaning for us than any concocted legend could possibly have.

October 19, 1937

Biography of Business

A History of the Businessman, by Miriam Beard

Despite the title, despite the publisher's talk about "the biography of a type," this is essentially a history of business. In her preface Miss Beard suggests that the businessman of 1938 has much in common with the businessman of 1000 B.C. or 1300 A.D., but fortunately she does not often permit this idea to get in her way. Her theme is necessarily what businessmen have done. Her theme is business, not a "type."

The book begins with the traders of ancient Greece and the traders and bankers of Rome. A third of it is devoted to the medieval cities, to the rise of the merchants in the Middle Ages, the growth of such commercial centers as Lübeck, Venice, and Florence, the role of business in stimulating the renaissance, and the eventual decline of the oligarchs. A good-sized section is given over to the seventeenth and eighteenth centuries, and the remainder deals with the more familiar subject of the rise of industrialism.

It is worth emphasizing that half of the volume concerns the fourteenth, fifteenth, sixteenth, seventeenth, and eighteenth centuries, for it is in dealing with these periods that Miss Beard most clearly reveals her merits. Out of research of a very impressive kind she has constructed a detailed account of commerce, manufacturing, and finance before the industrial revolution. The chapter that contrasts the reality of life in Florence in the fourteenth century with Ruskin's conception of it is a peculiarly brilliant achievement, but the chapters on Holland are almost as illuminating.

As description, then, the book is, for the most part, excellent, but it fails as interpretation. The kind of psychological interpretation that Miss Beard occasionally offers is almost valueless, and with the actual dynamics of change she is rarely concerned. Like her distinguished father, she seems to delight in a kind of obscurantism. She apparently shudders at the very idea that there may be laws of change, and it is no wonder that, although the book would be inconceivable without the historical analyses of Marx and the Marxists, most of Miss Beard's scattering references to Marx are unfriendly.

We are not surprised, therefore, to find the book ending in a fog of phrases. The last chapter begins with an excellent analysis of fascism: Miss Beard has no doubt that fascism is a device to preserve capitalism, and she sees that it will fail. But she goes on talking about the future of the businessman as if it were likely to stretch into infinity.

It is not enough to say of this book, as one can say of so many, that it would be better if it were based on a Marxist analysis. One has to go further and point out that Miss Beard's frequent reliance on Marxist methods simply cries out for consistency. Often one feels, of an excellent piece of research, that it would make a first-rate book if the author had known the right questions to ask, but Miss Beard appears to have known the right questions and simply refused to ask them. That the book has great value, and especially for Marxists, ought to be clearly said, but it nevertheless leaves us with a sense that we have been thwarted, for what Miss Beard has done is so much less than she had the opportunity to do.

February 1, 1938

The Superman and the Socialist

More than twenty years have passed since Jack London's death, and yet Mr. Stone's biography (*Sailor on Horseback*) is the first that even approaches adequacy. Part of the explanation is the attitude of Mrs. London, who, after writing her own valuable but partial account, refused to aid other biographers, until Mr. Stone somehow overcame her objections. Then, too, publishers have been at fault, insisting— how erroneously Mr. Stone has proved—that interest in London was dead. Five or six years ago Dr. Fulmer Mood's study of London unsuccessfully went the rounds of the publishers. Less briskly written than Mr. Stone's biography, it was superior as a critical analysis, and, though the author had been denied access to the London papers, it contained almost all the information about London's life—and more especially his birth and his death—that one finds in *Sailor on Horse-*

back. The *Saturday Evening Post* would never have serialized Dr. Mood's book, nor would the movie rights have been purchased, but an enterprising publisher would have found that London still has his thousands of readers.

Mr. Stone's book is, of course, a better publishing venture, for it makes the most of London's extraordinary personality and his fabulous career. Perhaps too much influenced by the vices of London's style, Mr. Stone has at the same time caught its chief virtue—its irresistible vigor. The story is one that London would have loved to tell—and thought of telling—and it is right that it should be told in his way. It is also told to a considerable extent in his own words, a fact that has produced an absurd article in *Ken* and much pointless controversy. What matters is that Mr. Stone has managed to make us feel about this oyster pirate, hobo, sailor, prospector, and author as he felt about himself, and he was a master of self-dramatization.

The readability of the book is something to be grateful for. The story as a story is well told. But London's career has meanings for the present that Mr. Stone only imperfectly catches. For one thing, in dealing with the mainspring of London's actions, he is misled by views on heredity that could scarcely stand scientific scrutiny. He was excited, of course, at discovering that London's father was a Professor Chaney, an astrologist, and he wanted to make the most of his discovery, but that does not excuse his excesses. Jack, we are told, inherited from his father not merely "a warm human nature, a sensitivity to the hardships of others, a personal liberality, and an imagination," but also such qualities as "the passionate desire to be quit of the brutish labor of the machines" and "a special knowledge enabling him to anticipate the future."

When Mr. Stone is not under the influence of such notions, he does give some useful clues. Amid the hardships of his early life London had to struggle to survive and he was well equipped for victory: "He had good health, hard muscles, and a stomach that could digest scrap iron; he exulted in his young life and was able to hold his own at work or fight." Then, when he was a hobo, he learned that men as strong as he had been beaten in the fierce competition and thrown on the scrap-heap. His first impulse, as he has told us, was to find some other way of surviving, and he determined to rely on his brains. But another idea had also been implanted, the idea that the rules of the game were unfair, and he was generous enough to want to see them changed.

As soon, then, as London understood the nature of the capitalist system, he planned a dual triumph. He was resolved, he wrote Rose Strunsky, "to beat the capitalists at their own game," and at the same time he proposed to work for the establishment of a saner social order. In a sense it was a natural decision: any Socialist has to function within the system while he works against it. But the decision had peculiar implications for one of London's temperament. There have been many men who, once sincere Socialists, have succumbed to the capitalist world. There have been others who have learned how to subordinate the demands of the system to their chosen task. London, for many years, did not achieve either kind of integration, but remained a divided personality.

He was an eager and uncommonly retentive student of social theories, but each side of his nature found its own logic. His humanitarian impulses seized upon one body of theory, the Marxist; his egotistical impulses drew upon Nietzsche, Spencer, Darwin, and Kipling. He could talk about the anarchy of capitalism and the need for cooperation, or he could talk about the superman, atavism, and the mission of the Anglo-Saxon race. He was not always unconscious of the contradiction, but he could do nothing about it: he had to cling to both sets of ideas.

Individualism predominated in his writing. Although he became a Socialist five years before his first book appeared, there was no suggestion of Socialism in *The Son of the Wolf* or in any of its immediate successors. It was not until he published *The People of the Abyss*— his eighth book—that he gave an inkling of his views. The next year, 1904, he brought out *The Sea Wolf*, maintaining, to the amazement of critics who had charged him with inconsistency, that it showed the failure of the superman. *The Iron Heel*, in 1908, was, of course, explicitly Socialist, and London insisted that there were Socialist implications in *Martin Eden*. These novels, however, were followed by many others, in which Nietzsche speaks and Marx is silent.

Nietzsche's voice was heard even in the Socialist novels. Indeed, it might be argued that, though London was at times an effective Socialist propagandist, he was never a Socialist novelist. *The Iron Heel* contains magnificent expository passages, but the reader will be disappointed if he hopes to find a picture of the Socialist movement.

Ernest Everhard bears no resemblance to any Socialist Party organizer that was ever known, but he is strikingly like the superman in London's other novels and therefore like London himself. He is, indeed, Jack London in one of his favorite roles—the brilliant expounder of Socialism to whose marshaling of facts and reasons the apologists for capitalism succumb in helpless confusion. Events have proven that, in his conception of the violence with which the exploiting class would resist Socialism, he was wiser than his generation, and there is much in the novel that shows both his sincerity and the competence of his mind, but Nietzsche—or, rather, that side of London's character that seized upon Nietzsche—is not absent.

It would be difficult to exaggerate London's inconsistency. *The Valley of the Moon,* for example, contains his best pictures of proletarian life but, if one did not know, one would be sure to assume that it was written from an anti-Socialist point of view. One could compile from his letters either a Socialist or an anti-Socialist anthology. But in spite of all this we cannot charge him with insincerity. He declared himself a Socialist at a time when such a declaration was costly to him and invaluable to the movement. He wrote, lectured, and gave generously of his money.

Yet, much as he meant to the movement, it meant even more to him. Though it did not dominate his life, it was a curb upon his extravagant temperament, and the only curb. As one reads Mr. Stone's account of his prosperous years, when he was being paid larger and larger sums and always spending more than he earned, one's first thought is that he was a bad Socialist, but all through these years he did have a conception of values other than the making and spending of money, and without it his life would have been unthinkably barren. The influence of Socialism on his life, which so terribly needed some kind of balance, is more important than its direct influence on his books.

It was impossible, however, for London to escape the consequences of the split in his thinking and feeling. Mr. Stone greatly overrates his literary achievements, speaking of *Martin Eden* as "one of the greatest of all American novels," describing *The Star Rover* as "a magnificent literary accomplishment," and praising other novels in similar terms. London's abilities are not to be lightly dismissed, but his failure to create character above a certain rather simple level is enough to bar him from the first literary rank. Mr. Stone admits that few of his women are wholly credible. He might have added that there is scarcely a hero who is not an obvious projection of Jack London— a character, by the way, that he did not understand. What he could do, in the way of portraying action and recreating the primitive emotions he loved, has won him millions of readers. It is foolish to claim for him virtues he did not have.

If London had been a better Socialist, he would, other things being equal, have been a better novelist. That does not mean that political soundness is equivalent to literary excellence. It does mean that, in this particular case, the qualities that weakened his political thinking also weakened his literary talents. If he had been a better Socialist, that is, it would mean that, either as cause or effect, he had become a more integrated person, and with greater integration he would have done better work.

There is evidence for this view in what happened at the end of his life. "Martin Eden," he wrote, "died because he was an individualist, I live because I am a Socialist and have social consciousness." He made this statement in 1912, when his social consciousness was already dwindling. It was not enough for him to prove that he could beat the game by earning a huge income; he must constantly surround himself with proofs of his success. He bought more and more land, built more and more elaborate homes, entertained on a more and more lavish scale. He became cynical about his writing and bored with his success. The World War turned him into an apoplectic chauvinist who admired Theodore Roosevelt and borrowed his phrases. In March 1916 he resigned from the Socialist Party, ostensibly on the ground— so dear to renegades—that it was not militant enough. A few months later he committed suicide.

Much of this tragedy might have been averted, as Mike Gold has recently said, if London had not been so terribly alone. Mr. Stone, in one of the few downright stupid sentences in the book, says, "He was determined to be a Socialist writer in the days when it took as much courage to be a Socialist writer as it does nowadays not to be one." Much as Mr. Stone may admire the courage of his fellow-contributors to the *Saturday Evening Post*, we can assure him that the path of the Socialist writer today is not altogether easy. But it is easier than it was in London's day, and a great deal clearer. The superman in London might have found it less exciting to have scores of comrades, but the Socialist would have appreciated them. If there had been other writers with his problems, if other men had been using the same means towards the same ends, if his individualism had not been so augmented in the very act of avowing Socialism, the superman might have succumbed. "The strength of organized labor lies in its brotherhood," he wrote, knowing that comradeship with members of his craft was something denied him. If it had been possible for him, as it is possible for us, there is no telling where his talents would have taken him.

October 11, 1938

The Letters of Henry Adams

The keyword of the second volume of *Letters of Henry Adams* (1892–1918, edited by Worthington C. Ford) is catastrophe. Catastrophe, collapse, crisis, chaos—the words appear on every second page. The election of McKinley, the Dreyfus case, the Spanish-American War, the Boer War, Roosevelt's presidency, and the war between Russia and Japan successively harassed his mind. By 1914, when worldwide collapse actually came, he was so worn out by his prophecies that he was unable to do justice to the calamity. What he would say in 1938 can only be guessed. More than once in the course of the year editorial writers have quoted the last sentence of the *Education:*

Perhaps some day—say 1938, their centenary—they might be allowed to return together for a holiday, to see the mistakes of their own lives made clear in the light of the mistakes of their successors; and perhaps then, for the first time since man began his education among the carnivores, they would find a world that sensitive and timid natures could regard without a shudder.

The irony of this, which must have tickled the malicious autobiographer, becomes perfectly clear in the *Letters*. Almost any other prophet of doom would feel vindicated by the world as it is in 1938, but Adams anticipated even more flamboyant terrors.

It is not to be supposed that he was quite indifferent to what—at least between 1892 and 1914—appeared to be the ludicrous aspects of his melancholy. But he did expect, from year to year and almost from day to day, the collapse of civilization. It is the persistence with which he strikes this single note that makes the second volume of the *Letters* less interesting than the first. Reading the letters he wrote in the sixties and seventies, one could take considerable pleasure in contrasting what he had actually thought and felt with what he saw fit to set down in his autobiography. But here we have, sustained over twenty-six years and more than six hundred pages, the precise mood of the *Education,* and it does become tiresome.

There is little here to explain the genesis of Adams' mood, which was well formed before 1892. Adams' despair grew out of his own defeat, the defeat of his family, and the defeat of his class. The earliest letters in Volume I showed him as a student in Germany, planning a political career. He saw no reason to doubt that his father was on his way to the kind of prestige and influence that the Adams family had long enjoyed, and he believed that he and his brothers would emulate their father. It was not until the end of the sixties and the early seventies that he began to realize how few rewards there were in the post-Civil War world for the virtues of the Adamses and how little tolerance for their shortcomings. The process of disillusionment was a gradual one, but it was finished long before his fiftieth year.

Volume II, if it explains little in itself, does confirm this interpretation. Adams' mind, for years after he believed it to be above such foibles, was deeply concerned with politics. He longed to be one of the powers behind the throne, and he relished the opportunities to influence foreign policy that came when John Hay was Secretary of State. Of course he indignantly refused office when it was offered him, and he made a fetish of avoiding publicity, but he was pleased to have power, and he would have liked recognition if he could have had it on his own terms. In the *Education* it is made to appear that aloofness was his choice, but it was a necessity and a very distasteful one.

To the effect of political failure was added the sense of personal insufficiency that came with the suicide of his wife. In the eighties Adams assumed the defensive, consciously cultivating attitudes that became habitual. He talked much of his ignorance and his lack of success. He refused all honors, pretending that he was unworthy of them. Like Carlyle, he admired silence, calling it "the only sensible form of expression," and, though silence was more than he was capable of, he had his books privately printed. Always he was guarding himself against further blows from a fate that had already proved too unkind. And in particular he scorned the world that had scorned him once and might again.

Yet it would be wrong to think that Adams' pessimism was merely a private vengeance. By all the Adams standards the world of the post-war plutocracy was bad—and not by Adams' standards alone. He had his own reasons for searching for signs of decay, but they did exist, and he did find them. In 1894, for example, he was writing: "Here, in this young, rich continent, capable of supporting three times its population with ease, we have had a million men out of employment for nearly a year." In 1895 he observed that "religion, art, politics, manners are either vulgarized or dead or turned into money-making agencies." He called the press "the hired agent of a moneyed system," and the moneyed system itself "one vast structure of debt and fraud." Having watched the rise of the plutocracy after the Civil War, he knew that politicians, including his friends, were its servants. He put no faith in reforms, for he saw that "the whole fabric of our society will go to wreck if we really lay hands of reform on our rotten institutions."

Adams was not unaware that others had preceded him in the exploration of the rottenness of capitalism. He said of *Capital:* "I think I never struck a book which taught me so much, and with which I disagreed so radically in conclusion." He admitted that he and his brother Brooks owed their conception of history to Marx, and he was astute enough, when Brooks Adams sent him one of Edouard Bernstein's books, to see the implications of revisionism: "He throws up the sponge in the whole Socialist fight. . . . He preaches the bankruptcy of the only idea our time has produced." Always he knew that the Marxists, and only the Marxists, looked at events as he did: "I have been to the *salons* and the restaurants and the weddings and the little private talk-talks," he wrote from Paris in 1909, "and have seen nothing but what the Socialists see."

He realized, of course, that the Socialists not only saw the breakdown of his society but worked for the creation of a new one, and at times he felt them to be his allies.

For my part [he wrote in 1893], hating vindictively, as I do, our whole fabric and conception of society, against which my little life has squeaked protest from its birth, and will yell protest till its death, I shall be glad to see the whole thing utterly destroyed and wiped away. With a

Communism I could exist tolerably well, for the Commune is rather favorable to social consideration apart from wealth; but in a society of Jews and bankers, a world made up of maniacs wild for gold, I have no place. In the coming rows, you will know where to find me. Probably I shall be helping the London mobs to pull up Harcourt and Rothschild on a lamp post in Piccadilly.

It is a nice picture, but there was really no danger of Adams' being found on the barricades. In 1898 he stated his position more accurately:

Not that I love Socialism any better than I do Capitalism, or any other Ism, but I know only one law of political or historical morality, and that is that the form of Society which survives is always in the Right; and therefore a statesman is obliged to follow it, unless he leads. . . . One need not love Socialism in order to point out the logical necessity for Society to march that way; and the wisdom of doing it intelligently if it is to do it at all.

Having associated with and struggled against the ruling class for a good many years, he had no illusions about its inclinations and its methods. When Cleveland used troops to break the Pullman strike, Adams commented: "Now that the gold bug has drunk blood, and has seen that the government can safely use the army to shoot Socialists, the wage-question is as good as settled. Of course, we silver men will be shot next, but for the moment, the working men are worse off than we." He even understood that the capitalist class would be ready, if profits demanded, to abandon the pretense of democracy:

The reaction of fashionable society against our old-fashioned liberalism is extreme, and wants only power to make it violent. I am waiting with curiosity to see whether the power will come—with the violence—in my time. As I view it, the collapse of our nineteenth-century J. S. Mill, Manchester, Chicago formulas, will be displayed—if at all—by the collapse of parliamentarianism, and the reversion to centralized government.

As far as this Adams went, but no farther. He did understand the nature of capitalist control and its debasing effect, but it is not easy to imagine an Adams in alliance with the proletariat. "Much as I loathe the regime of Manchester and Lombard Street in the nineteenth century," he wrote, "I am glad to think I shall be dead before I am ruled by the trades unions of the twentieth." Any friendliness he had for labor vanished when his own comfort was affected: "The labor of our common sort," he remarked during the strikes of 1903, "seems to have developed a system of blackmailing society which society submits to. The capitalist robbed us, but had an interest in letting us have what we wanted. The laborer blackmails us under pretense of robbing the capitalist. His strikes are always against us, in order to impoverish us, and so affect capital. To me, it is all one. Between the two gentle tyrants, I was long ago squashed. My class is quite extinct, as a class." His prejudices against organized labor grew, and by 1912 he was speaking of its leaders as "scoundrels."

His views on Socialism were similarly subject to modification as his prejudices reasserted themselves. As early as 1896 he said, "The growth of Socialism is obviously only disintegration of society." On occasion he seemed to realize that Socialism was the disintegration merely of his kind of society: "Only Socialists can now oppose with effect, and Socialism is a strange world to us." But he could also rant: "I can't go out of my cheap garret here in Paris, for an hour, without being throttled by some infernal Socialist, leveling, humanitarian regulation which is intended to kill me and to keep some syphilitic abortion alive."

If this sounds like the senile viciousness of the well preserved gentlemen who write letters on club stationery to the Boston *Transcript* and the New York *Sun,* if it reminds one all too unpleasantly of the pathological fury currently visited on Franklin Roosevelt, it is necessary to remark that that is precisely the tone of an uncomfortably large number of letters. In all Europe and America there were, he said, no more than five hundred persons with whom he was capable of sympathy or from whom he could expect appreciation of himself and his books. Towards the alien millions he tried to maintain a sufficiently objective attitude, but without success. As he shuttled back and forth between Washington and Paris, he was always encountering "impossible neighbors." "I spoke to no human beast," he wrote of one voyage. "My neighbors at table were all singers at variety shows. I stayed in my own room, and read Mme. de Sévigné day and night." At Mont St. Michel, one summer's day, he found "a mob of tourists of many kinds of repulsiveness. Odious Frenchwomen, gross, shapeless, bare-armed, eating and drinking with demonstrative satisfaction; and dreary Englishwomen, with the usual tusks; and American art students, harmless and feeble." If they noticed him at all, no doubt they wondered who this old gentleman with the drooping mustache was and why he was in such a pet.

The philosophy he had so carefully cultivated and the modesty of which he made such a show did not save him from provincial snobbishness and the cheapest of New England prejudices. Readers of the first volume of the *Letters* will recall disparaging references to the Jews. Such references occur on almost every page of this book. At first Adams is chiefly talking about Jewish bankers, and the term seems little more than an objectionable kind of slang. Increasingly, however, its connotations are starkly anti-Semitic, until, in his comments on some New York customs official who had provoked him, he is on the Streicher level.

All this permits us to see the *Education* in better perspective. Adams had, with the customary growls, given his consent to its publication after his death, and it appeared in 1919. As with Samuel Butler's *The Way of All Flesh*, posthumous publication was a blessing, for pessimism was in vogue after the war, and the *Education* became one of the bibles of the twenties. It has always seemed rather querulous and affected, and we can now understand why, but it has been a force in the process of degeneration with which its author was preoccupied. Adams saw that the older American culture was dead, killed by its own child, industrial capitalism, and he made others see it.

That there were ways in which what was valid in that culture could be kept alive, he did not see, or saw only fitfully. His family had reached its highest point when John Quincy Adams, humbling himself to serve in the House of Representatives after having been President, had stubbornly fought the slave-owners in defense of the right of petition. Then an Adams had stood beside Channing and Emerson and Parker and Garrison and Thoreau, in the forefront of American culture. By comparison the reformist activities of Charles Francis Adams were a feeble gesture. The great tradition of American culture had passed into other hands, hands that an Adams viewed with scorn. The younger Adamses were out of the battle, and the best they could do was to preside over the obsequies of their clan. Nobody will deny that the funeral sermon Henry Adams preached was superb.

October 25, 1938

Expatriate's Autobiography

Unforgotten Years, by Logan Pearsall Smith

It is easy to call Mr. Smith an old fogy, so easy that he has thought of it himself, and it is just that quality that makes his autobiography better than it might be. He is everything that an expatriate might be expected, by an enemy, to be, except that he is aware of how he seems to other persons. His years of British residence, antiquarian research, and preoccupation with style have left a kind of tough honesty in him, which is perfectly incongruous but which makes him an uncommonly good observer of his own species. His thin, flaccid style, with which he is so much concerned, drops into a plaintive whine whenever he talks about culture in America, but he can bring himself up short, and he really knows how vapid he is. Just as his mother, an evangelist of remarkable piety, could occasionally voice a hearty paganism, so he, evangelist of culture that he is, is sometimes capable of a gesture of strength that is almost, from his point of view, vulgar.

The early part of the book is best: the story of Philadelphia Quakers, with a talent for making money. There is a fine account of Walt Whitman that really adds something to our understanding of the poet, some not unjust animadversions on Harvard, and a picture of American business methods. It was his dissatisfaction with the family business that sent Mr. Smith to Europe. His account of Balliol and Jowett shows us how the British ruling class is trained. But after Balliol, as he drifted into the making of anthologies, the search for manuscripts, and the writing of *Trivia*, Mr. Smith has little to say. He seems in these later years a less talented Henry James, with just the redeeming touch of critical humor that gives the book its special virtue.

The chapters of *Unforgotten Years* undoubtedly provided a rare treat for readers of the *Atlantic Monthly,* and the book is bound to appeal chiefly to Anglophiles and other snobs, but there is just enough in it to give other persons a pleasant surprise. Mr. Smith offers a warm defense of the expatriates. It would be more convincing if he had not succeeded in making us realize that he himself has something to say, not because, but very much in spite of, his English residence.

January 31, 1939

A Brave Man Is Dead

There was a death over on Staten Island the other day, the death of a great man. The newspaper obituaries did not say he was great, and perhaps his greatness would be hard to prove; but I think most of those who knew Bob Hallowell feel about him as I do. One could not talk with him for five minutes without recognizing the almost unique integrity of the man and sensing his infallible discrimination between shams and realities. Though he was well on in his forties when I first met him, he had zest for new experiences, an unflagging capacity for heroic decisions, and tremendous courage. It was what these qualities demanded of him in a world such as ours that killed him at the age of fifty-two.

Robert Hallowell belonged to the class of 1910 at Harvard—the class of Walter Lippmann, T. S. Eliot, and Jack Reed. Unlike those three contemporaries, who were to become famous in their various ways, Hallowell fitted into one of the typical Harvard niches. There was a Harvard pun in those days, "Hallowell be thy name," and, though Bob belonged to one of the less prosperous branches of the family, he had no difficulty in winning the kind of social position in the college that Reed, for example, craved, fought for, and did not achieve. He was not an outsider, but he was something more than a conventional insider.

Hallowell and Reed both won places on the staff of the *Lampoon,* Hallowell because of his relatively good drawings, Reed because of his absolutely bad jokes. They became and remained close friends. Bob Hallowell could not do what Jack Reed did. He was incapable of the slashing gestures and irrevocable commitments out of which Reed's life was made. He stood a little aghast at Jack's college pranks, and marveled at the saga of the Dutch Treat Club, Paterson, Mexico, the War, and Russia. But he laughed at the condescension with which Lippmann, for instance, signalized his unlikeness to Reed. He never denied that he wished he could be like Jack. And he told me once that he had never made an important decision without asking himself, not what Jack would have done but what Jack would have thought he ought to do.

On his side, quite obviously, Reed felt an admiration for Hallo-well, but it was accompanied by a certain anxiety. Knowing well the temptations to which he was subjected, Reed feared that Bob might succumb to convention. He kidded him gently, in *The Day in Bohemia,* and he advised him, for his own good, to accept the treasurership of the *New Republic.* He also cursed out Bob's Wall Street–Harvard Club friends with passion and thoroughness.

As a matter of fact, Reed need not have worried about Hallowell, who had a kind of stubbornness that made it just as impossible for him as it was for Jack to sink into the easy ways of upper-middle-class banality. The proof of his fearlessness came after Reed's death, which was a pity, for Reed would have applauded the decision that most of Bob's friends viewed with skepticism. In 1925 he resigned as pub-lisher of the *New Republic* and turned to painting. I am no critic of art, as Bob, with a good many shakings of his head, would have been the first to say. But I know that his water-colors deserved the praise they won and that the wisdom of the man got itself expressed in his portraits. Beyond all that, however, I know there was superb courage in his becoming a painter. He was not merely doing what he wanted to do; he was dedicating himself to the proposition that beauty is the birth-right of all the American people.

During the years that I knew him he was far more concerned with this social problem than with his own painting. He saw that the depression had put an end to the patronage of art by the wealthy, and, though the process had brought many artists, himself included, to penury, he welcomed it. He ardently wanted artists to find their sup-port in the people, and he evolved dozens of schemes, practical and impractical, to achieve this end. It was this interest in a people's art that led him to applaud the Federal Art Project, in which he served for two years as an assistant director.

I would not suggest for a moment that Hallowell was interested only in giving people a chance to see good pictures. He had an alert conscience as well as the sensitivity of an artist, and he was aware of all the suffering that goes on in our country and in the world. To me, as he knew, his political thinking never seemed to go far enough, for he believed that something less than a complete economic change might suffice. But I knew that his work was on the right side, and I knew where he would stand in whatever struggles the future might bring. He himself admitted freely that the Communists might be right, and he was always ready to unite with us in fighting for the ends in which he believed.

Because of his political outlook, he thought it possible for artists to find some satisfactory adjustment to the existing economic order, and, misdirected as his efforts often seemed, his spirit was magnificent. His last enterprise, if it had its pathetic as well as its tragic aspects, was proof of his sincerity and of a kind of recklessness that Jack Reed would have approved. Like William Morris before him, he became convinced that, if the public was not ready or able to patronize the fine arts, perhaps it would patronize the handicrafts. He set himself, therefore, to the task of making quasi-useful articles, such as andirons and door-knockers, that were works of beauty. By the use of machine techniques, he discovered, the work of first-rate craftsmen could be sold as cheaply as the hideous objects carried by department stores. Into this enterprise he put all his financial resources as well as his abundant energies. Here, he believed, was a way in which the artist could maintain his integrity within the framework of our system, and he wanted to prove his point to other artists. It was in this struggle that he exhausted himself.

It would be easy to point out that Bob Hallowell's premature death was one more of the tragedies of art under capitalism, just as it would be easy to dwell on his failure to understand the system in which he was forced to do his work. But it is better to make clear where his greatness lay. You could not know Bob Hallowell without realizing the terrible human importance of the revolution—all the more strongly because he was not, in any sense of formal avowal, a revolutionist. I have said and I believe that the revolution would justify itself if it meant no more than decent physical conditions for all the people. But it does mean more than that. It means the release of human capacities that cannot function in the world we have now. Bob Hallowell's life was evidence of how much of magnificence there is to be released.

February 21, 1939

Frances Wright

Frances Wright: Free Enquirer, **by A. J. G. Perkins and Theresa Wolfson**

Gradually the story of American radicalism in the 1830's and 1840's is being told, and to that story this book makes an important contribution. Frances Wright made her first visit to America in 1818, when she was twenty-three, and she immediately became the staunchest defender of republican institutions. She returned to the United States as a close friend of Lafayette. Then came the Nashoba experiment, the lectures in New York, and—most important of all—the founding of the Workingmen's Party. The end of her life was an anticlimax, but she had figured in some of the most important and least understood episodes in American history.

Except for W. R. Waterman's Columbia thesis of 1924, this is the first modern biography of Fanny Wright. Miss Perkins and Miss Wolfson have drawn upon many sources, including some hitherto unknown manuscripts, and they have brought forth much significant new material. But there are some surprising gaps in their research, and this is by no means a definitive biography. Unfortunately, also, it is badly written, and it is far from successful in the difficult job of interpreting its heroine's character. The student will find in it much that is of value, as well as much that must be criticized. The general reader will still await an adequate treatment of Frances Wright and her period.

September 19, 1939

A Great American

Benjamin Franklin, by Carl Van Doren

From the time he made his first success as printer until, in his will, he established a long-range philanthropy on a basis of loans to industrious young men, Benjamin Franklin was a good business man. It was his shrewdness, embodied in the maxims of Poor Richard, that endeared him to many bourgeois generations. His was the first American success story, and the saga of the poor apprentice's rise to power and wealth was an important part of the American legend. So completely, indeed, did attention focus on the Rotarian aspects of Franklin's thought that when, in this century, there was a revolt against Rotary, he was one of the victims.

Nothing, as this biography shows, could be more ridiculous. What, however, Mr. Van Doren does not seem quite to grasp is that the qualities he admires and those beloved by the Rotarians were naturally and logically united in one person. Franklin himself could have seen no incongruity in mingling rules for getting rich with speculations on science and philosophy. He was representative—in, of course, the rather special sense in which exceptional men can be representative—of a class that was rapidly conquering power throughout the world. The basis of the power of that class was the accumulation of wealth by various methods, including those Franklin recommended. He was, then, attentive to what, in his times, could only be regarded as legitimate means to a legitimate end.

The fact that he was concerned with money-making did not, to be sure, mean that, like the money-makers of subsequent generations, he had no other concern. On the contrary, his interests were almost boundless. But even in this he was representative, for the bourgeoisie in those days was a revolutionary class, full of an eager sense of the infinite possibilities before it. Moreover, though he was certainly a bourgeois, Franklin had risen from the working class, and he never forgot it. He spoke not merely for the successful, but also for the aspiring. The great political and intellectual upsurge that swept him forward and that he expressed and dramatized was no narrow movement, for the masses were moving forward in one of mankind's significant advances.

Mr. Van Doren, needless to say, does not see all this. In fact, his whole effort is to make Franklin seem unique, and though he is right in insisting on his superiority, he loses much by thus isolating his hero. To be specific, I think Van Doren has by no means grasped the pre-revolutionary strategy of the colonies, and as a result he makes Franklin's mission to London seem futile, which it was not. He quite misses the point of the episode of the Hutchinson letters, and finds himself in the ridiculous position of apologizing for Franklin's ungentlemanly conduct. In general, though he industriously records all of Franklin's meetings with his contemporaries, he seldom seems conscious of his points of contact with his age.

But on the other hand he has given us a vast mass of material about Franklin, much of it in Franklin's words, and it makes an exciting record. The bourgeois, in the days before specialization, could afford to have a speculative mind, and none was more resourceful or bolder than Franklin's. He loved gadgets, and he loved equally well the construction of sweeping generalizations. In politics he had the combination of common sense and idealism that is possible only in a man who knows where he is going and by what route. (Far-fetched as the comparison seems, I was constantly reminded of Lenin as I read the book.) He had, too, the kind of confidence in himself and his class and his cause that permitted him to assimilate whatever seemed to him good in the culture of the class that was being superseded.

Repeatedly one reflects: how has the bourgeoisie fallen! It is not fair, of course, to compare the average Rotarian of today with Benjamin Franklin, who was an extraordinary man even in his own times. But it is unthinkable that a modern bourgeois could ever reach such a level. That is what makes it outrageous that, because he wrote the Almanacs, the Rotarians should have appropriated him. He doesn't belong to them, and Mr. Van Doren has made that clear. He has given us one of the greatest Americans, and we ought to be grateful.

December 6, 1939

VIII

EXCHANGES

During his association with the *New Masses* Hicks had touched off several literary controversies, as critics with large followings are wont to do. Two of these controversies still hold interest for us today and for this reason I have chosen to reprint the exchanges here.

The first involved Andre Malraux's novel *Man's Fate*. The translator, Haakon Chevalier, took issue with the *New Masses* review of September 1934. Hicks replied on behalf of the *New Masses*, giving a more judicious appreciation of *Man's Fate* than had the original reviewer.

The second exchange centered on Hicks's review of *New Letters in America*, edited by Horace Gregory, poetry editor of the *New Masses*, in October 1937. The full material of the controversy is reprinted here along with the original editorial notes from the *New Masses*. This exchange is perhaps central to the interpretation of the literature of the entire period. (It deserves to be noted that in the past year or so collections of the poetry and prose of Horace Gregory have led to a complete reevaluation of his role in American letters.)

André Malraux's *Man's Fate*

Haakon Chevalier Objects

To the *New Masses:*

In your issue of July 3, you devoted considerable space to the discussion of the book reviews appearing in the *New Masses*. In the same issue appeared a review by Alfred H. Hirsch of a rather important book—André Malraux's *Man's Fate*. One might reasonably have expected that this book, which has been highly praised by critics as varied as André Gide, Robert Briffault, Léon-Pierre Quint, Jean Audard, Edmund Wilson, Horace Gregory, William Troy and Clifton Fadiman, would receive a careful, judicious and (dare one say?) sympathetic appraisal. The novel, mind you, is wholly sympathetic to Communism. In fact it is more than sympathetic: it is a magnificent tribute to the Communist heroes who fought and died in the Shanghai insurrection in 1927.

How does Hirsch treat this novel? Does he give an honest picture of what the novel is? He does not. Does he give even a suggestion of the merits of the novel? He does not. Does he critically analyze its shortcomings? He does not. What does he do? In a 1,500-word review he devotes barely 500 words to the novel itself. He gives a superficial glance at the historic background of the novel. He summarizes the author's career. In this summary he picks out facts which are obviously intended to convey to the reader the impression that Malraux could not possibly write a revolutionary novel. He points out the author's obsession with the problems of the individual, quotes a statement by a character in a previous novel to the effect that he is at bottom a gambler, and quotes incidents from other novels which suggest that Malraux is interested in furnishing the French government with information on market possibilities and in vandalism for its own sake. The reader, having been treated to this portrait of a rather decadent adventurer, is now in a receptive mood for Hirsch's account of this loudly heralded revolutionary novel.

Well, Hirsch assures his readers, this is not a revolutionary novel. It is merely the last in a series of antics by this muddle-headed adventurer (which does not amaze Mr. Hirsch). He treats, Hirsch says, of the heroics of the revolution rather than of the revolution itself. Hirsch winds up his review by generously conceding that "they [Malraux's characters] are with us, Malraux is with us." But, he hastens to enlighten his readers, "neither they, nor he, knows the reason why." A well-meaning fellow, this Malraux. Just muddled, that's all. And there Hirsch leaves his readers, having said all his imagination could suggest that would thoroughly discourage the reader from reading the book. At the last moment, however, his ingenious mind conceived one more little dig. All the "bourgeois" critics (and some not so bourgeois) had praised the translation, when they had mentioned it at all. Why not take a crack at the translator? So he thought of this: "The translation . . . is literal to the point of stiffness, at times even at the expense of clarity." This criticism takes on added weight when one knows that Hirsch had not read the original, while most of those who praised it, including Robert Briffault, Edmund Wilson and Clifton Fadiman, had.

Inasmuch as I consider *Man's Fate* one of the finest revolutionary novels that has been written to date, I think it is worth while to point out some of the most glaring inadequacies and misstatements in Hirsch's review. For, unlike Hirsch, I believe *New Masses* readers should be encouraged to read the novel.

Hirsch agrees with *1933*, the French Fascist weekly, that the novel has no political or social conclusions. Well, any reader who is not blind can find them throughout the novel—and towards the end they pile up as a superb challenge:

> The Revolution had just passed through a terrible malady, but it was not dead. And it was Kyo and his men, living or not, vanquished or not, who had brought it into the world. . . . "A civilization becomes transformed, you see, when its most oppressed element . . . suddenly becomes a *value,* when the oppressed ceases to attempt to escape this humiliation, and seeks his salvation in it, when the worker ceases to attempt to escape this work, and seeks in it his reason for being. . . ." "Our people will never forget that they suffer because of other men, and not because of their previous lives. . . ." In the repression that had beaten down upon exhausted China, in the anguish or hope of the masses, Kyo's activity remained incrusted like the inscriptions of the early empires in the river gorges. . . .

And as the book ends the horizon opens wide upon the dawn of the Five-Year Plan, and Kyo's wife leaves for Russia to carry on the work in which he had participated. Throughout the novel the political and social conclusions are unmistakably pointed.

Hirsch says that "all Malraux's characters are intellectuals." Of seventeen principal characters in this particular novel, only two—Kyo and his father Gisors—are intellectuals. Kyo, the central character, is an intellectual of a special and, I may add, precious type: he has "the conviction that ideas are not to be thought, but lived." And he is in the highest sense a man of action. Hirsch's single long quotation from the novel is part of a speech of Gisors, who becomes a hop-head and whose character, after Kyo's death, completely disintegrates. Hirsch deliberately gives the impression that this speech sounds the keynote of the novel.

Hirsch asks a number of rhetorical questions after making the statement: "Much is missing in this book . . ." Every one of these questions can be answered by numerous page-references. I shall answer merely a few, as it would take too long to give all the references, and moreover, these things that he finds missing are not only present in specific passages, but an aware reader will *sense* them throughout the novel as a rich background; their presence contributes to the extraordinary intensity of the novel:

"Where are the underfed coolies . . .?" Hirsch asks. Answer: pp. 14, 24 ("Hidden by those walls, half a million men: those of the spinning-mills, those who had worked sixteen hours a day since childhood, the people of ulcers, of scoliosis, of famine"), 25, 27, 28, 41, 70, 75, 76, 83, 87, 90, 94, etc., etc.

"Where are the peasants, taxed to the breaking-point . . .?" Answer: pp. 146–148 specifically, and elsewhere.

"Where are the women of the poor, sold into prostitution? . . ." Answer: p. 49: "I've just left a kid of eighteen who tried to commit suicide with a razor blade in her wedding palanquin. She was being forced to marry a respectable brute. . . ." p. 191: "There was his wife: life had given him nothing else. She had been sold for twelve dollars . . ." Also, p. 221.

"And where are the workers, whose conditions are such that the principal *revolutionary* demands . . . were confined to: a ten-hour maximum day, etc. . . .?" Answer: p. 83: "To the right, under the vertical banners covered with characters: '*A twelve-hour working day.*' (!) '*No more employment of children under eight,*' thousands of spinning-mill workers were standing . . ." Etc.

But, says Hirsch, "there is hardly a glimpse of all this and without it the relationships between Malraux's characters are only psychological ones, arbitrarily conceived and unrelated to the real causes of the

Chinese revolutionary awakening." This is his final estimate of the book.

The readers of the *New Masses* are entitled to know that the French Communist review *Commune* (from which much is to be learned) gave the novel a highly favorable review, and that a number of French Communists whom I spoke to, including Henri Barbusse, expressed the opinion that it is an extremely important revolutionary novel. Jean Audard, the *Commune* reviewer, says in part:

The first reason why we like Malraux's novel is the manner in which he has portrayed the Chinese revolution. Whatever reservations one may make as to the historic role which Malraux attributes here to the Third International, the Communist revolutionaries obviously have the entire sympathy of the author. They are presented under an aspect which one would commonly call heroic, but which it would no doubt be better to call, with Malraux, the simple aspect of *human dignity.* . . . The book does not only depict the Revolution in its collective aspect, but makes us penetrate into the individual drama of the characters that are involved in it. It appears even that this is its essential object. One can look upon it in two aspects: first as the picture of an event, of which Malraux *has understood the whole historic importance* [italics mine]; second, as the analysis of the effort of a certain number of individuals to struggle against the anguish of their solitude.

Such a point of view, which penetrates into the consciousness of individuals, which consists in asking oneself why the individuals are involved in the events, and even why they cause them, and especially *why they justify themselves in their own eyes for causing them,* appears to me superior to the point of view which limits itself to showing the characters of a Revolution simply reacting to external events.

The objections that I have raised suffice, I think, to make abundantly clear that, both in what it says and in what it does not say, Hirsch's review is an extraordinarily inept piece of criticism. I consider it distinctly unfortunate that the *New Masses* should have dismissed, in a contemptuous, sneering way, a book that is a moving tribute to all that the *New Masses* stands for, and to which its colleague, the Paris *Commune,* gave unqualified praise.

There will be some disagreement as to the sense in which *Man's Fate* may be considered a revolutionary novel. The novel does not aim to present a comprehensive picture of the external events of the Shanghai insurrection. Yet the author does give considerable attention to these events. It is, I think, a valid criticism to point out that these events are at times quite confused. What the author aims to do, and what he does admirably, is to show how the revolution becomes a part of the lives of diverse individuals, how it affects them and how they in turn affect its course. The manner in which the Revolution takes on a dynamic value for these characters I regard as an extremely important achievement. It is a novel of revolutinary *will*, which involves profound issues for man today. Malraux shows *why* and *how* these representative individuals become revolutionaries, and to have done that, with brilliance and penetration and an extraordinary ability to create character, to convey the strain and confusion of a vast social upheaval, and to keep before the reader's eye the complex and vivid international background, is enough for one novel. The book is essentially concerned with *values,* but those values are inseparable from the revolution which molds them. It is in this sense that I regard the novel as one of the most profound revolutionary novels we have had.

Haakon M. Chevalier

Granville Hicks Comments

To the *New Masses:*

I have read *Man's Fate* since the review of it appeared in the *New Masses,* and I find myself in the position of disagreeing almost as much with the review itself as with the translator's attack on it. To me the reading of the novel, especially after Alfred Hirsch's review, was a startling experience. Hirsch had not given me the slightest inkling of the book's extraordinary intensity. From the description of Ch'en's emotions in the act of assassination to the battle in the police station, I felt a steadily mounting excitement, not unmixed with dread. And then came that extraordinary scene in the prison yard, with Kyo's suicide and Katov's gift to the two prisoners of the cyanide that alone could save him from death in the firebox of a locomotive. Of the quality of the effect that *Man's Fate* had upon me I shall have something to say later, but the intensity of that effect cannot be denied.

If Chevalier quarreled with Hirsch on the ground that he failed to suggest Malraux's sustained power, I could not but agree with him. I feel that Hirsch was at fault, whether he simply did not respond to the book or neglected to record his response. But it is not, by and large, on that ground that Chevalier's objections rest. With his detailed criticism I do not agree, and I cannot accept his final estimate of the book.

In the first place, Chevalier objects to Hirsch's summary of Malraux's life. The tone of that summary may, as Chevalier says, prejudice the reader against Malraux, but the facts are unassailable, and it is the facts that count. Malcolm Cowley, in his review of *Man's Fate* in the *New Republic* for July 4, described Malroux as "a man whose own mentality has strong traces of Fascism" (a statement to which, as far as I know, Chevalier has taken no exception). Hirsch did not make so flat an assertion; in fact, he carefully avoided all epithets; but he did give the facts and let the reader form his own estimate.

In the second place, Chevalier, with a venom that is more understandable than admirable, objects to Hirsch's comment on the translation. I can scarcely expect him to like that comment, but I am surprised at the form his objection takes. He gratuitously assumes that Hirsch had not read *Man's Fate* in French. "One knows," he says, "that Hirsch has not read the original." I don't know how "one" knows that, for I know that Hirsch had read the original. Chevalier also says that Hirsch attacked the translation because the "bourgeois" reviewers praised it. I know—and Chevalier might have realized it if he had thought about dates—that the review was written and in my hands before any reviews had appeared.

In the third place, Chevalier states that Hirsch agrees with "1933," the French fascist weekly. Hirsch, on the contrary, merely quotes the statement of "1933" as symptomatic and as a partial explanation of the success of the book in bourgeois circles. He specifically says that the fascist comment is "not entirely fair," though he thinks it "gives a hint of why this book was awarded the coveted Goncourt prize."

In the fourth place, Chevalier objects to Hirsch's statement that all the characters are intellectuals, and says that only two of the seventeen principal characters deserve to be so described. This seems to me mere quibbling. The important thing is that none of the seventeen principal characters is a factory worker or a peasant.

But these are comparatively minor points. The central issue is whether we are to regard *Man's Fate* as "one of the finest revolutionary novels that has been written to date," "one of the most profound revolutionary novels we have had," and, to quote Chevalier's introduction to the book, "the revolutionary novel that has been so long anticipated and so often foreshadowed in contemporary literature." I quite agree with Hirsch that we are not.

The first point to consider is the actual handling of the revolutionary material. The coolies, peasants, prostitutes, and workers are in the book, but they are there in mere phrases, as anyone who cares to look up Chevalier's references can see. They merely form the background. One does not get from the novel any impression that it is they who are creating the events that take place. Chevalier says that Malraux is trying "to show how the revolution becomes a part of the lives of diverse individuals," rather than "to present a comprehensive picture of the external events of the Shanghai insurrection." But, instead of regarding the two aims as incompatible, he should, I think, see that the first is dependent upon the second. Let him look, for example, at William Rollins' *The Shadow Before,* in which the individuals come to life precisely because they are so organically part of the mass movements that are the book's theme.

Hirsch, recognizing this failure of Malraux to reveal the forces that actually bind together the various characters of the book, says that "the relationships beween Malraux's characters are only psychological ones." If Chevalier does not like that way of stating the issue, he can take Cowley's: "The revolution, instead of being his principal theme, is the setting and the pretext for a novel that is, in reality, a drama of individual lives." The informed reader, of course, can make the necessary interpretations for himself, can fill in the blanks, but that does not alter the fact that the blanks are there. The uninformed reader, it seems to me, would never be left by *Man's Fate* with a sense of the purpose and historic necessity of proletarian revolution. He would have a sense of personal heroism, but that is a quality that can be expended in many causes.

There is one section of the book that does deal directly with political issues, Part III, in which Kyo goes to Hankow to protest against the policy of the Communist International. It is unfortunate, in view of the political capital that Trotsky, in his fight against the Comintern, has made of the relations beween the Kuomintang and the Communist Party of China, that it is precisely here that Malraux is so misleading in his analysis, as the subsequent history of Soviet China and the Chinese Communist Party (authoritatively given by General Victor A. Yakhantoff in his *The Chinese Soviets*) unequivocally establishes. I also think it unfortunate that Hirsch failed to deal with this point. I do not question Malraux's sincerity, and certainly I do not pretend to be an expert on the Chinese situation. I do know, however, that disaster came, not as Malraux and Trotsky say, because the Chinese

Communist Party followed the instructions of the Comintern, but because Chen Tu Hsieu and other leaders refused to follow them. A careful comparison of the instructions issued by the Executive Committee of the Communist International and the activities of the Communist Party of China shows that it is with the latter that responsibility for failure lies.

There is another passage that raises similar doubts. Chevalier says, "And as the book ends, the horizon opens wide upon the dawn of the Five-Year Plan." But if Malraux is hailing a new day for the revolutionary movement, I wonder why he includes in the last chapter the letter from Pei, which seems to carry the absurd suggestion of the Trotskyites that world revolution is being sacrificed to the industrial progress of the U.S.S.R. It is not difficult to see why Trotsky wrote a letter endorsing *Man's Fate*, though he was shrewd enough to give literary reasons for his praise.

It is impossible to ignore such issues in dealing with the book. Though Chevalier says in his letter that the novel does not try to give "a comprehensive picture," in his introduction he spoke of it as "a remarkable feat in the novelistic treatment of historic material," commented on the "essential accuracy" with which events were recorded, and said we were made aware of the "profound issues" involved. I agree that the picture of the insurrection is not comprehensive, and I think it should be. I think, moreover, that even as far as it goes, it is not correct.

The second point to consider is the spirit of the book. Trotsky, though he sees fit to praise *Man's Fate*, finds it necessary to enter a disclaimer. "In the final analysis," he says, "Malraux is an individualist and a pessimist." Both these qualities are fully reflected in the novel. According to Chevalier's introduction, the theme is: "Change the conditions of man's life, control the blind forces that shape human destiny—*man's fate*. Above all, give his life a meaning; give it dignity." But I think Malcolm Cowley is far more accurate when he says: "Malraux's real theme is a feeling that most men nurse, secretly, their sense of absolute loneliness and uniqueness, their acknowledgment to themselves of inadequacy in the face of life and helplessness against death—that is what he means by *la condition humaine;* this is man's lot, his destiny, his servitude. And he has chosen to depict this emotion during a revolutionary period because it is then carried, like everything else that is human, to its pitch of highest intensity."

Malraux's pessimism, closely linked, as Cowley's description shows, to his individualism, permeates the novel. Different persons, he seems to say at the end, make different adjustments to the tragic burdens of fate. May, Kyo's wife, goes to Russia, but Gisors, his father, says, "I am freed both from death and from life." For myself I can only say that I was left, though briefly, with a sense of hopelessness. If it is objected that this is the fault of the material, I can point to Agnes Smedley's *Chinese Destinies*.

Extreme, even mystical, individualism and pervasive pessimism are not qualities that make revolutionary fiction. I agree, in other words, with Hirsch's fundamental contention, regardless of the opinions of Haakon Chevalier and Jean Audard. When Audard says that Malraux "has understood the whole historic importance" of the events he describes, he is, I believe, wrong. When Hirsch says, "The world of this book is not above the revolution, but it is apart from it," he is, I believe, right.

Hirsch's mistakes are, as I have said before, mistakes of omission, but they are important mistakes, and they invalidate his estimate of the book. The revolutionary movement has always attracted a considerable number of bourgeois intellectuals, especially, because of the nationalistic issues involved, in China. Many of these intellectuals have been, as Chevalier says of Kyo, assets to the revolution. At the same time they have often been vacillating and sometimes opportunistic. Their whole approach to the movement is personal and certainly not representative of the desires and interests of the masses. It is with such elements that Malraux can most easily sympathize, and it is with characters of this kind that he is concerned. Even into such characters he has, I believe, projected his own philosophic pre-occupations, and as a result they are considerably more reflective and mystical than the average run of bourgeois intellectual revolutionaries. He does, nevertheless, have real insight into their mental processes, and, though he does not portray their role correctly, he does magnificently convey their emotions. Moreover, Kyo and his comrades are genuinely heroic and inspiring. Though a great deal of the revolution escapes Malraux, a great deal is in his book, and there are moments when he transcends his limitations and gives the reader a real sense of the power and greatness of the revolutionary movement.

That is why, though I cannot call *Man's Fate,* as Chevalier does, "the revolutionary novel that has been so long anticipated," I have no hesitation in hailing Malraux as a novelist who is capable of surpassing the limitations within which he is already powerful. The review of his book in *The New Masses* should, I believe, have dealt as generously with what he succeeded in doing as it did cogently with what he failed to do.

September 4, 1934

New Letters in America

"Those who quibble, bicker, nag, and deny"

Communism is good news. Once understood, once believed in, it holds out hope to all but capitalism's pampered few. If one accepts the Marxist analysis of history, one believes that the establishment of a classless society is not only possible but inevitable. Without minimizing for a moment the difficulties in the way of the building of socialism, Communists hold that socialism will be built, and, without assuming that perfection will be achieved the day after the revolution, they are confident that socialism will initiate a new era of human development. Communists offer no short cut to Utopia, but they are far from despair.

The essential hopefulness of Communism is a fact, no mere theory. The understanding of events that Communism gives does inspire a confidence that is capable of changing human lives. I have seen, among intellectuals, confusion and weakness yield to clarity and strength. I have seen a baffled and desperate day laborer transformed into a militant, capable leader of labor. I have seen men and women, working together for their class, transcend the pettiness and frailty observable in the conduct of each as an individual. There is nothing miraculous about this; it results quite simply from an insight that is confirmed alike by logic and by action.

Some of us have felt that left-wing literature ought to be able both to reflect and to communicate this hopefulness. We have, therefore, rejoiced when such writers as Grace Lumpkin, Jack Conroy, Fielding Burke, Josephine Johnson, Thomas Boyd, Edward Newhouse, and others tried to catch the militant spirit of the class-conscious proletariat. And we have regretted that such writers as Robert Cantwell, Erskine Caldwell, and John Dos Passos so frequently failed to communicate—and even, so far as we could tell, to perceive —a warmer mood than the desperation and disgust expressed by such avowedly defeatist writers as Thomas Wolfe and William Faulkner. It seemed to us particularly unfortunate when these writers, having apparently felt for a time our kind of confidence, lapsed into their old despair.

Because we kept steadily before us the fact that Communism was good news, some of us have been called sectarian and have been charged with prescribing content and treatment to the writers of the Left. Let us be candid about this. Possibly our criticisms have had harmful effects. Novelists may have pretended to a greater confidence than they felt—or, more probably, than they could communicate. Slogans have sometimes been substituted for reality, and stereotyped situations for data of experience. On the other hand, writers who dealt in despair have usually written with integrity and carried conviction.

Our critical opponents sometimes seem to assume that all the more positive writers have been guilty of slogans and stereotypes and that we have a preference for shoddiness and superficiality. I admit neither charge. I do not know that my opinions of the authors I have mentioned have changed in any fundamental respect, and I deny that their novels are in any important way shoddy or superficial. But I will grant that often I have not borne down so heavily as I might have on writing that, in one way or another, I recognized to be bad.

I should like to explain why. If I have tolerated, let us say, the formula of the conversion short story or the formula of the strike novel, it is because I know that there is a dramatic reality in conversion and a powerful story in a strike, and I have hoped that some day the formulas would be transcended. And if I have urged gifted writers to try to see as clearly the hope for the future as they see the causes for despair in the present, it is because I refuse to believe that the central fact in Communism can be without significance for those writers who, in some sense or other, call themselves Communists.

Yet there are certain facts that have to be examined. It is invidious to mention names, but there is no other way to escape vagueness. I think it has to be granted, for example, that Farrell sees all the way round his characters as Newhouse has thus far failed to do. Cantwell is a more competent craftsman than Conroy. Caldwell's people are memorable in a way that, as a rule, Josephine Johnson's aren't. There are passages in Grace Lumpkin's novels and Fielding Burke's that show less than complete mastery, whereas John Dos Passos almost constantly maintains a certain level of artistic excellence. Of course, having said so much, I ought to go on and say whether Josephine Herbst is more impressive when she is affirmative or when she is nostalgic. I ought to discuss the extent to which Farrell, Cantwell, and Dos Passos do try to reflect the militancy of the proletariat, and why they succeed or fail. I ought to talk about Halper, and Rollins, and Roth, and Leane Zugsmith. But perhaps our critical opponents will be satisfied if I say that, among writers on the Left, those who are more militantly affirmative are often guilty of faults from which the more passive and pessimistic writers are generally free.

We are told that this is because the more Communist writers find their creative powers thwarted by the Communist Party line. Earl Browder stated at the first American Writers' Congress that the party had no literary line, and the facts bear him out. It is a matter of record, for example, that certain rather starkly pessimistic writers are members of the party and that certain affirmative writers are not. It is conceivable that one or two writers pumped up a kind of artificial cheerfulness in response to the repeated assertion by myself and others that Communist literature ought to be able to reflect the Communist hope; but it is more likely that even these writers were led astray by their own feelings and not by critical admonitions.

The party-line theory, though convenient for party enemies, does not hold water. What seems, on the other hand, to be true is that it is much harder to express the Communist conviction of the triumph of the working class than it is to communicate a mood of disgust and despair. The explanation partly lies in the readiness of the more intelligent reading public to accept the latter. *Man's Fate*, for example, seemed fine and moving to many readers who could not accept *Days of Wrath*. Many of Farrell's admirers found the end of *Judgment Day* mechanical and unconvincing. Caldwell's "Candy-Man Beechum" was more easily accepted than "Daughter." Certain authors sense this lack of receptivity, and feel themselves incapable of making the effort necessary to overcome it.

A further explanation lies in the literary training of the present generation of Left writers. The average poet or novelist of the Left was brought up either in a bourgeois family or in a proletarian family under bourgeois influence. He knew little from early experience of what is called class-consciousness. His first gesture of intellectual revolt was, in all probability, directed against the complacent assumptions of his parents and their contemporaries: he became a militant pessimist and devoted himself to pointing out the innumerable causes for despair. Later he heard about Marxism and became intellectually convinced of its truth, but he continued to read the pessimistic writers and his first literary experiments were based upon their work. Almost against his will he became part of the pessimist tradition.

How true this is could not be better illustrated than by *New Letters in America.** Mr. Gregory has not limited himself to Left writers, but most of his thirty-six contributors would, I take it, accept the general thesis that capitalism can and ought to be superseded by some form of collectivism. Yet they could scarcely write more bleakly if they were avowed Spenglerians or felt, with Joseph Wood Krutch, that the triumph of the proletariat would mean the end of civilization.

Mr. Gregory to the contrary notwithstanding, this is not "new." Indeed, the volume seems strikingly like the first *American Caravan,* which was issued in 1927 before there was a depression or the political upsurge that Gregory speaks of. The clearest impression one got from the *Caravan* was that our young writers were distressed by the American present and quite without hope for the future. *New Letters* gives the same impression. From George Weller's sardonic piece of reporting to James Agee's hysterical scenario, the prose writers express disgust, bitterness, pity, cynicism, but seldom hope. Nor are the poets different. Their very imagery is significant: "like men before a firing squad"; "a hangman's hood"; "machine guns/Punching in dust their rows of periods"; "the carrion cry of gulls."

There are other things, of course, to be said about the book. Mr. Gregory believes that " pragmatic naturalism" is outworn and suggests that something like the fable may take its place. We are all a little fed up, I suspect, with naturalism, but I am afraid the fable is another blind alley, like symbolism, the stream of consciousness, and

New Letters in America, edited by Horace Gregory.

the revolution of the word. I am not impressed by Kafka's fable, and Elizabeth Bishop's "The Sea and Its Shore," with its false naïveté, is downright bad. To my mind the best story in the book is John Hampson's "Care of Grand Hotel," which is well within the realistic tradition. So are the other memorable stories: Eleanor Clark's "Call Me Comrade," Morton Freedgood's "Good Nigger," and Eugene Joffe's "Ballard." If by pragmatic naturalism Gregory means the maximum amassing of facts and the minimum interpretation by selection, the best one can say for the method is that it sometimes works. If what he wants is to feel the conscious functioning of the mind and imagination of the author, I can readily agree. To get this, however, it is not necessary to go outside the general realistic tradition. Perhaps the mind and imagination can function better in some other form, but that has not yet been proven, and certainly the fable does not seem the way.

Another question that the book raises is why most of the younger poets are so determined that what they write shall not be pleasing to the ear. Except for Kerker Quinn's "How Good as Listeners?" there is scarcely a poem that can be read aloud with pleasure. I am not sure that this is important, but it is puzzling. The easy answer about the modern mood scarcely seems to fit when one thinks of Eliot, MacLeish, and Crane, each of whom has his own kind of melody. One is sure that, with such poets as Muriel Rukeyser, David Wolff, and Marya Zaturenska, harshness is achieved only with effort, and one wonders why the effort should have been made at all.

As for criticism, the only critical essay is contributed by William Phillips and Philip Rahv, which seems a pity. Messrs. Phillips and Rahv have now discovered consciousness and intelligence and are recommending them to American writers. It is sound doctrine, but it would carry more weight if they practised what they preach. As it is, the essay is the mixture of platitude and pedantry to which we have become accustomed if not inured. Since Phillips and Rahv first entered upon their joint apprenticeship in criticism, their ideas have seemed not so much false as unimportant. Their new political allegiance may increase the falsity but is not likely to enhance the importance.

The essay has, however, some slight interest in so far as it voices the critical views to which I have been taking exception. Rahv and Phillips are now among those who argue that the party line has ruined left-wing literature. But, even if there were a party line, a discerning critic could see that the trouble lies much deeper. Here in *New Letters,* for example, there are writers, some of them far removed from the party, who try to suggest that they are aware of sources of hope. The net effort of these efforts is to intensify the impression of gloom. The symbolic suggestion of hope in Agee's scenario carries no weight against the cumulative horror of his picture of decay. Eleanor Clark comes closer to an affirmative mood, for she makes her ridiculous old maid almost heroic, but the emphasis, nevertheless, falls on futility. David Wolff, Arthur Ebel Steig, and John Malcolm Brinnin end their poems with affirmations, but they are mere assertions, whereas the mood of hopelessness is powerfully realized.

All this confirms the impression that it is difficult to render in literature the substance of the Communist hope. We should, therefore, be tolerant of those who do not make the attempt. There is truth in their pictures of decay, even if it is not the whole truth. But I do not think that we should acquiesce in despair or make a virtue of it. If, to put the issue much too bluntly, authors can deal most effectively with decay, we must take their work as it is and recognize its merits, but we can still hold to our belief that there is more to be said and that some day writers will know how to say it. We can, moreover, without being uncritical, encourage those writers who do try to say it, even when they are not wholly successful.

Communism is good news. We are still waiting for the author who will show in literature what we know that means in life. We may have to wait, as T. K. Whipple suggests, for yet another generation, one that has grown up in the struggle, but I have more faith in the present generation. A greater boldness, a greater willingness to risk failure, a greater resourcefulness in experimentation, a more determined search for knowledge, and a greater eagerness for experience would give us what we want. There are mighty themes in the world today, and a lofty spirit. And I think there are writers wise enough to know that the sectarians are not those who quibble, and bicker, and nag, and deny.

September 28, 1937

A Symposium

Two weeks ago Granville Hicks reviewed at length in our column
New Letters in America, an anthology of the work of thirty-six younger
writers edited by Horace Gregory, poetry editor of the *New Masses.*
In the course of his review, Hicks made some very forthright statements about realism and pessimism (among other things), statements
which found Gregory and some of the *New Letters* authors in hearty
disagreement. The *New Masses* prints these several expressions of
opinion, along with Hicks's reply, both for their merits as bearing on
the particular literary questions at issue and in the hope that the discussion will lead to clearer definitions of literary and artistic canons.
—The Editors.

October 12, 1937

By Horace Gregory

Because I believe that a headstrong, slashing attack on young
writers is sometimes tonic for their work, I read Granville Hicks's
review of *New Letters in America* with considerable interest. And for
me, as editor of *New Letters,* he opened wide a central issue in my
divergence from his point of view. That issue should be fought out
here, in the pages of the *New Masses* and nowhere else, for I believe
that today young writers of anti-fascist conviction should read and
use the *New Masses* to discuss their work in creating a growing literature, a literature that embraces among many others the work of
Thomas Mann as well as Martin Anderson Nexö, that includes such
poets as W. H. Auden, Muriel Rukeyser, and Robert Fitzgerald, as
well as such widely divergent novelists as William Rollins, Grace
Lumpkin, and André Malraux. It includes myself and Granville
Hicks, and has included both of us consistently for many years.

One reason for my interest in Mr. Hicks's review was because,
as I read it, it seemed to be another example of the same technique
that D. H. Lawrence used in his exciting peacock-tail essay attacking
Edwin Muir. Lawrence, you remember, talked about the beauty of
the peacock's tail, and about his love of splendor, which no one could
deny, nor wish to deny, nor would ever deny in a thousand years. He

did not answer Edwin Muir's questions, no more than Mr. Hicks reviewed *New Letters,* but he talked bravely, courageously, and truly about his own vitality, which I believe in as firmly as I believe that "Communism is good news," whether we heard it back in 1924, as I did, or whether it is heard today by a growing number of younger writers.

Lest Mr. Hicks and the readers of the *New Masses* misunderstand me, I want to say at once that I do *not* believe that Mr. Hicks has written, or intended to write, a political review: there is about as much allegiance to an imaginary "party line" in his review as could be found in the entire works of D. H. Lawrence. But what I do find in Mr. Hicks's review is a curiously sectarian loyalty to the kind of writing that once was the delight of H. L. Mencken and his followers, and with it the same stark, staring blindness to what is valuable and useful in poetry. What I mean by this is that he prefers the hope of converting a Sinclair Lewis to our beliefs to reading carefully such younger writers as I have published; in writing of them, he gave them exactly four paragraphs in a seventeen-paragraph review.

I refer, of course, to Hicks's inordinate praise of Sinclair Lewis in the *New Masses* when *It Can't Happen* here appeared. His position then was not greatly different from that of those who, for a living, are forced to write hastily, thoughtlessly, and with the hope of being readable in newspaper columns and Sunday book sections. Was it good news that Mr. Hicks was praising a writer whose recent work, I insist, is "shoddy and superficial"? It is good news that Mr. Lewis is now reported to be writing an anti-Communist play? Is it good news for young writers, many of whom were completely ignored by Mr. Hicks and then told the good news that neither they nor I would deny? Is it good news when Mr. Hicks crashes down on David Wolff, a young poet whose unpublished manuscript is one of the best books of verse I have read this year, and who must find time to write in the short hours left him after working on a job?

I am not being sentimental here, but employing what I believe to be a cleaner, more humane form of realism than the kind that Sinclair Lewis writes. I know that sources of David Wolff's work lie in the same good news of which Mr. Hicks writes and then waves before us quite as D. H. Lawrence waved the peacock's tail. I also know that David Wolff is a better poet than many who receive inordinate praise from tired men and women whose work is often hasty and at times ill-paid. Mr. Wolff should expect a more thoughtful review from Mr. Hicks, and so should Muriel Rukeyser and Miss Zaturenska, who are grouped together on the fantastic charge of harshness. This charge is as crazy as Franz Kafka's picture of bourgeois justice in *The Trial.*

And if I say this, am I bickering, quibbling, or denying Mr. Hicks's good news? I have confidence that I am not, for I admire Mr. Hicks's central convictions, which are not actually the core of his review, but are the peacock's tail. The actual center of Mr. Hicks's review is a defense of a kind of realism that was ably practiced during the 1920's; and again, I do not deny the masters of that technique, but insist that Mr. Hicks seems to use it as his only scale of measurement. And there are many times when I suspect that he is trying to flog dead horses back to life. In the case of Sinclair Lewis, the dead horse got up and ran away, ran, in fact, straight in the direction of Leon Trotsky's friends, those who detract from all the good work done in recent American literature, who attempt to break up union activity as well as bewilder fledgling intellectuals, and who consistently quibble, bicker, nag, and deny.

In the *Herald Tribune Books* of September 20, 1936, one may read what Mr. Lewis has to say of Isidor Schneider and Robert Forsythe.

Mr. Hicks, with his strong bias in favor of a so-called "realistic" literature, made an honest, but grave mistake in *The Great Tradition* when he hoped for a poet who would be a combination of Walt Whitman and Emily Dickinson, a creature which, I fear, he will not find in his lifetime or in the next five thousand years. Does this detract from his admirable work in the rest of the book? Only so far as poetry is concerned. Does it disqualify Mr. Hicks as the authoritative biographer of John Reed (an important American biography that some day should be reprinted in the Modern Age reprints)? Not at all. But it does get in the way of his reading and understanding of contemporary poetry. As he glances through *New Letters,* he finds himself reading gloom and lack of musical quality in all poems but one. That poem, of course, is a good poem, because if it wasn't, I wouldn't have published it. But only one poem out of twenty-eight! Isn't Mr. Hicks, with his rusty slide-rule of realistic fiction, doing the real quibbling, bickering, and denying? And has the slide-rule anything to do with politics or "party lines," or good news or bad?

It has not, and will never have, as long as he and I believe that the U.S.S.R. is building an enduring civilization, and that Trotskyism is a disease, and that good writers today are united to fight fascism.

In his attitude toward poetry, it would seem that Mr. Hicks (quite unintentionally, of course) forms a united front with Edmund ("Poetry-is-dead") Wilson and Robinson Jeffers who finds "our verse troubled or frowning" and who then delivers an attack on strikes and the new Russia. I can scarcely believe that Mr. Hicks read Richard Eberhart's "Poem" in *New Letters,* particularly the concluding stanza:

> Who talks with the Absolute salutes a shadow
> Who seeks himself shall lose himself;
> And the golden pheasants are no help
> And action must be learned from love of man.

This assertion is neither mechanical nor forced; nor is the verse harsh or unclear; nor do I believe for one moment that Muriel Rukeyser's poem, "The Cruise," is uncharacteristic of her quickening style, which readers of the *New Masses* had an opportunity to discover for themselves in "Mediterranean." Would Mr. Hicks prefer *Conversation at Midnight* which is comparable to the quality of Sinclair Lewis's recent prose? Would he rather try to "win over" Miss Millay than to encourage a number of younger (and, I believe, cleaner and better) writers? If so, then I leave him (as far as poetry is concerned) in the company of Edmund Wilson and Robinson Jeffers; for my good news, along with Mr. Hicks's good news, is that poetry is reviving under the stimulus of more than one literary tradition, and if Mr. Hicks doesn't believe me, I strongly recommend that he re-read Stephen Spender's "The Destructive Element" and C. Day Lewis's "A Hope for Poetry."

The good news means more than the survival of a single group of novelists; it has meant far more than that for the past seven years. I thought it was good news when S. Funaroff's *We Gather Strength* appeared in 1933, and said so at once, in the pages of the *Herald Tribune.* I thought it was good news when *Trial Balances* appeared in 1935, in which I introduced T. C. Wilson and Malcolm Cowley introduced Alfred Hayes. That good news began to undermine the feeling of despair held by a number of critics in 1930, who had read Hart Crane and couldn't understand a line of anything he wrote. And today, I believe that it is very good news that the following poets have appeared in the "Social Poets" number of *Poetry* (May 1936): Edwin

Rolfe, Alfred Hayes, Kenneth Fearing, David Schreiber, David Wolff, T. C. Wilson, John Wheelwright, R. P. Blackmur, Hildegarde Flanner, Josephine Miles, S. Funaroff, Muuriel Rukeyser, and in the *Forum* for February 1937, additional names included: Archibald Fleming, Eunice Clark, David Schubert, William Stephens, James Agee, Clark Mills, Elizabeth Bishop, Winfield Scott, and Robert Fitzgerald; and in *New Letters*, eight of the above and Etta Blum, Tony Palmer, Naomi Raplan, Arthur Ebel Steig, Lionel Abel, Richard Eberhart, Emma Swan, John Malcolmn Brinnin, Kerker Quinn, Louis Grudin, Frederic Prokosch, and Marya Zaturenska.

And today I find my own work in *Chorus for Survival* (after it had been condemned as "gloomy" and God knows what else by a *New Masses* reviewer in 1935) described as "cheerful" in a college textbook. I know that the reviewer who attacked me then didn't follow a party line or was malicious or dishonest. All I know is that he couldn't read poetry, and should have been told to read it with interest and care. The reviewer should not have been bickered at and nagged; nor should Mr. Hicks be badgered for his refusal to read poetry if he doesn't like it. But I agree with Mr. Hicks about good news; I think the time is coming when he will change his mind, and change it with the same forthright courage that he has shown in modifying his specific opinions of John Dos Passos and of Sinclair Lewis. I think the time is coming when he will find the verse of David Wolff no less depressing than Grace Lumpkin's enduring (but not altogether cheerful) *To Make My Bread*. I am inclined to agree with Mr. Hicks in his appreciation of John Hampson's work in his review, but I wish he had helped me when I reviewed Mr. Hampson's memorable first novel in the *Nation* in 1931 and when again I praised his book in the *New Republic* in 1933. It was a pity to see *Saturday Night at the Greyhound* go out of print for lack of adequate critical support. Again, I think it would be good news to see that book in the Modern Age reprint series.

Meanwhile *New Letters in America* will be published twice a year. This should be good news for younger writers. Walt Whitman once wrote: "The poetic area is very spacious—has room for all— has so many mansions." He too had confidence as I have today that poetry is a living art; and it was he who also said: "To have great poets, there must be great audiences too." These statements may sound platitudinous to Mr. Hicks, but I believe that now and in the face of his review, they should be said again. I believe that those who "quibble, bicker, nag, and deny" will be doomed to a hell of their own making, but I am certain that very few of the thirty-five young poets I have published in *Poetry,* the *Forum,* and *New Letters* are of the sort that Mr. Hicks describes. It is a pity, I think, that they should be tarred with the same brush that he intends for his critical enemies.

Though I may disagree deeply wih Mr. Hicks concerning the present vitality of realism (as I think it should *not* be applied to criticism of poetry), I have confidence again that he and I shall stand together against the dangers of a split among the violent sectarians; and that we shall stand together as we have for the past seven years in praise of anti-fascist literature.

As I said at the beginning of this letter, Mr. Hicks's review might well be tonic to young writers but its essentially negative spirit should not be encouraged in the future.

By Muriel Rukeyser

Granville Hicks, in his review of *New Letters in America,* speaks of his "tolerating" the conversion story in his search for hope in literature. It seems to me that the time for such tolerance gives way now; that application of a rigid standard of the (moral) happy ending is useless and has been proved so every time it has been applied to left-wing literature. A great many people feel now that whatever excellence the left-wing writers have depends more on their sensitive straight facing of present scenes and values than on the happy posturing of their theses. Whatever is inert is hopeless, now as always; whatever is living and aware contains its base of hope. And that's no discovery or denial.

Mr. Hicks has recommended, curiously, that critics practice what they preach. This has been turned against critics before, but always by the enemies of criticism, and comes as a disappointment from Mr. Hicks who is a critic and friend of letters.

He harks back to the first *Caravan,* calls for "a greater eagerness for experience," says "it is much harder to express the Communist conviction of triumph of the working class than it is to communicate a mood of disgust and despair," complains bitterly that the poems in this book are hard for him to read aloud with pleasure.

But the book *New Letters* has sources of joy, for it has good writing in it. "Behold a Cloud in the West" has a true picture of the case for peace; "The Man in the Jail Is Not Jesus" contains a vision; the introduction calls for entertainment as well as use in the contents. In the poems, read for hope Schubert's

> Imagine, imagine, America, from the poet Alberti
> The veritable roots of a Christmas tree:
> Gladness and singing and the warm south
> In your mouth. . . .

or David Wolff's

>   . . . It is of you, broad hand,
> I sing, I sing of you, how near
> your mountains, after beautiful toil
> I stood under drooping pears in fine starlight. . . .
>   . . . so turn, begin
> speech with the darkening nations; and with all who
> stamp agains evil, hating death; with
> strikers especially; and with the tall plowmen of pioneer hills.

  The hope in this book is not the familiar one, for the next strike to be better than this last; or the survivor of calamity to be not so much alone, now that he has found his group; but another, profounder one, by which writers can touch their time and their country and find not the sweetness and light here called for, but its life and a steadier, less blatant hope than Mr. Hicks demands—a hope to be worked for continually, not shouted before its time.

By Marshall Schacht

  But when was lyric poetry ever more than a lagging barometer of social thought, a subconscious, heightened picture of an individual's reactions to individual experience, colored by chance influences and the fashion of the time? Most of it has no concern with social consciousness, and doesn't need to have—like the poems of Donne, or Emily Dickinson, or Robert Frost. Poetry isn't supposed to do what the mind thinks it should. The mind may go Communist, but the poet can't learn so fast. Communism is a rational philosophy, like utilitarianism, as well as a religion and an experience of love. The rational part isn't the business of poetry at all, and as for the rest, worshipful lyrics and lyrics of love for an idea can be very bad indeed. What can a poet do but be what he is, and let the color of his rational life fall through to stain, when it can do so poetically, the much over-rated importance of his song?

Isn't the only positive song, outside aesthetics, the labor chant?

The rest is up to thinking and doing—not verse, or even aesthetic prose.

By Granville Hicks

Mr. Gregory's story of the peacock's tail fits my review of *New Letters*. I did use the review as an opportunity to make a certain number of general statements about left-wing literature. I can understand why Mr. Gregory, who is statistically correct in saying that I devoted only four out of seventeen paragraphs to the writers in his book, is a little distressed, but I don't think he ought to have jumped to the conclusion that I hadn't read the writers carefully. I am willing to be charged with bad proportions or bad judgment, but not with having written about something else because I hadn't read the book.

With the bulk of what I say in the thirteen paragraphs that aren't about the writers in *New Letters* Mr. Gregory is apparently in agreement. That is, he agrees that Communism is good news and that left-wing writers ought to be able to communicate the hope that they feel. I never really doubted this, but I am delighted to have him say it. What he doesn't make clear is how he feels about the success or failure of our writers in expressing, in giving imaginative substance to, that hope. He is full of hope because many new poets are being published, which seems to me very fine, but isn't what I was talking about. I was saying that Communism is good news, and that most of our writers don't make me feel that they know and believe that in the very depths of their imaginations. I still would like to know whether Mr. Gregory agrees or disagrees, and if he disagrees, I should like to see the evidence.

Miss Rukeyser does disagree and says so clearly and cites two short stories and two poems to show that *New Letters* does not give a general impression of despair. The two stories seem to me to express nothing whatsoever, let alone the kind of hope I am talking about. One of the poems she mentions I also mentioned, but I said that the affirmation was less convincing than the setting of reasons for despair. I could have said the same thing about the other.

Mr. Gregory, Miss Rukeyser, and Mr. Schacht all attach a

somewhat disconcerting amount of importance to the paragraph I wrote on poetry. I asked, in all sincerity, a simple question. Why, I inquired, is there so little in contemporary poetry that can be called melody? I did not say there ought to be melody. I did not say that poetry without melody was valueless. I did not even say that I disliked poetry without melody. I merely said that much modern poetry seemed to beat rather harshly on the ear, and I wondered why. I thought Mr. Gregory might give me an answer. Instead, he says the charge is crazy. Well, maybe, but I put this innocent question to a whole roomful of critics one night, and they offered lots of ingenious explanations, without one of them denying the assumption I was making. The assumption may be wrong, of course, but I can't account for the heat it raised in Mr. Gregory and Miss Rukeyser.

I feel the same way about Mr. Gregory's comments on realism. It is true that Mr. Gregory thinks realism is played out, whereas I don't. It is true that he would like to see realism supplanted by something else, whereas the most I can say is that I should be glad to have it supplemented by anything else that works. It is true that he has suddenly become devoted to the fable, which I regard as just another blind alley. But I don't believe that a defense of realism is the core of my review. Instead, it seems secondary to the theme to which I devoted those thirteen paragraphs.

It is probably a fact that I admire Sinclair Lewis more than Gregory does, but he might have reread my review of *It Can't Happen Here* before speaking of "inordinate praise." I began by saying, *"It Can't Happen Here* is not a great novel. It is a political tract, a novel with a message, and it can no more be judged by ordinary standards than could *Looking Backward* or *The Iron Heel."* I said, "The various characters just barely serve their functions in the tract and that is all." I said that I was writing "a political review of a political book." It might be, I ventured to say, that Lewis was looking at America with new eyes. If so, "he ought to give us the kind of book that *Babbitt* promised, a book alive with understanding, warm with sympathy, a full, rich, honest, courageous book. If *It Can't Happen Here* is an event in American politics, that would be an event in American literature." This is praise, but not exactly inordinate.

Miss Rukeyser thinks the "conversion" theme should be simply ruled out. I don't, because I know there is a great story there that hasn't yet been written. And the same is true of the strike theme. As for asking critics to practice what they preach, I think that, if Miss Rukeyser will look again at the context of the remark, she will feel less cause for disappointment.

I am very sorry that Mr. Gregory feels that I was including the thirty-five poets among those who "quibble, bicker, nag, and deny." That sentence and the whole last paragraph referred back to the currents of criticism I was discussing in the beginning of the review. It was not meant to apply to the contributors to *New Letters,* and is applicable only to a few of them.

Mr. Schacht's remarks I, feeling rather chastened by the onslaught my simple query has brought upon me from the poets, would like to leave to them. In case anybody is interested, I don't agree, but I should like to hear what Mr. Gregory and Miss Rukeyser have to say.

I should like to hear what they—and others, of course—have to say on all the points raised by my review. There is a great deal in Mr. Gregory's letter with which I agree, but nothing with which I agree more heartily than his statement that the critical issues of the day should be fought out in the pages of the *New Masses.* We can argue, as this correspondence proves, amiably and perhaps not unfruitfully. Let us by all means continue.

READER'S FORUM

To the *New Masses:*

Granville Hicks's review of *New Letters in America* [Sept. 28], Mr. Gregory's, Miss Rukeyser's, and Mr. Schacht's replies to it, and Mr. Hicks's rebuttal [Oct. 12], raise once again the question of the function of left-wing literature. While Mr. Hicks, in his rebuttal, has modified certain of his original statements and adopted a less dogmatic tone, he still adheres to the general position set down in his review. He and Mr. Gregory, therefore, despite their willingness to reach a common ground, are still in disagreement on a number of important

points. In the interests of Communism and good writing it is essential
that the difficulties in the way of a common understanding be resolved
—and they can be resolved only by being stated, examined, and
analyzed. For that reason, I should like to reopen the discussion.

Fortunately we are all agreed that Communism is good news.
We accept the Marxist analysis of history and society, and as Marxists
we believe that social and economic forces should be reflected in our
literature. What we are not agreed on is the way in which these forces
should be reflected, the exact form that our acceptance of "the central
fact in Communism," as Mr. Hicks puts it, should take. Mr. Hicks
contends that it is the business of left-wing writers to "communicate
the essential hopefulness of Communism," and maintains that the
contributors to *New Letters* have failed to do so. He does not say
that these contributors are bad writers, nor does he deny that they treat
of contemporary reality; his objections to them is that they fail "to
render the substance of the Communist hope" with sufficient militancy.

Mr. Hicks again states this objection in his rebuttal and says he
"still would like to know whether Mr. Gregory agrees or disagrees."
But that is not the point at issue. The point at issue is, as I see it,
whether or not these writers have failed to express the Communist
hope because they have not expressed it *in the particular fashion
approved by Mr. Hicks.* Now I certainly disagree—and I think so do
Miss Rukeyser and Mr. Gregory—that Mr. Hicks's kind of hopefulness is the only kind that exists within the framework of Marxism, and
I no more believe that it is a necessary component of left-wing literature than I believe that writers who lack it are therefore cynics or
defeatists. I contend that there are more ways than one in art of
expressing one's belief in the validity and necessity of Communism.
I agree with Miss Rukeyser that "whatever excellence left-wing writers
have depends more on their sensitive straight facing of present scenes
and values than on the happy posturing of their theses." I think,
further, that the critic who makes optimism about the future rather
than clear-headedness about the present his chief criterion in judging
new work is going to fall into every sort of *non sequitur.* He will be
forced as was Mr. Hicks in his review of *New Letters,* to divide
current writing into the all-too-convenient categories of optimism and
pessimism (or despair), and having made the division, he is likely to
find that his favored category will accommodate only those works
which he himself admits to be inferior efforts. Such a division, in any

case, is critically meaningless. Mr. Hicks cannot, I am sure, point to a single literary work of the first order which does not contain both elements, which does not have sources of hope as well as sources of despair. Any enduring work of art—perhaps unhappily for Mr. Hicks —is not by any means so simple as to fit into one or the other of these categories.

Mr. Hicks says he has tolerated the formula of the conversion short story and that of the strike novel because he hopes and feels that some day the formulas will be transcended and a great story and novel will result. I have no objection to his tolerating these formulas and agree that eventually they will be transcended and we shall have the great story and novel he hopes for. Whether he will recognize them once they have transcended the formulas is another matter. Meanwhile, nothing would seem to be gained when a critic becomes so devoted to a particular formula or thesis that he neither can nor wants to see anything else—which is what Mr. Hicks was guilty of in his review of *New Letters*. The assumption behind his review was that all left-wing writers should attempt to express his own kind of hopefulness. That hopefulness, I think I am right in saying, he identifies with the two formulas already mentioned. In his anxiety to find that hopefulness he disregarded other positive qualities, and for the sake of a thesis placed these young writers in a category conveniently labeled "pessimism."

In doing so he excluded many elements from their work and simplified their "message" beyond recognition. His assertion that the *New Letters* authors express the same emotions—despair, defeat, bitterness, etc.—as did the contributors to the first *American Caravan* is simply not a true presentation of the facts. What he significantly neglects to point out is that whereas the young writers of the twenties were generally content to express those emotions and stop at that, the young writers in Mr. Gregory's collection, though they may convey a feeling of despair, also attempt to reveal its underlying causes. They neither identify themselves with this feeling nor acquiesce in it. They all say, either explicitly or by implication, "These things must be changed!" If Mr. Hicks will forget his categories and formulas and examine the work before him, I think he will discover this important difference in attitude between the young writers in *New Letters* and those of an earlier generation. By indicating the conditions responsible for our present anarchy, brutality, and chaos, these writers are helping to prepare the way for a new and better kind of society. To what extent they have succeeded is another matter, but at least the attempt is an affirmative gesture. It is to this kind of affirmation, I think, that Miss Rukeyser refers when she speaks of a "hope to be worked for continually, not shouted before its time."

Marxism holds out more than a hope for the future. It is an instrument of analysis which enables the writer to discern the dialectical interaction of forces and events. The young Marxist writer has at his command a vision of the world that is at once more inclusive, more penetrating, and more integrated than other *Weltanschauungen* today, and for that reason he finds it desirable to employ a form more suited to the expression of that vision than the realistic method, at least as we find the method exemplified in most American writing of the twenties and early thirties. He would dispense with what Mr. Gregory calls "pragmatic naturalism"; he would extend the method of realism to include perceptions and awarenesses impossible to convey within the confines of naturalist fiction. Henceforth, the amassing of data will give way to the selection of the *significant* fact. Documentation will have its place, but wherever possible its work will be done by interpretation.

Such procedures are quite in line with Marxist thought. Marxist literature does not need to include everything, for it is provided with a center of reference around which facts can be ordered and given perspective and illumination. Realism as practised during recent decades was the method of men who had no center of reference, no well-ordered and defined viewpoint; consequently they had no way of telling what was truly significant and were obliged to include everything. Today's younger writers—or a good many of them—are attempting to render an object, a scene, an event, or a character so that it will possess both a factual and a symbolic meaning. Writing will thus contain another dimension—one it has been deprived of far too long. The fable will again be pressed into service, not of course by all young writers, but by those whose vision can be best expressed by that form. I say "will," but as a matter of fact the fable has already been employed by some of the most distinguished of the younger talents. Mr. Hicks will even find that two or three Soviet stories included in John Lehmann's *New Writing* are essentially fables. Mr. Gregory, then, is not asking writers to adopt a method he "had suddenly become devoted to," as Mr. Hicks incorrectly remarks; he is approving a method whose usefulness has already been demonstrated. A broad definition of the fable, moreover, would include much of the finest writing of the last fifty years or so. It would include the work of Franz Kafka which, whether or not Mr. Hicks is "impressed" by it, is worth all of American realistic fiction put together. It would include Henry James's study in good and evil, *The Turn of the Screw,* and the greatest of Thomas Mann's shorter works, *Death in Venice* and *Mario and the Magician.* What I want to stress here is not the fable as such, but the process, common to all writing of the first order, whereby the objective fact is made to stand as a symbol of some emotion, ideal, or belief that is larger than itself—as Hamlet or Don Quixote does, or Kassner in *Days of Wrath* or Spina in *Bread and Wine.*

An unfortunately literal approach and interpretation, it would seem, has prevented Mr. Hicks from recognizing these facts. It is in his comments on the poets' imagery that his literalism is most plainly revealed. Poets who introduce images like "men before a firing squad" and "machine guns" are lacking in hope, he says; such images signify "disgust, bitterness, pity, cynicism." Does Mr. Hicks really believe that firing squads and machine guns are unrelated to the Communist hope? Does he think that getting people to realize their import is not a function of Communists? What is the value of making readers optimistic about the future if one has not clarified the present for them? To say that poets should not employ images and symbols of this kind is very like saying that Communists should not write about fascism. Does Mr. Hicks want left-wing poets to be dreamers? Does he want them to avoid the less pleasant aspects of their world? His answer is probably that he does not, but that he wants them also to project the Communist hope. As I read the poets in *New Letters,* I think a good many of them do convey this hope, though not in the particular fashion approved by Mr. Hicks. That is no reason for calling them defeatists. The affirmation in their verse—a more valuable quality, incidentally, than hopefulness—is much stronger than Mr. Hicks has made out.

As for the charge of "harshness," I confess I also find it fantastic, especially when brought against a poem of such sustained music as Marya Zaturenska's. True, neither Miss Zaturenska nor the other poets in *New Letters* (unless it be Frederic Prokosch) can or should care to boast the mellifluence of, say, Elizabeth Barrett Browning. That kind of vacuous melody would scarcely be appropriate to what

they have to say. Perhaps Mr. Hicks's failure to recognize the music of
these poets is traceable to the fact that he has trained himself to listen
for a conventional kind of music—that to be found in most of the
poets of the nineteenth century—and when he does not hear it, he
concludes that the verse is harsh. Many persons, he will remember,
found the romantics crude and harsh because their prosody was less
tight than that of the eighteenth century. It is largely a matter of what
the ear has learned to expect. I suggest that if Mr. Hicks abandoned
his preconceptions as to what is "pleasing to the ear," if he familiarized
himself to a greater extent with the poets whom these young writers
have in many cases taken as models—among others, Langland, Hopkins, Pound, W. C. Williams—and then read the verse in *New Letters,*
he might find more cause for enjoyment than for complaint. I admit
that the music of most of this verse requires a trained ear in order to
be thoroughly appreciated, but I do not consider that a fault. The
matter is a technical one, of course, and to persuade Mr. Hicks that
his charge is unjust, one would really have to discuss such things as
quantity, stress, alliteration, the musical phrase, etc. That, however,
would require considerable space, and I have already written enough.

To repeat: my own and I think Miss Rukeyser's and Mr. Gregory's
chief objection is to Mr. Hicks's very literal, unimaginative interpretation of "the substance of the Communist hope"—an interpretation that
is dubious Marxism as well as a denial of some of the most important
and useful functions of literature. I do not say that Mr. Hicks's kind
of optimism is inadmissible or that it should be scrapped, but I do say
that the least he can do is to realize that there are other ways of
expressing the Communist hope, ways just as acceptable as his own
and more likely, at any rate at present, to produce good writing.

Let me conclude by suggesting that as a basis for an intelligent
approach to these and other problems we all might make use of Kenneth Burke's brilliant and extremely valuable *Attitudes Towards
History,* in my opinion the most important contribution to Marxist
criticism yet made in America.

T. C. Wilson

By Way of Answer

To the *New Masses:*

I do not see how there can be any intelligent disagreement with Mr. Wilson's contention that "there are more ways than one in art of expressing one's belief in the validity and necessity of Communism." But it seems clear that Mr. Wilson, in his anxiety to stress the variety of forms in which revolutionary content may be expressed, has fallen into a double error. And Mr. Hicks's remarks on the subject, while tending to slur over this æsthetic axiom of multiformity, did possess the virtue of isolating and examining these errors.

Mr. Wilson assumes in his letter, as he did in his review of *New Writing* last week, that "We accept the Marxist analysis of history and society and as Marxists we believe that social and economic forces should be reflected in our literature." Mr. Wilson feels that a few years ago it was inevitable that Marxists writers should emphasize two qualities: a well-developed political consciousness, and an intense hatred of fascism. "That battle has now been won," says Mr. Wilson, "at least where young writers are concerned." I believe that this is a somewhat optimistic conclusion. That battle, it seems safe to say, will not be won until an international classless society is achieved. The world of literature is not exempt from the conflict of social purpose which is the crucial phenomenon of our time. Nor are young writers, even the gifted ones, universally persuaded of those truths which are central to Mr. Wilson's own political consciousness. Mr. Wilson is satisfied that "we are all agreed that Communism is good news." It is true that in this respect Mr. Hicks, Mr. Gregory, and Miss Rukeyser do agree. But they represent a group which will for some time be on the offensive. A casual glance at the books and magazines most widely read in America is a sufficient reminder that to not a few writers the news remains unbroken. Indeed, some of the young contributors to *New Letters* neither behave nor write as if the news had reached their ears.

It is one thing to note "political consciousness" in writers and another thing to analyze the real nature of that consciousness. I mean, quite simply, that there is a difference between a man's saying or thinking he is a Marxist and his being one. Granting for the moment that it is not as necessary as it was a few years ago to convince writers that they ought to be against fascism, it still remains true that it is more necessary now than ever before to dissipate confusion as to what fascism actually is and how precisely one should fight it. When a Trotskyist writer attacks the people's front or the Soviet Union in the name of "anti-fascism" and "socialism," he betrays a political consciousness, to be sure, but not the kind that can be accepted with either complacency or gratitude. Literary criticism at the present time which escapes the responsibility of such analysis is just as distorted as literary analysis which fails to take up the social problem at all. Marxist criticism does not benevolently observe that there are different types of approach to socialism; it separates the genuine from the spurious. I am sure that Mr. Wilson agrees with this as a generalization. What he does not seem to recognize is its importance as a practical technique of criticism in precisely this period.

The second error of emphasis in which Mr. Wilson finds himself is of a more strictly literary order. It is undeniably true that Marxists cannot be satisfied with what Mr. Gregory calls "pragmatic naturalism." Marxists are neither pragmatists nor naturalists; they are dialectical materialists. We do not tell a novelist that beyond Zola or Dreiser he must proceed at his own risk. On the contrary, we welcome and are ready to assimilate new æsthetic techniques. But it seems nonsense to say that the work of Franz Kafka "is worth all of American realistic fiction put together." Nobody will be hanged for writing "fables." But surely one may be pardoned for feeling that the heritage of realistic fiction in America is more significant for us than the work of Kafka. Realism must be enriched by new sources; art which falls into a routine is deadly. As Ralph Fox pointed out in *The Novel and the People,* the tradition of realism in fiction has been a flexible one, expanding continuously in terms of new social structures and corresponding social attitudes. This expansion will continue. Naturalism is only one of the forms of realism, and it does not seem to follow that in abandoning naturalism we must all fly to the fable. I agree with Mr. Hicks that what we want is "a greater boldness, a greater willingness to risk failure, a greater resourcefulness in experimentation, a more determined search for knowledge, and a greater eagerness for experience. . . ." If Kafka or Hopkins or James can stimulate writers, there is no need to turn one's back on them. But it is hard to understand why one must be compelled to mistake enriching streams for great historical sources. There is a kind of literary sectarianism in which none of us can afford to flounder.

Samuel Sillen

Discipline in Verse

To the *New Masses:*

Since Granville Hicks has invited further comment, I might as well stick in my two cents' worth. It seems to me that the man who has spoken least in the controversy so far has said the most. But I cannot agree with Mr. Schacht in a tendency to minimize the importance of lyric poetry: I think such an attitude is a betrayal, not a defense, of culture. The ardor that goes into pure song, like the ardor that goes into revolution, is a vital and important manifestation of the human spirit; and no one devoted to either should ever disparage the other. There are times when, for economic or other considerations, the one, rather than the other, is indicated; but I hope, even in this day and hour, the same man may be a good lyric poet and a good Communist.

I should like also to support Granville Hicks's charge that modern verse is too much lacking in melody, and to add my note of explanation. It seems to me that too many revolutionary poets are politically sound in their politics, but politically unsound in their poetry; that is to say, they are still Bohemians, or, at best, anarchists, who consider themselves superior to prosodic discipline. If it is fair to insist that poetry, among other things, must consist of "human speech wrought by art into musical utterance," then I should say that about 90 percent of *New Masses* (and other Left) verse fails to be poetry for this reason alone.

For this defect, editors must assume their share of responsibility. There will be a howl of rage from the poets at my saying so, but the fact is that editors are far too easy. Their position has been like that of complaisant hotel clerks who admit to their hospitality all too readily anyone who bears the outward and visible signs of respectability. The poet who appears with what is alleged to be the muse on one arm, and a suitcase with the proper stickers on the outside dangling from the other, has no trouble in finding a room in the house. But too often all there is in the suitcase is a very minimum in the way of the necessary technical apparatus for such occasions, and a couple of copies of last year's phone book.

Rolfe Humphries

The letters printed above are representative of the viewpoints expressed in those received thus far in the discussion initiated by Granville Hick's review of *New Letters*. Other letters, which could not be printed for reasons of space limitations, were received from Robert Gessner, William Jennings, Stephen Mangin, Thomas del Vecchio, James Neugass, Arthur Ebel Steig, Roland Polsley, and Myra Marini.

—*The Editors*

IX

I LIKE AMERICA

In the fall of 1936 Hicks had withdrawn as literary editor of the *New Masses,* although he continued to write reviews and occasional essays and he remained as a contributing editor. His time was taken up with the research of British literature.

The editor of Modern Age Books had been pressing Hicks to do a book for this series and in 1937 he agreed. *I Like America* came out in mid-1938, and, as Hicks later described it, was "a venture in propaganda." *I Like America* is a classic statement of the Communist position in the popular front period (1935-1939) in which the slogan was "Communism Is Twentieth Century Americanism." Evangelical yet totally undogmatic and devoid of the Stalinist jargon, *I Like America* is a description of exactly what Hicks liked about America (focusing on New England and adjacent New York) and what he did not like (depressions, poverty, poor housing, inadequate food, education and medical care.) His thesis was that America could be a nation of peace and prosperity if the working class and the middle class could unite to support a planned economy. This thesis was neither sectarian nor revolutionary but reformist in the progressive tradition.

I Like America was the first (and last) of Hicks's books that the Communist Party endeavored to promote seriously. This, of course, was due to the book's reiteration of the Party line.

Quite popular, the little book engendered a considerable volume of correspondence from individuals all over the country. Most people wrote to the author simply to ask questions. Hicks used the *New Masses* to grapple as best he could with some of the more important questions raised in the letters. He wrote four essays to this end between August and November of 1938. The essays are forthright, lucid and tell us as much about the author as about the times.

Why Not Be Selfish?

Some three months after its publication, *I Like America* has had only a handful of reviews. So far as I know, no New York newspaper except the *World-Telegram* and the *Times* has noticed the book. *Time*, the *Nation*, and the *New Yorker* have ignored it. Most of the reviews that I have seen appeared in small-city newspapers scattered through the country.

But if the book has had few reviews, it has brought me more letters than *The Great Tradition* and *John Reed* put together. More than fifty strangers have written me about it: a manufacturer in Ohio, a teacher in Tennessee, a lawyer in Colorado, a worker in New Jersey, a student at Harvard, a doctor in Vermont, an engineer in New York.

Two of these correspondents expressed vigorous disapproval. Several limited themselves to kind words. The majority asked questions. I have tried to answer the questions in letters to my correspondents, but it has not always been easy to find time for adequate answers, and I find, moreover, that the same questions are asked again and again.

What I am going to try to do in *New Masses*, then, is to answer some of those repeated questions. If some persons have been enough troubled by them to go to the bother of writing me, the chances are that they have occurred to many other readers of *I Like America*.

The question I want to deal with this week was raised with peculiar cogency in a long letter that came from Boston. The author begins by saying that he believes in Communism—"as an ideal, as a wonderful theory." "I should like to have Communism," he goes on, "but I have abandoned hope of such a phenomenon in this country in my lifetime—and my lifetime is all that matters to me. Animals are selfish by nature, and I am an animal. Why should I become a crusader, a martyr for a benevolent cause, or even an enthusiastic believer in an ideal that I am convinced I shall never see. Hitch your wagon to a star in flights of theory, I say, but stay out of the wagon."

I wish this correspondent had told me how he earns his living, for I should like to know why he is so sure he is acting in his own interests in acquiescing in the capitalist system. He apparently believes —and there are still many like him—that he can make a choice between Socialism and the status quo. Millions of Americans thought that in 1929, and a year later they were walking the streets. Millions

of Germans thought that in 1932, and a year later they were tighten-
ing their belts and trembling before Nazi brutality.

The system does not stand still. As capitalism declines, there is
unemployment, and, unless people struggle for relief, there is starvation. Let it decline still further, and, unless the people resist, there is
fascism. Perhaps this gentleman has nothing to lose by economic depression, nothing to lose under fascism, nothing to lose if the United
States goes to war; otherwise I cannot see how he can pretend that his
immediate interests are not involved. An intelligently selfish man
has got to consider the kind of world there will be five, ten, or twenty
years from now.

I believe, then, that this correspondent of mine is, from his own
point of view, betting on the wrong horse, but I can see why he may not
think so. He might say something like this: "I am a reasonably intelligent and resourceful member of the middle class. I am not counting
on becoming rich, but I have a comfortable income, and, if I am
discreet, it is likely to increase as time goes on. I realize that, as the
capitalist system declines—and I know it will decline—my income
may be reduced. Nevertheless, I think I am smart enough to keep on
top for a long time, and certainly I will be better off than I would if I
endangered my job here and now by taking an unpopular stand. As
for the revolution—well, if it comes in my time, which I doubt, I guess
I'll manage to get on the bandwagon, and, even if I don't, I'll have
had a good many years of easy living, whereas you guys will have
worked hard and lived miserably, and you'll probably be just damn
fools enough to go on working hard after the revolution."

But perhaps my correspondent wouldn't say this. A lot of people
actually live according to some such principles, but very few express
them. Instead, they defend their opposition to Communism on all sorts
of fancy intellectual grounds.

Why should they bother? At the risk of seeming preachy, I venture the guess that it's because they know they have other interests
besides easy living.

I suspect that my correspondent recognizes this. I observe, for
example, that he goes on to talk about "the primitive mass-mind," and
suggests that the nation "is composed largely of imbeciles." Why does
he do this? Even if his estimate of the intelligence of the American
masses were correct, it would still be irrelevant. He has what he

claims to be a good case. Why, then, should he try to justify his attitude by talking about the stupidity of the masses?

It seems clear that he is trying to bolster up his argument because he is not so sure of himself as he pretends to be. If the American people are morons, then they probably deserve to be exploited, and in any case nothing can be done about it, and so he might as well go his own pleasant way. Of course he says that he intends to go his own sweet way anyhow, but it's much easier if he can convince himself that it won't really make any difference.

In *I Like America* I tell about a man I met on a train, who, after a long and intelligent discussion of literary topics, turned to politics and said, "People are corrupt, and you can't do anything about it. In thousands and thousands of years you can't do anything about it. I know there are injustices under our system, but there are injustices under every system, and always will be. Human nature is bad." And I go on to tell how I discovered that this man was a lawyer engaged in rather shady practices. He had to believe human nature was bad in order to justify his own conduct.

No Marxist would deny that men are motivated by self-interest, but what every Marxist knows is that self-interest is a complicated thing. Marx realized that capitalism would be abolished only by those who had an interest in superseding it, but he knew, if only from self-analysis, that an interest in the abolition of capitalism might be of many kinds. The Russian Revolution meant simple material things— peace, land, bread—to the masses of the Russian people, who therefore fought for it, but to the Bolsheviks it meant justice, equality, and a new civilization, and without the Bolsheviks there would not have been a successful revolution.

The complexity of human motives still baffles the psychologists, but we do know that they are complex. People do want comfort, even luxury, and many are willing to sacrifice everything else in order to have comfort and luxury. But they usually know that something has been sacrificed, something that could give their lives richness and meaning. We Communists object bitterly to the fact that millions are undernourished in a land of plenty, but we also object, just as strongly, to the fact that men and women are not allowed to develop the capacities within them. What my correspondent proposes to do is deliberately to stultify some of his capacities in order to have an easy life.

I wonder if he has ever looked carefully at men who have done this. When I was writing the biography of John Reed, I examined the book in which his classmates told what had happened to them in the twenty-five years since graduation. It is the most depressing reading I have ever done. One man after another confesses that he finds his principal satisfaction in golf or bridge or drinking. Actually they make clear that they find no satisfaction at all. Many of these men could not have been different from what they are. Their circumstances were such that there was no alternative to the kind of life they followed. My correspondent sees an alternative, and yet he talks about rejecting it—believing that he is following self-interest in doing so.

What we know is that, if the masses of people don't do something about it, the world is going to be an increasingly uncomfortable place to live in. Unless, as I have said, my correspondent has somehow convinced himself that he will be untouched by depression, fascism, and war, I do not see how he can deny that. What he can deny is that it will be to his immediate personal interest to be one of the millions who struggle. In terms of dollars and cents this may or may not be true, but in terms of other values it is not true. I doubt if many psychologists would laugh at me for maintaining that self-respect is a value. We have all seen what happens, psychologically, to the people who sell out, and it's not a pretty spectacle. After a fairly extensive experience with people who live according to my correspondent's principles and with people who are working for what they believe in, I am willing to say that, whether you call their motive altruism or enlightened selfishness, the latter are the winners.

August 16, 1938

What Can I Do?

Some reviewers have complained because *I Like America* offers no detailed plan for the remedying of the conditions it describes. I can see why the reviewers are disturbed. If I had laid down such a program, they could have spent their time in picking it to pieces, and thus pleasantly distracted themselves and their readers from the real problem the book raises. The book, however, is intended as a challenge, not a blueprint. It is all too easy for some people, if they have found what they regard as a flaw in this program or that, to convince themselves that they don't have to do anything. What I wanted to do, if I could, was to make my readers feel the need for change so urgently that, if they turned down one program, they would immediately start hunting for a better one. More than that I wanted them to do certain immediately possible and practical things and to keep on doing them while they made up their minds about the next steps.

Because of all this, I am not troubled when critics rebuke me for not laying down a program of action. But when readers take the trouble to sit down and write me letters, I realize that I must answer their questions as best I can. "Your book has got under my skin," one writes. "Tell me what I can do." "What can I do?" asks another. "Don't tell me to join the Communist Party. I'm not ready for that. Maybe I ought to be. Maybe some day I will be. But right now I'm not. There must be hundreds of thousands of people who, for good reasons or bad, feel as I do, and yet agree with your account of what is wrong with the United States today and want the kind of America you want. What are we to do?"

Any regular reader of *New Masses* knows the right answers, and yet I have found that they are not so easy to put into words. One thing is clear: We all ought to be educating ourselves so that we can find our way round in this complicated world of ours. I shall, therefore, deal in another article with the subject of getting a Marxian education. But in this article I shall try to outline a program of action.

It is a program for the kind of people who have been writing me letters; so let us see what they do believe and what they don't. They believe that a large proportion of people in America are badly fed, badly clothed, badly housed. They believe that the majority of Americans have no security. And they believe that poverty and insecurity are unnecessary. In short, they see that our economic system is functioning badly. Some of them, however, are not sure that the system cannot be patched up, and others, who are willing to admit that it is a failure, have only the vaguest idea of what should take its place.

Is there any program that will satisfy those who have a lingering faith in capitalism as well as those who have varied ideas about supplanting it? And is this program specific enough to give my correspondents something to do?

Such a program is at least hinted at in *I Like America*. We must insist that capitalism serve the interests of all the people. We know that the United States can produce enough for everybody. We believe, therefore, that the private individuals who own the productive resources of the country have a responsibility. What we propose to do is to see that they fulfill their social obligations.

How can this be done? Well, there is one way that has proved successful. It is obvious that, from my point of view and that of my correspondents, an employer who pays inadequate wages is not fulfilling his social obligations. When, therefore, his workers get together, form a union, and use their united strength to raise wages and improve conditions, they are not merely serving their personal interests. Labor unions are instruments for forcing private capitalists to fulfill public obligations.

The first thing, then, that we can say to the kind of individual who has been writing me is, "Join a trade union. If there is no union in your field, then join whatever organization most closely corresponds to a union—the Lawyers Guild, say, or the Authors League. But don't stop there; don't content yourself with signing your name and paying your dues. Give the union your best support. And if it happens, as it might, to be a rather ineffectual, or even a rather corrupt type of organization, don't withdraw in disgust, but do your best to make it serve the purposes it ought to serve."

There is another thing. I am shocked to find people who call themselves liberals calmly walking through picket lines. If you admit what I have been saying about the role of unions in the capitalist system, the success of all unions is important to you. The losing of a strike is your loss.

The whole job, however, cannot be left to the unions; the government, which is supposed to be our government, must help. Experience shows us that the capitalists resist all attempts to raise the standard of living, and the capitalists are very powerful. When they can, they use the government to serve their purpose. We all know, for example, how local and state police and national guards have been used to break strikes. So have courts, through the abuse of their power of issuing injunctions.

The federal government at the present time does not propose to be used for such purposes. It has, moreover, created machinery—the National Labor Relations Board—to protect the rights of workers to organize. And it has also adopted a wages-and-hours law, which, though the standards it sets are very low, indicates one way of making capitalists do their duty to society.

Anyone can see that it makes a great deal of difference what kind of government we have in our city, state, and nation. The government may help us in our attempt to secure abundance for all, or it may thwart us. The progressive individual, therefore, must look for a progressive government. The capitalists prefer profits for a few rather than plenty for everyone, and they are aided by many short-sighted persons who ought to know better. These reactionaries would like to get rid of whatever progressive measures the Roosevelt administration has adopted, and they will therefore seek to elect their candidates this fall. They can be defeated if the progressives are united and energetic, but, as the defeat of Maury Maverick shows, we must not lie down on the job.

There are other types of essential political action. For many years now there have been millions of men who could not get jobs. We say, "If a capitalist system cannot give these men work, then the government must do so, and it must raise the money by taxing the capitalists." The reactionaries would give the unemployed the smallest possible amount of relief, would let them starve if they dared. We, on the other hand, propose not only to give these people the means of subsistence but also to use their strength and skill for the benefit of society. The administration of relief today is often inadequate, but it is on the right track, and it is up to us to keep it there. Nothing is more important in our program than the raising of relief standards, for, if they go down, the whole standard of living suffers.

I have dwelt on the fact that there is a group of people—I call them reactionaries—who are working, consciously or unconsciously, for a program of scarcity rather than a program of plenty. These people know that they are in a minority, and they therefore try to divide the majority by skillful propaganda in the newspapers they control. They also stand ready to use violence to check the majority.

We have seen exactly this done in Jersey City, in Johnstown, Massillon, and many other communities. My correspondents, I am sure, think that freedom of speech is a good thing in itself, and so do I. But there is an added reason for working for the liberties of the masses of the people, and that is that they are a guarantee of the maintenance of the American standard of living. If our civil liberties are taken away from us, we cannot hope that the American people will secure the abundance that is their birthright.

This is so obviously true that many reactionaries desire above all else to destroy the freedom of the masses. They see that in Germany and Italy, under fascism, labor unions have been destroyed, the leaders of the people have been murdered or imprisoned, and all democratic rights have been abolished. They see that in those countries it has been possible to drive the standard of living lower and lower. And they would be glad to see fascism established here. The progressive citizen, who hates fascism, is quick to oppose those organizations that are openly fascist, but he does not always realize that any successful attack on democracy is a step towards the hated dictatorship. Whenever a Mayor Hague gets away with his anti-democratic misrule, it emboldens those who would like to see the total destruction of democracy.

The threat of fascism at home cannot be separated from the threat of fascism abroad. The progressive citizen wants peace, and he usually knows well enough that fascism constitutes the great danger of war. There are three ways in which he can combat that danger. First, he can fight every manifestation of fascism at home. Second, he can give practical assistance to the people of Spain and China, who are at war with fascism. Third, he can work constantly for the adoption by his own government of a policy—such as that outlined by President Roosevelt in his Chicago speech—that will unite peace-loving nations against the fascist aggressors.

I wrote something like this to one of my correspondents, and he replied, "But what do *I* do?" So I recapitulated: "Join a union and work in it. Take part in the campaign for progressive candidates this fall. If there is a local group that protects civil liberties, work within it; if there isn't start one. Organize meetings for Spanish relief, get people to boycott Japanese goods, and join the American League for Peace and Democracy."

But, somebody wants to know, what has all this to do with Communism? Just this: If we Communists are right in believing that capitalism is going to decline further and further, then it will become clear in time that the only way to protect the American standard of living is for the people to take over the means of production. In other words, we believe that these very measures will lead to the establishment of Socialism, which is our goal. If we are wrong, if abundance for all is compatible with the continuance of the capitalist system, then you win In fact, as I see it, you win either way.

August 30, 1938

What Shall I Read?

In a previous article I tried to describe a program of action for readers of *I Like America*. A number of my correspondents, I pointed out, had accepted the major premise of that book, namely, that poverty and insecurity could and should be abolished. Now they wanted to know what they should do about it. There were, I said, two things to recommend: study and action. Having dealt in that article with the subject of action, I want to deal in this one with the subject of study.

The two subjects are more closely related than my correspondents are likely to realize. I believe, as I have said, that gradual reforms can lead to drastic change. But anyone who knows history is aware that, during the past thirty or forty years, various organizations—for example, the British Labor Party—have put forth some such program as I outlined. Yet, far from bringing about Socialism, these organizations have actually failed, in the long run, to secure the moderate and wholly reasonable reforms they asked for. How can we be sure that we will not be similarly disillusioned?

A book has been written to answer this all-important question, and I have been recommending it to my correspondents—John Stra-

chey's new volume *What Are We To Do?* Strachey does not demand
the immediate and unconditional overthrow of capitalism. On the contrary, his practical program is very much the same as that I proposed.
What he maintains is that such a program cannot succeed in the hands
of those who do not understand the nature of the capitalist system. It
will work, but only if its adherents are led by men who know exactly
what they are doing.

I realize that some of my correspondents are not going to be
interested in study. That is a pity, but the fact remains that they can
go on doing useful work for the progressive cause. But there are others
who will want to master their job. They will want to see where they are
going and why. It is for them that I am writing this article.

In lectures I have told how a young Italian once said to me, "It
is only by study that an intellectual can raise himself to the level of the
proletariat." This is no empty paradox. Of course proletarians have to
study too, but the victim of exploitation undeniably has an advantage
in understanding its nature. Union activity does not teach a man all
he needs to know about the capitalist system, but it does teach him a
great deal that the rest of us have to get by intellectual effort.

Most of my correspondents, however, have no idea of under-
taking an ambitious program of study. They want to be given the
name of one book that will tell them all they need to know. Usually I
recommend John Strachey's *The Coming Struggle for Power,* because
of its eloquence, its clarity, and its scope. Dealing as it does with
history, economics, politics, philosophy, and literature, it is bound to
touch the interests of any reader.

But the book was written some years ago, and today it needs
some kind of supplement. The book that I would put beside it is *The
Peril of Fascism,* by A. B. Magil and Henry Stevens. This deals more
specifically with American conditions, and it is up to date. When you
have read these two books, read Strachey's new one, which I have
already mentioned, *What Are We to Do?* The three volumes will give
you an excellent guide to the understanding of your own country and
the world.

I hope, however, that many of you will want to go to the fountain-
head of Marxian thought. I am aware that some of my correspondents
have an initial prejudice against Marxism. But today, whether you
agree with the Marxists or not, an understanding of their position is
essential for any man or woman who pretends to be educated.

Two aids to study might be mentioned first. Strachey's *Theory and Practice of Socialism* has an excellent list, with comments, of the Marxian classics. Then there is the *Handbook of Marxism,* which contains extracts from the major works of Marx, Engels, Lenin, and Stalin. A careful reading of its thousand pages would certainly be an education, and yet, as Strachey says, extracts cannot be substitutes for the works themselves. Moreover, in my experience, the extract, because it is set off by itself, and often seems rather abstract, is frequently harder to read than the whole work. Finally, many of these works are available in cheap editions, and the reader can therefore begin his study without much expense.

The Communist Manifesto is the obvious starting point, and, though it was written ninety years ago, it is still the best starting point. From its famous beginning—"A specter is haunting Europe—the specter of Communism"—to its famous ending—"The proletarians have nothing to lose but their chains. They have a world to win. Working-men of all countries, unite!"—it is eloquent, exciting, and revealing. The forces it describes are still the forces that struggle for control of the world. Its analysis of the weaknesses of capitalism is, in its essentials, proven true every day. The types of non-scientific Socialism it describes are still with us in various forms. It is not only an historical document that every educated person ought to read because of its influence on world history; it is relevant to our world, and will be so long as capitalism survives.

Where do you go next? If you are interested in economics, you turn, of course, to Marx's *Capital.* Only the first volume was published in Marx's lifetime. The second and third volumes were edited by Engels. A fourth volume, edited by Kautsky, has never been translated into English. The second and third volumes are available only in the edition published by Charles Kerr. The Modern Library has published the first volume in the Kerr translation. Everyman's Library has published the first volume, in two of their volumes, in a new translation by Eden and Cedar Paul. This edition, which has a rather pointless and misleading introduction by G. D. H. Cole, seems to me easier to read than the other.

Capital is hard reading, but not so hard as many people suppose. The chapters of economic theory must, it is true, be read again and again to be understood, but the historical chapters are vivid and lively. And all through the book, even when the reasoning is closest, there is a sense of Marx's extraordinary personality. "Why didn't you—or any-one—ever tell me that Marx's writing has some charm?" asked a cor-respondent to whom I had somewhat hesitantly recommended *Capital*.

Because Marx's historical writings are easier to read than his economic theory, you might prefer to begin with his pamphlets on France. *The Eighteenth Brumaire of Louis Bonaparte* begins this way: "Hegel says somewhere that all great historic facts and personages recur twice. He forgot to add: 'Once as tragedy, and again as farce.' " This suggests the tone of what is at one and the same time a brilliant polemic and a magnificent analysis of social forces. *The Civil War in France,* dealing with the Commune, shows the same analytic power, and also discusses proletarian tactics.

Or perhaps you would get more out of Engels' *Socialism, Scien-tific and Utopian,* which is an abbreviation of a book called *Herr Eugen Dühring's Revolution in Science,* usually referred to as *Anti-Dühring.* The longer work carries on a running controversy with a gentleman who has thus been immortalized, and this makes it hard reading. The shorter version is excellent reading, and its preface is one of the best things Engels ever wrote. It is the easiest way of coming to understand the scope and distinguishing characteristics of Marxism. The reader who is especially interested in philosophy and science will go on to read *Anti-Dühring* as a whole, and then Lenin's *Materialism and Empirio-Criticism.*

Franz Mehring's *Karl Marx* deals quite as much with Marx's ideas as with his life, and is admirably done. I suspect, however, that you would get more pleasure and more information from the *Selected Correspondence* of Marx and Engels. The letters deal with economics, history, philosophy, with contemporary events and persons, with every development in the Socialist movement from 1846 to 1895. Of course ideas are seldom developed fully, but you constantly come across com-ments that light up this aspect or that of Marxian thought.

There is much more of Marx and Engels that you will want to read, but, long before you reach this point, you ought to begin making the acquaintance of their great successor, Lenin. Twelve volumes of his *Selected Works* have been published in this country, but I should like to mention three tremendously important pamphlets. *Imperialism,* written during the World War, is a precise description of why the war took place. *The State and Revolution,* written on the eve of the Russian Revolution, is the classic account of both the immediate and the ultimate aims of the proletarian revolution. *Left-Wing Communism* discusses the problems of the Communist Parties of the world after the establishment of the Soviet Union.

Lenin's *The Teachings of Karl Marx* is a good introduction to Marx and Engels, and Stalin's *Foundations of Leninism* is an excellent approach to Lenin's writings. Stalin's *Marxism and the National and Colonial Question* is the authority in the field that Stalin has made peculiarly his own. His "Address to the Graduates of the Red Army Academy," included in the *Handbook of Marxism,* takes up problems that have arisen in the later stages of Soviet development.

Speaking of the Soviet Union, I realize that this is a subject on which more information is always desired. There are innumerable books of personal impressions, ranging from the enthusiastically favorable to the bitterly hostile. The works of Walter Duranty, Anna Louise Strong, and Maurice Hindus are, I gather, reliable on the whole, and I can testify that they are interesting. However, to one who, like myself, has never been in the Soviet Union, the Webbs' *Soviet Communism* is the indispensable book, for it covers all the ground and answers all the questions.

What about the Communist Party in the United States? Certainly the student ought to begin with William Z. Foster's *From Bryan to Stalin,* which is an account of thirty years of the American labor movement by one of its best-loved and most active leaders. This book gives the background for Earl Browder's *The People's Front,* which discusses the aims and accomplishments of the Communist Party at the present time. This, in turn, provides the proper setting for the pamphlet that, at the moment, everyone interested in Communism ought to read—Browder's report to the tenth convention of the party, *The Democratic Front.* One other book must be placed with these: Dimitrov's *The United Front,* which explains Communist policy throughout the world.

October 4, 1938

What About the USSR?

It may as well be admitted at the outset that no reader of *I Like America* has asked me this question. Perhaps there is no reason why a reader should. The book makes it clear that I am talking about American conditions and American needs. The problems I describe have to be solved regardless of what is going on in the USSR.

It is the reviewers who have been talking about the Soviet Union. I think I know why. Here, let us say, is a young man who has been asked to review the book for Section Five of the New York Sunday *Times*. On the one hand, he knows that J. Donald Adams will not be pleased if he praises a book by a Communist. On the other, he finds the book's arguments fairly watertight. What is he to do? Well, Communists are not, to say the least, enemies of the Soviet Union. Moreover, I state in the book that I find the accomplishments of the Soviets encouraging. What is easier than to damn the USSR, hoping thus to damn the book?

If the reviewers spoke for themselves alone, I should not bother to devote an article in this series to the Soviet Union, but I am afraid that some of the 25,000 readers have the same objections. And I am also afraid that they do not write me for the very reason that they feel they have settled something when they say, "Bolsheviks! Stalin! Purges!" That is why I want to make this point clear.

I am not an expert on the Soviet Union. I have not spent even the traditional six weeks in Moscow and Leningrad. This is not something I boast about; on the contrary, I regard it as a misfortune. I should like to go to the Soviet Union—for six weeks or, if possible, longer. But it may as well be pointed out that, at the moment, my information, like that of most of my readers and reviewers, is secondhand.

I should like to go to the USSR, but I do not think my not having been there lessens the value of my book. One does not have to be an authority on the Soviets in order to understand that, if the average annual income of one-third of all American families is $471, there must be a great deal of misery in the United States. Nearly half of all our citizens are inadequately housed, clothed, and fed. Only one American in ten lives in comfort. And this is perfectly unnecessary, since we are capable of producing enough for everybody. These are facts about America, and one can interpret them without having set foot in Moscow.

I Like America seeks to call these facts to the attention of the American people. It describes a situation and asks, "What are you going to do about it?" As I have said in an earlier article, its aim is to emphasize the need for action, not to prescribe a particular program. I tell, of course, what I think we ought to do, but I put my program in the form of a suggestion. "If you do not like my proposal," I say, "have you a better one? We must do something."

I am not trying to deceive anybody, however. I personally believe that only Socialism can give us the abundance that is our birthright, and I make this quite clear. This ought to indicate for what reasons and to what extent I am interested in the Soviet Union. There Socialism has been tried for more than twenty years. I should be altogether a fool if I did not ask myself what this trial has proved about the nature of Socialism.

It has proved a good deal. It has shown that Socialism can steadily increase production, can eliminate depressions, can banish unemployment, and can raise the standard of living of a whole people. This is what we want to know. In a sense, other achievements of the Soviet Union—the emancipation of women, for example, the abolition of illiteracy, and the elimination of race problems—are irrelevant. If Socialism can use a country's productive resources, as capitalism cannot, that is all that is necessary for the purposes of our argument.

You see how silly it becomes to complain that the USSR is not Utopia. Only crackpot romanticists have ever said that it was. The friends of the Soviet Union are well aware of its shortcomings, and, if they usually seem more concerned with defending than with criticizing it, that is because they naturally hasten to answer the lies of its enemies. Many of the stories circulated in supposedly reputable newspapers are so fabulously false that all one can do is brand them as slanders. But to deny flatly such canards is not to maintain that all is perfect.

Never having been in the Soviet Union, I cannot pretend to talk about details, but I can recognize general tendencies. And what amazes me is that, in the face of such handicaps, so much has been accomplished. After years of czarist corruption and maladministration, after world war and counter-revolution and foreign intervention, the Soviets undertook not only to rebuild a devastated Russia but also to establish a new kind of social order. And they have had to do their work while surrounded by desperate enemies.

If Socialism had been tried under ideal conditions and had failed, then it might be legitimate to object to any advocacy of the socialization of the means of production. But Socialism has been tried under almost the worst possible conditions, and has succeeded. That is the one fact that is relevant to my argument in *I Like America*.

If we examine more closely the reasoning of the reviewers, their fallacies become perfectly clear. They say in effect that, because conditions are less than perfect in the Soviet Union, we must put up with an economy of scarcity in the United States. Their account of conditions often seems to me mistaken, but I am willing to waive that point for the moment, for, even if the situation in the Soviet Union were much worse than they maintain, my argument would be unaffected.

Take, for example, the question of civil liberties in the Soviet Union, a question that often agitates those who are singularly indifferent to violations of the rights of American citizens. I am in no position to make a first-hand pronouncement on this point. Friends who have been in the Soviet Union tell me that the average worker there has far more liberty than the average worker in the United States. Knowing a little about what happens to workers in the big factories and the company towns, I can believe this. And freedom of speech on the job is about as important as anything can be.

But I know that this won't satisfy the liberals. They are thinking about their own middle-class privileges. They say that over here they have a right to criticize the government, whereas in the Soviet Union they wouldn't have. To a certain extent they are, so far as I can tell, right. Certain types of criticism are tolerated in the United States that aren't tolerated in the USSR.

It would be easy to say a good deal about the limitations on freedom of speech that exist, even for the intellectuals, in the United States—the economic restrictions that are more potent than laws can ever be. But I don't want to raise that argument. What puzzles me is why anybody should expect complete freedom of speech in the USSR. We have Nazi agents in this country, with which Germany certainly does not expect to go to war in the near future. Who can doubt that Germany is using every opponent of the Soviet regime to undermine a nation against which it is plotting immediate warfare? And who can blame the Soviet Union for using every method at its disposal for checking them? I am not a bloodthirsty person, and that is why I wish the Spanish government had taken severe measures to restrain its foes as soon as it came into power.

No doubt mistakes are made and injustices are done, but I wonder if we have the right to demand perfection. I grow somewhat impatient with persons who make so much of the little mistakes and fail to recognize the great achievements. You may say that the achievements of the Soviet Union are a matter for argument. Look, however, at its role in the international situation, which is something that anyone can understand, whether he has been to the USSR or not. Who has helped the Spanish people? Not the United States, for all its vaunted love of democracy. Who has helped the Chinese? Not our country, not England, or France. Who staunchly stood by treaty obligations to the Czechs? Not the so-called democracies of the West. The critics of the Soviet Union might try to imagine what the world situation would have been, these past five years, without the influence of that country. Today, when the moral bankruptcy of the British and French governments has been so devastatingly exposed, the defenders of democracy and peace everywhere know that their great reliance is the USSR.

I am not trying to balance the good and the bad, so that I can prove that the bad is slightly outweighed. I believe that the fundamental tendencies of the USSR are all good. But, on the other hand, I do not want to appear to minimize whatever evils there are. It is unnecessary to minimize them, for the Soviet Union is big enough to acknowledge its shortcomings and try to overcome them.

As for the argument that, if we try to introduce Socialism in the United States, we will have precisely the same evils, that seems to me nonsense. Wherever Socialism is attempted, it will have to be developed in terms of the situation that exists at that time and that place. When the oppressors use violence, they make violence the only weapon that can be employed against them. It is obvious, for example, that, when the revolution takes place in Germany, it will be a bloody affair.

So far as the United States is concerned, it is conceivable that, if we do not resolutely resist them now, the profit-makers will succeed in fastening their economy of scarcity upon us by the use of force. They may establish a despotism as terrible as the czar's in pre-war Russia or Hitler's in present-day Germany. If that happens, a time will come when the only salvation of the American people will be a conflict as cruel and exhausting as the War of Independence or the Civil War.

Socialism, that is, may come through a war, with war's characteristic disregard of individual rights and war's inevitable destruction of life and resources. If Socialism comes that way, it will be because it is the only alternative to a tyranny even more terrible.

But nothing could be more stupid than for us to believe that at this point we are committed to such a development. If we permit the profit-makers, who are faced with a disintegrating capitalist system, to put heavier and heavier burdens on the rest of us, we will reach a point at which violent revolution is the only way out. Today, however, there may be still time for us to effect a peaceful transition. At any rate we must use our democratic rights to curb the powers of the capitalists and to force them to serve the interests of the people. I believe, as I have said, that such a program will eventually lead to the abolition of capitalism, but the important thing is to act now, in the interests of the 90 percent of the American people who do not have an American standard of living.

The establishment of Socialism in this country will involve plenty of problems. Whether it will also involve hardships and sufferings and terrible losses depends on us. If we have sense enough to keep on moving in the direction of an economy of abundance, we can make the transition with a minimum of disturbance. If, however, we wait until Socialism is the only alternative to tyranny, we will have to pay for our folly.

In any case we are not going to duplicate the history of Russia. We can learn from its history, but its development is neither to be taken as a blueprint nor regarded as a bugaboo. "I have seen the future," Lincoln Steffens said when he went to Russia soon after the revolution, "and it works." That is the important thing: Socialism works. It is a good thing for us to believe that we can make it work better than the Russians have, and probably we can. The important fact, however, is that we know it does work.

I would not want anything I have said to obscure my admiration for what the Soviet people have done or my gratitude to them for their defense of world peace. I think I recognize as clearly as anyone the importance of studying the Soviets. But our job, after all, is over here. And even if I held very different views on the Soviet Union, I should still believe that job ought to be done.

November 15, 1938

X

ON LEAVING THE COMMUNIST PARTY

The signing on August 23, 1939 of the Nazi-Soviet non-aggression pact put to rest the popular front strategy and, in the process, threw the international Communist movement into disarray. Coming late to the recognition of the dangers of fascism (the German Communists on Stalin's orders had helped the Nazis seize power in 1932-33), the Communist parties throughout the world had grown tremendously in membership by being in the forefront of the struggle against fascism. The appeal of antifascism having disappeared overnight, the Communists faced major desertions in their ranks in the months that followed.

Hicks remained a few weeks longer in the Party and then resigned quietly. He sent a letter to the *New Republic* giving his reasons for leaving the Party. He also took his leave from the *New Masses* and a six year relationship came to an end. Thus it is appropriate to conclude this collection of Granville Hicks's writings for the *New Masses* with this letter.

The letter is not the last word Hicks has written on his involvement with the Communist movement in the 1930s. During the McCarthy period of 1954 he wrote an evaluation of that earlier experience entitled *Where We Came Out* and in which he criticized the McCarthy "red scare" tactics. Ten years later in his autobiography, *Part of the Truth*, Hicks placed the period of his Communist experience within the context of his entire life.

Letter to the Editor of the New Republic

SIR: I joined the Communist Party, after long hesitation, because I believed in its aims and because it seemed to offer the best way of working for those aims. As a party member, participating in its work on many levels, I became more and more convinced of its effectiveness. I am now resigning from the party because it is no longer an organization in which I can be effective.

The occasion of my resignation is the Soviet-German pact, but that does not mean that I am prepared to condemn the pact and its consequences. I see the validity of some of the arguments put forth in its defense. Furthermore, the record of the Soviet Union compels me to suspend judgment. It is possible that history will prove the soundness and wisdom of the Soviet leaders. I am still ready to give them the benefit of the doubt. The truth is that I do not know what is happening in Europe, and until I have far more information than I have now I cannot come to any conclusion about Soviet foreign policy.

That is my immediate quarrel with the Communist Party of the United States. If the party had left any room for doubt, I could go along with it, at least for the present. But defense of the pact is now an integral part of the line and, indeed, has inevitably become the most important item of political belief. Leaders of the party have generously urged me to take all the time I wanted to make up my mind. They have sympathized with the difficulty of my decision, and have not made the slightest effort to force my adherence to the party position. But they have made it clear that, if I eventually found it impossible to defend the pact, and defend it in their terms, there was nothing for me to do but resign.

In common with many of my friends, I have been much more disturbed by what has happened in the American party in the past month than by what has happened in the Soviet Union. I cannot now defend the pact, but I can conceive of history's justifying it. I can see no justification for the behavior of the party.

The party is now telling us that the pact was a necessary and wise move. If that is true, the leaders of the party should have prepared the American people for such a possibility. They tell us now that Stalin's speech last March to the eighteenth congress of the CPSU foreshadowed this development. This is wisdom after the event. No

429

party leader, prior to August 21, had ever drawn such conclusions from the speech. On the contrary, when journalists predicted such a pact, they were indignantly denounced. I am not saying that advance notice should have been given to the world by the Soviets; I am saying that an analysis which ruled out the possibility of a pact was false.

Moreover, so far as one can judge from all the evidence, the leaders themselves were completely unprepared for what has happened. They were unprepared for it, and they did not understand it. If they had only said this, if they had only admitted their ignorance, the Communist Party of the United States would be intact today. But instead they insisted that the Soviet-German non-aggression pact was the greatest possible contribution to peace and democracy, and offered anything that came into their heads as proof. They rushed into print with apologetics completely devoid of clarity and logic. Only one conclusion could be drawn: if the party leaders could not defend the Soviet Union intelligently, they would defend it stupidly.

If anyone had any illusions about Moscow gold, which I may say for the sake of the record I never saw the slightest evidence of, these recent weeks should have destroyed them. Nothing could be clearer than the fact that Communists in this country had not been given the slightest inkling of what was to happen. If the leaders had frankly admitted this, if they had simply pointed to the record of the Soviet Union and asked people to wait and see, they would have strengthened the party. But they insisted on giving the impression that they were under orders from Moscow, without having the authority that a close tie with the Soviets would have given them.

The leaders of the Communist Party have tried to appear omniscient, and they have succeeded in being ridiculous. They have clutched at straws, juggled sophistries, shut their eyes to facts. Their predictions have almost uniformly been proved wrong within twenty-four hours. They have shown that they are strong in faith—which the future may or may not justify—and weak in intelligence.

One thing that particularly concerns me is the fact that, as the party has retreated from one untenable position after another, it has revealed the likelihood that its domestic policy may be drastically altered. Though I have been a warm supporter of the democratic front, I have not been uncritical of the way in which the democratic-front line has been applied, and I have been willing to listen to more fundamental objections. If the American situation had greatly altered,

I could conceive of adopting a different position. But I cannot accept a change that is dictated by the exigencies of Soviet foreign policy. It still seems to me essential to aid the Soviet Union, but I believe that can be done, not through stupid, unconvincing apologetics, but through the building of a stanch bulwark against reaction in America.

How much strength and influence the Communist Party has lost remains to be seen, but it is my belief that the events of these past weeks have in large measure destroyed its effectiveness. I think the party did a magnificent job in building the united front. I have seen for myself that the most intelligent leaders and the hardest workers in trade unions and in every type of progressive organization were Communists. The present policy of the party is going to make such work vastly difficult, perhaps impossible. Even if the party does not abandon the policy of the democratic front, as it may, its members will be unable to build that front. When the party reverses itself overnight, and offers nothing but nonsense in explanation, who is likely to be influenced by a Communist's recommendations?

I can understand those who have been made bitter by a sense of betrayal, but I feel no impulse to denounce the Soviet Union. After all, the Soviet Union is a socialist commonwealth, and, even if it makes mistakes, its fate is of the utmost concern to every believer in socialism. I shall continue to defend its achievements, and I think my defense may be all the more effective because I am not committed to the proposition that every detail of Soviet foreign policy is necessarily and demonstrably wise and beneficent.

Furthermore, I propose to do my best to defend the Communist Party. Nothing distresses me more about leaving the party than the realization that I am leaving it at a moment when it is in extreme peril. I know as well as any party member that the pact is not the cause of the present drive against the party, and I know too that no progressive movement is safe if the party is suppressed. The whole progressive cause has suffered, and we must repair the damage as rapidly as possible. Defense of the full legal rights of the Communist Party must be an important part of the redoubled fight against reaction.

Leaving the party is as serious and difficult a step as joining it. I value my years in the party not only for the experience and the associations, but also for the opportunity they gave me of fruitful work for a cause I believed in. My problem now is how to continue that work.

October 4, 1939
Granville Hicks

INDEX

432